SPIRITS
& Cocktails

Dedicated with all my love to my wife Jo and in memory of my father, William (Bill) Broom, a gentle man who loved his dram.

THIS IS A CARLTON BOOK

This edition published in 1998

10 9 8 7 6 5 4 3 2 1

Text and design copyright © Carlton Books Limited 1998

A CIP catalogue record for this book is available from the British Library

ISBN 1 85868 485 4

PROJECT EDITOR: *Martin Corteel*
PROJECT ART DIRECTION: *Diane Spender*
PICTURE RESEARCHER: *Alex Pepper*
PRODUCTION: *Sarah Schuman*
DESIGN: *Heather Blagden*

AUTHOR'S ACKNOWLEDGEMENTS

This book wouldn't have been written without the help of a huge number of people across the globe. There simply isn't enough space to thank them all in full, but particular thanks must go to: Christine Logan, Morrison Bowmore; Jim Turle, John Ramsay and Alan Reid, Edrington Group; Campbell Evans, Scotch Whisky Association; Colin Scott, Chivas Bros; Ian Grieve and Jonathan Driver UDV; Stuart Thomson, Bill Lumsden and Kirsty Mellish, Glenmorangie; Mike Nicolson, Lagavulin, Mike Winchester, Aberlour; Deni Nicholl; Jennifer Stewart, Seagram; Jean Crossley, Simon Soothill and Chris Nadin, IDV; Sheila Reynolds and Mark Hunt, Allied Domecq; Adrian Lane, Jose Cuervo; Claire Powers and Ken Hoskins, Hoskins PR, Kentucky; Booke Noe, Jim Beam; Jim Rutledge, Four Roses; Max Shapira, Heaven Hill; Bill Creason, Brown-Forman; Catherine McDonald, Wray & Nephew; Jean Longueteau, Mon Repos; Susannah Grant, Wines from Spain, Bartolo Vergara; Jacopo Poli; Antonio Moser, Bertagnolli; Desmond Payne, Beefeater; Hugh Williams, Gordon's; James Rolls and Sean Harris, Plymouth Gin; Willie Phillips & Patrick Heron, Janneau; Yves Grassa, Château Tariquet; Alain Braastad-Delamain; Bernard Hine; Dr Boleslaw Skrzypczak; Dr Dimitri Hajinicolaou; Dr Richard Herzog; Carlos Read; Neil Mathieson; Mark Savage; James Tanner; Rupert, Rosamund and Ricardo at R&R Teamwork, Nicky Forrest, Phipps PR; Vanessa Wright, Campbell Distillers & David Hume, Richmond Towers; Chloe Wenban-Smith, Sopexa; Su-Lin Ong, Remy; Gilly Mackwood & Henny Taylor, Moet-Hennessy.

Thanks also to Adam McLean and Anthony M. House of the Alchemy Discussion Forum. To my friends in Brighton and Edinburgh for the use of their palates and their patience in listening to various madcap theories. To Bi Jackson for bringing back obscure bottles and Aggs for keeping me going. To fellow hacks for their selfless offers of help, in particular, Charles MacLean, Richard Neill, Nigel Huddleston, Jonathan Goodall, Barbara Cormie, Chris Losh, Fiona Sims and all at *Decanter and Wine*. Cheers guys!

To all the distillers around the world who have communicated the love and passion they have for their job. For their patience and most of all for their product that's proof of their care. Some should be singled out. Jim McEwan at Bowmore who has taught me more about distilling than anyone else – and who showed me that it's people that matter; David Robertson, at Macallan at the forefront of the new wave of malt distillers; Marek Brniak, at the excellent Polish Vodka Website, for help beyond the call of duty; Ron Cooper for restoring my faith in mezcal; Jimmy Russell, Bill Samuels and Gerard White guardians of quality in Kentucky.

To my editor, Martin Corteel, for his endless patience, gentle nudges and cheerful and constructive help – and for having faith in a first-time author. I hope it's proved justified! To Alex Pepper for her tremendous work in the picture research and Diane Spender for her attention to detail in the design.

Finally to my beloved wife, Jo, for putting up with my increasingly crazy and obsessive behaviour during the writing of this book and for being a constant and loving source of support.

SPIRITS
& Cocktails

DAVE BROOM

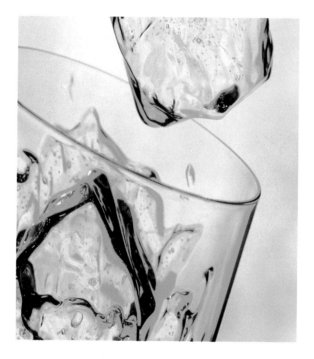

CARLTON

Contents

INTRODUCTION

PAGE 6

Chapter 1

AN AGE-OLD ELIXIR

A spirited tale of the arcane art of distillation. Alchemists, monks, disaffected clansmen, moonshiners, peasants and aristocrats – all have had their own part to play in the evolution of today's spirits.

PAGE 8

Chapter 2

THE ESSENCE OF SPIRITS

An introduction to the basic ingredients, the fundamentals of distillation and how today's industry mixes tradition with hi-tech production methods.

PAGE 18

Chapter 3

WHISKY

From Scotland to Kentucky … . Here you'll find out about the very different evolution of malt and grain whisky, why no two malts taste the same and how to make your own blend. Why Irish whiskey once had the world in its pocket and then lost it – and its glorious revival. How Bourbon finally won its place on the world stage by talking about quality – and what the rest of the world is up to. Learn to mix a Manhattan and a Mint Julep.

PAGE 24

Chapter 4

BRANDY

Discover why *terroir* and the Dutch have made Cognac, Armagnac and Brandy de Jerez all taste different. See how Italy's grappa producers have given their product a new gloss. Learn how to mix a Sidecar and a Pisco Sour.

PAGE 70

Chapter 5

RUM

How rum was built on the back of the slave trade – and helped start the American War of Independence. Go island-hopping to discover the differences between the rums of Barbados, Jamaica, Trinidad, Brazil and Cuba – and why the French Antilles do it their own way. Relax with your own Daiquiri or Rum Punch.

PAGE 92

ABSO

Chapter 6
GIN

Chart gin's progress from a cure for the Plague to an essential ingredient of the first glittering "Cocktail Age". Learn about botanicals and the medicinal origins of pink gin and gin and tonic.

PAGE   112

Chapter 7
VODKA

See how Russia, Poland and Scandinavia all put their own interpretation on how vodka is made and how flavoured vodka isn't a modern invention. Read about the battle between neutrality and quality. Find out what goes into a Bloody Mary and why the Moscow Mule changed the world.

PAGE   132

Chapter 8
TEQUILA

Discover the mythic roots of mezcal and tequila and see how today's top brands are going back to the future. Dispel the fallacies about worms and cacti and learn how to make a Margarita.

PAGE   152

Chapter 9
ANISE

Unearth the truth behind the legend of Absinthe – and how Rimbaud didn't help. Follow anise as it captures the hearts of drinkers in the Mediterranean from Lebanon to Provence.

PAGE   160

Chapter 10
OTHER SPIRITS OF THE WORLD

From bitters to fruit *eau-de-vie*, from India to Norway, hangover cures and the rarest drink of them all, the world's specialities are brought together.

PAGE   168

Chapter 11
LIQUEURS

Try to untangle fact from fiction as medieval elixirs and modern concoctions are exposed. Sift through herbs, nuts, seeds and secret recipes to discover the sweet spirits that are at the heart of every great cocktail.

PAGE   180

Chapter 12
COCKTAILS

What is a cocktail? Chart the progress of mixed drinks from the hotel bars of the last century, through the Jazz Age and Prohibition to today's post-modern mixes. Find out what ingredients and implements you need to make the world's top 100 cocktails.

PAGE   198

APPENDIX

The Bartender's checklist: the essential "tools of the trade" for the well stocked home bar.

PAGE   216

GLOSSARY

PAGE   218

SELECT BIBLIOGRAPHY

PAGE   220

INDEX

PAGE   221

Introduction

MAYBE IT WAS THE OVERPOWERING SMELL OF WHISKY IN THE BOTTLING HALL AT 7 A.M. THAT DID IT, MAYBE IT WAS THE FACT THAT, AS FOR MOST SCOTS, DRINKING WHISKY WAS AN EVERYDAY SUBJECT – NOT OVER-INDULGED, BUT A RECOGNIZED AND ENJOYABLE WAY TO SOCIALIZE. WHATEVER, SPIRITS HAVE BEEN PART OF MY LIFE FOR AS LONG AS I CAN REMEMBER.

Then, when the opportunity came to write this book, it was clear how vast the subject was. Every time I walked into a bar, an off-licence or a restaurant, there would be some bottle leering at me, saying: "Ha! Forgot about me, didn't you!" There were too many for the brain to cope with. But then, slowly, strange connections began to appear – patterns which linked styles and countries. It became apparent that the question wasn't just what makes, say, whisky, gin and Cognac different – which is mainly down to production – but *why* they are different. That's the starting point.

A lot is down to the simple fact that the earliest distillers distilled from ingredients that were to hand – grapes, sugar cane, barley or agave – but in time these spirits took on a human element, became rooted in the physical environment and more abstract national identity. The greatest spirits have always drawn their character from this melding of the environmental and cultural landscape.

But in the recent past this element has been missing. As technology and communications improved, so there was nothing to stop the same spirits being made everywhere in the world. As this happened, so the whole category was in danger of becoming homogenized. The sense of belonging was in danger of disappearing.

At one time, spirits were thought to be quintessential in the truest sense – the mysterious fifth essence, the physical manifestation of the stuff of life itself. These days many people see them as interchangeable own-label brands on the supermarket shelf.

But the more I looked, the more people I met for whom the magic was still there. The distillers with a passion for their product, who don't see it as a commodity, but as a palpable mystery; the people for whom there is still mystery – and a human element. Thankfully, these are the spirits that are growing in popularity.

Why has it happened? Maybe it's part of a millenarian desire to try and rediscover naturalness. Maybe it's thanks to a change in attitude by drinkers who have rediscovered the joy of flavour. We have realized that we don't need to accept mediocrity any more; we have the chance to revel in diversity.

Look at it in musical terms. John Coltrane, Lee Perry, Earl Scruggs, Patti Smith, Brian Wilson and George Clinton are all wildly different, but they are all equally relevant to anyone who is truly interested in music. Real music lovers are always searching for that flash of genius, can be thrilled by one note from Miles Davis, savour the way Aretha Franklin bends a phrase. Spirits are the same. Malt whisky, tequila and rum are different, but the greatest examples of each contain a spark that transcends the category and allows you to compare their similarities and delight in the contrasts. The greatest spirits act like Proust's madeleine – a taste that inspires a flood of memories and associations.

The writing has taken me across the globe from Orkney to Jerez, from the numbing cold of a Kentucky winter to the heat of the Caribbean. It's been virtual travelling as well – the world wide web has proved its worth. Along the way a weird and wonderful cast has been acquired – gods, kings, pirates, slavers and slaves, bootleggers, spice merchants, the odd US president and Highland crofters. The book isn't, however, a comprehensive list of every brand in the world or a visit to every distillery. I apologize to those which weren't included, but a line had to be drawn. Hopefully there's enough to keep everyone happy – until the second edition!

SLAINTE!

THE PINNACLE OF THE BARMAN'S ART

1 An *age-old* Elixir

DISTILLATION FUSES THE PRACTICAL AND THE PHILOSOPHICAL. IT'S BEEN USED BY THE ALCHEMIST TRYING TO REVEAL THE MYSTERIES OF EXISTENCE, THE DOCTOR ATTEMPTING TO FIND MEDICINES, THE PERFUMER CREATING SCENTS FOR HIS MASTER AND MISTRESS – AND THE PRODUCER OF ALCOHOL. BECAUSE DISTILLATION HAS HAD SO MANY USES, IT'S IMPOSSIBLE TO SAY WHO THE FIRST DISTILLER WAS.

THE ANCIENTS DRANK WINE – BUT DID THEY ALSO DRINK SPIRITS?

The earliest days

All we can say is that alcohol has always been used by man. It was probably discovered by chance – someone ate some fermenting fallen fruit, and discovered the strangely pleasurable effect. All ancient peoples drank some form of fermented drink – grape beer and palm wine were being produced in 4000 BC in Mesopotamia and Egypt, and by 1000 BC the Greeks and Phoenicians were trading in wines throughout the Mediterranean.

All of them used whatever crop was native to their region. In time, distillers would do the same, thereby establishing the main differences between the major styles of spirits. But where does distillation come in? From a twentieth-century perspective, it doesn't seem to be a huge

THE SEARCH FOR THE SECRET OF LIFE – ALCHEMY

jump in logic from fermenting to distilling, yet it's widely believed that distillation didn't start in Western Europe until the Middle Ages.

There are tantalizing snippets of information that encourage you to put two and two together … and end up just making five. By 800 BC, most Eastern and Caucasian cultures used two terms to differentiate between their fermented and stronger drinks. In China, rice beer was called *tehoo*, and the "distillate" was *suatchoo*; in India "toddy" palm wine became *arrack* when processed

a second time, and the fermented mare's milk drink of the Tartars, *kumiss*, was given the second name *arika* or *skhou*. It seems plausible that distillation may have taken place. The trouble is, there's no evidence that it did.

The evidence

To find the first possible written evidence of distillation of spirits, you have to go to fourth-century China, where the alchemist Ko Hung wrote about the transformation of cinnabar in mercury as being: "like wine that has been fermented once. It cannot be compared with the pure clear wine that has been fermented nine times". Is he talking about distillation? It seems possible. How do you ferment a wine nine times unless you distil it?

IOÁNES
STRATENSIS
FLANDRVS
1570

By that time, the Alexandrian Greeks had already discovered that by boiling you could transform one object into another. Pliny writes about distillation being used to extract turpentine from resin, while Aristotle recounts how sea water could be turned into drinking water in 4 AD, but at no point is wine mentioned – despite the fact it was being made. Perhaps they never made the leap. There again, they might have, but in 290 AD the emperor Diocletian ordered that all the records of the Alexandrian School should be destroyed, and any possible record of spirits production vanished with them.

So who were first: the Chinese, the Egyptians or the Greeks? Alchemy historian Anthony M. House takes a sensible middle ground. "It's entirely possible that these cultures were simultaneously experimenting with distillation in roughly the same period, unknown to each other."

Secret ALCHEMY

You see, alchemy lies at the root of it all. These days, the most common image of an alchemist is some bearded madman lurking in a laboratory trying to turn base metal into gold. That's a misunderstanding. Alchemy is a school of thought that tries, through a variety of disciplines, to capture the mysteries of life itself. It tries to make sense of the world by, among other things, working with the elements to transform matter and attempt to strip away the extraneous and capture its purest essence.

Alchemists camr from every religion, and all approached this quest in slightly different ways, but they were all trying to comprehend the mysteries of the world by somehow making the substance of existence visible. Out of their investigations came perfume, make-up, medicine, the ability to gild metal, mummification and, in time, alcoholic spirits. When alcoholic spirits were "discovered" by Raymond Lull (*see* page 11), they were seen as a powerful elemental creation – a possible answer to this abiding mystery.

As Denis Nicholl points out in his paper on the history of distillation, alchemy's founding father was the Egyptian god Thoth (in Greek, Hermes). Both are symbols of mystical

A DISTILLATION OF BASE MATERIAL – AND THOUGHT

knowledge, rebirth and transformation – Hermes' staff could turn base material to gold, but both gods could also turn death into life.

Alchemy appears to have started in Ancient Egypt (*al-khem* means the art of Egypt in Arabic) but in time, after being influenced by the Alexandrian Greeks, it became central to the philosophical and scientific investigations of the early Islamic scientists. In this way, Arab scholars became the guardians of the secret of distillation. Because Islam banned alcohol, scientists used distillation in *al-ambiqs* (our alembics) for different ends – making perfume, make-

up (*al-kohl*, our alcohol) and medicine.

The most notable of these scholars was the eighth-century scientist Rhazes, the founder of modern medicine, who is credited with being the first to use alcohol for medicinal purposes, while his compatriot Avicenne invented the condensing serpent. If you are looking for a name, Rhazes' is as good as any.

The art of alchemy travelled with Islam as it spread across Northern Africa and into mainland Europe with the Moorish invasion of Andalucia. There are records showing that stills were being used in Andalucia in the tenth century.

That said, you can't put your finger on any one location as being the birthplace of spirits. The reality is that it probably sprang up in a number of places at around the same time. While stills were being used in Moorish Spain, the Benedictine monks of Salerno were beginning to translate Arabic and Greek texts. Inevitably, they came across the secret and started their own experiments.

There is also evidence that distillation was being practised in the far north-west of Europe at the same time. As Islamic scholars were starting modern-day medicine, the Celts were distilling, rather than just fermenting,

RHAZES, A FATHER OF MEDICINE – AND SPIRITS?

honey into mead. In his "Mead Song", the Welsh bard Taliessin refers to "mead, distilled, sparkling", while Skene's *Four Ancient Books of Wales* refer to the Celts of this time as being: "distillers, furnace distillers or kiln distillers".

So how did it get all the way up there? There are hints that the Celts knew not just of making beer, but distilled spirits as well – though, sadly, there's no concrete evidence. It is far from impossible, though, given the evidence that knowledge of distillation had started in China and spread through India and the Caucasus, that the Celts – who were originally a tribe from this area – had carried the art with them as they wandered through Europe, finally reaching the rugged shores of the West.

Monkish habit

From these three centres of knowledge – Andalucia, Salerno and Ireland – a web of information began to be established, with monks taking over from alchemists as the guardians of the art. Monasteries were the great centres of learning of this time, and during the Dark Age, Ireland was a key centre of knowledge. It was Irish monks – wandering the roads of Europe, along with their brethren in Salerno – and the Moors who spread knowledge of the art across Europe.

We now reach a time when written descriptions of distillation begin to appear. The Salernan school was distilling by the eleventh century, and when Henry IV invaded Ireland in 1174 he found the natives making *aqua vitae* – unknown in England at the time.

Although drinks like mead would have been drunk for celebratory reasons, at this point spirits were still being used as medicines. Alcohol was used not just as a marvellous new remedy in itself but, as Rhazes had discovered, it was the perfect medium for medicinal herbs.

The monks, therefore, were dispensing cordials and elixirs – one is still made by the monks of Chartreuse – produced from spirit made from whatever grew around them. Those in the south used grapes; in the middle, fruit was more common; while in the cold north, grains and honey were the bases for spirits. These broad divisions still remain.

Spirits only started becoming the property of the people when the tight control of the monasteries was loosened. As the knowledge of spirits spread, so the art split into three camps. Monks and early medical scientists like Thaddeus Florentus (1223–1303), a medical lecturer at Bologna, made remedies; alchemists were still trying to capture the essence of existence; while the people – Highland crofters, Polish landowners and the European peasantry – were beginning to take an interest in spirits as a social pleasure.

The father of European distillation is, for some reason, still given as the thirteenth-century Moorish scholar and alchemist Arnold de Villanova, who taught the art at Avignon and Montpellier. His pupil Raymond Lull (or Lully) is credited with producing the first true alcoholic spirit – a distillation of wine using double

MONASTERIES WERE ALSO VINERIES AND DISTILLERIES

BATHING IN THE WATER
OF LIFE

of this time were a long way removed from the pure distillates we know today. Virtually all whiskies and vodkas at this time would have been flavoured with herbs and spices to mask the off-flavours produced by poor-quality distillation.

Spirits by now had escaped from the cloisters and arrived in the homes of the people. As they did, so their usage began to change dramatically. While they were still used as a beneficial medicine – *aqua vitae* made from *genever* (the precursor of gin) was used as a cure for the Plague in the fourteenth century – there's little doubt, when you look at who was making them, and what was going into them, that they were also being drunk for pleasure.

The art of distillation was vital to gracious living. "From medieval times (until the eighteenth century at least) the rich had a still-room, run by the still-room maid, where she would prepare potions. She managed the herb garden and orchard and made sure they were harvested at the right time, in tune with the phases of the moon", writes Rosamund Richardson in *Country Wisdom*.

Alcohol therefore easily slipped off the shackles of medicine and became part of daily life and celebration. As Terence McKenna points out in his *Food of the Gods*, alcohol was nothing less than the first synthesized drug, predating heroin, cocaine and mescalin by hundreds of years.

A major international expansion in spirits production took place in Renaissance times for two main reasons. Firstly, the marriage of Catherine de Medici to Henri II brought the Italian mastery of liqueur production to France. Meanwhile contact with Italian monks had brought the hitherto arcane techniques of pot-still distillation into both Poland and Russia.

distillation and a cold-water condenser. He was so astounded by the potency of the spirit, that he believed it could bring about the end of the world. Lull was looking for ether, the elusive fifth element (quintessence) regarded by alchemists as being the element that was latent in all things. It must have seemed as if he had succeeded. Lull is credited with bringing the art to England when John Cremer invited him to visit the court of Edward I.

Drinking For Pleasure

Spirits were now firmly established. In 1483, Schrick of Augsburg published the first printed book on alcohol, while 12 years later Friar John Cor bought his famous eight bolls of malt and, allegedly, started off whisky production in Scotland.

Although gins and liqueurs were becoming identifiable as similar to the spirits we now know, many of the spirits

Commercial ENTERPRISE

By the end of the sixteenth century, commercial distilleries began to appear (immediately followed by taxation). Many were no more than a still in a great house, but some distillers, such as Amsterdam's Lucas Bols, were already involved in large-scale commercial production of *genever* and liqueurs, while vodka distillers in Poznan had begun to export their new vodkas.

Distillation equipment was becoming more advanced. Hieronymus Braunsweig's 1519 manual, *Das Buch zu Distilliern*, has illustrations showing stills with up to four retorts. In Scotland triple distillation was common practice, while in Poland and Russia quadruple distillation was used as part of those countries' never-ending quests for the purest spirit possible.

Every country was beginning to sow the seeds that would eventually flower into the great spirits we know today. The expansion of the "industry" allowed greater experimentation and the development of national and regional styles. As ever, this was predominantly a matter of developing and perfecting the spirit made from local ingredients, but each country (and region) had a slightly different idea as to how to do it. In the East, the goal was a pure spirit base that could then be flavoured with various exotic ingredients ranging from grass to gold. In the West, in Scotland and France, distillers were beginning to use distillation itself (rather than botanicals) to produce powerfully flavoured spirits.

Impact of empire

Although export was beginning, with the exception of the Dutch and English trade in brandy, spirits remained local specialities which were becoming increasingly popular with the growing population – and with governments, who were delighted at this easy target for raising revenue for wars.

The world was becoming smaller, and the spread of the European empires provided the next spur to spirits' development. The Spanish and Portuguese had established their colonies in Brazil and the Caribbean in the fifteenth century, and started sugar production almost immediately. The new settlers wanted a spirit to drink – it took too long for brandy to reach them from Europe – and so they did what all distillers have done throughout history: they used the local crop, in this case sugar cane. Rum started off as a drink for slaves but soon became an important profit-making industry, particularly when the British, French and Dutch began colonizing the other islands and starting their own sugar industries.

By the end of the sixteenth century this fermented sugar beer was known as "kill-devil", and within 100 years it was being produced commercially across the Caribbean, and England was trading in sugar and rum.

In the American Colonies, the early settlers started out by drinking Caribbean rum, but soon realized that they could make it more cheaply at home, and so began importing molasses, distilling rum and, following England's example, using it to buy slaves.

In Mexico, the Spanish settlers who were spreading inland from the cane plantations on the coast had started experimenting with distilling the local fermented drink, *pulque*, that was drunk throughout the country. In time, *mezcal* joined the other fast-growing spirits of the world.

In Peru, Chile and Argentina, meanwhile, settlers brought grape cuttings with them (*vitis vinifera* is not indigenous to South America) and began producing brandy (*Pisco*). Every wave of immigrants brought new knowledge and new spirits. The Scots

RUM, DISTILLED BY THE SLAVE TRADE

AS EMPIRES GREW, SO DID SPIRITS

13

and Irish, arriving in America and Canada, started replicating what they had done at home – making whisky from grain (although in this case it was rye rather than barley). Within a short period of time the world of spirits had become increasingly diverse.

One of the main catalysts for this development was the influence of the Dutch mercantile empire. Not only were their ships bringing back flavouring spices from around the world, affording gin and liqueur producers an ever-growing range of flavourings to play with, but they kicked brandy production into life. The Dutch needed spirit to keep the water on ships drinkable during long sea voyages. In the seventeenth century they therefore started to buy wine from the region close to the French port of La Rochelle, and then started to make brandy *in situ*. In this way, Cognac was born.

Drinking to forget

By the eighteenth century spirits were being consumed in vast quantities across the world. It was a time of excess, and it was the beginning of the exodus from the country to the city. The new urban poor needed something to take their minds off their wretched existence and mass-produced, cheap alcohol was the drug of choice. Suddenly it was a long way from the mystical aims of the alchemists.

By the beginning of the nineteenth century drinking spirits was a serious business that was enjoyed by all classes in virtually every country. The next development was to increase this mass-appeal still further. For years, distillers had been faced with the fact that to make their drinks they had to use pot stills. That meant distilling once, collecting the spirit, recharging the still and redistilling a second, or

third time. It was time-consuming, it was expensive and the return was small. If only a way could be found to produce large quantities of good-quality spirit at low cost.

Aeneas Coffey is credited with being the inventor of the answer to their prayers, the continuous still, although it seems likely that different scientists were all coming up with similar ideas across Europe. These stills solved the problem, and continuous production of high-strength, clean, light-flavoured alcohol had arrived. It was to change the face of spirit production. Over the next 150 years pot stills became rarer and spirits became lighter. As huge volumes of this new spirit were produced, so many of the small distillers found they could no longer compete. The industry began to shrink in numbers as it increased in volume. The age of the global spirit loomed.

SPIRITS BECAME THE
MASS-PRODUCED DRUG
OF CHOICE

Mass PRODUCTION

At that point, though, pot-still brandy was the world's best-known spirit. Then, in the 1870s the *phylloxera* louse infested and killed off the European vineyards. The sudden cessation of supplies forced drinkers to look elsewhere – and there were the new blended Scotches that could be produced in huge quantities, thanks to the continuous still. The Scots (and Irish) stepped into the gap left by brandy, and within a few years whisky was the world's top-selling spirit, with gin – the essential base for the new cocktails – following hard on its heels.

The world shrank that little bit more when America embarked on the lunacy of Prohibition. By effectively killing off its whiskey industry, it allowed British firms to flood the market, first after Repeal and once again after the Second World War. By then, though, a subtle change had taken place. The post-war consumer – particularly in America – was looking for a lighter spirit to drink long and mixed. It was the start of vodka's rise from the obscurity of Eastern Europe to overtake whisky as the world's favourite spirit.

The global market

It wasn't long before the larger distillers thought, "What's the point of shipping our spirit from A to B; why don't we just establish distilleries in other countries?" Smirnoff, Gordon's and Bacardi ceased to be regional or national spirits, and became international brands. Some of the ancient ties between country and spirit had been severed. The continuous still meant that neutral base spirit could be made in any country – allowing gin and, more commonly, vodka to be produced by anyone with the requisite equipment. No longer was it necessary to make a distillate purely from local ingredients and expect it to taste of them. Stateless neutrality was fast becoming the theme.

Scotch was holding its own, however. The affluent USA and Britain of the 1960s were happy to drink a whole range of spirits. Everyone was happy – especially the major distillers who, by taking the next logical step into a truly global market, began to treat their brands as commodities.

Their marketing and distribution had been so effective that soon everyone in the world was drinking more or less the same thing. National and regional differences existed, but they were significantly less pronounced than they had been 50 years previously. This meant, from the distillers' way of looking at things, that all spirits could be treated in the same way in every country.

The market was buoyant. In the eyes of the multinationals, if their whisky brands were declining, then as long as their vodka was growing at the same rate, what was the problem?

As the 1970s and 1980s wore on, that shift from whisky to vodka was beginning to accelerate. In general, since the late 1970s "brown spirits" have fallen – most significantly, in their oldest markets. To be strictly accurate, it's "old spirits" that have fallen, as gin and rum (with the exception of Bacardi) have also hit the slide. Part of this was down to the fact that the new generation of drinkers that was emerging didn't want to drink the same spirits as their parents – in the 1980s, many of them didn't want to drink spirits at all!

The arrival of multinational drinks firms opened up the market and made what used to be national specialities into international brands. As this has happened, however, so many have simply become commodities – their specialness, their history and strangeness being lost to the strict framework that uninspired marketing theory applies to everything, whether it's baked beans, nappies or malt whisky. In spirits it meant that Cognac was sold in the same way as vodka, rum, whisky and gin. So we ended up with greater choice but less understanding than ever before. Never have spirits been so far removed from their spiritual homes.

Craft revival

Of course there were exceptions. The small industries of Cognac and Armagnac managed to retain their individuality, while some far-sighted malt distillers in Scotland realized that people might just be interested in old-fashioned tradition and hand-crafted quality after all.

This return to "authenticity" has underpinned the major shift in spirits since the end of the 1980s. It started with malt, but soon moved to small-batch bourbon, premium imported vodka and top-aged rums, and now tequila, mezcal and even gin are in on the act.

Today's younger drinkers are looking for spirits with flavour and with a story to tell; spirits that speak of their place. Spirits are being looked at in the same way as wine. Drinkers don't only want to know where they come from and what they taste like, but why they taste the way they do and who made it. Distillers are now more important than marketing managers. At long last the human element in distillation is being given the attention it deserves.

Today's consumer is able to choose from the largest range of high-quality spirits the world has ever seen. Along the way spirits may have lost their mystical quality, but in recent times they have regained something equally important – their sense of place.

Chronology of Spirits

3500BC Mesopotamian perfumers using distillation to extract essential oils.

1000BC Chinese using distilled rice wine in manufacture of gunpowder.

800BC Arak allegedly being distilled in India. Eastern and Caucasian cultures using two terms to differentiate between fermented and stronger drinks.

4AD Aristotle recounts how sea water can be distilled into drinking water.

290 Diocletian orders the records of the Alexandrian School to be destroyed and erases any record of spirit production.

c. 320 Chinese alchemist Ko Hung writes about wine, "fermented" nine times, possibly the evidence of spirits distillation.

c. 500 Welsh bard Taliesen's "Mead Song" mentions distillation. Skene refers to Gaels of this time as being "distillers".

c. 700 Distillers in Poland and Russia use freezing to separate water from alcohol.

c. 864–930 Arab philosopher–scientist Rhazes becomes the first person to use alcohol for medical purposes.

c. 900 Distillation starts in Jerez [for perfume].

c. 1050 Distillation starts at the monastery in Salerno.

1174 Henry II of England records the drinking of *aqua vitae* in Ireland.

1235–1312 Arnold de Villanova. He teaches alchemy at Avignon and Montpellier. Often seen as the father of distillation.

1235–1315 Vilanova's pupil Raymond Lull(y) produces alcoholic spirit from wine.

1296 Sir Robert Savage, lord of Bushmills, gives "aqua vitae" to his troops.

c. 1300 Stills being used in Scandinavia.

c. 1348 Black Death treated by juniper-based elixirs.

1405 First written record of vodka production in Poland.

1411 First written record of Armagnac production.

1430 A Russian delegation visits Italian monasteries and is shown the art of distillation.

1474 Ivan the Great restricts production and sale of vodka in Russia.

1483 Schrick of Augsburg publishes the first printed book on alcohol.

1494 First written record of whisky production in Scotland. Columbus plants sugar cane in the Caribbean.

1510 Benedictine created by Don Bernardo Vinvelli.

1519 Hieronymus Braunsweig publishes *Das Buch zu Distilliern*. It's translated into English in 1527.

1533 First written record of Calvados production.

1534 Polish herbalist Stefan Falimirz lists 72 different types of flavoured vodka.

1546 King Jan Olbracht decrees all Poles can legally distil.

1556 First written record of Irish whiskey.

1572 First record of *eau de vie de genièvre*, by Franciscus Sylvius, a physic of Leiden. Polish vodka production restricted to the gentry and landed classes.

1575 Lucas Bols establishes his distillery near Amsterdam making genever and liqueurs.

1590 Fynes Moryson records whisky being exported from Scotland to Ireland and the use of triple distillation in the Scottish Western Isles.

1598 Goldwasser first made in Gdansk.

1603 An ancient recipe for an elixir given to the Carthusian monks in La Grande Chartreuse.

1627 Robert Haig starts producing whisky on his Stirlingshire estate.

1638 First mention of Cognac.

1644 The Scottish Parliament levies the first tax on whisky.

1647 Richard Ligon writes his history of Barbados, including descriptions of the production of "kill-devil" (aka rum).

1648 End of the Thirty Years War and the arrival home of English mercenaries, bringing with them Dutch genever.

c. 1650 Start of rum distillation in mainland United States.

1651 John French's *Art of Distillation* is published.

1653–1702 The Worshipful Company of Distillers decrees that all spirits should undergo rectification (i.e. a second distillation).

1663 Samuel Pepys takes: "strong water made of juniper" as a medicine for his upset stomach. William Gay buys a plantation in Barbados complete with still house.

1672 Start of brandy production in South Africa.

1675 De Kuyper's distillery founded in Rotterdam.

1681 State monopoly imposed on Russian vodka production.

1687 The English Navy gives ratings a ration of half a pint of rum a day.

1689 William of Orange bans imports of (French) brandy to England, ushering in the gin era.

1690 Rhum producer Dillon founded.

1694 Père Labat, the father of rhum distillation, arrives in Martinique. Beer duty increased in England making gin the cheaper drink.

1715 Jean Martell moves to Cognac. Duncan Forbes granted duty-free status for his Ferintosh distillery in Scotland.

1717–18 First wave of Scots and Irish settlers arrive in North America and start distilling from rye.

1730 One fifth of London's houses are "gin shops" (home distilleries).

1733 The first of two Molasses Acts imposing heavy duties on imports of "non-British" molasses into American rum distilleries.

1740 Philip Booth starts his gin distillery in Clerkenwell. Admiral Vernon orders the navy rum ration to be diluted with two parts water.

1745 Prince Charlie (allegedly) gives the recipe for Drambuie to the Mackinnons of Skye. Start of the Highland Clearances, precipitating the next wave of Scots into North America.

1749 First mention of Jamaica's Appleton Estate as a rum-producing plantation.

1750 Gin consumption in England peaks at 20 million gallons. Hogarth prints "Gin Lane".

1758 Don José Antonio Cuervo is granted land by the King of Spain to farm agave in Jalisco province, Mexico.

1765 Catherine the Great creates two-tier system of vodka production in Russia with the gentry producing the top quality styles and state distilleries producing poor quality spirit for the masses.

1769 Alexander Gordon founds his gin distillery in Southwark.

c. 1770 Settlers arrive in Kentucky and Tennessee. Potatoes begin to be used for vodka production in Poland.

1774 British Government bans wash stills smaller than 400 gallons and spirit stills less than 100 gallons. Start of the "Smuggling Era" in Scotland.

1780 John Jameson establishes his distillery in Dublin's Bow Street.

1782 J.A. Baczewki distillery in Lvov making 123 different styles of vodka and exporting to 20 countries.

1783 Evan Williams starts production in Louisville, Kentucky.

1784 The Wash Act in Britain restricts the sale of malt whisky to above the Highland Line.

1787 The Henriot sisters sell their recipe to Major Henri Dubeid and commercial production of absinthe starts.

1789 George Washington earns $1,032 from his spirits production. America's first temperance society founded in Litchfield County, Connecticut.

1791–2 The Whiskey Rebellion in the United States.

1793 The Coates family founds Plymouth gin distillery.

1795 Jacob Beam founds his distillery. Don José Maria Guadaloupe Cuervo granted a licence to produce "mezcal wine" in his La Rojena distillery, Tequila.

1806 The first record of the term cocktail: "a mixed drink of any spirit, bitters and sugar".

1814 Excise Act bans stills under 500 gallons in the Highlands.

1817 The first Pistorius three-chambered column still installed in Poland.

1818 Peter Heering, a Copenhagen grocer, creates his cherry "brandy".

1820 James Pimm opens his oyster bar in London and starts serving his No. 1 cup. John Walker opens his grocery shop in Kilmarnock.

1823 James (Jim) Crow begins working at the Oscar Pepper distillery, Kentucky. In Britain, excise is reduced and licences for distilleries introduced. The start of today's whisky industry and the end of the "Smuggling Era".

1825 First mention of The Lincoln County Process [charcoal filtration] in Tennessee, credited to Alfred Eaton. John Wray founds Jamaican rum producer Wray & Nephew. Dr Siegert trademarks Angostura Bitters.

1827 Robert Stein invents a continuous still for whisky production.

1831 Aeneas Coffey improves on Stein's continuous still and patents the invention.

1837 William Teacher opens his first grocer's store in Glasgow. Swedish Temperance Movement founded.

1838–48 Father Matthew's crusade against the evils of

drink halves the number of pubs in Ireland and closes distilleries.

1845–9 The Great Famine in Ireland reduces the amount of grain available for distilleries, crippling production and forcing a mass exodus abroad.

1846 John Dewar starts up as wine and spirit merchant in Perth.

1849 Cointreau created by Edouard Cointreau.

1850 M. Verdier invents the Armagnac continuous still.

1853 The first Scotch blend, Usher's Old Vatted Glenlivet, launched.

1860 The Alberti family creates Strega. Home distillation banned in Sweden.

1861 Piotr Smirnov starts to produce vodka in Russia.

1862 James Burrough starts distilling gin in Chelsea. Don Facunado Bacardi installs the first Coffey still in Cuba. Professor Jerry Thomas publishes *The Bar-Tender's Guide and Bon Vivant's Companion*. Russia removes monopoly on vodka production.

1865 Arthur Bell starts his own whisky-blending business.

1867 Walker's Old Highland Whisky copyrighted and trademarked.

1869 National Prohibition Party founded in America.

c. 1870 The height of absinthe's success.

1871 Poland's first rectification plant opens in Starograd.

1871–1885 Plague of *phylloxera vastatrix* devastates European vineyards.

1873 Sauza starts distilling in the La Perseverancia distillery.

1874 Fundador becomes the first Brandy de Jerez brand.

1877 Six grain whisky distillers found the Distillers Company Limited (DCL).

1879 Lars Olsson Smith produces Sweden's first rectified spirit, Absolut Rent Brannvin.

1880 Louis-Alexandre Marnier-Lapostolle creates Grand Marnier.

1882 Harry Johnson publishes

New And Improved Illustrated Bartender's Manual, Or How to Mix Drinks of the Present Style. James Buchanan creates "Buchanan Blend" (later Black & White).

1890 Russia reimposes full state monopoly on vodka production.

1894 Matthew Gloag launches "The Grouse Brand" (later The Famous Grouse).

1908 Royal Commission decrees that a blend of grain and malt can be legally called whisky.

1909 Walker's Old Highland renamed Johnnie Walker Black Label and is joined by a new brand Johnnie Walker Red Label.

1915 Tennessee and Kentucky become "dry" states. Dewar's and Buchanan merge.

1915 Absinthe production banned.

1917 Vladimir Smirnov flees Russia and establishes a distillery in Istanbul, soon followed by one in Lvov. Russia's Bolshevik Government bans production of vodka.

1918 Prohibition imposed in Canada.

1919 Sweden places production and sale of alcohol under control of a state monopoly, Vin & Spirit. Finland imposes Prohibition. Canada repeals Prohibition. Polish vodka production comes under state control.

1920 Prohibition starts in the United States.

1922 Tanqueray-Gordon joins DCL.

1925 Dewar's and Buchanan join DCL. Partial lifting of Russian prohibition allowing vodka to be sold at 20% abv.

1927 Johnnie Walker and White Horse join DCL.

1928 Pernod launched. Vladimir Smirnov arrives in Paris.

1931 Bacardi builds a distillery in Mexico.

1932 Ricard launched. Prohibition repealed in Finland.

1933 Prohibition repealed in the United States.

1934 Rudolph Kunett starts distilling Smirnoff in the United States.

1936 Lem Motlow reopens the Jack Daniel's distillery in Lynchburg, Tennessee.

1937 Rudolph Kunett sells Smirnoff to Heublein.

1939 Finnish distilleries start producing alcohol for Molotov cocktails.

1941 US distilleries stop producing spirits and switch to making alcohol for the war effort.

1952 British rights to distil Smirnoff sold to W&A Gilbey.

1960 Bacardi moves from Cuba to Puerto Rico after Fidel Castro nationalizes spirits production.

1962 IDV formed when W&A Gilbey, Justerini & Brooks and United Vintners merge.

1966 Jameson, Power and Cork Distillers join forces to form Irish Distillers Group (ID).

1970 The British Navy rum ration abolished. Finlandia exported to the United States for the first time.

1971 William Grant & Sons starts marketing Glenfiddich.

1973 Bushmills, the last independent distillery in Ireland, joins Irish Distillers. Polmos, the Polish state vodka body, founded.

1975 Bailey's Irish Cream launched by IDV.

1979 V&S relaunches Absolut.

1983 IDV buys Heublein.

1986 Guinness buys DCL to form United Distillers (UD).

1987 Cooley Distillers starts operations in Ireland.

1991 Polish vodka distilleries become independent.

1998 Guinness and GrandMet (IDV) merge to form Diageo, the world's largest spirits firm. Bacardi buys Dewar's, Bombay Sapphire and four whisky distilleries for £1.15 billion.

the Essence of spirits

DISTILLING IS MEANS OF CONCENTRATING THE ALCOHOL IN A FERMENTED LIQUID. THE THEORY IS SIMPLE: ALCOHOL AND WATER BOIL AT DIFFERENT TEMPERATURES – WATER AT 100°C AND ALCOHOL AT 78.3°C. THEREFORE, WHEN A FERMENTED LIQUID IS HEATED, THE VAPOUR THAT CONTAINS THE ALCOHOL IS RELEASED FIRST. THIS CAN THEN BE TRAPPED, COOLED AND CONDENSED INTO A SPIRIT AT A HIGHER STRENGTH.

WATER FOR THE WATER OF LIFE

Heating is not the only way to achieve this result. Early "distillers" in eighth-century Poland (and later in Canada) used freezing to separate water from alcohol. This is known as fractional crystallization, although they didn't know that at the time. A fruit wine, or cider, would be left outside to freeze and the (brutally strong) liquor would be removed. This works because water freezes at a higher temperature (0°C) than alcohol. It's an inexact science, however, as it first requires the temperature to hover around -15°C, and still doesn't remove any potentially harmful alcoholic compounds.

The early distillers therefore used small glass flasks, which were soon to be replaced with copper pots. These were filled with the fermented liquid, heated and the vapour would rise along

a thin tube, which ended immersed in a vat of cold water.

"It is to be understood that distilling is nothing else but a purifying of the gross from the subtle, the subtle from the gross each separately from the other to the intent that the corruptible shall be made incorruptible and to make the material immaterial." So begins the first

A SEA OF GOLD – READY TO BE TURNED INTO WHISKEY

great treatise on distillation written in 1500 by Brunschwig, a physician of Strasbourg. That principle remains true today.

Alcohol contains a huge range of chemical compounds, the main one being ethyl alcohol. However, there is also a wide range of by-products such as aldehydes, amyl alcohols (fusel oils), esters, acids and methanol, all produced by a combination of the raw material and fermentation.

Some of these are harmful, others are what gives a spirit its taste and smell – the congeners. The question facing distillers is how many of them they want to retain.

In simple terms, the distillers of those spirits that use pot stills – such as malt whisky, Cognac and some top rums – will be aiming to produce a more flavoursome spirit with a higher

percentage of flavours of the raw material than those which are distilled in continuous stills.

The pot still

In today's terms, a pot still isn't an efficient method of distilling. The base (wine for brandy, or a crude beer for the grain spirits) has to be distilled twice – sometimes three times – in order to remove the harmful elements. At the end of the day, though, the distillate will still contain relatively high amounts of congeners. The downside is that these heavy alcohols are a major contributory factor in producing hangovers; their advantage is that they are the elements that give the spirit its complex flavour.

Normally two, sometimes three, distillations take place in batch distillation. The first distillation gives a light concentration of the fermented liquid resulting in a spirit of around 20 per cent ABV. The second distillation is where the distiller concentrates the spirit further and discards or captures the congeners.

The distillation is divided into three different parts: heads, heart and tails. The first alcohols to be condensed (known as the heads) are highly volatile and are retained and redistilled with the next batch. But then, usually at around 72 per cent ABV, the heart begins to reveal itself. This is what has to be captured by the distiller.

This starting point of the heart of the spirit run is vital to the final flavour of the spirit. Make it too early and you'll end up with heads in the spirit; too late and you'll miss the most delicate, floral and fruity esters, which arrive just after the volatile elements have disappeared.

As the spirit flows, not only does the strength drop, but the aromas begin to change from being light to heavy. Logically enough, the last alcohols to come across (known as the tails) contain the heaviest alcoholic compounds with the richest and most powerful aromas.

Some of these are desirable – they contribute palate weight and bass notes to the final spirit – but capture too many and you'll end up with a rank spirit. The tails are also retained and added to the next batch.

Knowing when to start and stop collecting the heart is an art, for while there are undesirable elements in heads and tails, they also contain flavours that the distiller wants to retain. The secret is to capture just enough of the last of the heads and the first of the tails to give each spirit its identity.

Needless to say, this will vary between distillers. Those who want to produce a light and delicate spirit will, by and large, collect the spirit at a higher strength. Those who want something with weight and guts will allow more of the latter part of the distillation to be collected. There again, the less you collect the more expensive the operation is, so economics often have their part to play in the decision.

The size and shape of the still and the speed of distillation all have a hugely important role to play. The effect of the shape of the still is seen most clearly in malt whisky distillation. No two distilleries have the same shaped stills, and every distillery manager will have his or her own theory on how they impact on the vapour to help produce the distillery's signature flavour.

In general, the smaller the still the heavier the spirit; the taller the still, the lighter the spirit. This is because only the lightest, most delicate aromas can rise to the top of a tall neck; the other, heavier elements fall back and are vaporized again, a process known as reflux. Some stills have large goitre-like balls that encourage this process.

Of course in reality it's not quite as simple as that. The speed of distillation (which corresponds to the temperature of the heat applied to the still) will also have a significant impact on flavour and quality. The slower and gentler it is, the more effectively the congeners are separated. As one distiller says: "It's like stewing fruit. The lower the flame on the stove, the more intense the aromas released." You don't want a hot, fast distillation where all the aromatic elements come rushing across like children at the end of the school day; you want a slow, even procession. This is how a distillery with small stills can still manage to produce a complex and delicately flavoured spirit.

The continuous still

Until the beginning of the nineteenth century, all spirits were produced in pot stills, but distillers were already searching for a more cost-effective method of producing larger volumes.

This was particularly important in Scotland, where the distillers in the Lowlands wanted to produce huge volumes of cheap whisky for the growing urban population, and in Eastern Europe where vodka producers, always searching for ways to make their spirit as pure as possible, had to distil three or four times in pot stills to obtain the required result.

The solution was the continuous still. This is usually credited to whisky distillers Robert Stein and Aeneas Coffey, but similar apparatus was popping up at the same time in Armagnac and Poland. All of these stills worked to the same principle. As

long as you put a fermented liquid in one end, you'd get high-strength spirit out of the other.

Most continuous stills consist of two linked columns called the analyser and the rectifier, each of which is divided with perforated horizontal plates. The cool fermented wash enters the top of the rectifier and runs down inside a pipe to the bottom of the column and up to the top of the analyser, where it sprays out and starts to descend through divisions in the horizontal plates.

At the same time, hot steam is being constantly fed into the bottom of the analyser. This rises through the perfora-

DISTILLING IS A HIGH-TECH BUSINESS

MAKING CHARCOAL AT JACK DANIEL'S

tions in the plate and meets the descending wash, then strips the alcohol vapour off. As the wash travels down the analyser, therefore, it becomes progressively weaker.

The steam and alcohol vapour rise to the top of the analyser and pass along a pipe to the bottom of the rectifier, where they are released and start to rise once more. At this point they come into contact with the pipe containing the wash with which they perform a sort of heat exchange. The steam and vapour warms the pipe up, while the pipe begins to cool the vapour down, and this causes it to start to condense.

Continuous distillation works on the principle that not only do water and alcohol boil at different temperatures, but the different congeners also boil (or, to be more precise, vaporize) at different temperatures as well. Therefore as they rise up the column, so the different components begin to separate (fractionate). The column is therefore a far more efficient way of separating almost everything except the higher alcohols, which are collected on a solid plate. This can be placed at any point in the column, allowing the distiller to collect spirit at whatever strength he wants. The end result is a spirit of, on average, 90

per cent ABV or more with most of its congeners stripped out. Here speed is important as well. Just as in pot-still distillation, the best-quality spirit will come from those stills that are run slow and steady, achieved by varying the flow rate of the wash and the pressure of the steam. Too fast, and you'll end up with burnt aromas.

There are various types of continuous still. In vodka, gin, most white rums and grain whisky – where the aim is to have a low-flavour, high-strength spirit – linked columns will be used. In the case of some vodka and all gin, the spirit will be rectified once more to produce what is known as neutral alcohol. Some rum and vodka distilleries have three, four or five linked columns, giving the distiller a huge range of possibilities, from neutral spirit to flavoursome.

It's often thought that continuous distillation gives a uniformly bland spirit. Not true. Although the vast majority of vodka distillers will distil to the same strength, a tasting of a cross-section of brands will reveal totally different flavours. Part of this comes from the raw material used (and proves that they aren't neutral), but also is the result of the skill of the distiller in capturing the style and personality of the spirit that he wants.

In Kentucky and Tennessee, the spirit isn't rectified but comes off a single column still and into a basic pot-still apparatus called a doubler, which concentrates the alcohol to around the same as a malt whisky or Cognac. In Armagnac and some islands in the Antilles, meanwhile, they use tiny single-column stills which, although working on the same principle, produce a spirit of lower strength than one from a pot.

To age, or not to age

In general, white spirits (vodka, gin, white run, silver tequila and mezcal) are reduced in strength, given time in a vat to mellow and are then bottled. Brown spirits (whisk(e)y, brandy, aged rum, reposado and anejo tequila) are given some time in oak barrels.

Each country and region will have its own specifics when it comes to what type of oak to use, what size of barrel, whether it is new or not – and, if not,

what it has previously held. Oak and oak maturation is probably the area that is receiving the greatest attention in Cognac, Scotland, Ireland and Kentucky. A popular statistic that's being bandied about at the moment is that up to 60 per cent of a malt whisky's flavour will come from the wood it is kept in. Good reason to pay close attention to the barrels.

The aim of maturation is to give the spirit a period of controlled oxidation,

and also to allow it to mingle and extract the flavour and colouring compounds that are contained in the barrel. Oak contains a huge range of phenolic compounds, which are easily broken down by high-strength alcohol. These include tannins, (giving fragrance and grip), lignins (which give spiciness) and cellulose (light sweetness), all of which build complexity in the spirit as they break down.

As the spirit matures, it moves in and out of the layers of wood, sucking

up the wood compounds and colour and absorbing them into itself.

Each spirit has a different approach to wood and maturation. By law, bourbon can only use new, heavily charred American oak. New wood is brimful of flavouring such as vanillins, which American oak is particularly high in, and colour extracts. Cognac and Armagnac producers usually only give their brandies a couple of years in new wood in order to extract some of these compounds, before transferring the brandy to older barrels, where the level of extract is lower. They can then start slowly oxidizing and breaking down the remaining flavouring compounds in the wood.

The thrifty Scots only use second-hand wood – either ex-bourbon barrels or sherry butts, both of which impart their own distinct character on the spirit (*see* Whisky).

It's already evident that there's no one correct way in which to make a spirit; what's important is knowing which technique is the most appropriate, given the local conditions, ingredients and environment. You couldn't copy bourbon techniques in Scotland or Ireland and expect to produce the same spirit, just as you couldn't replicate Scottish or Irish techniques in America – that has already been proved, because it is what the early American distillers attempted to do. Raw materials are different, as are ferments, distillation techniques and maturation. Diversity is the welcome result.

At their root, the greatest spirits are human creations that are inextricably linked to their place of birth. They distil human experience and the physical environment – and amplify them both.

THE FINAL ELEMENT – THE BARREL

3 Whisky

THE WILD COASTS OF NORTH WESTERN EUROPE HAVE LONG SHELTERED PEOPLE FOR WHOM SPIRITS ARE PART OF THE NATIONAL PSYCHE. SCOTLAND AND IRELAND HAVE GIVEN THE WORLD MANY THINGS – BUT WHISK(E)Y REMAINS THEIR GREATEST GIFT. IT WAS EMIGRANTS FROM THESE CELTIC NATIONS WHO TOOK THE ART OF DISTILLING TO NORTH AMERICA AND HELPED MAKE THE DRINK THE WORLD'S FAVOURITE SPIRIT. WHISKY'S STORY ENCOMPASSES LEGEND, INTERNAL STRIFE, THE PAIN OF FORCED EMIGRATION AND THE TRIUMPH OF VICTORIAN CAPITALISM.

That said, whisky is the same as every other category when it comes to trying to get tabs on who first made it. In all of the major categories there will be plenty of conjecture, a smattering of rumour, some hypotheses, a touch of speculation and numerous leaps of logic. Bloody-minded national pride will rear its head occasionally, but at no point will we be able to say that a certain type of spirit was first distilled on this date, in this year, by this person.

OPPOSITE: JAZZING UP WHISKY WITH TEACHER'S

MAKING THE "CRATUR" 16TH-CENTURY STYLE

Scotch whisky is typical of this state of affairs. It's true that in 1994 the whisky industry celebrated the 500th anniversary of Scotch, but to be strictly accurate the cause of this worldwide rejoicing was actually the 500th anniversary of the first documentation of distilling taking place in Scotland. This was a record in the Exchequer Roll of 1494 that said: "To Friar John Cor, by order of the King, to make *aqua vitae*, VIII bolls of malt." There you have it; the first distiller was a man of the cloth domiciled in Lindores Abbey, near Newburgh, Fife.

But hang on a minute. A boll of malt is 140 lb. Eight bolls are enough to make 400 bottles of whisky. This suggests that Friar Cor wasn't just conducting an experiment, but had already mastered the art and was making commercial quantities. He was a distiller, of that there is little doubt, but the first? Unlikely. It's more probable that he was continuing a practice that had already been refined and perfected.

We still can't say who it was that first distilled whisky in Scotland, but Friar Cor provides two clues. The first is that he was a monk. Monasteries in this period were the universities of their time – places not just of prayer, but laboratories, hospitals, centres of philosophy, writing and art. As we have seen, the secret alchemy of distillation is most likely to have spread along a network of learning, being passed from its origins in Arabia to the wandering monks of the early Church.

One conjecture about Scotch is that distilling was brought to the country by the monks of the Celtic Church who sailed from Ireland to the Western Isles, making their first landfall on Islay in the sixth century. From there they sailed north, establishing their first religious base on Iona, before spreading the word of the gospel (and the other holy spirit?) into the Highlands and Central Scotland.

This theory implies that distillation was already being practised in Ireland – legend says that it was taken there by St

Patrick when he arrived from France in the fifth century, although this seems unlikely. What's possible is that Irish monks, roving across Europe, were taught the art and brought it back with them. You could even speculate that information about distillation could have arrived in Ireland via the trade with the Phoenicians, who brought viticulture to Europe. If distillation was being practised in the Middle East at this time, then why shouldn't that science be shared as well?

The second theory, most famously proposed by Scots author Neil M. Gunn, is that whisky-making was known to the Celts as they trekked from their Indo-European homeland to the fringes of the utter west. There's a logical argument here as well. If distillation was known to the Chinese, the Huns, the Indians and the Scythians, then why not to the Celts as well?

Julian the Apostate (Roman Emperor, 361–363 AD) taunted the northern "barbarians" when, on trying a "barley brew", he said: "For lack of grapes, from ears of grain your countrymen, the Celts, made you." Some scholars have seized on this as meaning spirits, but it could be beer. There's a more intriguing mention by the early Welsh bard Taliesen who wrote in his "Mead Song": "Mead distilled sparkling, its praise is everywhere." Given that Taliesen also wrote at length about brewing and didn't use the term "distil" in that treatise, it is possible that the art of making spirits was known in sixth-century Celtic Britain.

Whoever was first, by Friar Cor's time spirits were being distilled in considerable quantities in monasteries. Significantly, he distilled in the reign of James IV – a true Renaissance king,

fuelled by a lust for life, loved by his people, a patron of the arts. He was the king at whose court Scots poetry first flowered, and who financed investigations into alchemy. He spoke Gaelic, as well as French and Scots, and visited Islay to try to quell a rebellion by the Lords of the Isles. The strands come together. Islay, monks, a lost art, and an alchemist king whose mind was on higher learning.

Perhaps it's best that the birth of Scotch remains obscure. There's nothing better than debating the possible truth over a few drams in a Scottish bar. You can be guaranteed that everyone will have their own pet theory – not surprisingly, as this spirit is everyone's drink. It is inextricably bound up with the development of Scotland as a nation, it has dictated the national psyche, and echoes the land from which it springs.

THE PURE WATER OF HIGHLAND BURNS: ESSENTIAL FOR GREAT SCOTCH

Malt and the LOWLAND PLOT

All early distillers made their original compounds from readily available ingredients. Malt whisky came into existence because Scotland's climate produced a hardy grain (barley) and plenty of water, which, thanks to the country's geological structure, was virtually pure. There was also a plentiful supply of fuel (in particular, peat) to fire the stills and dry the barley. Malt came about when these natural ingredients, peculiar to Scotland, were manipulated by man.

Don't think for a minute, though, that the early whiskies would be anything like the malts we enjoy today. The stills, although they had developed from crude alembics to something equating to today's models, were small. Malted barley – from the archaic, indigenous strain of the plant called bere – was used, but so were other cereal crops, while plants and flavourings would also have been added. These early whiskies were not only used for celebrations, but also as medicines.

It was only after the dissolution of the monasteries that whisky-making became a people's art. Initially it was practised by ex-monks who became apothecaries, barbers and surgeons, but it was soon taken into the crofts and great houses of the Highlands. By the sixteenth century, not only was triple distillation common practice in the Western Isles, but exports had started to Ireland and France.

By then, *uisge beatha* (the Gaelic translation of *aqua vitae*, from which is derived today's whisky) was a central part of the rhythm of Highland life. Crofters would make it with surplus

grain, and the by-products were fed to the cattle wintering indoors. It was a spirit that fuelled dancing and celebrations, drowned sorrows, numbed the hard life and helped to pay the rent. It became part and parcel of life itself.

Although the bulk of Highland whisky was distilled in small batches for personal use, either on the croft or in the larger houses, distilleries were beginning to appear. The first notable example was Ferintosh in the Black Isle, which, thanks to the political allegiance of its owner, Duncan Forbes of Culloden, was granted duty-free status in 1715. The capital generated by this allowed Forbes to build three more distilleries and sell this first "brand" across Scotland. He had a ready market. Whisky consumption was booming and, for the first time, Lowland distillers had begun to produce spirit in significant amounts. Whisky was Scotland's drink.

Then disaster struck. The failure of the 1745 rebellion ushered in a new era for the Highland distiller. After Culloden, every aspect of Highland life and culture was systematically and ruthlessly crushed. It wasn't as simple as English versus Scots; it was aristocracy against peasant, Protestant against Catholic, Lowlander against Gael. This process of ethnic cleansing culminated in the Clearances of the nineteenth century, when a people who had made their life on the land were either herded into new towns on the coast and forced to learn new trades, or shipped to Nova Scotia, America and Australia – leaving the glens where they had farmed and distilled for centuries silent, apart from the bleating of sheep.

The post-Culloden repression took place on many fronts and directly affected how whisky developed. Crofter-distillers on islands like Tiree or Pabbay, who had exported whisky to the mainland, found themselves caught in a pincer movement of increased governmental legislation and a culture of depopulating rural areas. They were given no option but to shut down their stills, thereby losing a significant percentage of their income, and to move.

The taxman cometh

Almost inevitably, tax played its part. The saying is that "Freedom and Whisky go together", but to be strictly accurate it's taxation and whisky that have been inseparably linked since 1644. Tax had been used to fund wars and curb drinking; now it was being used to help eradicate Highland culture.

To be fair, the taxation measures affected Lowland producers as well, and the effect of a law in 1774 banning stills smaller than 200 gallons effectively drove distilling underground (often literally). This ridiculous ban made the small Highland stills illegal overnight, so smuggling increased. The Wash Act of 1784 made matters worse for the Highland distiller, for although duty was cut and smaller stills could be used in the North, it was on the proviso that only local grain be used, while the whisky produced couldn't be sold below the Highland Line.

Not surprisingly, the smuggling war intensified, mainly because by this time Highland whisky (by now similar to today's malt whisky) was considered to be better quality than the rough firewater produced by the large distillers in the Lowlands.

Then, in 1816, the Highland Line was scrapped, restrictions on still size and shape were dropped and duty was cut. By the time a further act was passed in 1823, legal distilling was not only an option but a desirable one. Whisky-making had become the preserve of the rich, often the very landowners who had forced the crofters from their land. It had ceased to be a cottage craft, but had been moulded (some would say deliberately) into an industry that could be effectively legislated by the government and controlled by relatively few men of capital.

The death-knell for single malt came with the invention of the continuous still and the rise of the blenders. Some distilleries managed to hang on to their markets – most notably producers in Campbeltown and Port Ellen on Islay, who had built up trade with America – but they were the exception. Malt was considered too heavy, too much of an acquired taste, for the world markets. As the Victorian capitalists took control of a fast-expanding industry, malt was relegated to providing the fillings for the new-fangled blends that were to make Scotch the world's favourite spirit category. Malt would remain virtually forgotten until the 1970s.

BLENDS TOOK ON THE WORLD – AND WON

The blenders

Lowland producers were always working to a different agenda from that of the Highlanders. Whisky played less of a central role in the cultural life of the cities, where the bottom line for distillers was to supply as much alcohol as possible as a palliative for Scotland's growing urban proletariat.

The Lowland distillers had always thought "larger" than their counterparts in the Highlands. The latter preferred to use small stills and malted barley, while the Lowland producers (richer, and therefore able to comply with the legal requirement to produce only from large stills) used rapid distillation and any cereal that came to hand. The grain spirit that cascaded out of their stills was undoubtedly a deeply unpleasant creation, but so what? It wasn't a drink for the refined bourgeois palate – they still drank wine and brandy (or illegal malt).

Then, in 1827, Robert Stein invented a still that not only made distilling less labour-intensive, but improved the quality of the grain spirit and allowed this more palatable drink to be mass-produced. His invention, adapted in 1831 by Aeneas Coffey, was the invention for which the Lowland producers were crying out. The continuous still had arrived, and with it the grain whisky we know today.

Much of this new drink was exported to England to be turned into gin, but it was only a matter of time before someone with a bit of imagination worked out that if they added some flavoursome malt to the light grain, they might come up with the best of all worlds – a drink that would be ideal for everyday drinking across Scotland, maybe even in England, perhaps across the world.

Crude blends would undoubtedly have been made in pubs, but after the launch of Usher's Old Vatted Glenlivet in 1853, it was grocers and wine merchants who first refined the art – men like Johnnie Walker in Kilmarnock, George Ballantine in Edinburgh, James Chivas in Aberdeen and William Teacher in Glasgow – while in Perth, Arthur Bell, John Dewar and Matthew Gloag made the town the blending capital of Scotland. Whisky was ready to be sold to the world – ironically, initially to the expatriate communities founded by the same Highlanders who had been turfed off their land.

Today's market

It needed a further stroke of fortune, in the shape of a louse, to turn blended whisky from a national into an international drink.

In the 1880s, just as the blenders were perfecting their first brands, the root-eating parasite *phylloxera vastatrix* was happily munching its way through the vineyards of Europe. When the louse destroyed the entire Cognac vineyard (the international spirit of choice at the time), blended whisky stepped into the breach and never looked back. By the time the brandy-producing regions were up and running again, blends had taken an unassailable lead.

The blended boom initiated a frenzy of distillery-building in the best locations in the Highlands – but these new whisky palaces weren't built to produce bottled single malt; they were filling stations for the new blends. While malt distilling had become a profitable business, it was the blenders who called the shots and, despite a rearguard action by the malt distillers to define "whisky" as being a spirit produced only from pot stills, in 1909 Scotch whisky was defined as being malt, grain and blended whisky. The road was clear for blends to take over the world.

Even the onset of Prohibition in the USA (1920–1933) ended up helping blended whisky, as the best-quality brands were considered to be Scotch. Prohibition may have crippled domestic production in the United States and devastated the fortunes of Irish whiskey, but blended Scotch simply shrugged off another inconvenience and just carried on growing.

Partly this was due to the distillers' canny strategy of establishing their brands in a number of international markets, rather than just relying on sales at home and in one export market in order to survive.

The combination of the Depression and the Second World War severely restricted production and most malt distilleries closed – but in the post-war world (despite high taxation in the UK) blended whisky took advantage of a more optimistic outlook and growing consumerism. New distilleries were built, while old ones reopened and increased in size. Tied to a boom in consumer spending and the development of multi-media communication, blended whisky grew rapidly throughout the 1960s and early 1970s, but a slump was not far off.

An air of complacency descended on the distillers in the late 1970s. They thought that they only had to say "drink whisky" and people would, but before they knew it the young generation in the old markets like the United States, Australia and the UK had turned away from the drink – seeing it as old-fashioned and out of touch, the drink their parents enjoyed. A combination of high oil prices, world recession and a downturn in the biggest markets saw distilleries closing again.

Thankfully, as old markets have struggled, so new ones have opened up. Europe has proved a fertile selling ground where young people have been turned on to the "new" taste of blended Scotch by the very marketing strategies that could well have turned around the decline in the old markets. The Far East, too, has clasped whisky to its bosom – particularly at the de luxe end of the market – while South America is also booming. The industry, although growing, is approaching life cautiously.

Intriguingly, as blends have declined in the old markets, new drinkers have switched their allegiance to malt. Single malts have always been available, thanks to the work of independent bottlers like Gordon & MacPhail and Cadenheads, while some distillers always bottled their own product. But until the early 1970s malt was unknown on the mass market.

Then, in 1971, William Grant & Sons decided to actively market its single malt Glenfiddich by advertising, promotions and opening the distillery to the public… It's all old hat now, but 30 years ago Glenfiddich was hugely innovative – it caught the rest of the industry on the hop, and emcouraged the development of single malt.

Malt may still only account for around five per cent of Scotch's sales, but as far as image is concerned it's leading the way forward. Increasing numbers of new whisky drinkers of both sexes aren't starting their whisky education with blends and then "graduating" to malt, but are going straight into malt.

It's become a full-time occupation to try to keep tabs on the new brands and variants that are appearing. Each week brings new malts, not only from established players, but from distilleries that were forgotten by their owners. There are malts from long-closed plants, malts that have been "finished" in different types of wood, cask-strength malts, special bottlings – the list is endless. Blends may remain all-powerful, but malt, after a century of languishing in the shadows, is now showing its true colours and may yet prove to be Scotch's saviour – not in volume, but in image.

WILLIAM GRANT LED GLENFIDDICH TO COMMERCIAL SUCCESS

Malt Whisky

Malt whisky is produced from three ingredients: malted barley, water and yeast. The barley is germinated, dried over a fire, ground, mixed with hot water, fermented and then distilled twice in pot stills. The spirit is then aged in oak casks for a minimum of three years. Simple.

How it's made

If it were just a matter of following a recipe, then all malt whiskies would taste pretty much the same. The fact that they don't have exactly the same flavour as one another is a fundamental part of malt's magic, and every distillery manager will have his or her own theory as to why each one is different. Every aspect of production is subtly different in each distillery. The same process is happening, but each site will have its own unique take on proceedings – from the type of grain used to the shape of the stills.

Take barley. There is a rumbling debate about which strain is the best. The days of bere are long gone. These days, malt is made from super-strains. Since whisky-making is an industrial-scale process, distillers are looking for a type of barley that not only gives consistent quality, but which can deliver a minimum of 400 litres of alcohol per ton.

That requires the barley to be ripe, dry, high in starch, but low in protein and nitrogen, and able to break dormancy easily. Despite the large number of strains available, a distillery will use only one or two at a time, as each type has to be processed slightly differently. There are even some romantics, most notably Macallan and Glengoyne, who insist that barley contributes to the final flavour of the spirit. Both insist on using the "old-fashioned" (and expensive) Golden Promise.

Each grain has a genetic memory of a plant within it. Malting fools the grain that it's time to start growing, and then

A SEA OF GOLD: BARLEY BEING FLOOR MALTED

stops that growth when the starches are suitable for whisky-making. This is done by first steeping it in water and getting it to start germinating – when two of its three enzymes are triggered, converting the starches into soluble sugar (maltose).

The sight of a traditional malt barn is a glorious one – the stone floor covered in a sea of gold, rucked up into waves, the barley softening, bursting out of its shell, the whisky itself starting to come alive – but these days you'll find floor maltings only at Bowmore, Laphroaig, Springbank, Benriach, Balvenie, Glen Garioch and Highland Park – although there's a chance that Ardbeg will start up again.

The rest use malt from the commercial maltsters (with the single exception of Tamdhu, which uses a system called a Saladin Box) who can process the malt in one machine. Commercial maltsters may not be as romantic, but they are highly skilled operators – vital for an industry that has to keep pace with demand.

Whatever the method, the germination has then to be stopped. Traditionally, this took place in the kiln, and even though few distilleries malt their own barley, most of them have retained the kiln's pagoda-shaped roofs.

In floor malting, a fire is lit below the floor of the kiln, which is perforated to allow hot air and smoke to rise. Traditionally the fire would have been lit with peat whose smoke, on entering the barley, permanently locks in its fragrant reek.

These days the majority of distilleries start drying with either hot air or coke, and then add a specific amount of peat for a set number of hours. The length of time the malt is under the blanket of peat smoke dictates how many phenolic parts per million (ppm) will be

in a malt. Heavily peated malts like Ardbeg, Lagavulin or Laphroaig have between 40 and 50 ppm; medium-peated examples, like Bowmore of Highland Park, have 20 ppm; while lightly-peated Speysides, like Aberlour, Glenfarclas or Cragganmore, are all around 2 ppm. There are malts such as Glengoyne and Deanston that have no peat at all.

The malted barley, crisp and fragrant, then goes to the mill – where it's crushed to a specific grind. Too fine a grind, and you get a thick porridge that won't drain; too coarse, and you won't have exposed sufficient sugars. A percentage of husks is also needed to act as a natural filter in the mash tun.

Once in the mash tun, hot water is poured over the grist, completing the final conversion. Since Scotch is only allowed to use the natural enzyme in the barley, the water has to be at a temperature that can do this without killing the enzyme.

This sweet water (worts) is drained off, and a second and third waters are poured on. The first of these gets rid of those stubborn starches that cling to the husk. This, too, is drained off and kept with the first water. The third water is kept as the first water of the next mash.

The worts are then cooled and pumped into fermenting vessels (washbacks) made either from steel or Oregon pine. Yeast is then added, and here's another area that's open to debate. The wine industry accepts that yeast imparts flavours, as do bourbon producers. Most Scotch distillers reject this and use whatever yeast gives the best yield. But if the flavour of the water, the aroma of peat and, perhaps, the flavour of the barley impart tiny elements of flavour, then why can't yeast?

The washbacks seethe as the ferment starts. Huge, puffy bubbles form on the scummy surface and pop in nose-tingling explosions. This goes on for between 48 and 60 hours, by which time the worts have been transformed into a strong wash.

31

The key is knowing when to stop – a rule of thumb is that the lightest, most fragrant whiskies tend to be cut at a higher strength than the phenolic, almost oily malts, which are cut significantly lower. Each distillery will do it differently. Macallan is notoriously tight with its cut, while the unctuous Laphroaig lets it run for longer than most.

Once the heart is collected, the feints are run into the low-wines receiver to join the foreshots, ready for the next charge of the spirit still. Then the new spirit is poured into casks – made either from ex-bourbon or sherry butts – for its long, slow maturation. [see box]

While distilleries may now be equipped with computers that can calculate quicker than the human brain, whisky-making is a human activity. For, despite all the research and increased technology, no one knows quite what makes each malt special. For Mike Winchester at Aberlour, it's quite simple: "As understanding increases, so we'll realize why we are here, but the fact is we're here already! There's still a lot of witchcraft and magic to it all."

You need spend only a short time with the men in a distillery to realize that this isn't an industrial process – it's a labour of love; producing whisky taps into living folk wisdom. It's about guys who care about their product: the maltmen, who know that the malt is ready to be kilned when they can write their name on the wall with the soft grain; the stillmen, who can tell when to make the cut just by the look of the swirl the spirit makes in the hydrometer; the coopers, obsessively caring for each cask. That isn't industry, it's love – generations of knowledge being passed down from father to son. At the end of the day malt whisky, like all great spirits, is still about people.

THE STILLMAN WATCHES THE NEW SPIRIT LIKE A HAWK

Now comes the final transformation: distillation in large, copper pot stills. The first distillation gives a spirit called low wines, of around 21 per cent ABV. This is collected and, once the distillation is finished, is pumped into the spirit still for a second distillation.

Like all forms of batch distillation, this process is concerned with separating the heads and tails (here known as foreshots and feints) from the heart of the spirit – or "making the cut", as it is known. Once the cut has started, the speed of the distillation is slowed down, and the heart is allowed to flow into a receiving tank until the distiller has decided that the true character of his malt has been captured.

WATER

This, the first element in the creation of a malt whisky, is also the most mysterious. Why does water affect how a whisky tastes? It comes down to purity. What you want in good 'whisky water' is an absence of elements such as iron, but beneficial minerals such as calcium and zinc. Scottish water also has a low pH level – often because it contains traces of acidic peat – which will help with fermentation. What the water flows over on its way to the distillery will also have an impact on flavour. The three peaty monsters on Islay's south coast – Ardbeg, Lagavulin and Laphroaig – all use water that has run for miles over peat and picked up phenolic elements. Every little thing makes a difference.

WOOD

The whisky industry has always used second-hand casks to age its product. In the early days these would have been wine, rum or sherry barrels that had been shipped to Scottish wine merchants. The Celtic nations are known for their thriftiness, so it made sense to re-use the casks.

The industry now uses two main types of cask: ex-Bourbon barrels, and butts that have previously held sherry. Good casks will then be refilled once, or maybe twice, and some may be recharred to give them a new lease of life after the second fill. Components for blends, by and large, are filled into second- or third-fill barrels, while malts will go into a combination of first- and second-fill.

Some malts, like Glenmorangie, use only first- and second-fill ex-bourbon barrels, while Macallan will use only sherry wood – although most distilleries use a combination of the two.

In the old days, choosing the percentages of bourbon and sherry was about as far as it went. These days, distillers are looking at how the two different woods behave and what quali-

ties they give. It's been estimated that between 50 and 60 per cent of a whisky's flavour comes from the wood, and Glenmorangie has taken the radical step of designing its own casks – the logic being that if you know which wood works best, you'll be more likely to get consistent whisky.

The conclusion was that they wanted air-dried, 100-year-old, white US oak from north-facing slopes of the Ozarks. Why? Air-drying eliminates the acrid astringent notes that kiln-drying can produce, while trees from north-facing slopes have a slower rate of growth, giving the right pore size and structure.

Macallan is equally obsessive. Its research showed that it got greater colour extraction and a more even maturation from Spanish, rather than American, oak. Now Highland Distillers (Macallan's parent) gets casks built to order. Macallan, Highland Park and Glengoyne all use Spanish oak, as does Bowmore.

Where the whisky is matured makes a difference as well. It is generally agreed that the old, low slung "dunnage" warehouses with their earth floors perform the best – retaining humidity and giving good air circulation. Trouble is, there isn't enough space to build this

style, and many distillers now age in rack warehouses. Macallan invested heavily to ensure its new racked sheds performed as its old-style warehouses, but others are suffering from the shortcuts they took.

Where the whisky matures is the final element in its building a sense of place. It has received its personality from the water, the peat, the barley and the shape of the still, and now wood. As a spirit sits in a cask, it is slowly drawn in and out of the wood, not only taking in the colours and flavouring compounds of the cask, but the air as well. A little bit of the microclimate is captured.

PEAT

Peat, technically, is decomposed vegetation that has been carbonized by water. It's the fuel that's widely used in the Highlands and Islands, and the black incense that gives many whiskies a flavour that immediately whisks you back to their place of birth.

There are also different types of peat, giving different aromas. Islay's contains seaweed and moss and gives a denser, more aromatic nose; that on the mainland has more wood and heather, and is lighter; while on Orkney – where they even have different names for the different layers – heather is the main constituent.

The days of distilleries using nothing but hand-cut peat are long gone. Bowmore uses 150 tons of peat a year in its own kiln, but the maltings at Port Ellen, which malts most of Islay's barley, needs 2,500 tons of peat each year. To get that, it has to rip the peat up with industrial tractors.

The question of (ab)using a non-renewable natural resource arises. In fact, the whisky industry uses just 0.1 per cent of the peat cut every year. A nagging doubt still remains though. The old peat banks allow the heather and grasses to regrow which, in turn, protects a fragile ecosystem. The slash-and-rip technology leaves nothing behind. Surely another method needs to be found?

The sense of PLACE

THE MOST HEAVILY PEATED AND ARGUABLY THE MOST COMPLEX OF ISLAY'S MALTS

IF IT'S FULL-ON PEAT YOU WANT – LOOK NO FURTHER

The issue of whether malt whisky regions actually exist is another topic best discussed over a few drams with a fire blazing in the grate. The "antis" argue (rightly) that since each malt uses different water, has a slightly different malting specification, distils in a unique set of stills and matures in its own selection of casks, it's impossible to quantify what effect the environment has on the final product. There are too many variables – and it's too easy to manipulate.

Ah, but while it's difficult to bind together distilleries from a disparate region, there are some parts of Scotland where the "regional" argument holds up.

For example, the reason that the majority of Islay's malts are peaty and have a bracing iodine aroma is because on Islay there was no option but to use the local fuel, which was (and is) peat. The composition of the water will also have a minuscule, but significant, effect. Phenolic water will impart a different flavour to the purer water on the mainland. There's also little doubt that you find a saltiness in malts that are matured by the sea – no great surprise there. Casks that have been matured in a salt-laden atmosphere will have sucked in some of that air to mingle with the spirit as the wood inhales.

In other words, there are regions where you can say the physical environment has dictated some of the malt's final flavour. The rest? Well, perhaps it's just romantic nonsense to claim that there's a pasture-like quality to the malts from the gentle Lowlands, a softness in those from the rolling hills of Perthshire, and a dry heatheriness to the ones from the harder lands in the north – but somehow, once you have visited the distillery, the landscape becomes inextricably linked with it.

Islay and Jura

If you accept the theory that distilling was brought to Scotland by Irish monks, then it's more than likely that the island of Islay was the first place in Scotland to distil whisky. It is only 28 miles by sea from Ireland, it is an ancient Christian site, and was the political focus for the virtually independent west-coast islands until the mid-seventeenth century. Even today, Islay manages to stand apart from the rest of Scotland – particularly in its whiskies. Relatively prosperous, it's a place where whisky continues to bind the community together.

This is something that the bean counters in head offices seem to forget. Malt whisky is made in rural parts of Scotland, places where there is little alternative employment. It provides an infrastructure of jobs, from distillery workers to coopers, coppersmiths, transport firms and farmers. When the distilleries of Ardbeg and Bruichladdich were mothballed on Islay, 20 people lost their jobs on an island of only 2,500 inhabitants.

The human dimension to whisky is clearer on Islay than in many other places because there are seven distilleries (one of which is mothballed) on this small island. Along with Edradour and Highland Park, this is where you feel closest to whisky's roots. All early distillers made their spirit from local ingredients – and Islay, as one of the most fertile islands in the Hebrides, could provide locally grown barley, water and fuel – as well as having natural harbours to get the whisky out and supplies in. This combination of self-sufficiency, and the fact that Islay was less brutally cleared than the other islands, helped whisky-making to prosper, while on other islands distilleries have either dwindled to one, or gone altogether.

What Islay is about is peat. When early blenders wanted a bass note of peat in their blend (look no further than White Horse, Bell's and Johnnie Walker), Islay was the obvious choice. Nowhere else can provide the rich, "iodiney", fragrant reek that Islay's peat gives to its malts, and nowhere else in Scotland is this more obvious than on the southern strip of the island, home to the three most powerfully peated malts of all – Lagavulin, Laphroaig and Ardbeg.

While the rest of the industry has scaled down peating levels, here they are kept up to between 35 and 50 ppm, but behind that immediate blast of peat smoke and seashore aromas lurks real complexity.

They do things differently on the remote north-east coast, where Bunnahabhain uses spring water and peats to a mere 2 ppm. It's a delicate dram, which, despite the low peating, still has a rich saltiness that fixes it on the coastal fringe. For too long its neighbour, Caol Ila, was a distillery whose peating levels flew up and down, depending on what the blenders at United Distillers wanted at that time. It's not an unusual state of affairs, but it did mean that the rare bottlings of the single malt were unpredictable. These days consistency is the key, and the single malt has improved immeasurably.

To get from Caol Ila to the island's capital, Bowmore, you have to pass by the ancient seat of the Lords of the Isles at Finlaggan, a seat of power since neolithic times. These days it's the distillers who look after the community, and nowhere is this clearer than in Bowmore, where an old warehouse has been converted into the local swimming pool, whose water is heated by waste heat from the distillery.

Sitting on the shores of Lochindaal, this is a distillery with a wood regime that's among the strictest in Scotland. The complex mixes of casks (only Spanish oak is used for the sherry butts) means that there's a mass of Bowmores available, but the finest of them all is, at 17 years old, as magnificent a malt as you'll find.

Bowmore looks across the loch to Bruichladdich, sadly mothballed but, in its day, capable of producing a lovely, lightly peated malt that still had a lick of sweetness and a tingle of salt air. It

was closed because its owner already had an island distillery – on the neighbouring island of Jura.

Despite the two islands being only 800 yards away by ferry, the contrast between them couldn't be greater. Islay has 2,500 people, Jura 250. It's

an otherworldly place, where golden eagles spiral on the thermals above the scree-streaked Paps. The distillery, framed by palm trees, produces a lightly salty 10-year-old, but the best stuff is found in occasional bottlings of sherry casks.

ISLAY'S DISTILLERIES ARE BUILT HARD ON THE SEA EDGE

Tasting Notes

ISLAY

Bowmore 17yo. Intense. Whiffs of peat smoke, orange peel/Jaffa cake and a hint of cigar box. Peat and ozone with mocha-accented fruit. Elegant, rounded, soft and very long. World class.

Laphroaig 10yo. Peat sodden, medicinal with slight biscuity crunch on the nose. With water, more smoke and seaweed emerge. A little lacking in complexity.

Laphroaig 10yo cask strength. Huge. Peat and fishy oiliness, a rich and powerful mix of seaweed and ozone. Very malty, powerful and weighty. A classy dram.

Ardbeg 17yo. Orange/lemon marmalade, chewy malt and integrated peatiness on the nose, giving a sense of richness with some vanilla mingling with the smoke. Smoulders in the glass. A tight start, then rich flavours laced with lapsang souchong tea and ripe fruit.

Ardbeg 1978. Big and grumbly, then a graceful unfolding of peat. The merest touch of peat oil on the palate then rich, smoky fruits with a hint of toffee, heather and salt. Very, very long. Glorious.

Lagavulin 16yo. A great waft of smoke mixed with leather and walnut. Slight green woodiness on the finish,

but an elegant, multilayered dram.

Caol Ila 15yo. A mix of medicinal, rooty notes with lanolin and soft peatiness. Full palate with a hint of tobacco leaf and peat smoke. Crisp, tingly finish with a touch of salt.

Bunnahabhain Chewy toffee/salt on the nose with a manzanilla tanginess. A bracing start, well rounded and gentle on the palate, with a sudden ping of gingerbread on the finish.

Campbeltown, Arran and the Lowlands

Occasionally the flight from Glasgow to Islay will touch down at the military airport at Machrihanish in the south of Kintyre. It's only a few miles to Campbeltown, one of those solid, respectable-looking towns that dot the Scottish Highlands.

It's hard to believe that this now apparently sedate town was once whisky's capital, with 21 distilleries pouring out malt, prompting whisky's first chronicler, Alfred Barnard, to comment that there were "almost as many places of worship as distilleries". Once, there was so much whisky in Campbeltown that they wrote a song about it; there are records of complaints that gangs of pigs, drunk on pot ale, were terrorizing the town. These days one distillery is open and another is in a sad state of repair (and not an inebriated porker to be seen); but there are still plenty of kirks… What went wrong?

Campbeltown's fall from grace was down to greed. In the early part of the

twentieth century it was a major supplier to the booming US market and, as demand increased, so distillers upped production, but they didn't keep their eyes on quality.

The second nail in the coffin was thanks to Prohibition. Campbeltown's

high reputation meant that it could command a higher price, so production was speeded up further. The fact that Campbeltown whisky soon became to be known as "stinking fish" is evidence that there was some pretty poor distilling going on.

To be honest, where the whisky originated from didn't worry the boot-

legger over-much; Al Capone wasn't too concerned with the niceties of appellation law. This combination of poor-quality, genuine Campbeltown and the ersatz Campbeltown killed its reputation – and distilleries. The only evidence of the quality that came out of Campbeltown's stills these days is Springbank. It is produced from hand-malted barley (a release of malt made from local barley is imminent), uses complex distillation, a selection of different woods (including rum casks) and bottles at the distillery without any chill-filtering. Springbank, quite simply, makes some of Scotland's greatest malts.

Lying between the east coast of Kintyre and the mainland, the island of Arran was once noted for its malt, but like so many parts of the Highlands its stills had long disappeared – that is, until 1995 when the brand new Isle of Arran distillery started operations. It's early days, but the indications are that it's producing a wee cracker, although we'll have to wait until 2001 before we can find out quite how good it is.

Sadly, the story of distillery closures is repeated across the Lowlands. These days only Auchentoshan and Glenkinchie are open to show the graceful, gentle style that defines this region.

The indications are that Rosebank is to re-open, which would at least mean that the Lowland's greatest malt is back in production, while Bladnoch, the most southerly distillery of them all, seems likely to be up and running again. There's a gentle stirring in the southern regions.

Tasting Notes

CAMPBELTOWN
Springbank 15yo. Very rich nose with roasted spices and a hint of peat. Powerful. A melding of bracing seaside air with sleek, deep, concentrated fruitiness.
Glenkinchie 10yo. Fresh, almost citric nose with grassy aromas. Crisp clean and smooth on palate.
Glenkinchie Amontillado finish
Rounded with a little malt loaf and some nut. Soft, sweet grass and a longer, sweeter finish with a nutty drive.

Auchentoshan 10yo. Delicate and ultra fresh. Very clean, dry – a good lunchtime dram.
Rosebank Appears light initially, but there's a deceptive richness behind. Dry on the palate, but balanced with elegant fruit. Some wood on the finish.

EDRADOUR: WHISKY-MAKING THE OLD WAY

Central Highlands

Although people's image of the Scottish Highlands is of stark mountains with stags and rabbits at bay, its southern and central parts are filled with soft, rounded mountains and fertile valleys.

The malts that come from this disparate region are similarly smooth – although they often share a firm, dry finish. The fact that there's plenty of water, wood and coal (and little peat), and that the major blending towns of Glasgow and Perth were within easy reach, made this the perfect area in which to build distilleries in the latter part of the nineteenth century.

The malts range from the unpeated duo of Glengoyne (an often overlooked malt which is one of the great lunchtime drams) and Deanston to the joys of Scotland's smallest malt distillery, Edradour. This is a fascinating place, which gives an insight into how whisky used to be made. Built as a co-operative in 1825 by farmers who had undoubtedly been distilling illegally for many years previously, it lies nestled, half-hidden in a small glen to the north of Pitlochry. Even today, it's easily missed – perhaps when the industry was closing down much grander places, it simply forgot it was there.

Right enough, the fact that the 90,000 litres that appear from Edradour's minuscule stills every year end up as a brilliant dram – with a typically Perthshire creamy, honeyed palate – might just have tipped the scales in its favour.

This character is echoed to some extent by Dalwhinnie, Scotland's highest distillery, which, walled in by the bulk of the Cairngorm massif, produces a soft, versatile dram that epitomises the rather graceful style of this region.

Western Highlands

Scotland's west coast is ripped by sea lochs that run (roughly) west to east, thereby making travel from north to south difficult. Because this meant it was not easy to get malt whisky to the Lowland blending houses, there's only a smattering of distilleries in this part of the country. The most notable is Oban which, although on the mainland, has its gaze set firmly out to sea – whose salty air inveigles its way into the malt, making it a delirious bridgehead between Highland and island.

From Oban it's a short ferry trip to Mull. Once a quarter of all the grain grown there was turned into whisky. Now there's only one distillery, found in the island's capital of Tobermory, and even that has had a pretty shaky few years (and produced some pretty shaky bottles as a result). Fortunately, its new owner is quality conscious.

Tasting Notes

CENTRAL HIGHLANDS

Glengoyne Edradour 10yo. Light, floral notes with a hint of sherry/honey richness. Touches of hay on palate, coupled with the crisp crunchiness of Bourbon casks. A rich, soft buttery finish.

Dalwhinnie 15yo. Light, a little nutty with a soft, smooth mix of honey and pepper on the palate.

Oban 14yo. Very clean and tingly nose of dried herbs and sea breezes. Gentle but with a marvellously refreshing quality.

Oban Montilla finish Cold tea, vanillin wood and a salty lanolin aroma. Very smooth, elegant on palate. Fresh, long, clean finish with a hint of redcurrant.

Speyside

The west coast couldn't be in greater contrast to the region that lies at the top of the Great Glen. Here, in Speyside, lies malt's golden heart. Nowhere else on the mainland can you find such a concentration of high-quality, complex drams. But why? For a start it's slap bang next to Scotland's main barley-growing region. In the old days the granite mountains provided pure water and peat – until the railway allowed coal to be brought in from the south and the peating levels dropped. During the smuggling war, Speyside's tight glens and wooded hills provided perfect cover for the illicit trade. In other words, all the ingredients were on hand to make great whiskies – and make them they did.

In many ways, Speyside's landscape mirrors its malts. It's a part of Scotland that only reveals itself in tempting morsels: birch and beech woods, the slanting light, the rapid rivers that swerve and jink through its tweeded valleys. Whisky is a lot like Speyside. Elusive, its secrets are never quite fully revealed. Its best malts have a complex mix of light, floral notes mingled with smoke, that somehow give a feeling of delicacy but remain weighty. They can also cope well with sherry wood – revealing chocolate, walnut and Dundee cake richness. With 50 distilleries to choose from, you're spoiled for choice.

The history of distillation in Speyside could go back to the earliest Christian times. St Drostan, an early missionary, is buried underneath Aberlour distillery, and distillery manager Mike Winchester has a hunch – though no more than that – that if monks did carry the secret with them,

then perhaps the good saint was the man responsible for first spreading the word of whisky (as well as of God) to the region.

In more recent times, Speyside has been the most pioneering of the regions. After all, this is where the malt revolution started. Ever since George IV decided that only Glenlivet could slake the royal thirst in 1822 (even though it was illegal), Speyside's reputation was sealed. Soon after the royal seal of approval was given, George Smith's Glenlivet distillery became the first licensed distillery in Scotland, much to the annoyance of the smugglers. As a result, Smith had to sport a pair of loaded pistols, just in case. The distillery's fame spread, so that everyone wanted to tag the appellation on to the end of their name, even if some were malt's equivalent of Spanish Sauternes. The first blend was an "Old Vatted Glenlivet", made by Smith's Edinburgh

agent. Even today, the concentration of distilleries in this part of Scotland is down to the fact that Speyside's elegance and complexity are exactly the qualities that blenders want for core malts in their blends.

Let's not forget, either, that this is where Glenfiddich is based. So-called malt lovers may scoff at the name, but if William Grant hadn't taken the initiative to market this single malt, then who knows where the market would be? Equally, when most of the industry had given up on sherry wood as an expensive luxury they couldn't afford, Macallan persevered and showed beyond a doubt what obsessive quality

control and exemplary wood management could do. A youthful Macallan is a huge seller on the Italian market – following in the footsteps of another great innovator in the region, Glen Grant, who opened up that important market with a cheeky little five-year-old. Ironically, Glen Grant is a malt that needs more time than most to reveal its true properties – look for independent bottlings for proof of this.

If pushed to produce a list of the top dozen, I'd plump for (alphabetically): Aberlour, Balvenie, Cragganmore, Glenfarclas, Glen Grant, The Glenlivet, Knockando, Linkwood, Longmorn, Macallan, Mortlach and Strathisla.

Eastern Highlands

You would perhaps think that the richly fertile Eastern Highlands would be home to a host of distilleries. You couldn't be further from the truth. Sure, they were once here, taking advantage of the mild climate and the fields of barley, and turning out medium-bodied, juicy malts, but now there's the merest smattering. Fettercairn, Glenadam, the meaty and muscular Royal Lochnagar and the recently re-opened Glen Garioch. There's a chance that Glendronach will re-open soon, while rumours abound that Montrose's Lochside may be up and running in the near future. We can only wait and hope.

*One of Glenfarclas'
enviable range*

Tasting Notes

SPEYSIDE

Tamdhu Crisp, grassy, biscuity with a touch of cowpat, hot bracken and a hint of freesia. Clean with a nice smoky touch.

Knockando 1980. Fragrant, delicate and a wisp of greek yoghurt and honey. A dreamy dram with a refreshing tingle on the finish.

The Singleton 10yo. Medium-rich fruit. The nose has a touch of peat, some vanilla and soft fruit compote and slight pepperiness. Some substance on the palate, but the wood is obtrusive.

Strathisla 12yo. Rich and deep. Soft bracken aroma, but with a layered mix of plum, dates, spice, toffee, almond and toasted hazelnut. Powerful, yet subtle. A multifaceted malt.

Glen Grant 10yo. Almost winey in its herbaceous/grassy aroma, but with a slightly dumb weight. A little astringent on the palate, but delicate and juicy.

The Glenlivet 12yo. Clean nose with plenty of US oak on show. Ripe fruits with a touch of smoke. Lightly heathery. Starts light on the palate, then smoke and wood begin to build.

The Glenlivet 18yo. Rich, with some sherry nuttiness on show, with aromas of nutmeg, damson, but with pears and apples giving it a gorgeous lift. Rich and unctuous, it flows through the mouth.

Longmorn 15yo. A dense nose filled with all manner of hairy things. Dark woodland fruit, treacle, Highland toffee, honeycombs. On the

palate it is hugely rich with dried herbs. A grave and complex glass.

Macallan 18yo. Warming richness, tending to sweetness. Exotic spices mixed with acacia honey and rich fruit and nut notes. Powerfully textured.

Macallan Gran Reserva Complex nose of pink grapefruit, butterscotch honey, walnut and a hint of cloves. Surprisingly delicate given its dark colour. Fresh with deep fruit. Elegant and long.

Cragganmore Highly perfumed, akin to incense with ripe red fruits behind. Very clean with a fine, complex mid-palate that has a strangely evocative sweetness, mingling with light smoke. A benchmark of Speyside complexity.

Aberlour 10yo. Nuttily rounded with toffee and vanilla, but a really fresh drive. A touch of peat on the palate mixed with herbal straw and a hint of anise on the finish.

Aberlour 18yo (Sherry matured). Rich Spanish sherry-wood aroma. Walnuts, figs and dates dominate the nose. Beautifully rounded on the palate, with a soft, smoky finish.

Balvenie Double Wood 12yo. Rich, dry and slightly smoky, with some grass and blooming heather. Very clean and gentle, with a subtle touch of sherry wood on the finish.

Mortlach Rich, smooth sherry nose. This isn't just big, it's an immense malt – a huge Highland hero. Complex and masterly.

Glenfarclas 15yo. Rounded, quite spicy, almost minty. Lifted, intense, delicious.

Glenfarclas 21yo. Rich and slightly honeyed nose that mixes butterscotch, currant fruit, a touch of smoke and orange. Great.

Glenfarclas 30yo. A feel of butter and raisin/prune on the nose, mixed with wild herbs. A gorgeous Seville orange lift that complements the walnut fruitiness superbly. Everlasting, and one to kill for.

EASTERN HIGHLANDS

Royal Lochnagar 23yo. Sherry sweet on the nose. A hugely muscular, sturdy number with good spicy notes. Rounded, rich and mellow.

Dailuaine 16yo. Slight rubbery notes with hazelnut behind. Big and rich on the palate. The finish is very clean.

Black Isle and above

The distilleries to the north of Inverness straggle out along the coast. There aren't many of them, but they do share a style – not surprisingly influenced by the sea air that wafts into the warehouses. Here you can find rarities like the heathery, citric Teaninich, the sadly underrated and mighty Dalmore – and Scotland's best-selling malt, Glenmorangie.

GLENMORANGIE: MASTERS OF WOOD MATURATION

Here, a pair of gin stills was converted for whisky distillation, and the spirit that comes over their graceful, tall necks is one of the most delicate in Sscotland, where pear-drops mix with oranges and gorse bushes. Glenmorangie is also one of the distilleries to lead the way with wood-management. Just as Macallan, Highland Park, Glengoyne and Bowmore specify Spanish oak for their

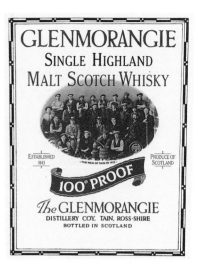

sherry butts, so Glenmorangie insists on air-dried white oak from the Ozarks for its supply of wood.

The malt hasn't the physique to cope with extended maturation in sherry, but it does have sufficient character to allow it to be enhanced with a short period finishing in a different type of wood. Port, sherry, Madeira and ex-red-wine barrels have all been used so far, and with great success. They are all different, yet part of the same family. There's no holding Glenmorangie at the moment – there are even plans to release an organic malt made from barley grown on its own estate.

North from the town of Tain you hit the empty, but fertile, straths that the Duke and Duchess of Sutherland so effectively cleared. The Black Duke was the first owner of Clynelish, having first used illegal distilling as an excuse for evicting crofters, only promptly to take over whisky-making to line his own pocket.

These days, Clynelish (and its northern neighbour, Pulteney) produce drams with a maritime edge – Clynelish going for the smoky, even seaweedy edge, while Pulteney is a cracking dram with bracing, salt-laden complexity.

BLACK ISLE AND ABOVE

Teaninich 10yo. Light, soft and heathery, with a hint of smoky wood. Sweet with very soft peatiness.

Glenmorangie Port finish Summer aromas, some citric spiciness and a hint of chocolate. Very soft on the palate – redcurrant jam and red pepper.

Glenmorangie Madeira finish Subtle, complex nose – hay, mint, cumin, cinnamon, toffee and a light burnt edge.

Dalmore 12yo. Concentrated nose with a whiff of coal gas. Smooth with fine weight mid-palate and a clean, dry finish.

Clynelish 14yo. Seaside aromas with touches of orange peel and smoke. Slight sweetness and some peat smoke on palate.

Talisker 10yo. Ozone, peat, seaweed, smoke and burnt heather on nose. Mouth-filling flavours. Peppery bite on finish.

Talisker Amoroso finish Heather and peat give way to fruitcake and peat fires. Rich and sweet.

Highland Park 12yo. Touches of heather, honey wax and cinnamon/ginger spice. Dry with sweetness of fruit on palate, before a long peat smoke finish.

Highland Park 18yo Powerful herb and honey aromas with some light smokiness. Soft and rounded in the mouth. A long seductive smoke-accented malt.

Skye and Orkney

This pairing may seem pretty tenuous – they may both be islands, and their malts both use peat, but they are on different coasts! They do, however, have a connection insofar as they both produce malts that are true distillations of their environment. You may have to suspend belief to marry many malts to their surroundings, but there can be no doubt that Talisker from Skye and Highland Park on Orkney rise from the land on which they are distilled.

Talisker is an elemental whisky, the distillery standing lonely on the storm-lashed west coast, glowering mountains behind. There are few other spots in Scotland where sea, rock, water and weather unite so dramatically. Nothing could be further from the distilleries which have sprung up in small towns. This is whisky-making in its original form, made by people in remote communities using the ingredients that come to hand. Skye is all strange mists and peat bogs, jagged crags, heather moors and seaweed-lathered coasts. All of that is in the glass, from the burnt-heather peat reek, the touch of iodine and a peppery finish that makes it the perfect match for haggis – uncompromising, and quite brilliant.

Orkney's environment is totally different. Low-lying, and green as Ireland, it's a collection of islands where civilizations have layered themselves on top of each other like the strata in rock. Orkney exists in its own time frame, a place where the cathedral and pagan religion seem to sit quite happily side by side. In fact, the only building in Kirkwall that's higher than the cathedral is Highland Park distillery – and there's as neat a symbol of Scottishness as you could wish for. Highland Park malts some of its own barley, uses its own peat and ages in a mix of ex-bourbon and sherry casks. All combine to give a malt with honey, heather, spice and smoke. It's as magnificent a dram as you could wish for.

At times, microclimate may seem a figment of the over-excited imagination, but when you encounter malts like these there can be little doubt that distillation doesn't just convert bere into spirit, but somehow manages to capture and refine the very environment on which the distillery stands.

TALISKER DISTILLERY: HOME TO SCOTLAND'S MOST ELEMENTAL WHISKY

Grain Whisky

The foundation for Scotch's international success is based on the blends which first appeared in the mid-nineteenth century. Blends and whisky would have amounted to very little without the invention of the continuous still and the arrival of grain whisky

How it's made

By the early nineteenth century, Scotland had woken up to the delights of whisky, and the growing urban population of the Lowlands had developed an insatiable thirst for it. Lowland distillers, though, had to cope with this growing demand by producing whisky by the slow and small-scale batch process. Some tried to get round the problem by distilling their grain spirit in huge flat-bottomed monsters, but that only ended up producing a vile concoction. If only whisky could be made in the quantities desired, but also to taste pleasant.

Enter Robert Stein and Aeneas Coffey. These two pioneering distillers invented stills that could produce a flavoursome light spirit, in large volumes and continuously. As long as you fed wash in one end, you'd get spirit out of the other. It was the invention the Lowland distillers had been waiting for.

What Stein invented and Coffey perfected was a distillation process that allowed grain spirit to be produced in huge quantities. So successful was Coffey's invention that his type of still is the main one that continues to be used in grain whisky production. Each grain plant will have its own variations on the theme, but the principle remains the same.

The process starts off relatively straightforwardly. The cereal is crushed and then cooked at a high temperature to release the starches. Then a small amount of ground-malted barley is added to the mash, along with hot water, and the conversion from starch to soluble sugar takes place. The resulting worts are then fermented into wash and distilled. This is where the genius came into play.

Coffey's still comprises two tall, linked columns called the analyser and the rectifier, each of which is divided internally into chambers by horizontal, perforated copper plates. Pressurized steam is pumped into the bottom of the analyser, where it rises and then passes into the bottom of the rectifier. The wash, meanwhile, is moving in the opposite direction. Cold wash, carried in a copper pipe, travels down the rectifier and is then carried up to the top of the analyser, being gradually heated by the steam as it travels.

The wash is now allowed to meander down the analyser through drip pipes that link the chambers, all the time coming into contact with the rising steam that's being pumped through the perforations in the plates. As the wash

GRANT'S GIRVAN DISTILLERY: WHISKY-MAKING 20TH-CENTURY STYLE

descends, the rising steam strips the alcohol from it, so that when the wash reaches the bottom of the column it has no alcohol left. The alcohol vapour, mingling with the steam, is then carried by it to the bottom of the rectifier. The steam and the vapour then begin to rise up the column, meeting the cold wash as it descends in its copper pipe. This causes the spirit vapour to condense slowly, so that only the highest-strength alcohols reach the top of the column. After removing the first alcohols to come off, the spirit is collected on a condensing plate at around 95 per cent ABV. The end result is a high-volume, high-strength spirit that is low in flavour.

The truth about grain

This interpretation has led people to believe that all grain spirits are the same. Nothing could be further from the truth. Sure, they don't have the powerful complexities and differences that you find in malt, but each grain has its own distinctive character. Part of this character is down to the cereal used. Maize (corn) is generally recognized as producing a better quality grain, although economics meant that in recent times most has been produced from wheat. Equally, each grain distillery will use a different percentage of malted barley.

The results are a fascinating range of spirits, ranging from the fragile Strathclyde (whose spirit, when further rectified, is the base for Beefeater Gin), through the smooth, soft Girvan, to the sweet, yet firm spirit that comes from Invergordon – the only grain distillery in the Highlands. Glasgow's Port Dundas is more weighty, Dumbarton has a fat, slippery quality, while Cameronbridge (where it all started)

EXPERT NOSES DECIPHER WHISKY'S DEFINING CHARACTERISTICS

has a rich elegance, though not as rich and full-bodied as the grain from North British in Edinburgh.

All are different, and all mature in a different fashion, which is great for blenders. At The Edrington Group, master blender John Ramsay will use grain from Strathclyde when it is young, as it matures quickly. Because the grain from North British (in which Edrington has a 50 per cent stake) has greater body and character, it can age well and is a perfect component for 12- or 18-year-old blends.

It is also a fallacy to believe that the exact same spirit flows from the stills every day. This was brought home to me when Alan Reid, blender at Robertson & Baxter, lined up four glasses. It's one of his regular tests to show journalists who's boss. All the samples were grain, but all nosed differently. Logic dictated that they all came from different distilleries. They didn't; rather, they were from the same distillery, but from different days. Grain changes – less obviously than malt, perhaps, but it changes nonetheless – and this is

another element that has to be taken into consideration when a blend is being assembled.

It is also widely believed that grain whisky doesn't age well. Perhaps that's because most blends use young whiskies to achieve the required character and to keep costs down. Grain's light character, however, hides an ability to develop fine qualities over long periods of time. "Of course you can age grain for as long as malt," says Colin Scott at Chivas Brothers. "The the important thing is to ensure that you are putting it in a top-quality cask."

Grain's finer qualities have long been overlooked. For years, only Cameronbridge was available as a bottled brand, but it has recently been joined by Invergordon's 10-year-old and Grant's Black Barrel. They may only be niche products, but they demonstrate that there's more to grain than you may assume. Says Scott: "I look at malt as being the cake, but grain is the icing. It enhances the malt." It's this malleable quality that allowed blended whisky to take over the world.

The art of the BLENDER

Despite the fact that blended whisky accounts for 95 per cent of Scotch's sales, it's a sector that is often dismissed as being second best and, with malt in the ascendant, blend's image looks like deteriorating still further.

We have almost returned to the days of Sir Robert Bruce Lockhart who, in his wonderful book *Scotch*, wrote: "Scotch malt is a he-man's drink, and goes with hard toil and strenuous exercise in the open air. Blended Scotch is for weaker stomachs."

Well, those weaker stomachs – not as used to the rigours of Highland life – have been the ones that took Scotch from a little-known local spirit produced in a small, wet country in the north of Europe to a world-conquering spirit. The reason they did was because blends have an instant appeal – at their best they are subtle, flavoursome, mixable. They can also be mass-produced.

Blends are a classically Scottish fusion of commerce and creativity, and their creators are unsung heroes who, armed with nothing more than a glass, their memory and their nose, are in charge of creating and monitoring every single Scotch whisky brand.

Blenders always play down their role. They shy away from publicity and see themselves not as artists, but as custodians of the brand. Their function is to ensure that the brand remains consistent year in, year out. But it cannot be denied, artists they are.

In simple terms, a blended whisky is a combination of grain and malt whiskies, with grain making up the lion's share. But blenders have considerably more to do than just follow an ancient recipe.

Each day's distillate is subtly different, each type of cask (sherry, bourbon, first-, second- and third-fill and rechar) will produce a different style of whisky, and each individual cask will also have its own personality. There's nothing fixed in whisky. Blenders need to maintain consistency, but they are working with ingredients that warp and shift continually. To add a certain *frisson*, distilleries have the habit of closing down, either temporarily or for good.

This means that holes can appear in inventories. The blender is left with no option but to replace the missing whisky with another that tastes like it. This can either be slowly blended in to gradually replace the missing component, or a new combination will be introduced that replicates the lost taste. In other words, while a blend should always taste the same, the whiskies that go into it may change. This involves having a mind and a nose that can not only identify each whisky, but knows what happens when you put whisky A with whisky B.

To start building a blend, the distiller decides how many grain whiskies to use, how old they should be and what percentage they should take in the blend. Then the malts are chosen. Each major blend will have at its core malt from one or two distilleries – usually the ones that were owned by the blend's original owner. Chivas has Strathisla, Famous Grouse has Tamdhu and Highland Park; Johnnie Walker has Cardhu; White Horse has Lagavulin; Dewar's has Aberfeldy. But you shouldn't be able to pick up a glass of Johnnie Walker and say: "Ah, the Cardhu comes striding out!" If you can pick out one individual whisky, then the blend has failed.

Imagine a blend being like a pyramid. The core malt is at the apex, buttressed by a small selection of supporting malts that complement the core malt and add flavour. Then comes a wider selection of "packers", which are more neutral in flavour. Although they don't contribute much in the way of taste, they give character and body. These are the elements that can be shifted. "You can use Glen Spey for one blend, and the next time substitute it with Strathmill, and it won't affect the flavour," says John Ramsay, master blender at The Edrington Group, which produces Grouse, Lang's and Cutty Sark (among others). "You can't leave either one out, though!"

Solid foundations

The grains are the foundations, and it's quite common for more than one grain to be used in a top blend. J&B Rare, for example, is a blend of 36 malts and six grains. A blend, therefore, is the success of the collective spirit, where the character of the individual is lost in order to benefit the whole. Each element plays its part; some give flavour, others texture, some others weight, some all three.

Wood has to be taken into account as well. A light blend like Cutty Sark needs a fragrant sweet wood, so Speyside malts aged in American oak are used at the core. Lang's Supreme is a richer dram, so Spanish wood plays a central part. A brand like Famous Grouse uses a combination of both wood types.

The blender also has to take the age of his components into consideration. Whiskies change as they mature, so while a distillery's single malt may be at its best at 16 years old, the style of the malt at that age is often more than likely to be unsuitable for a blend. You don't want too many dominant personalities shouting the odds – you want a quiet murmur of conversation. This means that blends carrying age statements will likely contain fewer, but older and richer, malts.

As if that were not enough, blenders are also in charge of ensuring the consistency of single malts. A 12-year-old malt isn't produced by opening all the casks of malt that happen to be 12 years old on that day and pouring them into a vat. Most single malts are a *mélange* of different ages and, often, wood types. It's only the youngest whisky that is the age that appears on the label. Once again, the trick is to maintain consistency, even though you are being faced with constantly changing variables.

Blends, however, are still dismissed as not being worth a second glance. Right enough, in recent years the downturn in Scotch's fortunes has resulted in cheap and nasty blends appearing on the market. At the top end, however, the best remain wonderful drinks. "If a single malt is that great, then why isn't a blend greater?" asks Chivas's Colin Scott. "After all, it's superior than the sum of the individual parts."

FILLING CASKS WITH ONE OF A BLEND'S MANY COMPONENTS

Famous BLENDS

Every Saturday from the 1870s onward my great-grandfather, Thomas Moffatt, would walk the five miles from Forgandenny (where he was schoolmaster) to Perth to meet friends and share a dram with them. His diaries don't note what brand he drank, but it's more than likely that it would have been one of the blends that Perth's grocers were offering. Scotland in those days was becoming an industrialized society, and the rise of blends mirrors not only the birth of the country as one of the heartlands of Victorian capitalism, but the rise of the British Empire. The times they were a-changing. People were moving off the land and into the new cities. It was the end of self-sufficiency, the beginning of consumerism and the mass market.

Thomas would more than likely have wandered into the shops owned by Arthur Bell, John Dewar or Matthew Gloag, the first of the great Perth blenders. But who were they? John Dewar had joined his cousin's grocery store to look after the cellar and then set up on his own; Arthur Bell had joined the firm of Thos Sandeman as a traveller. After Sandeman's death, Bell became a partner and started selling blended whisky in 1865. A few years later, Gloag created a blend for the shooting parties heading into the Perthshire hills – he called it The Famous Grouse.

In 1821, in the then boom town of Kilmarnock, John Walker had opened his grocer's shop, and soon started blending whisky, while William Teacher opened his grocery store near Glasgow Docks in 1837. He, too, produced his own blend.

These patriarchs were mere whippersnappers compared with the Haigs, though. Robert Haig started distilling on his Stirlingshire estate in 1627 and each successive generation followed in his footsteps, establishing distilleries across the central and eastern Lowlands. There were Haigs everywhere.

It was John Haig, though, who provided the catalyst that sparked the blended revolution. It was at his plant in Cameronbridge, Fife, that he first tried the new Stein still (the Steins, needless to say, being related by marriage) and then installed the first Coffey still in 1831. His first blend appeared in 1850, and by the end of the century he was producing more than one million gallons a year.

Brand building

A London wine merchant was also in on the act. Giacomo Justerini had arrived in London in 1749, and by 1779 was advertising in *The Morning Post*: "An extensive range of liqueurs in the greatest perfection and *Usque Beatha*." In 1831, the firm was bought by Alfred Brooks, who changed the name to the J&B that we know today.

These grocer blenders didn't want people asking for any whisky; they wanted them to ask for their own label. Brands were born. It was the next two generations, however, who took the new blends from the local market out into the world.

John Walker's Old Highland Whisky was taken to new heights by his grandsons, George and Alexander, who copyrighted and trademarked the brand in 1867. In 1909 it became Johnnie Walker Black Label alongside a new,

lighter blend called Red Label. By that time Alexander had already established export markets, and by the end of the First World War the Walkers were selling into 120 markets.

They were pretty circumspect when compared with the antics of Tommy Dewar, John Dewar's son, who established himself (and his whisky) in London, thanks to a series of spectacular stunts. In 1886 he drowned out all sound at the Brewers' Show by refusing to stop playing his bagpipes until the pibroch was finished (and he had attracted the attention of the press). He toured the world for two years, establishing agents in 26 countries, and ran the first-ever cinema commercial in the United States. By 1901 Dewar's was selling a million gallons a year worldwide. Twenty years previously, it hadn't been known outside Scotland.

Then enter James Buchanan. He had joined Leith-based Charles Mackinlay in 1879 as its London agent and founded his own firm soon after, selling his Buchanan Blend. He put it in a black bottle with a white label and, always dressed up to the nines, schmoozed his way round London, getting hoteliers and restaurant buyers on his side. He supplied all London's music halls, and won the exclusive rights to sell whisky to the House of Commons. Buchanan's Blend became Black & White in 1904.

All of the blenders were also either buying or building malt distilleries to give them the core malts they needed, but it was all a great gamble. Many of these great whisky dynasties borrowed heavily, and relied on quick thinking and slightly dubious business practices

SCOTLAND'S FAVOURITE BLEND – NOW SPREADING ITS WINGS WORLDWIDE

to build their empires ... but it worked. In fact, it worked so well that in time the blenders became the Whisky Barons, men of substance, pillars of the establishment. It was this proximity to the mechanics of power that undoubtedly helped whisky to stave off Lloyd George's prohibitionist tendencies.

Strength in unity

Times were tight after the First World War. Taxes rose inexorably and, despite export sales remaining buoyant, Prohibition had restricted sales in the United States. Amalgamation was the logical solution. The Distillers Company Limited (DCL) had been formed in 1877 by six grain distillers to avoid a potential collapse in the market. It was only a matter of time before many of the other major blends were brought into its orbit. Dewar and Buchanan joined in 1925, Walker two years later. This gave blended Scotch the financial clout to flood the US market when Prohibition was repealed.

Although production fell during the Second World War, the government allowed the industry to continue to produce whisky in order to generate much-needed dollars. Across the Atlantic, the American industry was closed down again, while the Irish had stopped exporting. Therefore, although sorely in need of investment at the end of the war, once again blended Scotch

was able to steal a march on its rivals.

Blends just kept on growing until the late 1970s, when the firms failed to notice that a new generation of drinkers was emerging – an advertising-literate generation who needed to be convinced that blended whisky was the drink for them, a task that the industry singularly failed to do.

The major markets collapsed. Although emerging markets like Spain, France, Portugal and the Far East have recently softened the fall, the loss in volume (and credibility) in the old markets has been considerable, and the industry has yet to find a way to get it out of the decline.

Thomas Moffatt wouldn't recognize today's drinks industry. Of his three local brands, Dewar's is the biggest seller in the USA, Bell's is the UK's top-seller, while Famous Grouse is, rightly, regarded as one of the best blends on the market. Not bad for three grocers' own-labels from a wee town in the Highlands. The question is, what's next?

CONSUMERS ARE ASKING TO BE SHOWN THE WAY TO THE NEXT WHISKY BAR

JOHNNIE WALKER REMAINS A BENCHMARK BLEND

Tasting Notes

Ballantine's Closed, quite hard with a whiff or cordite. Clean but undemanding.
Ballantine's 12-year-old Sweet rich nose, a heathery start, pure grain centre. Plush.
Ballantine's 18-year-old Clean grassy nose, well-balanced wood. Almost chewy weight on palate with some apricot fruit.
Bell's 8-year-old Fairly sweet, but well balanced, round and spicy.
Black Bottle 10-year-old Peaty, turfy nose. Sweet start, balanced, rich and smoky.
Chivas Regal 12-year-old Light hay-like nose, some smoke. Toasty, turfy and some sugared almond. Gentle.

Chivas Regal 18-year-old Big rich nose with mint, ripe fruit and a slight medicinal/phenolic edge. Lime on finish.
The Famous Grouse Smooth, rounded in mouth with a light smoky finish.
J & B Soft, light with good balance and a crisp finish.
Johnnie Walker Red Label Positive nose, good weight on palate, hint of peat on finish.
Johnnie Walker Black Label Rich, elegant fruity nose, full flavour and palate.

Irish Whiskey

Even the Scots admit that the Irish got there before them when it came to inventing whiskey, although at least they can say it was a Scottish emigrant, none other than St Patrick himself, who is attributed with its creation.

Whether the holy man – who also had time to establish Christianity, raise the dead and banish snakes from the Emerald Isle – actually was the first Irish distiller is unclear. To be honest, it seems unlikely.

The religious argument does have some basis in fact, however. If the Celts didn't bring the secret of distillation with them as they travelled through Europe, then it would have been brought to Ireland by monks. In the time of St Patrick, Ireland was a centre of learning without equal in Europe.

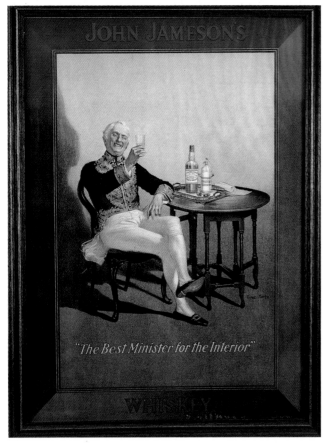

AN OLD SMOOTHIE FROM THE VERY START

JOHN JAMESON'S

"The Best Minister for the Interior"

WHISKEY

Monks travelled from Irish monasteries across Europe, getting their feet dusty on the information superhighway of the time, exchanging knowledge with other men of learning. It is entirely possible that they came into contact with Arab alchemists and learned the art of distillation. Certainly, there are records from the sixth century that a form of beer made from "the bruised juice of wheat and barley" was being drunk. If the art of distillation were known, then it would only be a matter of time before the monastic alchemists would have used it in their researches. In those days, *uisce beatha* would have been used for medicinal reasons, but a process of time and trial and error refined the art – and opened it up to wider, and more sociable, uses.

A boost to courage

The identity of the first distiller will always be unclear, but what is certain is that when Henry II of England paid an uninvited visit to Ireland in 1174, he recorded the use of *aqua vitae*. In 1296, Sir Robert Savage, the lord of Bushmills, was using *aqua vitae* to numb the minds of his troops as they entered battle while, in *The Annals of the Four Masters* in 1405, one Richard Magrenell, chieftain of Moyntyrolas, died of "a surfeit of *aqua vitae* ... or *aqua mortis*." Cynics suggest that the lack of written proof that this referred to whisky (à la Friar John Cor in Scotland) until 1556 means these are just fanciful tales, but

it does seem unlikely – given Ireland's position in the intellectual evolution of Western Europe – that distillation took so long to arrive there.

Whiskey became part of the staple Irish diet and immediately acquired an almost mystical quality. The ancient Brehon laws of hospitality have long been rooted in the Irish psyche, and whiskey would have been an integral part of this willing sharing of food and shelter with strangers. Just as in any agricultural environment whiskey became a form of currency, not just as an accompaniment to festivals and fuel for the craic, but as a handy way to pay the rent due on the land, or to use in a bartering system for supplies. For poor farmers, distillation was a vital way to supplement a meagre income.

Rural Irish distillers suffered in the same way as the Highland distillers in Scotland. While the 1823 Wash Act gave a leg-up to the rich distillers who could afford the £10 licence and be able to run stills of above 40 gallons, it was another nail in the coffin of the small, rural producer. That's not to say it stopped them outright. The Irish have always hung on to their love of illegal distilling. While you might chance upon the odd illegal still in Scotland, *poitín* is still widely available in rural Ireland. In the nineteenth century, however, it was more than just making a supply of alcohol on the cheap – it was an act of civil disobedience, a refusal to accept British rule, whose attempts to legalize distilling

BOOM TIME FOR IRISH
WHISKEY

were seen as an act of aggression by a foreign power. Making *poitín* was a political act.

The luck of the Irish

By that time a steady consolidation was starting, with major distilleries such as Dublin's John Jameson and John Power becoming increasingly important and successful on the export markets.

Although the famed luck of the Irish hasn't been with the whiskey industry this century, it wasn't always that way. In the nineteenth century Irish whiskey was holding its own quite nicely, thank you, and enjoyed a high reputation. In those days, Highland malts were in short supply and were heavily peated, while the Lowland grains were virtually undrinkable. The Irish pot-still brands, made from a mix of malted and unmalted barley, held the high ground and were the world's top-selling whisk(e)y.

Ironically it was an Irish invention that conspired against Irish whiskey's growth. When Aeneas Coffey invented his patent still, the get-rich-quick entrepreneurs of the Scottish Lowlands leapt on it as the answer to their need to produce large volumes of low-cost, lightly flavoured whisky. The Irish distillers initially rejected the new invention, seeing it as a cheap alternative capable of only producing a spirit that was inferior to the stuff coming off their pot stills. It's doubly ironic that one of those who rejected the patent still was John Jameson who had established his distillery in Dublin's Bow St in 1780. A Scot by birth, he had married into the Haig family, and was the brother-in-law of the first distiller to install a patent still.

The first Scotch blends appeared soon after and seized the initiative away from the Irish pot-still whiskeys. The Irish distillers soon realized their mistake and, somewhat reluctantly, began producing from patent stills, but it's fair to say that they had lost a golden commercial opportunity.

If you can understand their reluctance to alter their product, then they were powerless against the temperance movement of Father Matthew, whose decade-long evangelical crusade (1838–48) against the evils of drink managed not only to halve the number of pubs in Ireland in seven years, but to close distilleries as well.

Then came the Great Famine of 1845–1849. The failure of the potato crop reduced the amount of grain that was available for distilleries. Production slumped. The famine resulted in a mass exodus from the countryside, either to the towns or abroad. This combination of a falling population and little raw material was a disaster for distilling. When Alfred Barnard visited Ireland in 1887 he found 28 distilleries. There had been 2,000 (admittedly not all of them legal) less than 100 years before. Today there are three.

Although the industry continued to shrink, it was beginning to use patent stills, and the major Dublin firms were building up considerable trade with England, the British Empire and, increasingly, the United States with its massive expatriate community. Just over 100 years ago, there were 400 brands registered in the United States alone.

PART OF JAMESON'S EVER-GROWING PORTFOLIO

There was still considerable volume sold to England and the British Empire, but when the struggle for Irish independence finally succeeded in 1921, the Empire struck back, with inevitable results. The English (Scotland was never a significant market) and Empire markets went belly-up, thanks to a trade embargo placed on the new Irish Free State. Given that they accounted for 25 per cent of Irish whiskey's sales at this time, the industry was suddenly faced with a huge hole that couldn't easily be filled. In normal circumstances, efforts would have been doubled in the USA, but Prohibition was already in force, so that market was severely reduced. It didn't help that the bootleggers, recognizing the higher price they could get for bottles that

COOLEY'S BRANDS HAVE HELPED INVIGORATE THE IRISH SECTOR

claimed to contain Irish whiskey, began selling any old rot-gut and claiming it was Irish. By the time Prohibition ended, the reputation of Irish whiskey was in tatters.

Hard times

The 1930s and 1940s weren't a good time for any distiller. Depression, war, slow economic growth and progressively severe domestic taxation meant that Irish distilling was hit by closures, consolidation and an increasing concentration on the domestic market. It didn't help that, during the Second World War, the Irish government banned exports of whiskey. No one, it seemed, wanted to drink their whiskey. The industry imploded. A case in point is Locke's distillery in Brosna. A successful malt producer with a good reputation, it struggled to survive, and by the time the Irish government raised taxes steeply in the 1950s it had closed down. In time it became a pig-fattening centre and then an engineering plant, before being rescued by the new Cooley Distillers in 1987, which now uses it as a warehousing site.

There was a certain element of stubborn insularity that accompanied this decline. The post-war American market wasn't the same as that before

Prohibition; trade with England had started up again. The world was drinking increasing volumes of whisky. There was nothing to stop the Irish distillers going ahead and starting to sell and promote their deliciously individual whiskeys, but they remained strangely reluctant to dip their toes in the water. Perhaps they had simply had too many knocks. The end result was that the industry only produced sufficient whiskey to meet with domestic demand, rather than trying to re-establish itself as a world player.

The situation began to change when, in 1966, the old distilling firms of Jameson, Power and Cork Distillers amalgamated to form the Irish Distillers Group (ID). They didn't just merge head offices, but Jameson and Cork Distillers also closed distilleries and, in 1975, all of ID's production was switched to a purpose-built plant in Midleton, Co. Cork – one of the world's most remarkable distilleries. The ID merger left only one independent distillery, Bushmills, in Co. Antrim in Northern Ireland. In 1973 that too joined ID, though it kept its own distillery. One firm was making all the Irish whiskey in the world – and producing it from two plants.

This quasi monopoly remained in place until 1987, when a new player started up. Cooley, based in Dundalk, aimed to break ID's grip. The reaction was swift. ID tried to buy out Cooley (with the Cooley board's approval) and close the whole operation. This rather bizarre state of affairs was brought to a halt when the Irish Competition Authority ruled it illegal, and Cooley was allowed to start production.

The industry TODAY

Today, then, there are three distilleries in Ireland: Midleton, Bushmills and Cooley, and as wide a selection of brands and prices as at any time for years. With Tullamore Dew now owned by Allied Domecq and Cooley producing Hackler's Poitín for UDV, there is real competition in the Irish sector at last, and export markets are being sought out.

It's early days for the new-look Irish industry. Cooley has certainly stirred the sector up, but with its need for quick cash it had to hit the bottom end of the market and start supplying young, own-label brands – one of which remains one of the worst whiskeys I have ever tasted. That said, Tyrconnel, Locke's and Millar's are great brands and deserve worldwide success.

Cooley's aggressive approach has finally stung ID into action. For years its strategy was to push Jameson, mention Bushmills and forget about the rest. With limited resources you could perhaps understand the logic. But if you manage to search out ID's full range, the more inexplicable it seems that the firm isn't promoting world-class whiskeys like Crested 10, Power's and Redbreast. Whiskeys this good shouldn't be allowed

to languish in the shadows. Both firms have latched on to the fact that people are not only thirsty for whiskey, but for education as well. ID has three visitors' centres – the Whiskey Corner on the site of Jameson's Bow Street distillery in Dublin, the Jameson Heritage Centre next to its massive distillery in Midleton, Co. Cork, and Old Bushmills in Northern Ireland. Cooley, meanwhile, has opened Locke's distillery in Kilbeggan as a museum, and plans to get the plant up and running in the near future.

These days, Irish bars are opening up across the globe. Every town you go to, from Oslo to Bordeaux, Cape Town, Adelaide and Dubai, there's an "Irish" welcome – albeit not always an authentic one! Irish whiskey has the greatest opportunity it has ever had to find that crock of gold.

BUSHMILLS DISTILLERY, HOME OF SOME SEDUCTIVE WHISKEYS

COOLEY'S BRANDS ARE COMING UP FAST ON THE RAILS

Tasting Notes

MALTS

Tyrconnel Light in colour with a strangely gassy/peaty note on the nose. Clean and orangey but, while delicate, it lacks definition.

Bushmills 10yo Clean, gentle vanilla ice cream on the nose with subtle hints of liquorice and clover meadows. Nicely malted on the palate with a good mid-palate bite and a softly dry, fresh finish.

Bushmills Triple Wood Full, ripe and fruity on the nose with fine complexity. Starts molasses-honey sweet and then the damson fruity power washes in. Very fine indeed.

Connemara A peak reek, at a similar level to Lagavulin, but more aggressive. On the palate this damp peat fire dominates the rather aggressive orange/lemon fruit.

THE
TYRCONNELL
★★★★★
◆ SINGLE MALT ◆

Tyrconnell whisi 100%ol.

PURE POT STILL
IRISH WHISKEY
DISTILLED, MATURED AND BOTTLED IN IRELAND
ANDREW A. WATT & CO.
RIVERSTOWN, DUNDALK, IRELAND.
ESTABLISHED 1762

40% Vol.   PRODUCT OF IRELAND   1L ℮

How it's MADE

*A LAND OF LEGEND – AND
LEGENDARY WHISKEYS*

Every great spirit contains a little of the country that produced it. Ireland is no exception, and a sip of one of its great brands conjures up a soft countryside, a gentle smirr in the air, the aroma of grass and herbs – a feeling not of power and bravado, but of contemplation, time and space.

Each country has its own idiosyncratic approach to the basic recipe for making spirits, and the Irish aim is to produce a more gentle beast than the often assertive Scotch. Traditionally, Irish whiskeys have used only Irish barley, and each of ID's brands will have a different percentage of malted and unmalted barley going into its mash. Unmalted barley (along with oats and rye) was first used last century because malted barley was taxed, difficult to produce – and you got more alcohol from the mix.

These days, other grains, such as maize saccharified with some malted barley, are used for the lighter grain whiskeys that make up part of some brands. The ID brands have refrained from drying the malt over peat, giving the final product a lighter flavour. That isn't to say that peating has never been used in Ireland. The country, after all, is rich in the stuff, and it would be inconceivable that peat would never have been used – particularly in distilleries far from the coal-fields of the north, or out of the major towns. Indeed, Barnard mentions peat being used during his travels round the distilleries.

The other main difference between Irish and Scotch, until Cooley's arrival, has been ID's adherence to triple distillation. The essence of distilling is refining a spirit, and doing the process twice will do this; however, some heavier flavour compounds will remain. Doing it three times will give you a considerably lighter spirit – although you run the risk of stripping out all the character. There are, however, no regulations saying that Irish whiskey has to be triple distilled, and double distillation was common in the past – Barnard named only three distilleries out of 28 that were triple distilling in 1887. Cooley (much to ID's indignation) uses double distillation for all its brands and, equally controversially, peats some of them as well – most notably its Connemara single malt, which has a peating level close to that of Islay.

The remarkable thing about the ID brands produced at the Midleton complex is the way in which the distiller can produce such a vast range of highly distinctive brands on one site. This single distillery can produce 23 million bottles of up to eight different major brands (and a few smaller ones).

In simple terms, each ID brand will have a different percentage of malted and unmalted barley in the mash. Then, because Midleton's huge pot stills and column stills are interlinked, each charge can be distilled in a host of different ways. In general, the whiskeys are first distilled

*THE LARGEST POT STILL IN
THE WORLD AT THE OLD
MIDLETON DISTILLERY*

in a pot still, but can then be diverted for their second and third distillations in either column or pot (or a combination of both). All the component whiskeys in a brand are a product of this fusion of different types of distillation. Some will be triple pot still, some a combination of the two types of still – oh, and there is also some grain whiskey produced in the column stills. When you add in the fact that these are also aged for different periods of time in a range of different casks for, on average, five to eight years, the method begins to reveal itself.

It's mind-bogglingly complex, but this is why one distillery can produce a brand like Paddy, whose light character comes from a greater percentage of column still in the spirit and virtually no sherry cask; and Redbreast, where the oiliness of three pot-still distillations oozes out, along with lashings of sherry wood.

While most Irish brands are aged in ex-bourbon casks, there is a significant element of oloroso and rum casks used – Black Bush and Jameson both use a high percentage of sherry wood, as does Cooley's fuller-bodied brand, Millar's. The end result is a remarkable array of flavours, weights and styles.

Bushmills, situated only an hour from Belfast on the beautiful Causeway Coast, uses only triple pot still distillation; but while its malt is made from 100 per cent unpeated malted barley, the premium Black Bush is a blend of 80 per cent malt and a 20 per cent splash of aged single grain from Midleton.

The magic of distilling may have changed from the early times, and Midleton may look more like a science-fiction set than a distillery, but at the heart of this complex technological achievement is the skill of an artist and a desire to produce a spirit that speaks of its country. It's not fanciful to have a dram or two and realize that the soft Irish air and the grace and easy pace of the people have been captured.

Spoiled for choice

These days you can taste more Irish brands than at any time since the Second World War, and there are some magnificent specimens.

Cooley has burst on to the scene with a raft of brands, some of which are great and some not quite so great, but the fact that they've reached the heights they have with such young stock shows there's a quality-oriented ethos behind it all. Millar's is their equivalent of Power's, and is a juicily seductive whiskey; Tyrconnel malt is crisp and assured, while Inishowen has a light, peaty quality that's winning friends.

Bushmills' whiskeys are seen at their best in the richly fruity and complex Black Bush, with its mix of nuts, butter and sweet sherry wood, or the gentle 10-year-old malt with its aromas of vanilla and clover and a crisp, fresh finish. There's also a new Three Wood – that started life in ex-bourbon barrels, then spent two periods of finishing, first in sherry butts, then in port pipes – which is long, ripe and softly fruity with a long, powerful finish.

Midleton's production covers the entire spectrum of flavours that define Irish whiskey. You can start with the light, tangeriney, peppery Paddy's, or move through the ever-growing Jameson range – from the soft, malty (but slightly boring) standard Jameson, to the magnificent creamy, chewy, sherried 1780. Best, though, to keep digging because then you'll come across brands that represent the height of Midleton's achievement. There's the elegant Redbreast, with its pot-still hallmarks in evidence, coupled with pears, peaches and malt-loaf richness, a lick of bourbon wood and plenty of sherry cask; the rich, almost tarry Crested 10 and the magnificent Power's – the best-selling whiskey in Dublin. It's not expensive, but is the quintessential Irish whiskey, a soft, fruity, almost fat nose filled with peaches, apricots and vanilla. It's dangerously drinkable – Dublin sipping whiskey at its best.

BLACK BUSH – BUSHMILLS'
FINEST BRAND

Tasting Notes

IRISH DISTILLERS

Paddy. Slightly hot on the nose with a touch of tangerine. Firm, if a touch lean.
Bushmills Very soft fruity nose mixing pepper and orange. Delicate and toasty.
Jameson Soft, full and slightly malty. Fresh on the nose with a green edge mixed with slight sweetness.
Power's Full nose with apricot/peach fruit. Soft on palate. Weighty, apricot on finish and edgy backbone.

Crested Ten Fresh malt, earth and good weight on the nose. Broad on palate. Rounded, smooth and lingering.
Jameson 1780 Ripe fruit and dog rose aromas, creamy, long, soft with toffee palate and a long finish.
Black Bush Full, sweet nose, toffee and sherry wood. A rich smooth fruitiness.

COOLEY

Inishowen Beady and yeasty with green apples and pears and a lightly smoky flavour. A touch lean.
Kilbeggan Mix of camphor and grass on the nose, a pleasant middle-weight whisky.
Locke's Soft, clean and quite malty with a little orloso sherry running through the palate to the dry, peppery finish.
Millars Full with a gentle touch of sherry wood and fruit loaf on the nose. Spicy and nicely rounded with sugared almonds on palate. Dry finish. A great sipping whiskey.

Bourbon

A central character in Native American mythology is Coyote. He represents the maverick, the creative individual, the free spirit. Anarchic and mischievous, he is regularly killed, but always manages to put his body back together again. American whiskey has that Coyote spirit.

The history

Spirits across the world have been intertwined with the rise and fall of societies. They have helped form nations, becoming part and parcel of the living history of a country. Behind virtually every step in America's progress, from colony to nation-hood, is whiskey.

Spirits were distilled in the new American colonies from the word go, but to find the birth of American whiskey you have to wait for the second wave of immigrants who hit its shores. These were Scots and Irish fleeing clearances and famine, who carried with them the knowledge of grain distillation.

They distilled from the raw ingredients around them, and although barley proved difficult to grow in Maryland, Pennsylvania and the Carolinas, rye thrived on their hard soils, so rye it was. Good rye is a wonderfully bitter, lemon-accented spirit, but can have an astringency if not handled with care. You can just picture the early settlers sucking their teeth as the first slug of Pennsylvania rye hit their mouths.

Whiskey, just as with any spirit of that time, became a vital source of income. Transport was difficult, and grain was too heavy to lug by mule to the markets. However, if the grain could

be distilled, not only was it easier to carry, it was actually more valuable. So, while the east continued to drink rum, as the colonists slowly moved west, whiskey went with them.

So vital a contribution did whiskey make to the settlers' income, that when George Washington decided to tax distilling, the producers rose up in the three-year Whiskey Rebellion. There is a deep irony in this, as not only was Washington a distiller of note – he made a handsome $1,032 from spirits in 1789 – but it was the taxes applied to rum that had been a contributory factor in the Colonies rising up against the British. Washington's bottom line, though, was that the fledgling USA needed cash fast. Spirits (as ever) were the softest target.

So aggrieved were the distillers that they tarred and feathered the

tax collectors and marched on Pittsburgh, threatening to burn it down. Washington decided on a show of brinkmanship and mustered 15,000 men to march on the rebellious distillers, who backed down.

Some distillers gave up entirely, but more decided to flee west to Kentucky and Tennessee, which had not yet achieved statehood. This is the start of the whiskeys that remain America's national spirit.

The first settlers had arrived in Kentucky in the 1770s, taking advantage of the incentive of 400 acres for free if they could clear the land and plant corn. What they found was an environment that is almost unsurpassed in the world for the production of high-quality spirits. There was clear, limestone-rich water, there were massive stands of oak for barrels, there was a river for easy transportation and, vitally, there was a native crop, Indian corn (maize), which made a smooth, soft spirit. Kentucky whiskey (bourbon) was born.

These early distillers didn't hang around and soon began producing in commercial quantities. Evan Williams was producing good volumes in Louisville in 1783; Jacob Beam arrived in Kentucky in 1788 and founded his distillery in 1795; Robert Samuels arrived in 1780. Then there were Elijah Pepper, Daniel Weller and Basil Hayden, names that still appear on bottles today.

The invention of the "bourbon" style is generally credited to the semi-legendary Rev. Elijah Craig, who combined hell-fire Baptist preaching with whiskey-making. Craig may have acquired the same mantle for bourbon as Friar John Cor has for Scotch, but he wasn't the first distiller in Kentucky. It's also unlikely that he invented the charred barrel that gives bourbon some of its most distinctive characteristics.

Quite where the charred barrel originated is a mystery. It could have been an accident – a cooper toasting a barrel may have nipped off to the toilet and left the barrel over the fire for too long. It could also have been good, old-fashioned Celtic prudence, recharring a barrel that had previously held some other goods; or it could have been deliberate, with a distiller realizing that the charcoal on the inside of the barrel would help to leach impurities out of the young spirit. Waymack & Harris, in their *Book of Bourbon*, argue plausibly that, since charring was used for other goods to stop them going off, the technique was likely to be used for whiskey as well.

What's significant is that bourbon was known as an aged spirit from its birth, simply thanks to Kentucky's geographical situation. It would have been distilled in the fall, barrelled and left to wait until the rivers were navigable before it set out on the three-month river journey to New Orleans. That means a whiskey could have been up to a year old when it reached its final destination. Given that new spirit greedily sucks the colour and flavour out of a barrel as soon as it hits the wood, by the time the merchants in the south got their consignment of Bourbon County whiskey it would have acquired a reddish hue and lost some of the rough edges. Enter Red Eye.

It would still have been pretty rough stuff. Distillation remained an inexact science until the arrival of a Scottish chemist and physicist, James (Jim) Crow, who began working at the Oscar Pepper distillery in 1823. (The site is now Labrot & Graham's distillery.) What Crow did was to apply scientific rigour to whiskey production. He brought the first hydrometer, and he experimented with and perfected sour mashing, distilling, charring barrels and ageing. His breakthroughs tamed what had been a pretty archaic process, and gave consistency to the product.

The frontier was moving inexorably west and whiskey went with it, its

THE SPIRIT THAT FUELLED

THE PIONEERS

THE MADNESS OF PROHIBITION - INITIALLY AMERICANS DRANK EVEN MORE

progress speeded up by the building of railroads. It no doubt caused more than its fair share of gunfights, but then it helped to numb the wounded bodies. Whiskey helped build the West (and also made it wilder than it might otherwise have been). It also played a significant part in the genocidal annihilation of the Native American tribes.

After the Civil War Lincoln needed money fast – so a further tax was imposed, forcing many of the smaller distilleries into the arms of the larger concerns, starting the steady consolidation of the industry that continues today. Another significant change happened at this time, with the arrival of the first continuous stills. A lighter style of whiskey emerged – and there was also more of it. Despite the best efforts of the taxman, brands grew in strength.

But bubbling below the surface was a greater threat than the excise man: the Temperance Movement.

Temperance had started as an attempt to moderate people's drinking habits. The same thing was happening in Ireland, England and Russia – with some justification. People simply drank more in those days. In America, though, the two camps became polarized and, by the turn of the century, Temperance had given way to Total Abstinence. The industry didn't take the threat seriously or attempt to curb its more excessive stunts aimed at getting people to drink more and more, and somewhere down the line compromise was forgotten.

By 1910, Prohibition was common in every state – in fact, by 1915 Tennessee and Kentucky were dry. Even today, it's pretty damned hard to get a drink in certain counties in these whiskey-making states.

Full Prohibition came into force in 1919, and the industry has only just recovered from the blows it, the Depression and the Second World War dealt it. The twentieth century may be "the American Century", but it as sure as hell won't be known as the American Whiskey Century. These days you have to search hard to find good rye whiskey, and you'll be hard pressed to find any (legal) corn whiskey at all. There are now just over a double-handful of distilleries producing all of the American whiskey in the world. Prior to Prohibition there were 2,000.

Draconian measures have a habit of producing the opposite reaction to the one they intended. America actually drank more during Prohibition than it had before. The amazing thing is that the bean counters in the Department of the Treasury forgot just how much money whiskey taxes contributed to the economy – it has been estimated that $500 million per year was lost during Prohibition, a vast sum in those days, even for an affluent nation.

When you add in the jobs lost in distilling and its infrastructure, it's fair to conclude that Prohibition managed to establish organized crime in America, and was a contributory factor in precipitating the Great Depression.

The industry emerged blinking in the sunny uplands of Repeal in a sorry state. Many producers simply couldn't afford to restart operations. Some brave individuals, like 70-year-old Jim Beam, started up again from scratch. Others pooled their resources. Heaven Hill was formed in 1935, when a group of former distillers approached the Shapira brothers. "It was doggone scary," says current president Max Shapira. "This was an industry that hadn't existed for 16 years; it was full of bootleggers, its product wasn't respected and there wasn't any of it anyway."

This consolidation picked up pace after Repeal. More seriously, the quality of the whiskey wasn't great. The bulk of the stock had been held in barrels for 19 years, and there wasn't sufficient young spirit distilled on the brief distilling holidays to get the category up and running again. Booker Noe of Beam and Gerard White of UDV both gave me samples of whiskeys distilled before Prohibition and bottled on Repeal. Woody, oily and pungent, they hit the mouth with a rasping, sour quality. No one would drink that. Imported whiskies, which had been producing all through Prohibition, had no such problem and walked straight in.

Things may have been different had Roosevelt not decided to shut down production during the war and make distillers produce industrial alcohol to help the war effort. In Britain, Churchill had realized that sales of Scotch would generate much-needed revenue, and kept production going. The result was that in 1945 the American whiskey industry had to start up yet again. The result was more consolidation and a drive for the fighting end of the market. Once again, the distillers saw Scotch ride roughshod over "their" market. "This industry has had the worst record on being beat up of any I know," says Max Shapira. "We ended the War with no inventory – and then we made the mistake of not looking globally."

Initially this concentration on the domestic market was moderately successful, but, with some notable exceptions, much of the spirit produced was bottom-end stuff. Sales began to slide, but distillers just kept churning the stuff out. When the "brown spirits" crash came in the late 1970s, American whiskey went into freefall. If you drive down Distillers Row in Louisville today, behind the tatty strip joints are elegant, empty brick warehouses, the mausoleums of a once-prosperous industry.

Then, something miraculous happened. The Japanese, having already discovered malt whisky, woke up to the fact that aged bourbon was also a high-quality premium spirit. The same thing happened in Australia, Germany and, to a lesser extent, the United Kingdom. Much of the credit for this must go to Maker's Mark who, by word-of-mouth promotion – and paying attention to high-quality standards – had woken up the export markets to the top end.

Only once the export markets had begun demanding premium brands did the American public wake up to their heritage. This shift upmarket coincided with the emergence of Generation X – younger drinkers who wanted, well, flavour in their lives. Fine cigars, flavoursome beers, quality food and premium spirits have all boomed in the past few years. "It all came good when the last yuppie died," said Bill Samuels at Maker's Mark. "But it's been 40 years of struggle. Jeez, it was tough."

There's a new confidence in the industry, and American whiskey is finally being allowed to show what it can produce, but the booming top end can't bail out the industry. Things may be getting better, but the industry isn't out of the woods yet.

OLD-TIME WHISKEY FROM GOOD OL' BOYS – THE HADAN DISTILLERY

How it's MADE

*A GENTLE SEA OF WHEAT – SOON
DESTINED TO GIVE A GENTLE
EDGE TO BOURBON*

*THE GIANT FERMENTER AT
WILD TURKEY*

Why does bourbon taste the way it does? Like all of the great spirits of the world, it draws from its immediate environment. The reason settlers began to produce whiskey in Kentucky was because they had plentiful crops to distil with; they took advantage of a supply of pure, iron-free, calcium-rich water; oak trees to make barrels from; as well as a climate capable of producing a specific style of maturation; and a river system to get the product down river to market.

The water is as good a place to start as any. Kentucky sits on a bed of limestone, which filters out any minerals (most importantly, iron), but produces a water that's rich in calcium. This plays a vital role at different stages in the process.

Regulations state that Straight Bourbon must be made from a minimum of 51 per cent corn and a collection of "small grains" – usually rye and malted barley, but Maker's Mark and W. L. Weller both replace rye with wheat. Rye or wheat give flavour, while malted barley provides the enzymes that turn starches into fermentable sugars. When a whiskey contains more than 80 per cent corn, it becomes corn whiskey. Rye whiskey has a minimum of 51 per cent rye, while blended whiskey is 20 per cent straight whiskey blended with neutral spirit.

The exact combination of grains (the mash bill) will be different in each distillery – and, sometimes, different mash bills are used for each brand. UDV's Weller, for example, has 16 per cent wheat and 76 per cent corn, while its Old Charter has six per cent of rye and no wheat. Wild Turkey uses the highest percentage of small grains (mainly rye), while Heaven Hill has the highest percentage of corn.

The grains are checked for moisture content, mould and cracked kernels, and the corn is also nosed to see if it has the right sweet aroma. The grains, still kept separate, are ground into a roughish flour. The corn then gets cooked in scalding water to release its starches, next it's cooled and the rye (or wheat) is added. Wheat needs to be cooked at a lower temperature to preserve its aroma, while if you put rye in at too high a temperature you run the risk of rye balls forming, which can cause bacterial infection.

The mixture is then cooled before the malted barley is added. At Four Roses, some malt is added with the corn – not for enzyme activity, but to help liquefy the slurry.

The sweet mash is transferred to fermenters (made either of steel or cypress) where yeast is added. No other spirit holds yeast in such high regard. Each distillery jealously guards its own strain – and, for safety's sake, often has stashes in different sites. These yeasts are strains that have been developed and passed down through the generations. Booker Noe – Beam's master distiller emeritus – remembers his grandfather, Jim Beam, stinking out the house as he developed one of the yeasts that's now used in the Jim Beam brands. Some distilleries use one strain while others, like Beam, use different strains to suit different mash bills. What the old distillers knew intuitively was that yeast is a living organism that not only turns sugar into alcohol (and carbon dioxide), but imparts its own flavour.

The ferment, on average, lasts between three and four days, but this period can be extended to fit in with working weeks, or types of mash. Most distilleries now have a form of temperature control built into their fermenters to stop the heat rising above 90°F, when it would kill the yeast.

A third thing is then added to the fermenter – backset. This is the liquid part of the yeast and grain residue that is collected from the bottom of the beer still. This "sour mash" must make up a minimum of 25 per cent of the volume of the mash, but again each distillery will have its own recipe. Wild Turkey uses 33 per cent backset, while some – like Barton, Four Roses and Heaven Hill – add a percentage of backset at the cooking stage.

The tart, acidic backset does a number of things, most importantly killing harmful bacteria and lowering the pH of the ferment. Because Kentucky's water is calcium-rich, the mash has a tendency to become alkaline – which can lead to infection and off notes. Backset therefore provides an environment in which the yeast can propagate correctly, and give flavour and consistency from one mash to another. This could explain why,

although Scotland uses soft water and Kentucky uses hard water, they both produce such consistently fine spirits. Scottish water is naturally low in pH, so the mash doesn't need any backset; Kentucky's is higher, so it does.

The resulting 'beer' is distilled in a column still several storeys high called, logically enough, a beer still. The beer passes down the column, meeting steam, which is being pumped in under pressure from the bottom (although Beam pumps the mash in under pressure at the bottom).

As the steam rises, it strips the alcohol off the descending beer, so that by the time it reaches the foot of the still it is a non-alcoholic mix of water, dead yeast and spent grains – which is then used as backset.

The vapours are then condensed and passed through a second still called a doubler. Once again, each firm will have its own variation on this process. Maker's Mark condenses all of the charge from its beer still before redistilling it in the doubler. Others keep the flow going continuously, while some use a contraption called a thumper, which involves passing the vapour through water. The heaviest alcohols cannot break through because of the surface tension, and are retained – effectively giving a second distillation.

Only one distillery uses pot-still distillation – Labrot & Graham. The whiskey they produce is currently sitting in barrel – watch this space.

The rate of flow, and the strength at which the spirit comes off the still, can be regulated by adjusting the

pressure and the temperature of the steam. This strength is vitally important to the spirit's final character, and while legally it can be no stronger than 160° proof, everyone takes it off considerably lower. Four Roses comes off the highest – and produces a light, flavoursome spirit. Maker's Mark takes it off lower to preserve the delicacy of the wheat, while Wild Turkey is the lowest of them all – and the fullest flavoured. "It's like cooking a steak," says Jimmy Russell at Wild Turkey. "If you want a tasty one you have it rare, if you have it well done you won't get any flavour."

The 'white dog', as the new make is known, is diluted (again this varies between distilleries) and placed in new, charred American white-oak barrels. The level of char will also vary between distilleries. Ancient Age, for example, has recently moved to a heavier char after finding it gave greater consistency.

Increasingly, barrels are being made from kiln-dried timber, which is cheaper and quicker to produce, but some distillers, such as Wild Turkey, Labrot & Graham and Maker's Mark, all continue to use air-dried staves, as

RETURN OF THE POTS – THE NEW LABROT & GRAHAM DISTILLERY

they feel the barrels have none of the acrid notes that poorly kiln-dried timber can give. Even producers who use kiln-dried wood will admit in private that they prefer the other option.

The majority of distilleries age their spirit in huge rick warehouses up to nine floors high, with three barrels on each floor. It's at this point that Kentucky's climate once again enters the equation. Not only has it given ideal conditions for growing cereal crops and sufficient water for distilling, its temperature range has a huge impact on the way in which the whiskey matures. In other words, Kentucky's distillers harness their climatic conditions to produce their style of whiskey.

The state has cold winters and hot summers, which means that the whiskey will mature in a different way to Scotland. The physical shape of the rick warehouses also plays an important role. Think of it this way. Heat rises; therefore, in a hot and steamy Kentucky summer, when you should be sitting in a shady porch, Mint Julep in hand, the top of a warehouse will be as hot as hell, while the bottom will remain cool. In winter the top will be warm, the bottom cold.

The rate of passage in and out of the wood is therefore greater in the hot upper floors than at the bottom, so the same whiskey aged for, say, four years will look, smell and taste different on each floor. Distillers will also manipulate the temperature by opening and closing windows on each floor to cool or heat as required. Ancient Age and Labrot & Graham also centrally heat their warehouses in winter.

There are two ways to work with this style of maturation. One is to rotate the barrels, taking them from the top and putting them on the bottom – and

vice versa. It's a laborious option, but Wild Turkey and Maker's Mark insist it does have a beneficial effect. The other way is to leave the barrels positioned where they are and blend from a cross-section of floors. The barrels are therefore usually spread out on all floors and across warehouses.

This also means that not all your eggs are in one basket – an important consideration, given Kentucky's occasionally violent climate. One of Beam's warehouses was ripped apart by a tornado, while Heaven Hill lost five warehouses and its distillery in a fire.

The small-batch and single-barrel brands are nearly always taken from the middle floors, where the temperature fluctuations are less extreme. Ancient Age's Blanton always comes from the mid-section of its H warehouse.

Until recently, the word was that bourbon didn't improve much after eight years in barrel, but it's no coincidence that, at that time, most players were trying to sell young whiskey. Now that small batch and single barrels have been promoted – surprise, surprise – it's been shown that by careful wood management bourbon can age as long and as gracefully as any great spirit.

When you get down to it, the secret of the way bourbon tastes is contained in the souls of the master distillers – men like Jimmy Russell of Wild Turkey, Booker Noe of Jim Beam or Maker's Mark's Bill Samuels – and the young distillers who are taking over the reins, like Carl Beam at Heaven Hill or Jim Rutledge at Four Roses.

You know that a great whiskey is going to be produced at a distillery like Wild Turkey when you see the love that Jimmy Russell lavishes on his product. For him the distillery is a living thing –

and at times, with steam billowing out of chimneys, making strange whooshing noises, the whole plant seems to behave like a weird, antediluvian beast.

Russell can recognize the stage a ferment has reached simply by the appearance of the surface and the speed at which it the liquid swirls around the tub. The control room in the stillhouse may contain charts and controls and dials, but here, too, it's the personal touch that counts.

"In the old days, you'd be sitting here with one hand on the flow handle and the other on steam," he says. "People would think you were asleep. But do you hear that noise, hear how the still's whistling? Well, you'd be listening to that whistle, and if it changed you'd adjust either the flow or the pressure. We'd do it by sight and by sound – and we still do it all by nose and taste." The great bourbons are all produced by people who have this deep love. The final element is the heart.

Tennessee WHISKEY

Ironically, most non-Americans' favourite "bourbon" isn't one at all; it's from Tennessee – and Tennessee whiskeys are made in a significantly different manner from those of its neighbour.

In Tennessee's early days, whiskey-making evolved in much the same way as in Kentucky. The state was colonized by Scots and Irish, who were fleeing the imposition of Washington's first taxation of spirits. When they arrived they used the local corn, rye and barley, drew their water from the limestone bedrock and shipped their wares down river.

The split between the Kentucky (bourbon) and Tennessee styles came in the early 1820s when the Lincoln County Process appeared. Its invention is credited to Alfred Eaton who, in 1825, was reported as filtering his whiskey through several feet of maple charcoal, but there is evidence that the principle was already in use prior to

Eaton's "discovery". Whoever was first, it became the signature Tennessee technique by the middle of the nineteenth century.

There's still some mystery as to why this practice should spring up in Tennessee, and nowhere else. Although there is no concrete evidence, it's entirely possible that a Polish or Russian distiller had arrived in the state by that time. Water was charcoal filtered in sixteenth-century Poland before it was used for vodka production; and by the eighteenth century, most Polish vodka was being filtered through charcoal before being bottled or flavoured. This pre-dates any record of it being used in Tennessee. It can't be proved, but given that the history of distilling is about producers adapting and adopting techniques from across the world, it's entirely possible that this could provide the answer to how charcoal mellowing suddenly appeared in Lincoln County.

One of the first distillers to use the technique was the young Jack Daniel. He had started distilling at the tender age of seven, and by 1859 (aged 13) was running his own distillery, finally moving to the limestone water of Cave Spring Hollow in Lynchburg in 1866.

Eleven years later, George Dickel, a whiskey merchant and distributor,

wool blankets at the top and bottom. Certainly, the style is considerably more delicate than the rich, liquoricey Jack. This, however, may have something to do with the radically different ways in which the two distilleries age their whiskeys. While Jack Daniel's uses rick warehouses and rotates the barrels, Dickel ages in single-storey buildings that are heated in winter. This, in combination with the extra mellowing, means you get a considerably more delicate whiskey.

If there is one brand that has turned the world on to American whiskey, it's Jack Daniel's. It has somehow managed to cultivate a rock-and-roll image without ever advertising itself as a rebellious drink. It's a marketing success story without parallel in brown spirits – and one that no one can replicate. But there's more to American whiskey than one brand; perhaps now is the time to start exploring.

bought the Cascade distillery near Tullahoma (another town blessed with limestone water) – enough to supply eight other distilleries. By the turn of the century Dickel's Cascade distillery was the largest and most modern in the state.

It was a tricky time to be involved in the whiskey business. The Temperance movement was showing its teeth, and in 1910 it bit, turning Tennessee dry. Jack Daniel's, by then run by Jack's nephew Lem Motlow (after Jack had died from septicaemia, caused when he kicked a safe door), was forced to move to St Louis for the nine years before Prohibition shut down the rest of America. It managed to return to Lynchburg in 1936 only after a mighty struggle over the rights to the name.

George Dickel was faced with similar problems, and when Tennessee went dry it shifted production to Louisville – although it was still produced with the charcoal mellowing. It took a long time before Dickel could go home. After Prohibition it was made in Frankfort, only returning to Cascade Hollow in 1958. It and Jack Daniel

remain the only two distilleries in a state that once boasted in excess of 700.

By definition, a Tennessee whiskey must be made from a minimum of 51 per cent of one grain. Technically, it could be rye or wheat, although in practice both Jack Daniel and Dickel use corn – it makes up 80 per cent of Jack Daniel's mash bill.

While mashing, fermenting and distillation are the same as in Kentucky, Tennessee whiskey acquires its special character when the white dog is slowly filtered through 10–12 feet of ground-up maple charcoal. This is a double process – removing impurities from the new spirit, but also giving back a mellow sweetness, some say "sootiness", since sugars are retained in the maple when it is burnt, and are leached out when the spirit passes down the vat.

At Jack Daniel's, it takes fives days to filter out of the woollen blanket that's at the bottom of the vat. The firm also uses a double mellowing process for its premium Gentleman Jack.

Dickel has a subtly different approach, as its mellowing vats have

What it TASTES LIKE

Kentucky is home not only to America's indigenous spirit, but to America's first native musical instrument, the five-string banjo, the key instrument in Kentucky's own roots music – bluegrass. Just as bluegrass has its roots in Celtic music, but is a 100 per cent American creation, so whiskey is a fusion between Irish and Scottish knowledge, with an American twist.

Spirits evolve, and bourbon is no different. "Whiskey was the lubrication that allowed the West to be won," says Bill Samuels, President of Maker's Mark. "They didn't want any fancy frou-frou drinks in those days." Right enough; you can't imagine Wyatt Earp and Doc Holliday discussing the finer points of a single-barrel, small-batch bourbon in Tombstone. Red Eye was hard liquor for hard men, and most whiskey remained in that style until Prohibition.

Even after Repeal, the style of bourbon remained in the abrasive camp. You can understand why. The industry needed to build up its stock levels in ultra-quick time, so stills were run hot, hard and long to collect as much alcohol as possible. "I remember Dad sitting at the table before the end of the Second World War saying how he wanted to reinvent bourbon as a softer style of spirit," Samuels now recalls. "Someone at the table, I forget who, said: 'the last thing we need in this country is sissy whiskey'." Only when you see photos of some of the small, registered, pre-Prohibition distilleries does this all make sense. There's a photo of the Hadan distillery in Kentucky, which is nothing more than a

wooden shack with moonshining equipment inside it. The proud owners are standing outside, guns at the ready. You can bet your bottom dollar they wouldn't have been making no sissy stuff.

'Sissy' whiskey sure wasn't made here

There again, why should they have been? The majority of people who were drinking the stuff weren't high-flying executives, but the proletariat – scrabbling for jobs, working in heavy industry, digging for coal in the Appalachians – men who had been moonshining all the way through Prohibition. But things were changing.

Post-war, blended Scotch took the high ground in America, while vodka, gin and Bacardi all boomed. As drinking spirits long became the norm, so whiskey producers released their product young.

The top end of the market – with the exception of the small-scale Maker's Mark – remained untouched, and the category undersold itself. Then, in the face of the worst slump this century,

Old style, with a new attitude

Tasting Notes

BARTON

Ten High A strange mix of lemon cordial and young wood. Light and dry with dried herbs and a peppery bite.
Kentucky Gentleman Soft, juicy, though strangely mealy, fruit. Crisp, concentrated and simple.
Kentucky Tavern Creamy wood on the nose, some floral, orangey notes. Good feel and a zip of spice at the end.
Col. Lee Dry wood with some hazelnut and cream. Soft and oily to

start, then a crunch of small grains behind with a rye freshness on finish.
Tom Moore Muted with Juicy Fruit chewing gum aromas. Little feinty.
Very Old Barton Certainly old in the wooded stakes and certainly rich. Long and fresh, with crisp zippy acid/lemon finish.

HEAVEN HILL

Evan Williams 90° Balanced wood aromas of spice, cinnamon, caramel and a little smoke. A good, rounded feel with a mid-palate bite. Soft but lean.

Elijah Craig 12-year-old 94° Rich woodiness with spice, smoke and a hint of nutmeg. Firm in the mouth but enough soft fruit to carry it to great lengths.
Elijah Craig 18yo Almost heathery nose with touches of saddle soap and nuts. Soft and fruity in the mouth with great spicy, peppery length. Excellent.

FOUR ROSES

Yellow Label Gentle, slightly wooded, and lightly citric on nose. Clean, light,

fragrant with a gentle zippiness.
Black Label Firm on the nose with hickory wood smoke. On palate, light and clean. A sweet start, then a firm rye grip.
Super Premium In the house style, but with a richer undertow. Solid in the mouth and a fine tingle of zesty rye. Smoky and smooth. Good.

STILL THE BRAND
TO BEAT

people's palates changed again. They began drinking less, but drinking better. "It's fascinating to chart," says Gerard White at UDV. "There was a change in style after Prohibition, then it changes post-war when young whiskey appeared. Then from the mid-80s on there's this switch upmarket and we're back to the old style again. Now bourbon is a fundamentally American spirit again."

What hasn't happened, however, is a return to the fusel oil, over-wooded overload of the old days; the new premium bourbons take the best qualities of the old style, but add elegance, style and finesse to it – as long as they control the alcohol levels. They aren't sissy whiskeys, but Bill Samuels Sr's belief in quality has finally been proved to be correct.

These days, you are spoilt for choice – from the spice and nutmeg of Heaven Hills' Elijah Craig 12-year-old, and the saddle soap and heather of its 18-year-old version; the small-batch range from Beam that shifts from the zippy, crisp Basil Hayden; to Knob Creek's generosity and the all-out multi-faceted attack of Booker's. From UDV comes the beautifully balanced, intense Old Charter, and the rum and

RED BRICK FOR A
BLUE-COLLAR
WHISKEY

Tasting Notes

JIM BEAM

Basil Hayden 8yo 80° Powerful and rich. A zesty drive with chewy, tingly rye finish. Very good.
Knob Creek 9yo 100° Rich caramel/treacle nose. Fruity, elegant, ripe, rich.
Baker's 7yo 107° Firm, and heavy with some liquorice on the palate. An oily texture with a tingle on the finish.
Booker's 7yo 126/7° Rich, complex but alcohol-dominant nose with caramel, tobacco boxes, hickory and whiffs of lapsang souchong tea and

bitter orange peel. Powerful with an elegant orange/oak character.
Jim Beam Rye Zesty lemon lift with cumin powder spiciness. Tight and crisp that belts your tastebuds back into shape.

ANCIENT AGE

Ancient Age 4yo A quite delicate, almost nutty nose. Smooth with a touch of vanilla and a clean, corny middle.
Blanton Single Barrel Nutty, cereal nose, light perfume and high alcohol.
Ancient Ancient Age 10yo Rich,

elegant, plump with cinnamon, treacle and grassiness. Soft with good length.

LABROT & GRAHAM

Woodford Reserve Bitter orange, smoky wood and some sweetness on the nose. Fine grip on the palate with a melding of mint and honey.

WILD TURKEY

Wild Turkey 4yo Creamy, rich, vanilla notes with a cakey touch. Rich, clean

and spicy with a fresh finish.
Wild Turkey 101 8yo Ripe, rich with menthol and mint, rich vanilla, toffee and concentrated fruits. Mixes freshness with weight, instant appeal with ripe raisin and baked apple fruit.
Wild Turkey Rare Breed The wood shows on the nose, but the palate is all opulent, unctuous layered fruits. Rich and chocolately.

raisin, chocolatey W.L. Weller. Then there's Ancient Age's sweet single-barrel Blanton's; Maker's Mark's honeyed, buttery elegance; the orange peel and mint on Labrot & Graham's Woodford Reserve and, at the top of the tree, Wild Turkey's opulent, unctuous, flavoursome Rare Breed.

The two enforced shutdowns of the twentieth century killed two other truly American whiskeys – rye and corn. Rye, however, is a great style. The grain gives a bite to some of the best bourbons, but on its own it develops into a marvellously spicy, zesty drink, filled with the scents of cumin seed and citrus fruits, exploding in your mouth with mouth-watering acidity. These days, only Wild Turkey and Jim Beam make straight ryes, although Gerard White – trawling through UDV's massive inventory looking for possible limited-edition releases – discovered a

stash of 16-year-old rye from the George T. Stagg distillery. Powerful, spicy and lemony on the nose, it sets off a chain-reaction in the mouth, building up to an incredible intensity of bitter chocolate and lime zest. It might not be the prettiest drink in the world, but it reinforces the evidence that America makes classic, world-class whiskeys.

Corn whiskey labours under the image of being nothing more than moonshine, a whiskey without any finesse. Certainly, when you hear blues singers like Dock Boggs singing: "Give me corn bread when I'm hungry good people/Corn whiskey when I'm dry," you know he's not talking about top-end stuff. You'll be hard pressed to find (legal) corn whiskey these days, but UDV (again) has unearthed a small batch from the Old Quaker distillery in Indiana. Pale gold, it's fragrant, creamy and gentle on the nose, and lulls you

into a sense of false security with its dreamy start. Then it bites, before yielding again to a sweet, almost-malty finish. You wonder what Dock Boggs would have made of it – he'd probably have approved of the 130° proof.

The sad thing is that, as this is being written, it's unclear what will happen with this fascinating initiative. UD's merger IDV leads you to fear that small batches won't feature in the corporate plans. Let's hope and pray that they do.

You can't help but wonder what might have happened to American whiskey if Prohibition and the Second World War hadn't closed the industry for such long periods. For Booker Noe, small batch is like going back to the future. "Years ago it was aged for longer and distilled lower in proof, and you got a more concentrated whiskey. Booker's is what whiskey was 200 years ago. It's kosher whiskey." Let's drink to that.

Get in touch with your masculine side.

BRANDED FOR LIFE

Tasting Notes

UDV MAKER'S MARK

Old Charter 13yo 96°
Menthol, lemon thyme nose. On palate, very clean and zesty. Balances wood and floral fruit with a mouthful of spices that give a piquant, acidic attack. Brilliant.

W.L. Weller 10yo 100°
Rich mix of spice, butter, molasses and some rum and raisin. Rich and sweet start that mixes chocolatey fruit and spice.

George T. Stagg 16yo 110° Pungent and powerful. Lemon balm/lime zest leaning to aftershave. Clean, bitter chocolate spiciness that hits the mouth and then explodes and expands. Stunning, but not for the faint-hearted.

Taylor & Williams 15yo 115° Rich smoky wood with some plump fruitiness behind. Very smooth to start, then it builds into a powerful mouthfilling mix of fruit, treacle, orange and chocolate.

Old Quaker 21yo 130° (Indiana corn whiskey). Pale yellow. Fragrant and gentle with cream and clover aromas. Gentle and smooth to start, then an astringent bite which yields to mellow sweetness on the finish.

Medley 18yo barrel proof Wood-dominant with pungent whiffs of creosote and prunes. Dense and sweet on the palate with coffee bean, acid and chewy toffee wood on the finish.

Whiskies of the rest of the WORLD

Canada

Canadian whisky initially evolved in much the same fashion as American. Indeed, it wasn't made until emigrants from the Highlands of Scotland and Ireland began arriving in droves, bringing with them the knowledge of how to turn grain into spirit. Production first started around the Great Lakes, where it went hand in hand with the development of the farming of cereal crops. As in America, it was easier to distil the crops than to have to lug bushels of corn to market, and so whisky became Canada's national drink.

Distilleries were soon established, but, just as his counterparts did in every spirit-producing country the world over, the Canadian taxman soon got wise to the revenue that could be extracted from spirits production, and the industry became concentrated around a group of people with sufficient capital.

As Jim Murray points out in his *Complete Book of Whisky*, it made more economic sense in this high-tax regime

to be able to distil large quantities in a continuous still for high profit, rather than stick with the small-scale, labour-intensive batch process.

Although production was regulated by the end of the nineteenth century, Canadian whisky only really woke up to the wider world when Prohibition hit America. Canada itself had flirted briefly with this madness, but had lasted only one year – ironically Canada came to its senses in 1919, just as the United States was closing down. The result was that Canadian whisky

flooded across the Great Lakes and in doing so an export market was secured.

This triggered a boom that continued into the mid-1970s, when there were huge volumes of whisky coming out of Canada and disappearing all over the globe, before it, too, was caught up in the brown spirit slump. Now there are only nine distilleries in this vast country.

Canadian whisky is a style that is dependent on the blender's skill. You can't find the equivalent (yet) of a Canadian single malt, but you will find some great blends with a distinctive, soft sweetness that is livened up by the addition of rye.

Brands comprise, by and large, a blend of different grains: rye (for its bite); barley (for the enzyme, although enzymes are often used on their own); wheat (which gives sweetness); and corn (for softness). All are fermented with different yeasts, distilled in a range of different stills, to a selection of different strengths. Then they can be aged in a range of woods – ex-brandy or

Tasting Notes

CANADA

Canadian Club
Medium weight, but softly rounded in the mouth with a slightly over-firm finish.

Seagram V. O.
Fairly light on the nose, but attractive enough. There's good depth of flavour on the palate – a crisp, firm drive that's coupled to gently smooth, fruitiness that typifies Canadian style.

Seagram Crown Royal
Full on the nose with fairly complex smooth flavours – a touch of spice and citrus giving it lift. On the palate, a gentle, smooth character takes over.

JAPAN

Nikka All Malt
Decent malty weight on the nose, but not overly heavy on the palate, which has a clean crunch and a nudge of peat.

Suntory Hibiki
Proof that complexity can exist in Japanese whisky. More fruit dominant than most on the nose, there's some smoke, perhaps from the wood which gives the palate a decent grip.

Suntory Reserve
Substantial nose, with fruity, nutty character showing well. Rich and elegant.

bourbon barrels, as well as new and charred wood.

Each part of a blend will mature at an apposite time – the usual rule of thumb is that the corn spirit is distilled to a higher strength and aged for a short time, while rye is distilled to a lower strength and aged for longer. The blenders are attempting to build in as many possibilities as they can.

A brand like Black Velvet will combine a young rye that is blended with other base spirits and then aged together for another four years. Canadian Club uses three main components: a triple-distilled corn spirit that uses one kind of yeast, one double-distilled flavouring spirit and one single-distilled flavouring spirit from rye, malted rye and barley – both of which have been fermented with another yeast strain, and distilled in a combination of a column still and a doubler.

Seagram's classic brand, Crown Royal is made from a corn-dominant mash from a continuous still that's aged in new wood before being blended with aged rye. The older versions of Crown Royal will use a higher percentage of aged rye and a judicious splash of bourbon to add to its richness.

They are never too rich, though, never too forceful. The best Canadian whiskies are gentle spirits from a gentle country.

Japan

The existence of Japanese whisky is down to one man, Masataka Taketsuru, who arrived in Scotland in 1918 to learn the art of distilling. On his return to Japan in 1920, complete with Scottish wife in tow, he was employed by Shinjiro Torii, the founder of Suntory, at that firm's Yamazaki distillery, selling his first whisky four

years later. In 1940 (in retrospect, not, perhaps, the ideal time to start a new business venture) he started up on his own at his Yoichi distillery deep into the snowfields of Hokkaido.

On paper, Japan could produce great whisky (in fact, Yoichi does). It has pure water, there's peat in the hills, the country is fertile and the climate is suitable for even maturation. The Yamakazi and Yoichi distilleries both have the ability to peat their malt to different levels, distil in a wide range of stills and age in a vast range of wood types. The trouble is that there seems to be a fear that they won't be able to do it as well as the Scots, so malt whisky is brought over in bulk and blended in, resulting in the Japanese character being drowned out. With the Japanese public these days preferring single-malt and small-batch bourbon, it's going to be tough to change that mentality.

Other whisky-producing countries

In almost every country you come across you'll find someone making a drink that they call whisky. Some are the genuine article – DYC in Spain, for example, is a perfectly decent blend, while Tesetice in the Czech Republic has long enjoyed a good reputation.

Indian whisky, however, has not been so well received. Scottish distillers, including Glenmorangie and Whyte & Mackay, are entering into joint ventures, but you get the feeling it's more to get their brands a foothold in what could become a huge market for Scotch. That may be unfair, but Indian whiskies are rarely anything other than cheap spirits to be drunk quickly, then forgotten. Much the same can be said for the "whiskies" that come out of Thailand and China. Admire the labels, by all means, then buy something else.

STILLROOM AT SUNTORY'S HAKUSHU DISTILLERY

The
MANHATTAN
Classic Cocktail

MANHATTAN

2 OZ BOURBON

·

1 OZ SWEET VERMOUTH

·

3 DASHES ANGOSTURA

·

DROP OF MARASCHINO JUICE

·

MARASCHINO CHERRY

·

STIR OVER ICE IN MIXING GLASS AND STRAIN INTO COCKTAIL GLASS.

·

GARNISH WITH CHERRY.

HERE ARE TWO PILLARS OF SOUTHERN SOCIETY THAT ARE AS WELCOME AND REFRESHING AS A COOL BREEZE ON A WARM DAY RIPPLING ACROSS THE BLUEGRASS

There is always debate as to who was the first to make any specific drink, but the Manhattan's origins seem to be pretty clear. It was created in the 1870s at the Manhattan Club in New York for Lady Jennie Churchill (Sir Winston's mother) at a celebration dinner given when William Tilden became state governor. At its heart beat the essential ingredients of nineteenth-century cocktails: sweet vermouth and bitters.

There is almost as much debate over Manhattans as there is over Dry Martinis but, while the cocktail has undoubtedly become drier over the years, it should not be a dry drink. The magnificence of the Manhattan lies in the way the bitters and sweet vermouth join in an unlikely alliance to round off the whiskey's more abrasive edges.

The original recipe calls for rye – a style that sadly is hard to find these days – so most use the sweeter bourbon. Canadian whiskey is too light. But which brand? That's a matter of personal preference.

Speaking personally, I'd choose Wild Turkey when I need a weighty belt of liquor after a tough day, or Maker's Mark for sophisticated sipping. Knob Creek is equally good, although Booker's is, I feel, just too strong and tends to dominate the supporting flavours.

BARTENDER'S TIPS
For nearly a century, the mint julep has been the traditional beverage of the Kentucky Derby.

MINT JULEP NO. 1

3 OZ BOURBON

•

I OZ SIMPLE SYRUP

•

3 CUPS FINELY CRUSHED ICE

•

6 SPRIGS OF MINT

•

FILL A JULEP CUP OR GLASS TWO-THIRDS
FULL WITH CRUSHED ICE.

•

ADD BOURBON AND SYRUP. STIR TO
BLEND. PACK THE GLASS WITH MORE ICE
SO IT DOMES OVER THE TOP.

•

GARNISH WITH THE MINT AND INSERT
STRAWS. LET STAND UNTIL A THIN LAYER
FORMS ON THE GLASS.

Mint JULEP
Classic Cocktail

MINT JULEP NO. 2

3 OZ BOURBON

•

I OZ SIMPLE SYRUP

•

HANDFUL OF MINT LEAVES

•

3 CUPS FRESHLY FINELY CRUSHED ICE

•

6 SPRIGS OF MINT

•

COVER LEAVES IN BOURBON FOR 15
MINUTES. TAKE OUT AND PUT IN
MUSLIN CLOTH AND WRING OVER THE
BOURBON. PUT BOURBON AND SYRUP IN
ANOTHER BOWL.

•

FILL CUP, GLASS WITH CRUSHED ICE SO IT
DOMES OVER THE TOP. ADD BOURBON,
MINT, SYRUP MIX. ADD STRAWS AND
GARNISH. LET STAND UNTIL A THIN LAYER
FORMS ON THE GLASS.

If a Manhattan sparks debate, then a Mint Julep can incite war. Typically, its secret is simplicity, which is where the debate comes in. To crush or not to crush the mint, the quality of the ice, the receptacle, which bourbon to use. Every aspect causes argument.

On paper it's simple. All you need is fresh mint, ice, sugar syrup and bourbon. Ah, but if you are Bill Samuels of Maker's Mark, you pick mint only in April and use only the tenderest leaves, which you then tie up in a T-shirt, place in a container

IT MAY LOOK EASY, BUT MIXING A JULEP CAN LEAD TO BLOWS

holding the whiskey, batter with a mallet and then squeeze. Before he became a distiller, Bill designed nuclear warheads…

If you are one of those Julepians who doesn't believe in bruising the leaves, try gently squeezing the leaves instead or bruise them gently with a muddler. Jim Beam's Booker Noe only uses mint to infuse his

syrup, by pouring the cooled syrup over a jar filled with mint, refrigerating it and then discarding the mint.

There's also debate as to how much mint to use for the garnish. Six sprigs are about right. In his *Book of Bourbon*, Gary Regan suggests cutting the mint at the last minute and allowing some flavour to bleed from the stems into the drink.

A Mint Julep cools, refreshes and makes the world a beautiful place. Too many of them, however, and the soothing Southern experience turns into something bitter and twisted.

4 Brandy

IT WAS THE PHONECIANS AND THE ROMANS WHO TOOK IT UPON THEMSELVES TO SPREAD THE ART OF WINEMAKING THROUGHOUT THE WHOLE OF SOUTHERN EUROPE. MUCH LATER, IN THE SIXTEENTH CENTURY, LEARNED ITALIAN MONKS AND MOORISH SCHOLARS INTRODUCED THE REMARKABLE PROCESS OF DISTILLATION – AND, LO AND BEHOLD, A NEW SPIRIT WAS BORN – IT'S NAME WAS BRANDY

Cognac

Cognac, like any major spirit-producing region, is living proof of man's interaction with a beneficial environment. The Romans brought viticulture to this area around the Charente river (the Gaulish provinces of Angoumois, Saintonge and Aunis) in the third century, as they did across France. What made this particular area important was that it had access to the Bay of Biscay at what is now La Rochelle, thereby linking it to the trade routes with the Celtic nations and Northern Europe. In those days rivers were arteries that not only carried goods but ideas as well – a nervous system of intellect.

By late medieval times, coastal trade had become increasingly important and La Rochelle had been elevated to the status of a major port. Initially trade revolved around the salt that was produced there – salt, at that time, being as valuable as gold, and prized in Northern European states. As the salt trade developed, the region's wines also began to be exported to Scotland (Macbeth drank

Charentais wines), Ireland, England, Scandinavia, the Baltic States and, most significantly, Holland.

Importantly, La Rochelle – unlike Bordeaux – never silted up, which allowed merchants easy access to the interior and easy transport away – a fact that was to count against Armagnac (*see below*), and in time the Charente prospered. It wasn't to last.

In the thirteenth century, when the English and the French were battling for

ascendancy in France, the Charente found itself stuck between the (French-held) Loire and (English-held) Bordeaux. It allied itself with France which, as Axel Behrendt says in his book *Cognac*, was a "fateful" decision as the region became a battleground, the vineyards for ever being destroyed by the marauding English troops. Farmers gave up viticulture as a bad job and planted wheat in the chalky soil, and trees elsewhere.

Then fate smiled on the area. In the sixteenth century, La Rochelle aligned itself with the Protestant Huguenots, a move which, although isolating it from much of the rest of France, brought it close once more to the Protestant north of Europe. Trade (initially in salt rather than wine) grew, but in time the vines went back into the ground – then distilling arrived.

It's ironic that the world's premier brandy-producing region was such a late starter. The first record of brandy being made in the region was in 1638, when Lewis Roberts wrote about: "a small wine that is called Rotchell, or more precisely cogniake".

UGNI BLANC IS THE MAIN GRAPE VARIETY IN COGNAC

Although it's entirely possible that small-scale distilling was happening before this – after all, by then Armagnac and Jerez had been making brandy for two centuries – Cognac didn't produce brandy in commercial quantities until the middle of the seventeenth century. But why, then, did this late starter find itself elevated rapidly to the finest brandy region of them all? It was down to the Dutch. The sixteenth century had seen Holland becoming the most powerful trading nation in the world, controlling spices (*see* Gin), wine, rum and brandy, and the Dutch had been trading in salt and wine with the merchants of La Rochelle since the time of the Hanseatic League.

Now, with the Dutch mercantile empire encompassing Sumatra, the Caribbean and Northern Europe, they needed *brandewijn* (burnt wine) to make the drinking water on ships drinkable, and to fortify table wines in order to stabilize them. This led to the creation of Pineau de Charentes.

Although the Dutch initially imported the Charentais wine and dis-tilled it at home, it soon made economic sense to make the brandy *in situ* and then ship it – after all you can fit more barrels of brandy than barrels of wine on board a ship. Ever resourceful, they invented a pot still and switched production to the region around the towns of Cognac and Jarnac.

The quality of Cognac was apparent from the word go. English wine merchants were asking high prices for the new "cogniacke" almost as soon as it appeared on the market – and with some justification. Once again fate had looked on the region kindly.

Economic and social pressures had 'discovered' a region that was perfectly situated for the making of high-quality brandy. The wood to fire the stills and make the barrels was in the forests, there was easy access to the sea and long-established foreign trading links.

What made the difference, though, was the climate and the soil (particularly the chalky part around Cognac) which gave ideal conditions for viticulture, while the microclimate next to the river was perfect for slow, steady maturing. In 1669, when Louis XIV gave the inspired decree to establish oak forests in the nearby regions of Limousin and Troncais, all the elements were in place for a glorious future.

Cognac soon became established as the preferred drink of the Northern European bourgeoisie, especially in England. Even when boycotts were applied, it was smuggled in to England – either via Holland, or via Jersey, where one Jean Martell was a merchant. Martell moved to Cognac in 1715 to start ageing and blending his own Cognacs. The industry was fast becoming as recognizable as it is today.

The demands of a growing export market soon led to the development of the three tiers of trade which are still in place today. Growers cultivated grapes, made wine and occasionally distilled and shipped; others stopped growing grapes and became distillers; while the merchants bought *eaux-de-vie*, blended, aged and shipped.

As the merchants grew in importance (and size) in the nineteenth century, so they needed to control ever greater supplies, and in time built up considerable inventories of older Cognacs. Major houses, including Courvoisier, Delamain and Hine were founded at around this time.

The outlook was rosy. In a relatively short time, Cognac had become the world's premium spirit. Unlike most other major categories it didn't have to fight against prejudice and wait to gain the approval of the middle classes; it had that from the start. It was recognized as being of high quality, and there was a massive vineyard to support growing demand.

Then, disaster. In 1871, a vine pest called *phylloxera vastatrix* began gnawing away at the roots of the vines. Within a few years the entire vineyard had been destroyed. It took time to recover. Vines aren't like grain crops, or sugar cane. You don't just plant a new vine and harvest it a year later.

First, a way had to be found to make the vines resistant to *phylloxera* – which didn't happen until the mid-1880s, when it was discovered that grafting vines onto American rootstock had the desired effect. However, not all rootstocks could cope with French conditions; the rootstocks and the vines had to be paired up. While this research was scientifically done, it was still a matter of trial and error – and it was also expensive.

As the whole of the French vineyard was slowly obliterated, the demand

DELAMAIN REMAINS A PRODUCER OF ELEGANTLY RESTRAINED COGNACS

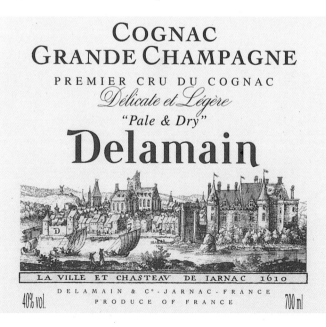

for rootstocks was high – and many growers simply could not afford to (a) buy the new plants and (b) wait for them to bear fruit. Given that it takes between three and five years for a vine to bear its first crop suitable for winemaking (and distilling), you can see why it took close on 20 years for Cognac to be replanted – and many growers didn't bother. By the time commercial quantities of Cognac were back on the market, Scotch and gin had become more popular.

Cognac, successfully, set its sights on regaining the top end of the market. While the effect of two world wars and an economic depression served to consolidate the industry, it also allowed the major shippers to tighten their control and, by developing major brands, they helped to rebuild Cognac's image as the luxury spirit.

This was augmented by the fact that Cognac has always been stronger in its export markets than at home. Even today 95 per cent of Cognac is exported, and the industry has always looked to sell into as many markets as possible. Therefore when the 1970s slump hit the European and US markets, the Cognac houses were already selling large quantities of deluxe brands to the Far East.

Even though the decline in the European markets necessitated a vine pull, the merchants thought that nothing could harm them, that the Far East would save them, and that Europe and the USA would, eventually, regain their senses and return to the fold. But they had grown complacent.

Now the Far East is in trouble and

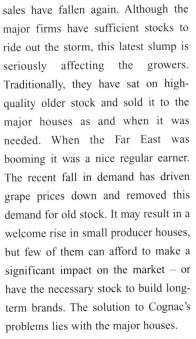

sales have fallen again. Although the major firms have sufficient stocks to ride out the storm, this latest slump is seriously affecting the growers. Traditionally, they have sat on high-quality older stock and sold it to the major houses as and when it was needed. When the Far East was booming it was a nice regular earner. The recent fall in demand has driven grape prices down and removed this demand for old stock. It may result in a welcome rise in small producer houses, but few of them can afford to make a significant impact on the market – or have the necessary stock to build long-term brands. The solution to Cognac's problems lies with the major houses.

There are a number of possibilities. Firms could emphasize the quality of the individual regions, they could promote VS (3-Star) Cognac as a mixable drink, or they could start releasing more vintage Cognac. The widespread introduction of age statements on the bottle is long overdue (indeed it is already being done by

firms such as Prunier), and would bring Cognac into line with every other premium spirits category. All approaches, thankfully, are being tried, but with varying degrees of conviction. The question remains as to whether people will buy it. No matter which way you look at the problems facing the region, you end up with the same conclusion. To prosper once again, Cognac must rid itself of its stuffy, elitist image.

It also needs to justify its price. Cognac has higher fixed costs than, say, malt whisky, which means that a VS (3-Star) Cognac is priced around the same as a malt – but it can't compete in quality terms. "Ah!," the houses say, "but if you pay a little more you'll find the finest brandies in the world." That's undoubtedly true, but the houses are not giving consumers a reason to do this.

The image of the most sublime brandies in the world is out of step with the new spirit drinker who is willing to lay out that little bit extra. The Cognacs are there; whether they can be sold is another question.

PHYLLOXERA IS STILL A MENACE – AS SEEN HERE IN CALIFORNIA'S NAPA VALLEY

73

How it's MADE

To try to understand what makes Cognac such an inspirational spirit, you have to start digging in the soil that makes up the six sub-regions (*crus*) of this tranquil, gently expansive region. The French have a word for it – *terroir*. To be accurate, it's more than just the soil. *Terroir* is about climate, altitude, exposure to the sun and how they impact on the vine – and then how man uses the fruit. Without the different *terroirs* of Cognac, the master-blenders of the region wouldn't be able to draw on such a diverse richness of *eaux-de-vie*. Certainly, different approaches to distillation will have an effect, but the fundamental difference between the *crus* lies in their differing *terroirs*.

It's all to do with the bands of chalk that run across the region. The two main quality regions, Grande and Petite Champagne, have the highest percentage of chalk – in fact, some claim that "Champagne" comes from the Latin *campania* (light, chalky soil), although others argue that it's from the old French *campagne* (open land). The *crus* radiate out from the town of Cognac,

the epicentre of the region, rather like rings on a target. To get to the heart of the region, therefore, you must start in the two Champagnes. As Alain Braastad-Delamain argues, their physical location and the resulting influence of climate are vitally important. His point is that, since Cognac is located between the Atlantic Ocean and the Massif Central, it's on the cusp of maritime and continental climates and also between northern and southern climatic conditions. This results in a mass of different microclimates.

Grande Champagne, lying to the south of the Charente, is at the axis of these different climatic conditions and this equable climate – combined with the highest percentage of chalk in the soil – results in *eaux-de-vie* which are the most delicate, subtle, elegant and refined in the region, but which need time before they reveal their full glory.

Petite Champagne is a semi-circular curve that encloses the southern part of Grand Champagne. Although twice as large, it only produces the same volume of *eaux-de-vie* as its prestigious neigh-

bour. There is less chalk here and slightly greater variance between east and west. The *eaux-de-vie* are correspondingly less intense and more floral and fruity. If a Cognac is made exclusively from these two *crus* – and a minimum of 50 per cent is made up by the Grande Champagne portion – it can be called Fine Champagne.

The small region of Borderies lies on the north bank of the Charente opposite the western part of Petite and Grande Champagne. Here the maritime climate has more of an influence, as does the higher percentage of flint and clay in the soil. The resulting distillates are highly distinctive, being rich, full-bodied and almost waxy, but with a flowery elegance. They are used by blenders to give roundness, guts and vigour to a blend. They are an important component for many of the major houses – in particular, Martell (*see* below).

These three central regions are encircled by the Fins Bois (so named, as the cru was forested when the vines for brandy were planted). Fins Bois supplies the bulk of Cognac, and is often unfairly dismissed as a result. Once again, situation is all-important. There are chalky strips running through the clay, which makes up most of the area, and the vineyards produce delicate, refined *eaux-de-vie*. Since this is the largest area, there are huge differences in climate between the eastern and western sections, as well as from north to south. In other words, it's dangerous to generalize.

Most firms use the robust, quick-maturing style for their higher-volume blends but the exceptions, such as Gourmel, show that Fins Bois can produce light, floral, graceful Cognacs, which can hold their own against the more prestigious *crus*.

Fins Bois itself is surrounded by the Bons Bois, and here quality begins to decrease, although again there are exceptions to this rule if chalk is involved. Most of the *eaux-de-vie* from here is used to give punch and drive to a blend.

The final *cru* is Bois Ordinaires, where the chalk has given way to sand, and the sea plays an important role. It's not the ideal combination for quality.

The proof of the influence of *terroir* is demonstrated by the fact that this vast range of spirits is produced by the same form of distillation, and by and large from the same grape variety – Ugni Blanc. The main pre-*phylloxera* variety, Folle Blanche, can still be found, but it proved to be difficult to graft on to American rootstocks and is prone to rot, so Ugni Blanc took over. It's not a particularly exciting variety as far as wine goes, but it has the advantage of being a late ripener, and therefore retains its acidity when it is being harvested.

High (though not excessive) acidity is essential for distillation for two reasons. Acidity acts as a natural preservative, making it more difficult for the wine to oxidize. Given that no sulphur (the normal protection against oxidation) can be added to a wine that's going to be distilled, the distiller must rely on acidity to guarantee that the wine is as fresh as possible. Acidity also has an impact on the aromas and flavours produced by distillation which, after all, is about concentrating the flavours and aromas in a fermented wash.

High levels of acidity mean that the wine is low in sugar (and therefore in alcohol), and a distiller wants a low-alcohol wine, as it is easier to concentrate. An alcoholic wine will give a flabby brandy. As Nicholas Faith points out in *Cognac*: "A wine of 12 per cent distilled to 70 per cent ABV is only concentrated six times, while a wine of 9 percent ABV is concentrated nearly 8 times." Cognac, on average, is made from a wine of around 8 per cent ABV.

A few producers distil on their own property, but most of the wine is taken to the professional distiller. Although the regulations allow distillation to be done until March 31 of the year after vintage, ideally you want to get the wine distilled as quickly as possible after the ferment.

All Cognac is distilled in the *alembic charentais*. This elegant, rather exotic-looking still consists of a boiler (*chaudière*), with an onion-shaped head (the *chapiteau*, which reminds you of the domes on Brighton Pavilion) and a long, thin neck (*col de cygne*) that swoops into the condenser. Some stills have a preheater, which sits in between the boiler and the condenser.

The vapour from the boiler passes through this preheater, which contains wine waiting to be distilled. The hot vapour gently heats the wine, while the cool wine acts as the start of a slow condensation. Not all distilleries like to use them. Martell, for one, has no preheaters, Bisquit uses one only for the first distillation, while Camus uses one for both. As ever, each producer puts a slightly different spin on proceedings.

This also applies to whether the wine is distilled on its lees or not. Some firms will distil some of their *eaux-de-vie* without lees, some with a little and others with the full lees. It all depends on the style of the distillate that's required. A wine with heavy lees will give an *eau-de-vie* with higher congeners which, in turn, take longer to break down in cask. If you are making an *eau-de-vie* destined for a young Cognac, you'll tend to cut down (or eliminate) the lees.

"A clear wine may give too lean a spirit," says Bernard Hine, master-blender at Hine. "Fine lees in the wine give fruity aromas, but too much may make the distillate too heavy. A proper balance between the average strength of

THE TIMELESS CALM OF A COGNAC DISTILLERY

Timothy hadn't realised forgetting the Martell was such a serious offence.

*A TRENDY TIPPLE AT LAST
— COGNAC TRIES TO BUILD
A NEW IMAGE*

the *eau-de-vie* and a reasonable quality of fine lees in the wine will give the aromatic Cognac, which contributes to the Hine style."

The first distillation yields a slightly cloudy spirit known as *brouillis*. Then comes the all-important second distillation (*bonne chauffe*), which must be done in stills that contain no more than 25hl of *brouillis*. As with any batch distillation, the aim here is to remove the heart (*coeur*) from the heads and the tails (*secondes*).

Each house will have its own specifications, and run the stills at different speeds and to different strengths, although on average the spirit comes off the still at 70 per cent ABV. The *secondes* are then added either to the wine or to the *brouillis* and, once more, the percentage added will vary between houses and distillates and give different results.

Normally, the spirit is placed in new, toasted, 350-litre Limousin oak barrels (although Martell prefers Troncais). Limousin is a medium-grained oak, (good for a long, steady oxidation), which is rich in tannin – again making it beneficial for long ageing.

COURVOISIER'S PARADIS

In general the young spirit will spend only one year in new wood – any longer, and you run the risk of it extracting too much from the barrel. It's then decanted into older barrels. Again, this will depend on the house. Frapin is unusual in giving its young spirit two years in new wood, while Delamain only uses used casks (*futs roux*) in its maturing, as the house feels that new wood gives excessive tannin.

Ageing

The process of ageing is a complex one (*see* The Art of Distilling). The spirit is extracting tannins, colour and flavouring from the wood, while also being slowly oxidized. A young Cognac will therefore be filled with the spicy vanillin character that comes from new oak, but in time the barrel begins to endow the spirit with its other components, making it richer, sweeter and more complex. After around 20 years in barrel the famed rich, raisined, fruit and nut (some think Roquefort cheese) *rancio* character begins to emerge.

Some barrels can continue to give this slow, steady exchange for 40 years, but they are the exception – and any longer than that will give too much wood character. These ancient Cognacs are decanted into glass demijohns and stored in an inner sanctum, the appropriately named Paradis.

Where the barrels are placed is important as well. The warehouse, too, has a microclimate. Relatively humid conditions are needed, which allow a steady, gentle maturation. Over-dry conditions mean that the spirit evaporates too quickly and becomes dry and hard. Too damp, and it absorbs too much water and becomes flabby. The siting of these ageing cellars is therefore a major contributory factor to the final quality of the Cognac – and the old ones by the river are demonstrably the best.

While old Cognacs acquire their colour and complexity from the exchange between spirit, wood and air, the law allows young Cognacs to be adulterated with caramel and a substance known as *boise* – made from wood shavings and brandy. This allegedly gives the Cognac the impression of being older than it is, but it doesn't. All *boise* and caramel does is to distance the Cognac from the *terroir*.

The Cognac also has to be reduced in strength before it is bottled, a process that some shippers feel is one of the most important elements of all. Reduction is a carefully executed technique, which can take years to complete. Methods vary and, although distilled water can be used, most of the top houses use a mix of Cognac and water (*faibles*) to bring it down to bottling strength. Delamain takes two years to complete the reduction, while Gourmel's Age des Fruits is slowly reduced over a period of three years, and its top brand Quintessence is brought down to bottling strength over seven years. "The quality of the Cognac depends on the quality of the reduction," says Pierre Voisin at Gourmel. "This long reduction creates a significant formation of fatty acids, essential oils and natural sugars."

It's often thought that Cognac is blended at this point. In fact, most Cognacs are blended from the word go. The master-blender will start making up his blend immediately after distillation, either mixing different distillates from the same region, or blending between regions. This process will continue throughout the ageing process, when it's decanted from new to old wood, and after reduction and prior to bottling.

The art of blending Cognac is the use of nose and memory to meld the different distillates from the various *terroirs* into a consistent house style – reflecting the gentle, unhurried beauty of the region.

The taste

Cognac has long been seen as the pinnacle of spirits. When bourbon or rum producers want to demonstrate how elegant and sophisticated their top brands are they invariably say that they are "comparable to a fine Cognac". You'll never find a Cognac producer saying that its wares are like a fine rum! However, if you ask the major Cognac houses why their region produces such magnificent spirits, invariably they'll start by defining the legal requirements of the *appellation*. It's a strange response, as AOC rules – which govern the boundaries of the *crus*, varieties, distillation and ageing – are there to guarantee typicity, and not to define quality.

Even the grading designations are there to set minimum requirements; it's entirely up to the individual house how it wants to make its brands. In theory a Cognac can be sold when it is 30 months old, but the youngest element of 3-Star/VS is usually between three and five years old (although there are indications that this has dropped in recent times). VSOP can be four-and-a-half years old, although most brands are between seven and 10 years. Brands carrying terms like XO, Napoleon, etc., can be as young as six years old, but are usually between 15 and 20. Then, at the top of the tree, that tiny group of astronomically priced Extra, Grand Reserve, etc., is likely to have as its youngest component a Cognac which is 40 years old or more. As you can see, it's vague, it's open to interpretation, and once you get past VSOP there are so many names that the only indication that you are getting something really old is from the expensive price tag.

In Cognac, as in any spirits-producing area/category, there are stunning, good and less-than-good examples. The joy is that there are so many extraordinary brandies produced in a huge range of styles. the question is, how do you choose?

The House STYLE

The simple answer is to find a house style you like – whether it's the richness of Courvoisier or the delicacy of Hine or Delamain – and then start to find other smaller brands that align themselves with these. In time, you'll find that there's a Cognac for every occasion.

Not all the houses own their own distilleries. Some, like Martell, contract distillation out to distillers in each of the *crus*, while others, like Delamain, select mature *eaux-de-vie* before buying. For a professional distiller it's a good income.

A producer such as Duboigalant, although making a magnificent range under its own name, actually distils the bulk of its annual production to the specifications of one or more of the major houses.

Each firm has its own preference as to the *cru* and also the method of distillation. It will also specify how the wine is to be distilled – an *eau-de-vie* destined for a short ageing will be made in a different fashion from one that's going to sit in the barrel for 40 years. The amount of lees used and the percentage of *secondes* will not only vary between houses, but between the distillates in each of the houses. This will also depend on sales projections. A major house such as Martell will have estimated how much VS it can sell in three years' time, so it can deduce how much quick-maturing *eau-de-vie* it needs from each vintage.

Of the major houses, Courvoisier is the heaviest (due to its running a high percentage of *secondes* through the stills), then Martell, followed by Hennessy, Remy-Martin, Hine and the smaller Delamain. As well as this style being dictated by small differences in distillation, each of the houses will have its own preferences in *crus*.

BERNARD HINE, A MASTER AT WORK

Martell, for example, while sourcing from the four main *crus*, uses a significantly higher percentage of *eaux-de-vie* from Borderies in the blend. The firm reserves 60 per cent of the cru's production each year, and the Borderies' distinctive fat quality is immediately apparent in all of its brands, giving a waxy roundness to a brand like Cordon Bleu.

Courvoisier will vary the percentage of *crus* depending on the brand. *Eaux-de-vie* from Fins Bois tend to be used for VS; the VSOP and the powerful, deep Napoleon are both Fine Champagne, while the top brands (the richly complex XO & Initiale) are Fine Champagne & Borderies. Remy-Martin and Hine, on the other hand, specialize in Fine Champagne *eaux-*

de-vie, giving their Cognacs a distinct delicacy. In Remy's case this is accentuated by the use of small stills and high lees content, which provides a signature citric element in all its brands, from the benchmark VSOP to the fruity, floral drive of the XO. Hine's range demonstrates the superb balance given by Fine Champagne Cognac, as refined a selection as you could wish for – with VSOP and Antique personifying the house's discreet charm.

Delamain chooses to use *eaux-de-vie* only from Grande Champagne – and has to age them for considerably longer before it can release them. Its youngest brand, Pale & Dry, is an average of 25 years old and personifies Delamain's signature of graceful poise. There are few better at crystallizing Cognac's elegance.

And that's just the start. There are close to 150 Cognac houses, each of which offers an extensive range. They range from the big-hitting, fruity Bisquit, the robust, cigar-smoke-accented Cognacs from the Polignac co-op, to the drier elegance of Camus and the spicy drive of Otard. This firm also now owns Exshaw, one of the great Grande Champagne producers, noted for its complex,

expansive style. Exshaw, along with Hine, is a specialist in Early Landed Cognac – light, dry, gentle vintage Cognacs, which have been shipped and matured in Britain.

Among the smaller producers is A. de Fussigny, whose range (which includes single-barrel bottlings) all share a sweet mouth-feel, tinged with the wild aromas of the countryside.

While Fussigny sources Cognacs from the two Champagnes and Fins Bois, Leopold Gourmel specializes in Cognacs from the best sites in Fins Bois. Owner Pierre Voisin's abiding obsession is with examining how Cognacs evolve and develop flavours during maturation – to the extent that he has abandoned the standard VS, VSOP, XO designations and named his brands after the dominant aromas that emerge with extended ageing. The youngest is Age du Fruit, then Age des Fleurs and Age d'Epices. There may be an element of auto-suggestion, but these are the aromas of these balanced Cognacs.

What Gourmel does for Fins Bois, Ragnaud-Sabourin and Duboigalant do for Grande Champagne. The former produces a superbly poised range – one of which is le Paradis, whose blend includes some pre-*phylloxera* Cognac. Duboigalant, meanwhile, is profound and elegant.

The tranquil, winding Charente is mirrored in the slow swirl of an amber-coloured Cognac in the glass. The region's calm and measured approach to life is reflected in the finest of its brandies. The greatest of them retain the purity of the distillate, the *terroir* and the wood. No single element is dominant; they are the personification of harmony.

Tasting Notes

COGNAC

Remy 1738 Fruit interlaced with mint, lemon balm and slightly hard wood. Great energy and drive.

Remy XO Tangerine peel and bergamot on the nose. Gentle, but with substance on the palate.

Remy VSOP Lightly herbal with some citric notes. Clean and appetising with fine weight. Well poised with a touch of quince. Benchmark.

MISCELLANEOUS

Ch. de Beaulon VSOP Ethereal nose Fruit-dominant refined and clean.

Delamain Pale & Dry Oranges and cashews with a hint of dates on the nose. High-toned and discreet.

Duboigalant VSOP Complex nose, mixing nuts, honey, raisins, cinnamon and ginger. Full and ripe.

Gourmel Age des Fleurs Clean and complex array of vanilla, fruit and the

merest hint of nut on nose. Complex and elegant with a very gentle core that has great concentration and grip.

Peyrat VSOP Light and very fine on the nose. Soft and floral.

Ragnaud-Sabourin VSOP Great depth. Long and stylish.

Armagnac

France's lesser-known brandy hails from Gascony – an unspoilt region, off the tourist track. Winding through the narrow lanes of its fourteenth-century villages is like stepping back in time – it's hardly surprising then that Armagnac claims to be France's oldest brandy.

The history

Armagnac takes its name from Hermann, an ancient feudal lord whose name was Latinized to Arminius when the Romans arrived bearing vines. Just like Cognac, it's a product of self-sufficiency – the grapes for distillation are grown locally, and the wood for the barrels originally came from

the local forests. Its best brandies retain this deep sense of identity.

The first recorded instance of spirits production was in 1411, and it's logical to assume that the secret of distillation was transported over the Pyrenees from Moorish Spain – though woe betide you suggest to a Gascon that distillation is anything but a French invention!

After a period producing medicinal potions, Armagnac's fame began to spread, so that by the seventeenth century the Dutch were buying the pot-still brandy. So, if Armagnac had this head start on Cognac, why isn't it more famous? One reason is its geographical situation. Cognac came into being because it had direct access to the sea. Take one look at a map, and you can see that Armagnac isn't anywhere near a port. Originally the brandies would have had to be transported by land to Mont-de-Marsan and then by river either to Bayonne or Bordeaux. The latter had a

tendency to silt up, so supplies were irregular for the export markets, while Cognac could always guarantee getting supplies out of La Rochelle. Because of this geographical disadvantage, Armagnac had to wait until the arrival of the railways and the building of canals before it could hit the affluent markets of the north. By the middle of the last century, production was booming, the vineyard area was growing and the bulk of the major houses was founded.

A significant development occurred at this time, which was to have immense repercussions on Armagnac's style – the arrival of the continuous still, credited to a M. Verdier, a chemist from Montpellier,. The new invention was an immediate hit with the producers, so much so that by 1936 it was the only type of still allowed to be used – although now pot stills are once again permitted. By the 1930s, though, Armagnac was once again a forgotton

area. Although it enjoyed a brief period of success when the Cognac vineyards were obliterated by *phylloxera*, the bug eventually decimated Armagnac as well. What with two world wars and a depression, it wasn't until the end of the Second World War that Armagnac started exporting in seriousness once more.

Even so, it remains a tiny producer when compared with Cognac but, while it can't compete in volume terms, it can offer a quality alternative. Armagnac isn't a poor man's Cognac; neither is it, as some seem to think, a more rustic version. It's a product of distinctive *terroir*, produced in a fundamentally different fashion, and is capable of reaching great heights.

At the moment, though, the region is burdened with a massive stock surplus. Convinced that the Far East was going to be a huge market, firms increased production – but then demand slumped. The BNIA, the region's controlling body, is currently trying to find ways of coping with the problem, but it seems obvious that the only way Armagnac will get itself out of its current crisis is to promote itself as a quality region.

ARMAGNAC IS ROOTED TO THE GASCON SOIL

ARMAGNAC VINES LADEN WITH THE GRAPES THAT PRODUCE THE PRIZED GASCON BRANDY

How it's MADE

Once again you are faced with that indefinable term *terroir* – the physical (and philosophical) interaction between soil, exposure, climate, vine and man. In clinical terms, Armagnac is divided into three regions: Bas-Armagnac, Tenareze and Haut-Armagnac, with the best-quality *eaux-de-vie* coming from the first two.

Bas-Armagnac is covered in forest and rolling hills, dotted with vineyards on the higher slopes. The sand and clay soil, stuck with large pebbles, produces a supple, relatively quickly maturing style of *eau-de-vie*. Tenareze, which arcs around Bas-Armagnac's eastern border, is higher and with a higher amount of chalk in its soil. Its *eau-de-vie* is significantly different – a more rounded, aromatic, fruit-driven style capable of long-ageing.

THE SMALL ARMAGNAC STILLS HAVE A SIGNIFICANT EFFECT ON THE SPIRIT'S FLAVOUR

Producers are allowed to make Armagnac from 12 varieties, but the majority make their *eaux-de-vie* from Folle Blanche, Ugni Blanc, Colombard and a hybrid variety Baco 22A, which has the advantage of being resistant to the mould that can hit the region in the autumn months. However, hybrids have now been banned by the EU, and while the Armagnac producers are fighting their corner, most are looking into alternatives – Ch. de Laubade has had success with the little-used Plant de Graisse.

Harvest normally takes place in October, and because Armagnac enjoys a slightly more moderate climate than Cognac, the grapes are higher in potential alcohol when they are picked, at around nine percent ABV. There is, however, still good acidity. Ideally distillation should take place as soon as the wines have finished fermenting, in order to preserve the light estery aromas, but until recently distillation could take place up until April 30. In an attempt to curb excess production, this date has now been brought back to January 31, which conceivably could have a positive effect on quality. The danger with letting wine sit around until the distiller – who is not always the grower or producer – is ready means that you run the risk of the wine oxidizing. Stale wine produces stale brandy.

However, it's the stills that produce the most significant difference between Armagnac and Cognac. The vast majority of distillers continue to use the "traditional" *Alambic Armagnaçais* or column still. This consists of two chambers, one containing a preheating chamber and the serpentine condenser, and the other a boiler (or boilers) and perforated plates. The wine is gently heated and flows into the distilling column, where it passes down through gaps between the plates, getting the alcohol stripped away by the rising heat. The vapour then passes back into the serpentine where it is cooled, condensed and collected.

On paper, this is no different from any other column still, but there is a significant difference between an Armagnac column still and most others. They are tiny. Because of this, the distillate is significantly lower than you would normally expect from a column still – it can be as low as 52 per cent ABV, but on average distillers collect the spirit at between 55 and 63 per cent ABV. Here is where many of Armagnac's rich, earthy characteristics come from. The problem is being able to control the quality of the distillate at this low strength. "It's true that single distillation can produce poor quality if it is distilled either too fast or at too low a strength," says Patrick Heron, *maître de chais* at Janneau. "But if you are looking for an Armagnac that you can sell in 15 years' time you'll distil to 55–60 per cent. If you want one to age for longer, you'll drop to 55 per cent, but no lower." It takes a master craftsman to be able to produce flavoursome, elegant spirit at this strength without collecting any pungent fusel oils.

Pot stills (or *double chauffe*) remain mildly controversial. They are permitted, but in practice only five or six producers use them. Janneau is the only house to release a pot-still Armagnac, although other firms, such as Laressingle, use pot-still *eau-de-vie* as a blending component. The type of still used is the same as that for Cognac, but because of the low-strength spirit that's obtained from the column stills, for once a pot still actually gives a lighter, higher-strength distillate which is better suited to a short period of ageing. But pot stills are mostly dismissed by other producers. Yves Grassa at Tariquet, for example, makes some of the finest Armagnacs in the region from an ancient wood-fired column still. "*Double chauffe* can eliminate the fruit esters, which can be the most interesting part of the distillate," he says. "And because you can separate the tastes at the beginning and end, you can get a more neutral result. I'd argue that if you use good wine you can get the finesse of pot still plus the richness of alembic from the continuous still – but then you have to age it for longer!"

The debate as to whether column is better than pot, rather misses the point. The bottom line should be whether it is of good quality and whether it has typicity. Good pot-still Armagnac, most notably from Janneau, just gives a different spin on that typicity.

Virtually every producer will distil wines from the different regions and varieties separately, and won't blend the *eaux-de-vie* until the Armagnac is ready to be bottled. Traditionally, Armagnac

was aged in the local Monlezun oak, which allegedly gave its own particular richness to the spirit but, due to expansion, most producers now use either Limousin or Troncais wood.

The new spirit will first be put in new wood, then after an initial period of ageing (which varies between producers) each batch will be decanted, mixed and then placed in older barrels.

As the Armagnac ages, so the spirit will regularly be decanted into progressively older (and often larger) barrels in order to cut down the impact of the oak, but still to allow slow and steady oxidation. The very top casks will be good for up to 40 years, but after that the Armagnac is removed and put into large glass jars and stored in the holy of holies – known as "Paradis".

The quality of the wood is central to the production of high-quality Armagnac. Yves Grassa, for example, insists on only using barrels made with air-dried staves, often sourced from different regions, and made by different coopers, with barrels being given different toasts.

Sadly, though, you get the feeling that the industrial-sized producers are more concerned with keeping costs

down, so the prevailing ethos is: get it made, get it in cask for a short time and get it sold. That means that not only is wood often only of secondary importance, but the spirit is given insufficient

CAREFUL WOOD AGEING IS ESSENTIAL IN PRODUCING TOP-QUALITY ARMAGNAC

Tasting Notes

VSOP

Baron de Sigognac VSOP Spent matches on nose. Fine, pruney weight. Plump, elegant and profound.

Ch Laubade VSOP Lightly wooded. Powerful fruits on the palate, good feel and fine weight. Mature, plummy depth.

Janneau VSOP Clean, light earthy tones with a touch of sandalwood. Easy.

Laressingle VSOP Well-balanced. Soft and round on the palate. Fairly simple.

M. de Caussade Big, fat and soft. Lightly honeyed with decent length.

AGE STATEMENT/VARIETAL

Janneau 8yo Soft and rich on the nose with some spicy wood. Walnut veneer and earth on the palate.

Janneau 15 yo A haunting aroma filled with dried roses, apples, cinnamon, butterscotch and nuts. Weighty.

Tariquet Folle Blanche 8yo Gold. picking up light mushroom notes and herbal toabacco leaf. Very soft and gentle with a precise lift.

Tariquet folle Blanche 12yo Graceful, deep, almost toffee-like nose. On the

palate, it's attractive with chewy, nutty fruits and really fresh finish.

M. de Caussade 30yo Some rancio character on a fairly elegant, well-rounded nose. Clean.

XO/RESERVE/REGION

Ch. Laubade Hors d'Age Nicely rounded with a touch of crème brulée. Soft in mouth with a fair bite.

Janneau XO Woodsmoke and earth with a hint of plum and light perfume. Good weight on the palate. Chewy, long, full and fat.

Janneau Reserve Complex aromas. Rich with a touch of rancio and a clear bell of fruit.

Laressingle 20ans Bas-Armagnac Soft, clean and long. A little woody, but good fruit and earth.

Laressingle Tenareze Rich, heavy and fruit-driven. Complex silky power.

Tariquet Hors d'Age Hints of sultana, vanilla and butterscotch. Supple in mouth. Clean, fresh finish.

VINTAGE ARMAGNAC, ALWAYS AN UNFORGET-TABLE EXPERIENCE

time to mellow and age. The fact that Armagnac is made from a low-strength distillate means it takes time to evolve in barrel. It is a spirit that is meant to be aged for a long time. Boise is permitted, and is widely used to give the impression of oak ageing, but it doesn't even do that. The consensus among top producers is that Armagnac only begins to give an indication of its true potential after a minimum of seven years.

The quality designations are assessed in the same way as Cognac, with VS being allowed to be bottled after 18 months, although in practice most producers hold it for around three years. The youngest brandy in a VSOP is on average seven years old, or 10 years for an Hors d'Age/XO. In private, most quality-oriented firms will tell you that they would love to see VSOP as the starting point, but that's extremely unlikely.

Armagnac, however, has another trick up its sleeve. Since the *eaux-de vie* are kept separate until they are ready to

be blended, it's possible to release Vintage Armagnacs. Most firms will have a regular range of vintages, but some small producers like Marcel Trepout have decided to specialize in this field. Walk into Trepout's "Paradis", and you are faced with a sea of raffia-covered jars with neck labels that date back to 1865. Paradis indeed for the Armagnac lover, although it has to be said that most producers, while seeing Vintage as a handy selling point (the market in Vintage has grown significantly in recent years) personally prefer their blends.

That said, tasting a great vintage Armagnac is an unforgettable experience. The extraordinarily complex Ch. Laubade 1967, with its rancio nose filled with violets, prunes and cinnamon and creamy, elegant palate; or the 1972 Ch. du Tariquet, with its nose of pine honey/beeswax and rich, plummy, walnut palate – are both proof of the region's ability to produce magnificent Vintage spirits.

It would be wrong to think that Armagnac is sitting back and waiting for people to (re)discover it. Go-ahead firms are trying to find new ways of generating interest in the region.

Janneau has, controversially, launched a three-strong, 100 per cent pot-still range – a soft and gentle five-year-old; an oily, earthy, rich eight-year-old and a hauntingly complex 15-year-old (from Tenareze) which mixes dried roses, apples and cinnamon with a nutty, pruney palate.

Grassa, meanwhile, has released a range of single-varietal Folle Blanche – a charming, toasty/smoky four-year-old; a gentle grapey/plummy eight-year-old that also has hints of tobacco leaf and mushroom, and a 12-year-old that has typical Armagnac richness mixed with beech nuts and an amazing fresh finish. Not to be outdone, Laressingle has gone down the regional route with its silkily powerful 20-year-old Tenareze.

The bottom line is that these (and other) producers are all driven by a passion for their region. They all want to produce brandies that speak of their place, and when you get your nose into a glass of old Armagnac and breathe in the aromas of violets, prunes, figs, plums, truffle and the beech wood mulch – you are instantly transported back to the woods of Gascony – The *terroir* is retained in the glass.

Tasting Notes

VINTAGE

Ch. Laubade 1975 Some rancio and a gorgeous mix of butter and crème anglaise among the prunes.

Ch. Laubade 1967 Exotically perfumed – violets, prunes, wild herbs and spice. Powerful and elegant, it expands in the mouth exposing a creamy heart. Extraordinary and complex.

Dom. de Boigneres 1984 Floor polish, saddle soap and earth. Massive concentration of multi-layered, dark fruit on the palate. Awesome.

Janneau 1976 Refined, with earth, nut and a dark undertow of beech-wood mulch. On the palate the fruit is soft and plummily rounded with a grip of chilli on the finish.

Janneau 1966 Pulpy fruit, with a whiff of musk. Smoky and subtle. High-toned with gorgeous length.

Janneau 1958 Great colour. The wood shows slightly on the cigar-box, rancio nose. Full and powerful with the high-toned elegance that's typical of the house style.

Laressingle 1942 Extraordinary dark

colour. A truffley, fungal nose with beechwood mulch. Subtle and soft, then beeswax. Amazing length.

Tariquet 1982 Buttery on the nose, with some vanilla and light plum. In the mouth the plum/prune fruit is almost honeyed before a hazelnut crunch finish.

Tariquet 1985 Earthy and rich. Heavy in the mouth with some nuts and flowers and really weighty fruit. Great structure.

Tariquet 1972 Touch of rancio – burnt matches, then treacle and

beeswax. Well-balanced wood. Soft and elegant with walnut veneer and plums. Superb.

Tariquet 1975 Some rancio, but deeper fruit on the nose. Rich, rounded, soft and plump. Smoky, spicy with great length of plummy fruits. A solid citizen.

Brandy de Jerez

When you think of the ancient centres of distilling spirits in Europe, you tend to consider Ireland, Italy and France; Spain doesn't get a second thought. But if you are looking for the origins of brandy-making, then you have to go to Moorish Andalucia and the city of Jerez.

It was the Phoenicians who brought vines to Southern Spain, but it was the Moors who brought their *al-ambiqs* (stills) and started distilling – initially for cosmetics, perfumes and medicines. Given that the Moors were benign rulers, it is inevitable that this art was practised by the non-Muslim occupants of Spain at that time. Certainly, there is evidence that stills have been used in Jerez since 900AD – long before anyone in Cognac had even heard of a still.

This early brandy was originally low-quality wine that was used solely for fortifying the local wine (now known as sherry), a process which stabilized it when it was transported. It wasn't until the arrival in the seventeenth century of those indefatigable traders and brandy drinkers, the Dutch, that exports of brandy from Jerez started. In fact, so much brandy was shipped in sherry casks to the Netherlands that the best *eaux de vie* used in Brandy de Jerez is still known as *holandas* while, in a direct link with its Moorish origins, the pot stills used are called *alquitaras*.

Jerez remained a supplier of bulk spirit until the nineteenth century, when a number of sherry firms decided to copy what was happening in Cognac and began ageing the brandy *in situ*. Domecq likes to tell the story of butts of brandy being sent back to Jerez after the *bodega* and its Dutch customer had fallen out. The casks mouldered in the back of a warehouse until they were

chanced upon. They were tasted and the first Brandy de Jerez brand, Fundador (the founder), was born.

These days, though, times are tough. Never rivalling Cognac in the export markets, Brandy de Jerez has relied on Spain's insatiable thirst for large glasses of brandy to be drunk after their meal. Brandy is inextricably bound up in Spanish culture. Keen filmgoers will recall how the action in the cult flick *Jamon Jamon* took place under the *cojones* of one of the black bulls advertising Osborne brandy that dot the hills across Spain. It's an image that, quite simply, sums up Spain.

But, in a repetition of what has happened to all the "old" spirits, in recent years young drinkers have decided that the time was right to look for something else. The ending of the Franco era

brought a wave of liberalization to Spain, and a newly affluent, young population was suddenly able to buy imported brands. Brandy was the main victim as the young turned to blended Scotch as their drink of choice. Spend some time at a bar in Spain (even in Jerez itself) and you'll find that almost everyone will be drinking Scotch and cola.

The domestic brandy market has fallen by 50 per cent in the past 20 years as young drinkers turn their backs on a drink they see as old, boring and representative of the Old Spain. To its credit, Brandy de Jerez's controlling body has started a promotional campaign to promote the style, while some top brands have been repackaged and promoted not just in Spain, but internationally. Only time will tell if it's too late.

IF IN DOUBT, CONSULT THE CARDENAL – ONE OF SPAIN'S TOP BRANDS

How it's MADE

The wine for today's Brandy de Jerez doesn't actually come from the chalky, dusty hills of Jerez, but the flat, hot plains of La Mancha. The reason is simple. Jerez is a demarcarted region – bodegas (producers) can't just keep planting vines and calling their wine sherry, so, when international sales grew for both sherry and brandy, it was impossible for the region to cope with the demand for both styles. The Jerez vineyards (and the Palomino variety) had to be kept for sherry production, but grapes for distilling could be found elsewhere. Now brandy producers either own, or have shares in, distilleries in the town of Tomellosa.

Although Brandy de Jerez is a distilled wine, it bears very little resemblance to any of Europe's other top brandies. For a start, the hot climate of La Mancha produces grapes – mainly from Airen, although Bobadilla and Gonzalez Byass (G-B) also use Palomino – which are considerably higher in alcohol and lower in acidity than those used in Cognac and Armagnac.

This base wine can be distilled in two ways – either using a pot still

(*alquitaras*) or column (continuous) still. This gives three types of distillate – *holandas*, which must be distilled in an *alquitaras* still to between 60 and 70 per cent ABV; and two types of *aguardiente* from the column – the first of which can be no more than 85 per cent ABV, the other between 86 and 94.5 per cent ABV.

Needless to say, the stronger the spirit, the lower the number of flavour compounds. To ensure that the final brandy is full of flavour, by law more than 50 per cent of the final blend must comprise spirits that are below 86 per cent ABV. The result of these regulations is that bodegas can then play with different percentages of the three distillates for their brands – some might be pure *holandas*, some a blend of the three, some a blend of the two *aguardientes*. A rule of thumb is that Solera brands (like Domecq's Fundador or G-B's Soberano) will be column-still *aguardiente*, while the top Gran Reserva brands (Domecq's Carlos I and G-B's Lepanto) are 100 per cent *holandas*.

The first blending takes place immediately after distillation, when the spirits are taken to Jerez to start their unique ageing process. The new spirit is blended according to the criteria for each brand. The young Solera brandies can be aged for as little as six months, but on average spend a year in *solera*; Solera Reserva can be bottled after more than one year, although most producers keep them in the *solera* for two-and-a-half years; the top designation of Solera Gran Reserva can be released after a minimum of three years, but the average is eight years, and the best brands are aged for consider-

ably longer. Conde de Osborne Cristal, for example, is an average of 10 years old, while the same firm's Dali is on average at least 20 years old.

But what is this *solera* system? It's another great Jerez invention that can best be described as fractional blending. Rather than ageing brandy in one barrel – or decanting it totally from young to old barrels – in Jerez the casks are never completely emptied, and no more than one third of the brandy can be removed from the cask at any one time. Once again, it gets a bit technical. Each *solera* comprises a series of collections of butts, each horizontal tier (or scale) of which holds brandies of the same approximate age. The *solera* scale itself is traditionally on the floor and contains the oldest brandy. This is where the brandy comes from when it is ready to be bottled. After brandy is taken from each barrel in the *solera* scale, it is refreshed with the same amount of brandy from all the barrels in the next oldest scale – the first *criadera* – and so on back down the system to the newest brandy being poured into the top scale.

The principle is fiendishly simple. The young brandy, rather than dominating the flavours in the cask, gets absorbed into the character of the old. Also, because the casks are never emptied, there will always be some of the original brandy in the cask – this becomes increasingly important as you move up the quality scale. The regular decanting also increases oxidation and changes the nature of the ageing process – but it doesn't, as many people think, speed the process up. Rather, the regular addition of newer spirit affects the interaction between wood and spirit.

THE SOLERA SYSTEM

INVOLVES A CONSTANT

MOVEMENT OF BRANDY

Equally, it's also thought that the best brandies come from the *soleras* with the highest number of scales. Not true. It's the number of times the brandy is moved that affects quality. Osborne's Solera Reserva brand Magno is moved fairly speedily through its *solera*, while the top brand, Gran Reserva Cristal, is moved very little. Inevitably, each bodega approaches brandy production differently. The initial distillate will be different, as will the blend between *holandas* and *aguardiente*. Each will manage the *solera* in its own way, and the kind of wood used will also differ.

The majority of bodegas use butts that have held oloroso sherry, but Gonzalez Byass prefers fino for its top brand Lepanto, while Sanchez-Romate goes to the other extreme and uses the sweetest sherry style of all, Pedro Ximenez (PX), for its Cardenal Mendoza. Osborne's Cristal *solera* comprises 25-year-old butts that have had PX maturing in them for at least five years.

Tasting through different *soleras*, you can see not only how the brandy

evolves, but how the wood has an impact on the maturing spirit. In Domecq's Carlos I *Solera*, the rich, walnut/sultana oloroso shows when the spirit is on average five years old. By the third *criadera*, the wood begins to appear, while on the first *criadera* and *solera* level, the three components – wood, sherry and spirit – have fused to give plummy, figgy aromas.

At Gonzalez Byass, the youngest scale of the Lepanto *solera* has vivacious fruit and aromas of grilled hazelnut. As it passes down the *solera* it begins to shed the crisp nuttiness and pick up a mellow fruitiness combined with the elegance you can only get from extended ageing in good-quality casks.

At Sanchez-Romate they put a slightly different spin on things. The young spirit is first aged statically for two years in PX casks before entering the *solera*. Now PX isn't exactly a subtle form of sherry, and it makes an immediate impact on the spirit, so that by the time it hits the first scale of the *solera* it's already filled with rich,

raisiny flavours. Then it seems to quieten down, slowly extracting the unctuous sherry flavours out of the wood. By the third *criadera* it's sexy, silky, with a mix of walnut whip and raisin. By *solera*, the wood has done its work, giving a clean bite to the brandy, while not masking its huge flavour.

These Gran Reservas then get a final addition of a brandy from an even older "mother" *solera*. Not only will this *solera* have gained in richness and intensity over the years, it too will work its magic on the younger brandies. For Cristal, this is a tiny *solera* of 28 butts from which a minuscule drop is taken and blended in. At Sanchez-Romate the cellarmaster took me to a venerable cask, used for the firm's top brand Non Plus Ultra, part of a *solera* that was laid down 150 years ago. The brandy was as dark as a Goya etching, and smelled of liquorice and treacle, but although dominated by PX, it had an astoundingly long, fresh, tangy finish. One drop is all that's needed. The flavour stayed in the mouth for hours.

TAKING A HANDS-ON APPROACH

Each house has its own approach, and it's little surprise that Brandy de Jerez is a totally different beast from Cognac or Armagnac. But are the brandies any good? Well, it's much the same as any category. The firms who take great care with their distillation and use the top-quality spirits get the best results. To be honest, if you are working with young spirit and you only give it six months in wood, then you'll end up with a young spirit no matter what – even in a solera system.

Sadly, there's an awful lot of Brandy de Jerez at the bottom end of the market that is nothing more than raw alcohol, a touch of wood and a splash of sweeten-

ing agent. Even at the top end there are firms who appear to take short-cuts in the ageing process and believe that "old" simply means "sweet", and don't concern themselves with producing aged brandies with the grip and structure that defines a high-quality style.

In order to prosper, Brandy de Jerez must turn its domestic problems around, and become a force on the international market. At home young brandies are now being promoted as the perfect mixer for cola, which is fine as they do mix well. They are also an essential part of the traditional Spanish breakfast – the *caragillo* (an espresso coffee with a shot of brandy). The top end contains some classy brandies that deserve more attention; brandies which are, quite simply, easier to drink than the Cognacs and Armagnacs of similar age – and of similar complexity.

The important thing during the process is to maintain tradition. Brandy de Jerez is a unique style, almost more akin to wine than spirits. It's not Cognac, but the best examples are easy-drinking, surprisingly complex spirits, which deserve to be better known.

The rest of Spain

It is not only Jerez that produces brandy. Catalonia is home to two producers, Mascaro and Torres – both with a high reputation. Catalonia shares several techniques with France in brandy terms, but neither firm slavishly copies what is done across the Pyrenees.

Torres has a six-strong range of brandies, two of which are made in continuous stills, the other four being made in Charentais stills. Torres 10 is the more obviously "Spanish", being a column distillate aged in *solera* in heavily toasted US oak, and can be seen as a halfway house between a Brandy de Jerez and an Armagnac. Miguel Torres Imperial, however, is double-distilled in pot stills, then aged statically in Limousin oak.

Mascaro, which distils entirely from its own wine, is proud to align itself with Cognac. Like the Torres brands, it is a Parellada distillate, the grapes picked at low alcohol, double distilled in a Charentais still, followed by static ageing in a mix of Limousin and Alliers oak.

Tasting Notes

BRANDY DE JEREZ

SOLERA RESERVA

Lustau Burnt, more than a touch of PX, some complexity and crispness from young spirit.

Magno Smooth, but not complex. Rich with a hint of plummy fruit. Soft in the mouth. Simple but attractive.

Fundador Young, nutty. Clean and simple.

SOLERA GRAN RESERVA
(1=DRY 5=SWEET)

Lepanto Clean, nutty and dry, but gently

subtle. Fresh finish.(1)

Cardenal Mendoza PX and coffee beans on the nose. Rich and deep with chewy complexity and a fresh dry finish.(5)

Osborne Dali Quite complex on the nose. Clean wood on show. Smooth, sweet as a nut. Very long and rich. (3)

Carlos I Imperial Soft, rich plummy/figgy fruit. Very soft to start, followed by lifted, delicate top notes. Long and clean. (3)

Carlos I Rounded, with walnut/Dundee cake notes on the nose. Chewy and clean with good range of flavours and soft, vanilla fruit. (3)

Senor Lustau Subtle, soft and elegant on nose with hint of burnt Madeira-like fruit. Very soft on the palate, but with decent grip. (4)

Conde de Osborne Medium intensity on the nose. A full, sweet, raisined impact with clean grip. (3/4)

Gran Duque d'Alba Full and sweet, little more than raisins steeped in alcohol. (5)

Grappa

For years grappa was one of those spirits that non-Italians tried to avoid. In fact, to be honest the majority of Italians tried to avoid it as well. It wasn't an issue of image or a lack of trendiness; it was, quite simply, that it didn't taste any good.

We have all tried to sip it at the end of a meal, but few of us have enjoyed the experience. Grappa, like its French equivalent, marc, had the astonishing effect of inducing a hideous hangover before you even got drunk. But that was then, this is now. Grappa, like some spirituous ugly duckling, has cast off its dull, unattractive past and emerged as a pure, elegant drink that deserves to take its place among some of the world's best spirits. The story of this fairy-tale transformation is a distillation of what has happened in Italian winemaking over the past decade.

How it's made

Italy has an ancient history of spirits production that dates back to monks in Salerno in the ninth century. Even today, it's a country where you'll find the widest (and most bizarre) range of spirits, from brandies to bitters, liqueurs to rustic concoctions that hark back to the earliest spirits of all. Then there's grappa. As ever, we can't be sure when the first grappa was produced, but it appears always to have been a speciality of the regions in the north of the country, from Piemonte in the west to Friuli and Trentino in the east. Grappa is certainly produced elsewhere, but this is its spiritual heartland.

Many spirits have started life as products of excess or surplus raw materials – barley, rye, potatoes, poor-quality wine. Grappa is similar, up to a point. In fact, it's closer to the rums of the British West Indies, as it too is made from the waste material produced by another process. In rum it's molasses that are left after sugar is made; in grappa's case, it's the pressings that are left at the end of winemaking.

Strictly speaking, therefore, grappa isn't a brandy as it isn't made from distilled wine. It's the runt of the litter, the afterthought. You can imagine how it first came into being. A winemaker was looking at the pile of skins (*vinaccia*) left over after his wine had been pressed. He could either throw them out, put them on the fields as fertilizer – or distil them. This has been grappa's greatest problem. Producers would only think of making their grappa after the important business of winemaking was finished, or when the mobile still came into their village. But *vinaccia*, like wine itself, oxidizes if left for too long. The result was that distillers were ending up working with poor-quality

raw material and, contrary to popular belief, distilling can't improve inferior base material. That didn't stop industrial-sized producers springing up and handling vast quantities of *vinaccia* which was sent to them from all over the country. Rural winemakers and farmers would quite happily sit back and knock down a few glasses of their own grappa, people would pour one into an espresso and drink this *coretto* as a heart-starter in the morning. But it wasn't pleasant stuff.

Quite what happened to turn grappa production around is a chicken-and-egg question. From the mid-1970s, Italian wine underwent a renaissance in quality. Great wines had been made for centuries before, but this was the dawning of a new era. Stainless steel and temperature control started being used in wineries, vineyards were better managed – the intention was to produce the highest possible quality. Importantly, grapes going into red wine production didn't have the life pressed out of them.

At the same time a Friulian distiller, Nonino, decided to make a grappa that reflected this new Italian stylishness. His grappas, packaged in clear, hand-blown bottles, were the catalyst for a revolution in grappa production. Nonino's example was soon followed by Jacopo Poli who, by the late 1970s, was sneaking into his father's

BETTER WINEMAKING RESULTED IN BETTER GRAPPA

THE GRAPPA REVOLUTION HAS ALSO EMBRACED PACKAGING

SMALL-SCALE, HIGH-
QUALITY PRODUCTION
TECHNIQUES

THE ITALIAN STYLE
PERSONIFIED

distillery late at night to experiment with these new-style grappas. The trend spread. In Trentino, Bertagnolli took up the cause, as did Maschio in Veneto.

All of a sudden the options were endless. The next step to take was logical enough. Since winemakers were beginning to separate each grape variety, there was a ready supply of different *vinaccia*. Nonino once again started single varietal off, with a grappa made from the rare Picolit variety. Winemakers then began producing single vineyard wines – the very same thing happened with grappa. The industry had changed from industrial production to something infinitely more sophisticated.

The starting point of this new grappa lies in ensuring that the *vinaccia* is fresh and moist, which means getting it from the winery to the distillery quickly. If the *vinaccia* isn't distilled within 24 hours of being pressed, then the aromatics disappear and the process of oxidation speeds up. It also means

ensuring that there are no stalks or stems in the *vinaccia*, as they produce methanol. Since Poli's stills, for example, only hold 15kg, he will only buy enough *vinaccia* to supply one day's distillation. "It means we are only buying 10,000kg every day," he says, "And we're going against our own interests by doing this as we can't satisfy demand, but we are making the best quality we can."

Getting this quality inevitably means paying more for the *vinaccia*, but it's a price they are happy to accept. "The quality is defined by the grapes," says Antonio Moser at Bertagnolli. "It depends on how hard they have been pressed and how healthy they are – we can't use any grapes that have had mould. It's only when the wines improved that grappa could as well." The *vinaccia* from red varieties, such as Cabernet, Merlot, Nebbiolo and Teroldego, can be distilled immediately, but the *vinaccia* from white grapes usually has to be

fermented first. This is because it's normal practice not to ferment the white wines with their skins when making new-style Italian white wine.

The top producers continue to distil in small pot stills (Nonino has 42 of them) or, in the case of Bertagnolli, a cunning combination of pot and column. This has a *bain marie* in the pot which allows the *vinaccia* to sit in an inner chamber surrounded by another wall that contains the steam. It allows a slow, even heating and avoids the problem of the *vinaccia* sticking to the sides of the still and producing off notes.

Each variety will also be handled slightly differently, as the aromatics appear at different strengths. It may seem far-fetched to a newcomer to grappa, but there are marked differences between all the different single-varietal grappas.

The majority are reduced in strength and then bottled, but there's a growing trend to barrel-age certain varieties. In Trentino, Zeni has recently made a stunningly delicate example, while in Piemonte, Barolo producer Rocche dei Manzoni has a superb, hugely aromatic range of barrique-aged grappas. Nonino is even experimenting with ageing in ex-sherry wood!

The most recent step has been to start distilling whole grapes. The grapes are fermented in vacuum-sealed stainless-steel tanks and then placed in the pot still. Nonino has Ue (and has established a vineyard planted to Picolit, Ribolla Gialla and Fragolino specifically for Ue production); Maschio has Prime Uve, while Bertagnolli makes a Grappino. These *eaux-de-vie* have a purity of fruit and lightness of character in contrast to grappa's firm grip, although to be fair we are talking degrees of delicacy here.

The innovations are endless. If you ask for a grappa these days in any Italian restaurant, a shuddering trolley will be dragged out laden with bottles. There will be grappas from well-known varieties like Chardonnay, Cabernet, Merlot, Riesling, Muller-Thurgau and Nebbiolo, but then there will be a raft of some of Italy's myriad other grape varieties – Prosecco, Teroldego, Torcolato, Picolit, Schiopettino, Pignolo, Ribolla Gialla, some of which have been saved from extinction by grappa producers.

The best grappas personify what a great spirit should be, the capturing of the essence of the raw material. The heart of the grape variety is revealed in the finest examples. They are not big spirits; rather they are fragile, contemplative drinks. But, as Philip Contini, of Edinburgh's shrine to Italian food and drink Valvona & Crolla points out, they remain an acquired taste.

"These days you don't need to drink stinking rotgut, but grappa's a taste you either love or hate. There's no middle ground; it's the spirit world's equivalent of truffles."

Some superb Italian-style grappas are being produced in the United States – most notably by Clear Creek and the Bonny Doon winery. Elsewhere, the production of pomace brandies remains relatively small-scale and often resuloutely rustic.

Most wine-producing regions have a speciality spirit made from the pressings of the year's vintage. However, most of Europe has yet to catch up with Italy when it comes to producing high-quality pomace brandy. There's nothing preventing them, though – they have the technology and the techniques. All that is needed is time and patience.

HOME TO SOME OF ITALY'S GREATEST GRAPPAS

Tasting Notes

WHOLE GRAPE

Jacopo Poli Uva Viva Fragrant with citric aromas. Soft, balanced with perfumed finish.
Bertagnolli Grappino di Uva Fragrant and gentle in mouth with some pepperiness.
Maschio Prosecco/Riseling Uve Clean, peachy, light earth. Juicy and delicate.

VARIETAL

Endrizzi Chardonnay Restrained, quite aromatic. Good palate weight. Elegant.
Maschio Chardonnay Depth of fruit, some apricot. Juicy mid-palate. Clean finish.

Giovanni Poli Nosiola Earthy nose with plums and some nut. Fresh and well balanced on palate with light walnut on finish.
Bertagnolli Nosiola Light, almost like a grain spirit. Strong start gives way to lingering marzipan/violet flavours.
Zeni Muller-Thurgau Autumn leaves, wood bark and aromatic yellow fruits on nose. Sweet start before dry finish.
Jacopo Poli Torcolato Honeycomb and fragrant herbs on the nose. Pure, sweet fruit on palate with tremendous feel.
Casa Girelli Moscato Lemon tending to aftershave, but with good richness.

The Pisco SOUR
Classic Cocktail

PISCO SOUR

2 OZ GRAN PISCO

1 OZ LEMON JUICE

1 TSP CASTER SUGAR

(OPTIONAL EXTRA: DASH BITTERS AND EGG-WHITE)

SHAKE WELL IN SHAKER — PARTICULARLY IF YOU ARE USING EGG-WHITE — AND STRAIN INTO GLASSES.

Sours are not normally the stuff of legend. They are one of the great workhorses of the cocktail bar. Any spirit can be combined with lemon juice and sugar to make a lip-smacking drink that wakes you up on a steamy day. The Pisco Sour is an exception to this rule. It's the national drink of Chile and Peru, and is used as a cooling glass during the hot South American summers. But behind a Pisco Sour's calming exterior beats the heart of a beast.

KEEPING COOL THE SOUTH AMERICAN WAY

It's deceptively easy to drink, thanks to the aromatic, apparently benign influence of the Pisco. So, you have another – and another. All of a sudden this gentle drink turns round and belts you on the back of the neck, distorting your vision, rendering all speech into gibberish. You might feel an overwhelming urge to dance like a crazy fool, you might feel a desire to have another. Be warned, once Pisco madness is unleashed it is difficult to keep under control.

Inevitably there's some debate over how a classic Pisco Sour is assembled. Getting the Pisco right is the first task. Use a top brand like Control or Capel, and go for the top designation of Gran Pisco. This is the strongest, but it is also the driest and most flavoursome – and flavour, after all, is the whole point of the exercise.

Most arguments revolve around whether to use egg-whites or not. I remain open-minded as it depends on the mood. Bitters can be used. If you must, try and use orange or Peychaud, rather than Angostura.

The
SIDECAR
Classic Cocktail

THE SIDECAR

1 1/2 OZ COGNAC

3/4 OZ COINTREAU/TRIPLE SEC

3/4 OZ LEMON JUICE

LEMON TWIST

SHAKE AND STRAIN OVER ICE INTO A CHILLED COCKTAIL GLASS WITH SUGARED RIM. GARNISH WITH A TWIST OF LEMON.

Theories abound when it comes to attempting to discover who first made this cocktail. What's beyond doubt is that it is a Parisian creation, but trying to find out who was the first to put Cognac, Cointreau and lemon juice together ends up with you following clues which only lead you up some blind alley in an obscure arrondissement being pursued by a homicidal monkey. According to David Embury, author of *The Fine Art of Mixing Drinks*, it was created by a military acquaintance in Paris during the First World War who travelled to drink "his" cocktail in a motorcycle sidecar. Sadly, the friend isn't named, nor is the bar to which the sidecar travelled so regularly,

DESPITE ITS OBSCURE ORIGINS, THIS DRINK REMAINS A TIMELESS CLASSIC

lending the whole tale an apocryphal quality.

It could have been a creation of Harry's New York Bar, the famous Parisian haunt where a host of cocktails were invented, including the Bucket of Blood (*see* Vodka), but in the end no one really knows.

The minimalist beauty of the sidecar makes it a classic drink – indeed it can be regarded as the spiritual father of the Pisco Sour and the Daiquiri. The important element is to get the correct balance between the mouth-puckering acidity of fresh lemon juice (lime won't do, which is why a Sidecar isn't just a Daiquiri made with brandy) and the clean, sweet orange richness of triple sec. If these sweet and sour elements are in harmony, they provide the ideal frame for the fruity richness and kick of the Cognac.

⁵Rum

THE MEREST MENTION OF RUM CONJURES UP IMAGES OF THE LUSH CALM OF THE

CARIBBEAN. A SWEET, EXOTIC SPIRIT THAT INSISTS YOU TAKE IT EASY, IT'S THE

ESSENCE OF RELAXATION. BUT BENEATH THIS BENIGN IMAGE LURK TALES OF

REVOLUTION, WAR, PIRACY, COLONIALISM AND SLAVERY. FEW OTHER DRINKS HAVE

SUCH A BLOOD-SOAKED PAST OR HAVE WALLOWED IN SUCH MISERY.

RUM STARTED LIFE AS A
MEXICAN WORKERS' DRINK

OPPOSITE: TAKING LIFE
EASY: JAMAICAN STYLE

COLUMBUS BROUGHT
CANE TO THE CARIBBEAN

Rum's hidden history starts 10,000 years ago when the sugar cane plant (*sacchorum officinarium*) began its migration from its home in the East Indies into China and India, acquiring a mythic power similar to the agave in Mexico. There are some commentators who believe that soma, the intoxicating, hallucinogenic drink of early Indo-European civilization, was the fermented juice of the sugar cane. "Like impetuous winds, like swift horses bolting with a chariot, the drink has lifted me up," it says in the *Rig Veda*, talking of a drink produced by crushing the stems of a long, leafless plant. Was it describing shamanic ecstasy brought on by drinking fermented cane juice? Certainly, Indian civilization knew of two other fermented sugar drinks, Sidhu and Gaudi.

As the plant spread west into Arabia, then North Africa, so it began to be cultivated for sugar production. The Spanish and Portuguese, who were cultivating it on the Canaries and Madeira in the early part of the fifteenth century,

then took it with them as they sailed across the Atlantic to newly "discovered" Brazil and the Caribbean islands. Columbus himself planted cane in Hispaniola and Cuba on his second voyage across the Atlantic. Sugar and the colonization of the Caribbean have been inextricably linked ever since.

Early days

Sugar cane became the main Caribbean/South American crop as soon as the early Spanish settlers realized that, contrary to their wishes, there wasn't any gold to be mined. When rum (or its early equivalent) first appeared is less clear, but since molasses will

ferment naturally if left to its own devices, it seems quite probable that the first people to discover the new alcoholic beverage were the slaves working on the plantations.

A distilled sugar cane brandy (chiringuito) made from molasses was made and drunk by slaves on Spanish settlements in Mexico, and in the Portuguese ones in Bahia almost as soon as they were established. It's probable, therefore, that the first Mexican spirit was rum, rather than mezcal. The same happened throughout the Caribbean islands.

By the end of the sixteenth century, this distilled sugar drink was building itself a fearsome reputation – one that led to it rejoicing in the name "kill-devil", a title that was also given to gin in West Africa.

By the seventeenth century, the French, English and Dutch had joined in the rush to colonize the small islands of the Caribbean. They too planted cane for sugar production, and where cane went distillation followed. It made perfect economic sense – by making rum from molasses, you'd get more money from one crop.

92

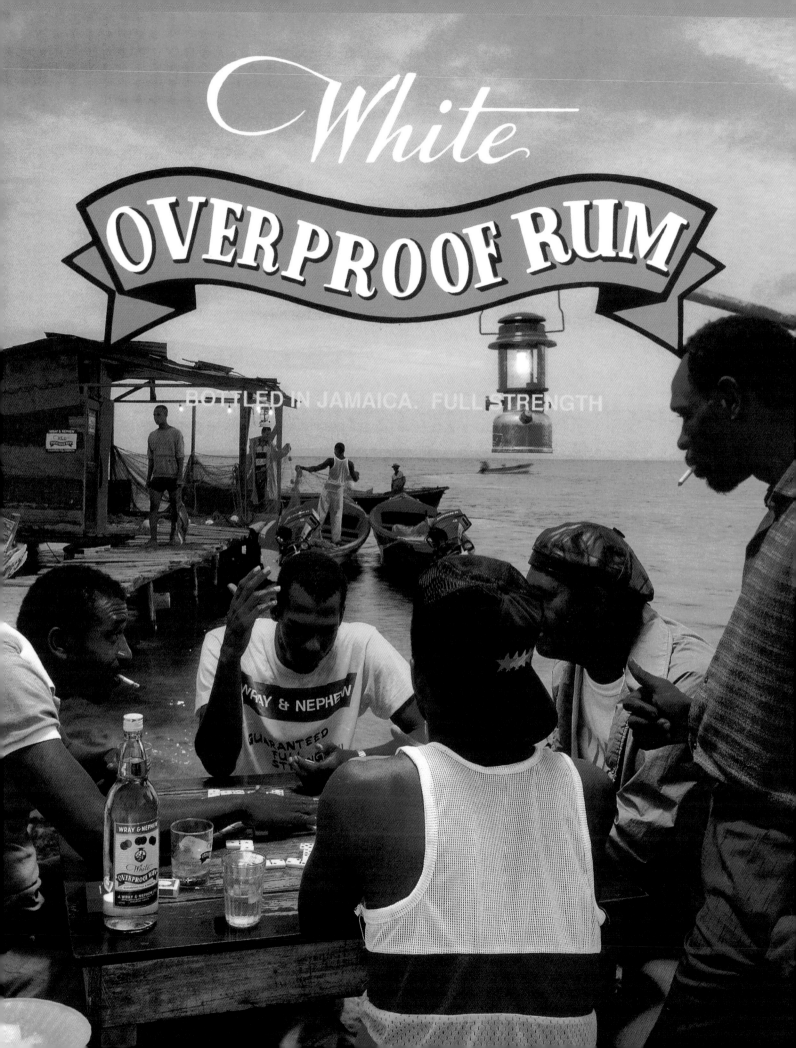

When Richard Ligon arrived in Barbados in 1647 and wrote his history of the island, he described the workings of a distillery and the taste of kill-devil, which he claims was a strong, unpleasant beverage, only consumed by the poor and "laying them asleep on the ground" almost immediately.

At this stage, the planters were still drinking imported brandy. Kill-devil was given to their slaves as a field medicine and as "payment" for their toil – a practice that was used by some employers in the South African wine industry during the years of apartheid. Another account of Barbados in the 1660s that is mentioned in *The Barbados Rum Book*, describes: "The chiefe fudling they make in the Island is Rumbulion, alias Kill Divill and this is made of suggar canes distilled, a hot hellish and terrible liquor."

Around the same time in French-owned Martinique, sugar cane was being used to make spirits such as Veson Guildive/Guildire and Tafia, again purely for consumption by slaves.

"It's all that savages, Negroes and modest inhabitants look for," said Père Labat, the father of rhum distillation, on his arrival on the island in 1694. "It is enough for them that this liquor should be strong and violent. It matters little to them that it is harsh and unpleasant."

By this stage, distillation was providing sugar planters a nice little extra income from kill-devil – Ligon claimed that a Barbadian distiller could make the vast sum of £30 a week from the spirit, which seems an unbelievable amount – and it was also starting to be sold to the crews of the ships which patrolled the Caribbean. By now the drink had begun to be known as rum, although there's a continuing debate over where the term came from.

Some believe it's a derivation of the Mala *brum*, meaning a sugar cane drink, a word that could have arrived via the Dutch traders. The Dutch at that time also drank from glasses called roemers or rummers.

Others think it comes from rumbullion which, according to who you consult, either means "an uproar" or is a Creole word which conflates the Andalucian *rheu* (stems) with the French *bouillon* (stew).

Whatever the correct derivation, by the late 1660s the drink was known as rum on the British islands and rhum on the French. [This is a spelling I shall use here to differentiate between these two very different styles.]

The slave TRADE

SLAVES PLANTING CANE IN ANTIGUA

By this time, rum had not only begun to be drunk by the Navy (*see* page 95) but was being exported to the American Colonies. Trade soon sprang up between New England and the important distilling islands of Barbados and Jamaica whereby supplies (including lumber for barrels) were shipped from New England in exchange, at first, for sugar and rum. In time molasses, rather than rum, was destined for the distilleries which had begun to be established in Boston, Rhode Island and along the eastern seaboard.

At this point rum entered the darkest phase of its evolution. Eighteenth-century European society was seized with sugar addiction. As Terence McKenna writes in his *Food of the Gods*: "Sugar is unnecessary to the human diet; it is a kick, nothing more. Yet for this kick, Europe was willing to betray the ideals of the Enlightenment by its collusion with slave traders."

The result was an evil triangle of "trade". Since the market demanded sugar, more people were needed to produce sugar cane, which by then was planted on every island in the Caribbean. Slave ships would leave New England loaded with rum and sail to West Africa, where they would trade the liquor for slaves and gold. (English-based vessels would do the same with gin.) The boats would then sail back across the Atlantic with their human cargo and the slaves would be sold in the Caribbean in exchange for molasses and rum, which was then taken to New England for distillation, and so on. Alcohol has long been used as a tool of barter, but never in such an obscene fashion.

Rum 'n' revolution

The molasses/slave trade was a main pillar of the American colonies' economy – so much so, that it was the curbs the British put on the molasses trade that caused the spark which was to explode into the War of Independence. The New England distillers needed a regular supply of cheap molasses to make sufficient rum to satisfy domestic demand and buy slaves. At that time the cheapest source for molasses came from either the French-controlled islands, since France banned the import of rhum to protect its domestic brandy industry, or those eternal middle-men, the Dutch.

The British wanted to force the New England distillers to buy (expensive) molasses from the British islands, and in 1733 and 1765 passed two Molasses Acts, imposing heavy duties on "non-British" molasses. When they then did the same with tea, the colonists had had enough. Tea may have been the final straw, but it was rum that was the catalyst.

Rum continued to play a significant role in the newly emerging America. George Washington allegedly swayed voters in Virginia by giving them free rum punch in exchange for votes, and he ordered a barrel of rum for his inauguration dinner.

Equally, Paul Revere's famous ride was notably silent until he arrived at Isaac Hall's house. Hall was the owner of the Medford rum distillery, and it was only after he gave Revere a few tots of a rum "which would have made a rabbit bite a bulldog" that the rider began to shout his warning that "The British are coming!" Who knows what would have happened without rum?

In the navy

The American colonists were not the only enthusiastic drinkers of rum. From the earliest days of distillation it had been given (or sold) to the crews of ships that guarded the Caribbean with quasi-legal authority. The French and British navies in those days were quite likely to be supplemented by boats stuffed with pirates, privateers and buccaneers. One side's guardian angel was the other's bloodthirsty pirate. What was clear was that supplying a ship with a few barrels of rum guaranteed that it would protect your waters.

If this slightly dodgy trade protected the colonists in what was a volatile region, the legitimate navy also enjoyed its rum – indeed Nelson asked for his body to be preserved in rum should he die at Trafalgar.

Rum's popularity with the navy was partly for health reasons. Beer soon went off in the tropical heat, as did wine. The Dutch had been early to realize that fortifying wine allowed it to be kept stable (*see* Cognac, pages 70–78), and in 1687 the English Navy had decreed that ratings be given the ration of half a pint of rum a day instead of the usual gallon of beer. Needless to say, it was a great success. The only trouble was that rum was also used as a reward for a particularly dangerous task – such as splicing the mainbrace. This meant that while ships may have had a happy crew, they also had a drunken one. The number of fatalities with sailors falling off the rigging made the Admiralty reconsider the practice.

In 1740 Admiral Vernon ordered rum to be diluted with two parts water (although he also increased the ration to a pint a day – and half a pint for boys). Later lime juice was added to help offset scurvy, giving the Navy their nickname of Limeys. This daily rum ration – called grog after Admiral Vernon's grogham cloak – continued until 1970, although by then it had been reduced to one eighth of a pint a day. The tradition lives on in the Pussers brand, a dark, intense, tannic rum produced in the British Virgin Islands.

PAUL REVERE FOUND HIS VOICE AFTER A TOT OF RUM

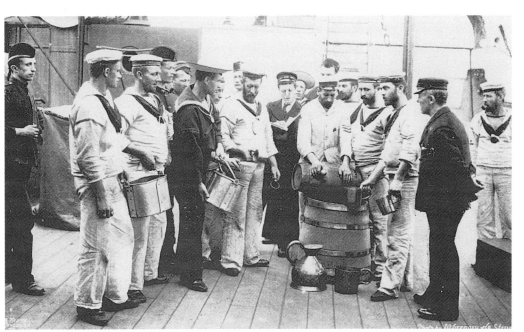

WAITING FOR GROG

Meanwhile in Britain

With the Navy supping at its rum ration and the Americans knocking it back with gusto, it wasn't long before English society became enamoured with the new drink, and rum became an integral constituent of the spiced drinks which were so popular at the turn of the eighteenth century. Elizabeth David, in her *Spices, Salt and Aromatics In The English Kitchen*, quotes Congreve's *The Way of the World* (1700) in which the playwright jokes about "all auxiliaries to the tea-table such as orange brandy, all aniseed, cinnamon, citron and Barbadoes (sic) water [a spiced rum cordial]".

Rum arrived at the start of the gin boom which had gripped England's urban poor and, as a result, rum became the acceptable spirit among the middle classes. Rum houses became fashionable watering holes for the literati, and rum punch – rum mixed with wines, other spirits and beers – was the fashionable "cocktail" of its day, drunk by such luminaries as Boswell, Garrick, Fox and Sheridan.

Not surprisingly, rum merchants like the interestingly named Lemon Hart became significant men of capital. Hart's grandfather had been a rum merchant in Cornwall, but Lemon moved the firm to London's West India Docks in 1804, as did fellow merchant Alfred Lamb. The two firms were to join forces along with the sugar refiner Booker McConnell after the Second World War to form United Rum Merchants (URM).

The industry TODAY

The mention of Booker McConnell underlines the fact that rum and sugar have always been linked. Indeed without a sugar industry there would be no rum distilling. Both businesses were badly hit in the nineteenth century when Europeans managed to produce sugar from sugar beet, and therefore no longer needed to rely on the Caribbean for their supplies. Planters had borrowed heavily to invest in sugar cane plantations (which always had a distillery attached), and when the market collapsed many distilleries failed.

Although the sugar industry received a boost after the First World War (when the European beet fields were blown up), by then most of the Caribbean islands were producing under strict quotas. Consolidation of the sugar/rum industry was the inevitable result, a process that accelerated after the "double whammy" of the Depression and the Second World War. These days, the rum industry is like any other spirits sector, with a few large players and a clutch of smaller producers who have somehow managed to hold on.

The decline in sugar cane production hit the smaller islands particularly badly and some, such as Antigua, now have to import molasses for rum-making. On many islands, farmers simply switched from sugar to bananas. Now, these independent Caribbean banana producers are being crippled by multinational firms, forcing farmers to pull up their plantations and turn once more to rum as an important money-earning industry.

Even a major sugar/rum producer like Jamaica was crippled by the emergence of the European sugar-beet industry and the starting of the massive Florida cane fields. With the post-war exodus of much of its workforce, Jamaican sugar's decline in profitability was severe – it was only saved when the industry was nationalized in the 1960s.

As distilleries have closed and molasses production has been nationalized, so distilling has become centralized, and much of today's rum is made in hi-tech distilleries that are among the most complex in the world. There are two each on Jamaica, Trinidad and Barbados, and one in Guyana. On Martinique, distilleries produce rhum for their neighbours, simply because it is more economical to centralize production. This is common practice these days, although it does make things pretty confusing, since you can find rums that seem to hail from an island which hasn't any distilleries, or from a producer who has no distillery.

All the way through this process of consolidation, one firm had taken on the world – and won. Don Facunado Bacardi had seen the potential for a light-style rum in 1878 when he brought the first Coffey still to Cuba and revolutionized the way the island's rum was made – and tasted. No longer did people have to drink heavy, rich pot-still rums; now there was a light, mixable alternative.

The fact that Bacardi rum was claimed to have cured King Alfonso XIII of Spain of a nasty bout of flu only helped its sales in Spain – and the extended Spanish Empire. The firm built a distillery in Mexico in 1931 and one in Puerto Rico a few years later. This latter facility allowed it to escape American import duty, and also enabled it to stay open during the Second World War, giving it access to an American market starved of any other domestic spirits. When Fidel Castro nationalized production in Cuba, Bacardi had already registered itself in Nassau and simply switched production to its other facilities.

It was Bacardi and Smirnoff who ushered in the era of the light, mixable drink which was virtually to kill off brown spirits from the late 1970s on, but Bacardi has achieved something that Smirnoff can only dream of – it has become a category in its own right. People ask for Bacardi and Coke, not white rum and Coke. In fact, to most people Bacardi isn't even rum: it's simply Bacardi.

In Britain, rum still meant (and still means) a dark, almost black, sweet spirit. URM and Seagram have long been shipping rums from Barbados, Guyana, Jamaica and Trinidad to Scotland, where they are aged and blended into brands like Lamb's, Captain Morgan, Lemon Hart, OVD and Black Heart. Even today on the rural west coast of Scotland, you'll more likely find people drinking Trawler rum than Scotch. Whisky specialists like Cadenheads also import rum and their bottlings, though little known, are among some of the finest on the market today. The firm, which is part of Springbank Whisky, then sends its rum barrels to the Campbeltown distillery for re-use.

The main UK brands, though, have been caught in the "old spirit" slump, and have yet to find out how to get out of the hole. The big dark warming style which was invented to suit the British palate (and climate) has been rejected in favour of something lighter.

Rum's future success may lie back in the Caribbean. Today's drinker is looking for authenticity, quality and flavour, and rum has all of that in bucketloads. White rums are hugely versatile – as Bacardi drinkers have long known – but it's the aged rums that may hold the key to growth. Firms like Mount Gay, Cockspur and Wray & Nephew have premium brands that are ideally suited to the new market. There's also growing interest in the aged and vintage rhums from Martinique and Guadeloupe. Only time will tell if this ancient, underrated spirit will get another lease of life.

How it's made

Rum is one of the few spirits that came into being as the by-product of another industry. In the past, sugar refining was the main business, while rum was made from the left-overs. These days, however, it has usurped sugar as the main income on a number of islands.

Caning it

To get to rum's starting point, you have to journey into the luxuriant plantations of the Caribbean and get to grips with sugar cane. The plant is a giant grass that grows quickly and vigorously – on average, young plants are ready for harvesting a year after they have been planted, although some new, quick-maturing varieties can be ripe in as little as six months.

Each island will have a selection of strains best suited for its soil and climate – there's terroir in rum as well as Cognac! It's claimed, for example, that Antigua's dry conditions give a sweeter cane, while on Barbados cane research has been developed into an agricultural science, with new disease-resistant varieties that give higher sugar levels in harsh conditions being developed. In Cuba, the producer of Havana Club claims that the climate in Oriente in the south of the island produces a particularly high-quality cane suitable for rum making, while the volcanic soil on Martinique is credited with producing particularly high yields.

Harvesting starts in February and continues (depending on the location) until June, when the canes are taken to the refinery to be turned into sugar. Or not, if you are in one of the French islands that produce rhum agricole from cane juice, rather than from molasses (*see* page 103).

The canes are cut and shredded to allow their sweet juices to flow. They are then crushed by a series of rollers, after which the juice is sent one way and the spent fibres (bagasse) go another. This is then used as fuel to run boilers and stills.

At this stage the cane juice is still dirty and has to be cleaned – traditionally by using lime and allowing the mud to precipitate to the bottom of a settling tank. This mud is then used as fertilizer on the fields. Once again, here's proof that spirits production is ecologically sound.

While technology has come to the assistance of the major refineries, in principle the next process remains the same as the one you'll find on the old estates. To produce sugar you need to boil the cane juice or syrup until it crystallizes. Traditionally this is performed in a series of progressively smaller pans. The cane juice is boiled, crystallized, then the crystals are extracted and the liquid is transferred to the next pan. Hi-tech refineries use centrifuges and vacuum boilers, but the aim is the same – to extract as much of the sugar solids as possible from the sweet syrup.

Eventually there isn't any more sugar to be crystallized, and you are left with a thick, black, sweet, gooey gunk – molasses. Now rum-making can start.

In the early days of sugar-refining, this waste product would have been left in pits until one day someone, somewhere, noticed that since it still contained the wild yeasts that grow on the joints of

HAND-HARVESTING CANE

the cane, it had started to ferment. It was probably in a Spanish colony, as molasses comes from the Spanish melazas, from miel meaning honey.

It wasn't a huge jump of logic to realize that if they used the same techniques as they had done to make brandy back home, they could make a stronger liquor.

Ferment and yeasts

All distillers will dilute the molasses to a sugar level of around 17° Brix and then pump the mash into fermenting vats where, usually, yeast is added. In the old days some acid (lime or vegetable ash) would have also been tipped in to lower the pH. These days, distillers wanting to produce a heavy, full-flavoured rum will add some of the acidic lees from the previous ferment – similar to the backset used in Kentucky and Tennessee. As this practice pre-dates Bourbon distilling, it's entirely possible that the technique was taken from the Caribbean to Kentucky.

It's not essential to add yeast to molasses, and some small distillers, such as Callwood on the British Virgin Islands, or River Antoine and Dunfermline on Grenada, still prefer to use the old technique of letting nature take its course. The result, needless to say, is a long ferment that can be difficult to control and can give variable yields of alcohol, but it's a style they prefer to use. Other firms, like Mount Gay and Wray & Nephew, have isolated their own yeast strains that they will use, while other distillers use industrial cultured yeast. It's horses for courses.

As with any other spirit, the length and temperature of ferment (and the

VAST CANE PLANTATIONS ARE NEEDED TO PRODUCE HIGH VOLUMES OF RUM, WHICH FOR MANY ISLANDS IS THE MAIN SOURCE OF INCOME

SUGAR PRODUCTION REMAINS CENTRAL TO THE LOCAL ECONOMY

"traditional" because originally all rums would have been made in pot stills – and some of them still use that ancient alchemical device, the retort.

The principle of pot-still rum distillation is the same as anywhere else in the world – to distil batches of a fermented wash and separate the heart (here called seconds) from the heads and tails (high and low wines). The retort is a way of doing the process in one batch, rather than redistilling.

A Jamaican pot still with two retorts works along the following lines. The fermented wash is heated in the still but the hot vapour, rather than being condensed as usual, passes into a chamber (similar to the doubler used in Kentucky), which is quarter-filled with the low wines from the previous distillation. The vapour heats the low wines, lifts off the alcohol and then passes into another retort, this time filled with the high wines. The process is repeated and further concentrates the flavours. Only then does the alcohol vapour pass into the condenser. The heads are then kept aside to fill the retort for the next run. There are variations of this basic rectifying technique across the Caribbean. Some use one retort, some three.

In Jamaica, pot stills are also used to produce a range of styles. As well as the "standard", rich, flavourful spirit, they can also give a high-ester distillate from a complex process which involves a long-ferment wash and concentrated spirit from the high wines retort being redistilled to give a high concentration of esters. This type of rum is predominantly used as a flavouring agent for rums in Germany, Holland and Austria, where they are mixed with local neutral spirit to produce rum verschnitt, or inlander rum. This style is also a significant part of the blend in URM's South African brand, Red Heart.

type of yeast) will have a direct effect on the flavour compounds produced, and this is a main difference between each island's rum. You can find ferments that last for as little as two days, while others rumble and grumble on for over a fortnight.

These days, the light rums that are distilled in column stills will be innoculated with yeasts that give a short ferment, and therefore lighter flavours. The heavier rums to be distilled in pot stills are given a longer ferment in order to build in richer flavours at an early stage.

The end result, wherever you are, is a wash of around 5 to 9 per cent ABV that is ready to be distilled.

Distilling

As ever, the distiller is faced with two choices: whether to use a pot or a column still. In general terms, light rums will be made from a short-ferment wash that's been distilled in column stills, while the big-flavoured "traditional" rums are from a long ferment, and are distilled in pots. I say

Column distillation is a far more complex process than it is believed to be. Every rum distillery, inevitably, will have its own recipe to work to. Each one will also have its own type of column, ranging from stills that wouldn't look out of place in Armagnac to the wooden Coffey still (the only one left in the world) used in Guyana to produce a smooth, light and balanced spirit. Then there are the technological marvels in place in Guyana, Trinidad and in Bacardi's various plants.

There you can find four or even five interlinked columns which the distillers can play like an instrument, taking off spirit at different strengths (and therefore capturing different flavours) then redistilling it, rectifying it or perhaps retaining it at low strength. One plant can therefore produce a seemingly infi-nite variety of flavouring spirits. They aren't just factories that churn out some flavourless whistle-clean product, but are set up to produce a range of styles in order to give the blenders as wide a range of basic ingredients as possible.

Ageing

Most white and overproof rums are kept in tank for a short period before being bottled. The other rums are normally aged in ex-Bourbon casks (although Cognac, whisky and wine barrels are also used), with light rums being in wood for no longer than one or two years (and then often charcoal-filtered to remove any colour). The heavier rums will spend from three to four years in wood, although some firms keep rums for 10 or more years in barrel.

The rate of maturation is affected by the climate. The Caribbean is a hot, humid area of the world, which means that the spirit extracts the tannins, colouring and flavouring agents from the wood quickly. Much of rum's character is derived from this rapid extraction.

The hot, humid conditions mean that the spirit fairly flies out of the barrel and into the waiting glasses of the angels (or duppies) hovering above the warehouses – producers in Martinique estimate that they lose eight per cent a year, meaning that they regularly have to top up the barrels with rhum from the same year. The standard British brands avoid this expensive option by taking their rums off the islands and into bonded warehouses in the far less romantic (but cooler) settings of Dumbarton or Leith.

AN ANCIENT STILL, USED FOR MAKING BAY RUM, REMAINS ON THE ISLAND OF ST THOMAS IN THE US VIRGIN ISLANDS

*WORKERS LABEL
BOTTLES OF RUM IN A
JAMAICAN DISTILLERY*

Blending

The rums are then blended – each to its own recipe. It's rare these days that you can find a rum which is bottled as it comes off the still – although Iron Jack (distilled in Trinidad) or River Antoine's Royale Grenadian are once-tasted, never-forgotten exceptions to that rule.

Blenders in the UK can use rums from different stills, distilleries, countries, ages and barrel types to make up their blends. Brands like Captain Morgan and Lamb's blend rums from Jamaica (for richness), Guyana (finesse and spice), Barbados (balance) and Trinidad that have been distilled in both column and pot stills, meaning that a typical "British" blend may contain 15 to 20 different types of rum. That said, each brand also gives emphasis to a certain core style – Lemon Hart, for example, is a light, golden "Jamaican" style; Black Heart is a dark Guyanan.

A blender like Mount Gay's Jerry Edwards uses different ages of rums from pot and column stills. For him, the column distillates give aromatics of oak and vanillin, while the pot-still rums are richer and more complex.

The rule of thumb is: the richer the aromatics and body, the higher the percentage of pot still in the blend. Other distillers, such as Trinidad Distillers, can use different rums from the same still. Caramel can then be added, to the blender's specifications. Some argue that the heavy caramel addition given to some rums is only appropriate, as caramel is burnt sugar. That may be the case, but caramel is too often used as a masking agent rather than a flavouring one.

Rum need not hide behind artificial sweeteners and colourings. At its best it is a glorious and complex drink which can compare with any of the world's finest spirits. For some reason however, it is often dismissed as a simple drink – useful for its kick, but not its flavour. Nothing could be further from the truth.

*SAMPLING MOUNT GAY
RUM AT THE BARBADOS
REFINERY*

Easy in the islands

Rum is the kind of subject you could quite happily spend the rest of your life getting to know. There's a mind-boggling variety of rums available in three broad styles: Light (white/overproof); Heavy (gold and aged); and Dark (the British brands).

There are also three main regional production techniques – the sugar cane distillate produced on the French islands; the molasses-based spirit from the rest of the Caribbean; and the UK-aged blends.

The French colonies

The story of rhum begins in 1694, when the Dominican priest, Père Labat, finally arrived on Martinique after a long voyage during which his ship was attacked by the English. Labat not only brought religion, but also knowledge of the very latest distillation techniques from France.

Prior to Labat's arrival, distillation in Martinique (like distillation everywhere else in the Caribbean) had been a pretty hit-and-miss affair, producing a strong rhum known as tafia – the French equivalent to the kill-devil coming off the stills in Barbados. Labat, quite simply, was the Jim Crow (see Bourbon) of rhum, bringing science to bear on an agricultural way of processing waste material.

In the early days, French rhummakers would have used molasses like everyone else – in the 1750s they were supplying molasses to the New England distilleries and playing their part in the ending of British rule in the American Colonies. It was only after the discovery of sucrose extraction from sugar beet

that there was a wholesale switch from molasses to cane juice. At that point, the French stopped seeing sugar as a commodity, while the British still continued to view it as the main crop.

The French are also very good (some would say obsessional) about regulating every agricultural product. Cheese, chickens, wine and brandy all have their own appellation controls, ostensibly to guarantee a minimum quality and (less clearly) ensure typicity.

Rhum, therefore, is produced under restrictions similar to those that regulate Cognac or Armagnac. The raw material, the method of production and the manner of ageing are all defined in law.

Only cane juice is used for Rhum Agricole, the stills must be pot, single or linked column, and the wood must be less than 650 litres in capacity (smaller than the large vats used elsewhere).Most commonly, rhum dis-

tillers use 250-litre barrels that have previously held Cognac, wine, bourbon or, occasionally, whisky. Rhums are themselves divided into two classes: Rhum Agricole, which is produced by sugar cane (or vesou) for roughly six months after the harvest (i.e. when the cane is fresh); and the less evocatively named Rhum Industriel, which is made from molasses during the rest of the year. Check the label when buying rhum; it's an important difference, and Rhum Industriel often tastes the same as its name suggests.

Within Agricole, there are two broad categories – the high-strength (overproof) white rhums that have been kept in tank for a minimum of three months, and which are usually used as the base for punches; and the aged rhums, which are lower in strength and have been barrel-aged.

There is also a rhum that has been aged for a shorter time (a bit like reposado in mezcal/tequila) which is called paille, after the straw colour it acquires as a result of this short period in wood, while there are also Vieux and Hors d'Age rhums which have been aged (often for considerably longer).

At the top end of the market there's Millessime, or vintage rhum. These are rhums that have been transferred from small to large barrels to allow a slower

Tasting Notes

WHITE

Appleton White Clean and a little green on nose. Coconut flavours on palate. Soft and mellow. Good.

Bacardi White Rounded and smooth but virtually neutral. A real needle on the palate. Crisp finish.

Wray & Nephew Overproof Rotten banana, heavy, oily and pungent. Oily in mouth, full and flavoursome. In time, a citric edge unveils itself. Clean and a weighty base for cocktails.

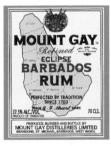

ABOVE AND RIGHT:

TWO BAJAN CLASSICS

maturation to take place – the vintage indicates the start of this secondary maturation, rather than the year in which it was distilled.

Rhum production remains, in essence, an agricultural creation with clear ties to the past; there's a timeless quality to be found in many of the distilleries. The products speak of this different way of doing things, having a finer, more floral and less pungent aroma than molasses rums, and a more delicate drive on the palate. Little known in the English-speaking world, they deserve a wider audience.

The regions

At one time, each island could be said to have its own identifiable style, but with inter-island blending now commonplace and more complex distillation practices in place, this is less clearly defined than it used to be. Still, there is a clear difference between rums from, say, Barbados, Jamaica and Trinidad. "It's always been thought that

rums from different countries had their own peculiar characteristics," says Jerry Edwards at Mount Gay. "Today, though, because most countries make rum in continuous stills, the difference in taste between rums from different countries is small. When they are blended with heavier rums, though, the difference between countries is detectable. I don't know why, but climate, soil, water and the preparation of the molasses wash and the ferment must all play their part."

Barbados

Barbados can claim to be the home of commercial rum; certainly it was producing kill-devil by the mid-seventeenth century, only two decades after the Dutch planter Pietr Blower brought cane from Brazil. It soon became one of the most famous rum-producing islands, whose spirits were requested by name, implying that the Barbados style was in place virtually from the beginning. By the end of the last

century every plantation on the island possessed its own distillery.

Traditionally this is the home of elegant, fruity rums, although these days you can find anything from light white to the classic aged rums. This is despite the fact that there are only two distilleries on the island, both of which

buy their molasses from the nationalized Barbados Sugar Industry.

Barbados is home to Mount Gay, a justifiably famous name in the premium rum market, and an estate that has been producing rums since 1663 at least. This allows it to claim to be the oldest rum brand in the world – although Calwood in the British Virgin Islands can put forward an equally strong case. When William Gay bought the plantation, he purchased "Two stone windmills, one boiling house with seven coppers, one curing house and one still house", so it seems likely that rum was already being produced when he arrived.

Although pot stills make up the heart of the Mount Gay brands, the firm also has a column still which can be used either to rectify the pot-still distillate or to produce a lighter style on its own, allowing Jerry Edwards three blending blocks. Compare the ever-popular Eclipse with the succulent, mellow Extra Old, and discover Barbados in a glass.

The other Bajan distiller is the less evocatively named West Indies Rum Refinery, which produces rum (and Gilbey's gin) under contract to the specifics of the other Barbadian bottlers – the best-known being Cockspur, (whose VSOR is one of the best aged rums on the market), and Doorly's.

Jamaica

The Jamaican rum industry was built on the back of the trade with the Navy and the privateers who guarded the island in the early days of the colony. After years of sugar being the dominant industry, these days – in common with many islands – it's rum that appears to offer a greater opportunity for profit. As in Barbados there are only two distilleries, including the excellent Wray & Nephew, which was founded in 1825 by John Wray. He owned three estates – among them the justifiably revered 250-year-old Appleton estate, a brand that proves that rum isn't just a white drink, but can age gracefully into a superbly balanced spirit. Its pot-still V/X, 12-year-old and 21-year-old are three of the finest aged rums in the Caribbean, building up layers of nutmeg, spice and luscious, mellow sweet ripe fruit as they age.

Though Jamaica remains most famous for its rich, pungent pot-still rums, like any other island it can produce rums to any style – Wray & Nephew's White Overproof and Sangster's Conquering Lion Overproof (from the National Rums of Jamaica distillery) are classics of their style, but be wary!

Trinidad & Tobago

Although late being colonized, Trinidad was still managing to produce half a million gallons of rum by the end of the eighteenth century. These days, however, it is best known as the home of Angostura Bitters (*see* Bitters, page 176–7), the flavouring ingredient that is used in every drink and dish made here.

If Jamaica and Barbados have retained their evocative estates and links with the past, on Trinidad you are brought face to face with the future. The two distilleries here (Trinidad Distillers, owned by Angostura, and Caroni) operate plants whose linked columns give a seemingly endless range of blending spirits from virtually neutral spirit to heavy, low-strength distillates. It may not be romantic, but for the spirit hunter this is a triumph of the distiller's art akin to Midleton in Ireland or Lancut in Poland.

Much of the production is destined for blending, but Trinidad's bottled brands range from the brutally strong Puncheon (Trinidad Distillers) and

AT THE PINNACLE OF JAMAICAN RUMS

Tasting Notes

GOLD

Havana Club 3 anos Lifted aromatic nose, spearmint and spices. Soft, initially crisp finish. Freshness personified.

Appleton Special Coffee and crème brulée with a touch of banana Good weight. Rich and smooth with a wooded fruity finish.

Bacardi Black Neutral.

Mount Gay Lifted and sweet nose with some banana/toffee notes and a hint of smoke. Very clean, elegant and long.

Mount Gay Extra Old Rich toasted wood, some coconut, orange and banana. Positive wood on palate, but balanced by sweet, complex layers of fruit flavours.

Cockspur Light and fragrant with touches of brown sugar and banana. Delicate and pleasant.

Cockspur VSOR Some walnuts and dates on the nose with some well-balanced fruity sugar. Rich on the palate and a good, lingering finish.

Appleton V/X Slightly vegetal with banana esteriness before a raspberry compote fills the nose. Good grip mid-palate before rounding out for a long, pleasant finish.

Appleton 12yo Immediate vanilla/ toasted coconut wood on the nose. On the palate, it's smokily complex and mellow. Very good.

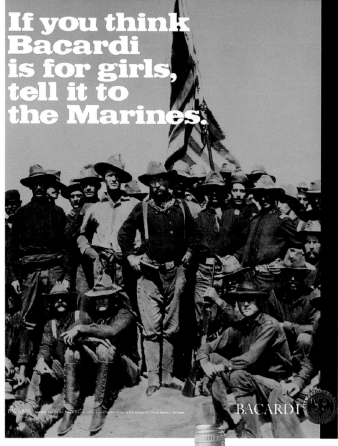

IN 1898 THE US ARMY JOINED forces with rebel troops to help Cuba win its struggle for independence. To celebrate their victory the allied soldiers created the Cuba Libre, a symbolic blend of Bacardi, Cuba's favourite spirit, and America's favourite soft drink. The Cuba Libre was proof that no matter which way you mix it the unmistakeable flavour of Bacardi always shines through. Which possibly explains why Bacardi went on to become the world's favourite spirit. As for the fizzy brown stuff... that's another story.

If you think Bacardi is for girls, tell it to the Marines.

BEFORE BACARDI AND THE USA FELL OUT WITH CUBA

THE WORLD'S FIRST SUPER-BRAND

Stallion (Caroni) to fine, blended aged rums like Caroni's Old Cask or Trinidad Distillers' Ferdi's. Trinidad Distillers also produces Iron Jack, a barrel-strength rum which deserves to be treated with considerable caution.

Bacardi

Bacardi isn't a national style; it's an international one – you could say state-less. The biggest spirit brand in the world, Bacardi has distilleries in Puerto Rico, Mexico, Spain and other places, all produced to the formula invented by Don Facunado Bacardi when he brought the first Coffey still to his original distillery in Santiago de Cuba in 1878.

What Bacardi (the man and the brand are inseparable) did was to revolutionize rum production – quite appropriate in Cuba – creating the first light, easy-drinking brand. When the firm moved to Puerto Rico in 1960 it had already started out on its aim of world domination. Tightly controlled – woe betide anyone who crosses swords with the Bacardi lawyers – it jealously guards its production methods.

All you can say is that Bacardi produces a hell of a lot of rum, it uses wood judiciously and it tends not to like caramel. You have to sit back in open-mouthed amazement that it has maintained such high quality control over such a vast empire.

In Puerto Rico, Bacardi supplies the spirit for the little-seen, but under-rated, Barrilito brands.

Cuba

One of the few places in the world where you won't find Bacardi is Cuba. No great surprise there, as it was Fidel Castro's nationalization of the rum industry that precipitated Bacardi's departure from the island. The revolu-

tion also meant the loss of the American holidaymakers who had been charmed by Cuba's vibrant nightlife and had fallen in love with those masterpieces of the Cuban barman's art – the Mojito and the Daiquiri.

But although the Americans still feel that this tiny island represents a threat to their national security, and have done everything in their power to bring the island to its knees for having the temerity to challenge their bully-boy tactics, the Cubans have survived, and if they haven't prospered they remain defiantly, proudly, Cuban.

These days Old Havana may be crumbling, and there may be no petrol and little food, but you can still sip a Daiquiri in its birthplace, el Floridita. It's also deeply ironic that at a time when the USA is going ga-ga over quality cigars and quality spirits, you can't (legally) puff on a Cohiba or sip a Daiquiri made from Havana Club. You can in Paris and London, though, and in these two cities Havana Club is one of the "hippest" brands.

Havana Club isn't Bacardi; it's a fine rum in its own right. It uses cane from the south of the island, a "secret" columnn-still distillation and a complex ageing in warehouses which are cooled by the sea breezes. For the three- and seven-year-old versions, this involves ageing the different distillates separately, then blending them and ageing them for a second time. It's America's loss.

Martinique

Along with Guadeloupe, this is the lush heart of the finest rhums, and there are more distilleries here than on any other eastern Caribbean island. It doesn't take long to get the feeling that this is how rhum has always been made, retaining the steady, easy rhythm of the seasons.

It may seem slow to a Western European, but there's an elegant tempo to life here (and on all the islands). What's the point of rushing in this heat? You'll find ox carts, water wheels and ancient stills, but don't be fooled into thinking rhum producers are lazy; their passion for their art burns through. The best of these rhums attest that no one is taking the easy option – they are beautifully crafted spirits.

But these small distilleries are under threat. You can produce more rhum at a lower cost from multiple column stills, but you get the feeling that some of rhum's quality is being lost in the process. Efficiency and volume are important, but these commercial aims must be balanced by producers who believe in the old ways.

Martinique is filled with ancient distilling firms. J. M. has been distilling since 1790, Saint James since 1765 and La Mauny since 1749. Dillon, the oldest of all, was founded in 1690 by the Girardin de Montegeralde family, the most famous of whom was Josephine de Beauharnais, the mistress and wife of Napoleon. It's entirely possible that the saying: "not tonight Josephine" may have been a polite refusal of a glass of her family's rhum.

Dillon, incidentally, was an Irish Jacobin who helped the French turf the Brits out of Martinique and married into the Girardin family. These days Dillon's Vieux and Millessime rhums are among the finest examples of their style you can find.

Rhum J. M.'s Fonds Preville distillery is one of the oldest on the island. The firm still produces its range from cane grown on the 30-hectare estate and distils in the only linked column still on the island – and ages, unusually, in ex-wine barrels, for a stunning range which includes Paille, Vieux and Millessime.

J. Bally also uses estate-grown cane, but its still is akin to an alambic Armagnacais in size – and therefore gives a lower-strength spirit for its excellent range of white, Paille, Vieux and vintages.

Guadeloupe

Cane arrived here in the seventeenth century and plantations still cover the northern part of the island, but these days there are only six distilleries. Among them is Bologne, which is notable not just for its high-quality rhum but for the fact it was the first plantation bought by a free black man. Also notable are

Mon Repos, which uses cane from its own estate to produce an excellent range of beautiful hand-crafted rhums, and Damoiseau, whose aged rhums (up to 15-year-old) rival those of Martinique for complexity.

Other islands

The US Virgin Islands was a significant supplier of rum to the New England distilleries, and currently one of its two distilleries is doing sterling work in trying to convince today's US consumer that rum has flavour.

Cruzan, owned by the US-based Todhunter – but still run by the Nelthropp family, which arrived in St Croix in the late 1700s – now has a wide range, including light (aged for two years), Estate (four-year-old), two high-strength brands (Clipper and 151 Proof), a single barrel brand as well as four flavoured styles.

These very different rums all come off the same highly sophisticated linked column still – here's another distiller that's looking to the future with confidence.

The rums from the neighbouring British Virgin Islands are less commonly seen, but rum lovers should seek out Calwood, from what claims to be the oldest operating distillery in the eastern Caribbean – and one of the few "British" rums which is made from cane juice rather than molasses.

There are a few cane rums from Grenada, although you're unlikely to find a bottle on the export markets. Grenada's fertile soil has allowed a wider range of crops to be cultivated and therefore sugar and rum production have never played the central role that they have on other islands. Although the bulk of the island's fragrant rums are overproof, like River Antoine's Royale Grenadian (allegedly the strongest rum on the market), Westerhall makes a delicate, clean, aged example that's worth searching out, as is Clarke's Court.

The final island of note is beautiful (but forlorn) Haiti, which can lay claim to be one of the oldest rhum-producing sites in the world – after all, it was here that Columbus planted the first cane. Rhum is made here in the French style by the quality-obsessed Barbancourt distillery. Its complex, aged rhums have a deservedly high reputation among aficionados, and are becoming more widely seen.

South America

Guyana is home to the rich, powerful Demerara rums, and to one of the world's great distilleries, a plant where rums of every description can be made by using pot stills, linked columns and the only remaining wooden Coffey still in the world.

The bulk of the production from Demerara Distillers is destined for blends – they make up the majority of the British brands – but the firm also releases underrated rums under the El Dorado label.

Sugar cane arrived in Venezuela in the sixteenth century and rum inevitably followed. In common with other South American rums, the Venezuelan style is lightly flavoured with delicate, fruity, aged (anejo) rums at the top of the tree. The first firm to age its rums in the country was Pampero, whose top brands have a graceful elegance. The other major distiller, Ocumare, produces a charcoal-filtered white and a three-year-old anejo, which uniquely has guarana added to it.

Rums from Nicaragua and Guatemala are along the same lines, though having a richer, more luxurious weight on the palate. The top Nicaraguan brand Flor de Cana is, sadly, now hard to find. You're probably more likely to chance upon the excellent Ron Botran from Guatemala.

Cachaça

It may come as a surprise to discover that the world's biggest-selling spirit style is a rum – although it isn't called that: it's known as cachaça.

Hailing from Brazil, this sugar cane juice distillate is drunk in vast quantities in its home country and is responsible for one of the world's finest cocktails, the caiparinha – the very mention of which gets knowledgeable drinkers salivating.

The cachaça market is dominated by brands such as 51, Pitu and Sao Francisco. Both are fine examples of the style. It's worth searching out the intriguing ginger-flavoured cachaça available from Dreher and, if you look hard enough, you'll find some aged pot-still examples, such as those from Ypioca.

Rum is also an important style in Mexico – indeed it's claimed that Mexicans drink more rum than they do mezcal or tequila, although here they call it aguardiente. Confusing? You bet.

Keep your eyes peeled for Aguardiente Juanito el Camineno from Pueblo, or mezcal/cane spirit mix El Tigre Aguardiente, which has had a short time marrying in wood. It qualifies as being an aguardiente, as it has more than 50 per cent cane spirit in the blend.

Rest of the world

Although rums are produced in Madagascar, Surinam and the French dependencies of Réunion and Mauritius, they are rarely found outside their home markets. More common is Bundaberg, Australia's native spirit. The distillery, situated close to the cane plantations of Queensland, has been in production since the late nineteenth century and remains an essential part of Australian life – and Australian drinking ritual. Although bottled at standard proof, "Bundy" has acquired a somewhat fearsome reputation – which is probably more to do with the way it's flung down the throat with reckless abandon than anything inherently wicked about the drink itself. Wherever Australians are gathered, a bottle of Bundy is never far away.

So, does rum have a sense of place? Maybe not in the way that Cognac, Armagnac, Bourbon and malt whisky do, but rum is part of the pulse of the Caribbean. It's not just the drink of the tourists in their protected all-inclusive compounds; it's as much the people's drink as it has always been. Rum started life as the drink of slaves trying to seek oblivion from their hellish existence. Now it's a drink of national pride – from the shacks at the side of the road offering unmarked bottles of illicit hooch to gaudy beachfront bars, the sipping of rum remains an essential part of Caribbean life.

Rum, more than any other spirit, has an image of eternal youth. If malt whisky is rather grave, Cognac sophisticated and bourgeois, gin middle-class, then rum is the drink of sunshine, of laughter, of relaxed sociability.

RHUM: EFFORTLESSLY STYLISH

Tasting Notes

Flor de Cana Mild and well-balanced with soft and lightly floral aromas. Good gentle character.

Dillon Tres Vieux Spicy and aromatic nose with touches of ginger and white pepper. Attractive depth and weight. A world class rhum.

Captain Morgan Dry curry spice on the nose. Sweet start, but with a good solid, firm grip. Commercial but very sound.

Bally 1986 Rose petals, anise and sugar on the nose. The palate is crisp and very clean with a lovely feel. Fruit-filled with tremendous drive.

El Dorado 15yo Deep, ripe and resonant. The aromas tend towards those of brandy. Highly complex with touches of Demerara sugar and some balancing wood.

OVD Sweet caramel and burnt sugar on the nose. Chewy, soft and young with a roasted coffee-bean palate. Rich, soft and undemanding.

Lamb's Navy Neutral, clean, young and hard. Hint of coffee, but green.

The
DAIQUIRI
Classic Cocktail

Rum's magical combination of delicate sweetness with an alcoholic kick makes it a wonderful base for cocktails, and in the 1920s the world's finest centre for their creation was unquestionably Havana.

There, in the el Floridita bar, barman Constante Ribailagua per-fected a cocktail that had originally been invented in the mines in the Daiquiri mountain range in the south of the country. It was there, according to legend, that two engineers called Pagliuchi and Cox mixed together rum, lime juice, sugar and ice. Simplicity itself, but the greatest cocktails always are.

Constante gave this a further dimension by creating the frozen Daiquiri, although his original is far from the mushy slush that's decanted out of blenders today. He used crushed ice, but strained the drink rather than letting the ice cause unwanted further dilution in the glass.

BARTENDER'S TIPS
Simplicity is the key to making a classic Daiquiri. Once truly mastered, try experimenting.

SIMPLE DAIQUIRI

2 OZ WHITE RUM

JUICE OF 1 LIME

1 TSP SUGAR

SHAKE AND STRAIN OVER ICE INTO COCKTAIL GLASS.

FROZEN DAIQUIRI

2 OZ WHITE RUM

JUICE OF 1 LIME

1 TSP SUGAR

PREPARE IN BLENDER WITH CRUSHED ICE.

His creation was to inspire Hemingway – still the most famous regular at the el Floridita – prompting Papa to launch into a beautiful, evocative and accurate description of the perfect Daiquiri in *Islands in the Stream*: "Hudson drank another frozen Daiquiri – and when he raised his glass he looked at the clear part under the crushed ice and it reminded him of the sea. The crushed-ice part was like the trail of a boat, and the clear part like when the boat cuts across its own trail when it moves over the sandy seabed in shallow water. The colour was almost the same."

All you need are the same ingredients as Pagliuchi and Cox – white rum, simple syrup or sugar and lime juice, but, as ever, balance is all-important. You have to hit that

HEMINGWAY'S FAVOURITE COCKTAIL AND A HAVANA HIGH POINT, DAIQUIRIS ARE IN A DIFFERENT LEAGUE TO THEIR SLUSH-PUPPY IMITATORS

precise spot where the tart lime counter-balances the alcohol and the sweetness of the sugar. Hemingway liked his Daiquiri cold and sour, and so to please the grumpy old devil

happy the sugar was replaced by dash of maraschino liqueur and some unsweetened grapefruit juice.

As blending became common, so the possibilities increased, with

fresh fruit being added. Try it with bananas, mango, strawberry, raspberry and, best of all, in an extension of that other Cuban classic, the Mojito – mint.

RUM PUNCH

*R*um punches are equally open to interpretation. It's the nature of the drink that every island, every bar will have its own variation on the theme, but all will be mixing sour, sweet, strong and weak components. Sourness is given by lime juice and bitters, sweetness from fruit juices, syrup and grenadine. Rum is the sole alcohol and most recipes dilute the punch with either water or ice. The end result is a gentle, soothing drink, not some confected mess. In Jamaica, Wray & Nephew dilutes lime, grenadine/syrup and overproof rum with water, and adds dashes of bitters and nutmeg. In Haiti they combine orange and passion-fruit juice as the sweet part, and use crushed ice for the dilution.

BARTENDER'S TIPS
Try not to get the mint leaves stuck between your teeth – a drink to avoid on a first date

MINT DAIQUIRI

2 OZ WHITE RUM

1/2 OZ COINTREAU

HANDFUL OF MINT LEAVES

JUICE OF HALF A LIME

1 TSP CASTER SUGAR

BLEND WITH CRUSHED ICE AND STRAIN INTO COCKTAIL GLASS.

6 Gin

THERE ARE ONLY A FEW LIGHTS GLIMMERING DEEP IN THE DARKNESS SURROUNDING THE ARRIVAL OF DISTILLING SPIRITS IN EUROPE THAT GIVE A CLUE AS TO HOW IT ALL STARTED. ONE BELONGS TO THE NINTH-CENTURY MEDICAL SCHOOL OF SALERNO IN ITALY, WHICH WAS FOUNDED BY BENEDICTINE MONKS. THEY WERE THE FIRST TO TRANSLATE THE WORKS OF GREEK AND ARAB SCHOLARS INTO LATIN, AND WERE DISTILLING ALCOHOL AT SOME POINT BETWEEN 1050 AND 1150.

ANCIENT DISTILLERS USED JUNIPER SPIRITS TO TRY AND CURE A HOST OF AILMENTS

At this time spirits were used purely for their medicinal properties, with various herbs, spices, roots and viscera being macerated in spirit and distilled either in crude pot stills, or in glass jars. While we can't be sure what the brothers were making in Salerno, it's certain that they would have used the restorative herbs and spices which were already being used in so-called folk medicine – and one of these was juniper (*ginepro* in Latin), which grows well and freely across Italy.

Juniper-based elixirs only became widely used during the fourteenth century, when the Black Death arrived in Europe. One of the potions which followed in its wake like some grisly camp follower was made from juniper. The Salernan monks had already discovered that the berry was effective against bladder and kidney disease, and it was alleged to strengthen the immune system as well as curing prostate problems. If it were taken to excess, it would more than likely have caused prostrate problems. Still, with the pustulant ravages of the bubonic plague laying waste to Western

Europe, what better than a patent cure-all?

The juniper drink is likely to have arrived in Flanders (then controlled by the Dutch) at some point in the late fourteenth century, although we have to wait until 1572 to find the first recorded distillation of an *eau de vie de genièvre* by one Franciscus Sylvius, a physic of Leiden. It wasn't long before *genever* (as it became known in Holland) had left the apothecaries' cellars and entered public use, not just as a health tonic but

as an enjoyable intoxicant. Lucas Bols, the father of commercial gin production, built his first distillery in 1575 near Amsterdam.

Genever soon became a staple part of the Dutch/Belgian diet, used not only to cure upset stomachs but also to give soldiers a certain numbed fearlessness in battle (after all, Sir Robert Savage, the Lord of Bushmills, gave *aqua vitae* to his Irish troops in 1296). This other side-effect of *genever* was discovered (and greatly appreciated) by the regiments of English mercenaries who went to fight on the side of the Dutch in the Thirty Years' War (1618–48). On their return to England they brought tales of this "Dutch Courage", and no doubt some bottles of it as well.

It's unclear whether gin was already being produced in England at this time. In fact, it's unclear what spirits were being produced there in the period that followed the dissolution of the monasteries. Certainly large houses would have had still-houses, but commercial production wasn't in place. If England

OPPOSITE:

FEED YOUR HEAD

wanted spirits, it imported them.

That isn't to say that there weren't keen distillers, although they still tended to be more embroiled in alchemical research than commercial production. John Doxat in *The Gin Book* quotes the example of The Worshipful Company of Distillers who in 1653, under the leadership of alchemist Sir Theodore de Mayerne-Turquet, issued a decree that all spirits should undergo rectification (i.e. a second distillation) to generate a purer end product. This enlightened quality control sadly lasted only until 1702.

In 1663 the famous diarist Samuel Pepys records taking "strong water made of juniper" as a medicine for his upset stomach, and gin might have remained no more than a medicine and a faddish drink – the equivalent of today's tourists bringing back bottles of retsina from their holidays in Greece – if the Dutch William of Orange had not been invited to become King. One of his first acts was to ban the import of French goods, among them brandies and wines. Scottish and Irish whiskies were little known outside their own borders and rum wasn't yet established. At that time brandy was the staple tipple of the English. What else was there to drink?

Opiate of the people

Why did gin become the English spirit? The art of distillation was known, there was a surplus of grain, but no one was forced to add juniper. Quite why gin emerged triumphant is more than likely due to a number of factors. With no

brandy to drink, people needed some spirit or other. Gin was being made anyway, it was also fashionable and the new king was Dutch. This combination of circumstances, fuelled by a certain new-found patriotism, made the English populace embrace the new-fangled "Hollands", or, as they eventually called it, "gin".

Certainly King Billy consumed his fair share; the Banqueting House at Hampton Court Palace became known as the gin temple.

To say that gin was an immediate success would be to make one of the greatest understatements of all time. Within a few years the major cities of England were awash with alcohol purporting to be gin, with the major ports of Bristol, Plymouth and, most importantly, London becoming distilling centres.

People living in the desperate slums of that time needed something to numb the reality of their situation, just as the soldiers needed a distraction from the horrors of the battlefield, and gin fitted the bill. The government didn't exactly stand in their way. In 1690, Parliament

decreed that all you needed to do to become a distiller was to display a notice of intent in a public place for 10 days, and four years later it also raised the tax on beer, making gin the cheapest option. With gin-making easy, by 1730 one-fifth of London's houses were "gin shops", and people were swilling back 11 million gallons a year.

These amateur distillers would have been making the spirit from anything they could get their hands on, although the constants were juniper, sugar and other flavourings. Juniper was particularly useful as its strong flavour would have hidden the "off" tastes in what would have been dangerously badly distilled spirits. Never mind; they worked, and they had the desired effect – oblivion.

It's difficult to conceive how heavy the drinking was. Gin was the drink of the huddled masses in their stinking slums, their fetid homes. It was the enemy of the upper classes, the opiate of the people. Gin was singled out as the root of all evil, while beer was an acceptable drink. Absinthe suffered in the same way at the turn of the nine-

PLYMOUTH RETAINS A TENUOUS LINK WITH GIN'S RELIGIOUS ORIGINS

GIN SOON BUILT UP AN UNWHOLESOME IMAGE IN ENGLAND

The GIN Shop.

teenth century, while in our own times marijuana is banned but tobacco is permitted. Some things never change...

By the 1730s the government had had enough, although it tried to get to grips with the problem in the most bizarre fashion: by decreeing that "intoxicating liquors" could only be sold in a dwelling house. The reaction was swift – and obvious. Every house became a gin shop. It wasn't until 1743, when legislation was introduced licensing distilleries, that the industry we know today began to take shape; being centred around a few reputable producers, among them Alexander Gordon, who started his Southwark distillery in 1769.

Consumption continued to rise, peaking at an astonishing 20 million gallons in 1750, before beginning to slide down to more reasonable levels as the double effect of licensed distilleries and high excise duties made cheap gin a thing of the past. Only people with sufficient capital and the ambition to succeed stuck with gin. The combined effect was an improvement in quality, and gin began to move very slowly up the social scale.

Gin, however, was far from the refined, rather bourgeois spirit it is today. It was still the drink of the poor, the desperate, the disenfranchised; the tipple of the mob, drunk in gilded and mirrored gin palaces. Not only was it a disreputable spirit, it probably didn't taste particularly great either. The most widely made style was still Old Tom, a juniper-laden drink flavoured with glycerine and sugar syrup.

Gin and gentility

How Old Tom got its name is a mystery – although it has brought various theories to light. John Doxat quotes two

GIN LANE.

tales: the cat in the vat (it fell in), and the more prosaic explanation that it was named in honour of Thomas Chamberlain, an early distiller. Stephen Bayley, in his book *Gin,* prefers the more lurid legend of one Dudley Bradstreet, gin distiller and all-round wide-boy, who had a wooden tomcat outside his gin shop. People put their money in the cat's mouth and their gin

trickled down its leg. You can still find Old Tom if you search hard enough, and allegedly it (or a version of it) is still made in Finland.

The first major shift in gin's fortunes happened when dry gin (the name meant "not sweet") was invented in the late eighteenth century – with Plymouth claiming to be the first distillery to produce a dry, crystal-clear gin.

HOGATH'S HELLISH VISION

115

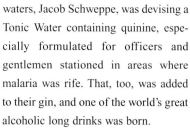

However, it was only when the continuous still was invented that gin began to take its first genteel steps toward respectability. As the quality of the spirit improved, so it no longer needed to be sweetened up, and this new dry style was a more sophisticated drink than Old Tom. This, Doxat argues, gave gin the leg-up it needed. Certainly, dry gin was a more acceptable style. It was lighter, drier and appealed to new drinkers. It was, to use a twentieth-century term, "trendy" – just like vodka became in the 1960s when it killed gin off. The Victorian middle classes could quite fairly say that they weren't drinking the same stuff as the working classes.

There was also the issue of peer pressure. The gin makers – men like Alexander Gordon, Charles Tanqueray, James Burrough and Sir Felix Booth were pillars of the community, men of substance. If the upper middle class were making it, perhaps it would be all right for the middle class to drink it as well; after all, it was miles away from the old "mother's ruin". It's an early example of the premium effect coming into play.

That's not to say it was all plain sailing. There remained some vestiges of snobbery; decanters of gin would carry neck-labels marked NIG, or White Wine. But the newly exotic, aspirational gin was becoming the drink not just of the emerging middle class; it was starting to be drunk by both sexes.

It was also embraced by the officers of the armed forces stationed in the far-flung reaches of the British Empire. Rum had been the drink of the Navy since 1687, but for some reason in the late nineteenth century, gin was embraced by the officer class. No one can be sure quite why; it may simply have been elitism – a way to differentiate themselves from the ratings. Whatever the case, gin became the wardroom's preferred tipple.

There was a practical reason as well, a distant echo of the monks of Salerno. Gin was a perfect medium in which to mix the Angostura Bitters which the Navy drank to prevent stomach problems – so that drink of retired admirals, the pink gin, was born. Equally, lime juice (taken as a preventative against scurvy) was mixed with gin, and the gimlet arrived. Meanwhile, a purveyor of soft drinks and mineral

waters, Jacob Schweppe, was devising a Tonic Water containing quinine, especially formulated for officers and gentlemen stationed in areas where malaria was rife. That, too, was added to their gin, and one of the world's great alcoholic long drinks was born.

The Navy also acted as representatives for the early brands, serving gin during the traditional drinks party on board the vessel when a ship first docked at a new port. It's no coincidence that the gin made in one of the major naval ports, Plymouth, could claim to be the most widely available gin brand in the world by the mid-nineteenth century, and was the naval officer's drink of choice.

In this way, by the turn of the century gin wasn't just acceptable, it was *de rigueur*. Cognac had temporarily disappeared thanks to *phylloxera*, and although blended Scotch whisky benefited most from this, gin wasn't that far behind it, and when the new American fashion of cocktails hit, it flourished. Gin had finally risen out of the gutter and on to a glittering stage. One of gin's greatest attributes is that its complex flavours are shown at their best when mixed. It's a classic cocktail base – after all, it's at the heart of the world's greatest cocktail, the Martini.

Gin remained the drink of fashionable London in the 1920s, and therefore became one of the main aspirational drinks in the United States of America during Prohibition. Despite the fact that bathtub gin (a concoction of industrial alcohol, juniper and glycerine that even an eighteenth-century Londoner would have thought twice about downing) was produced by bootleggers, gin managed to retain a sophisticated, almost decadent, image.

Gin came out of the restrictions

Tom & Jerry taking Blue Ruin after the Spell is broke up.

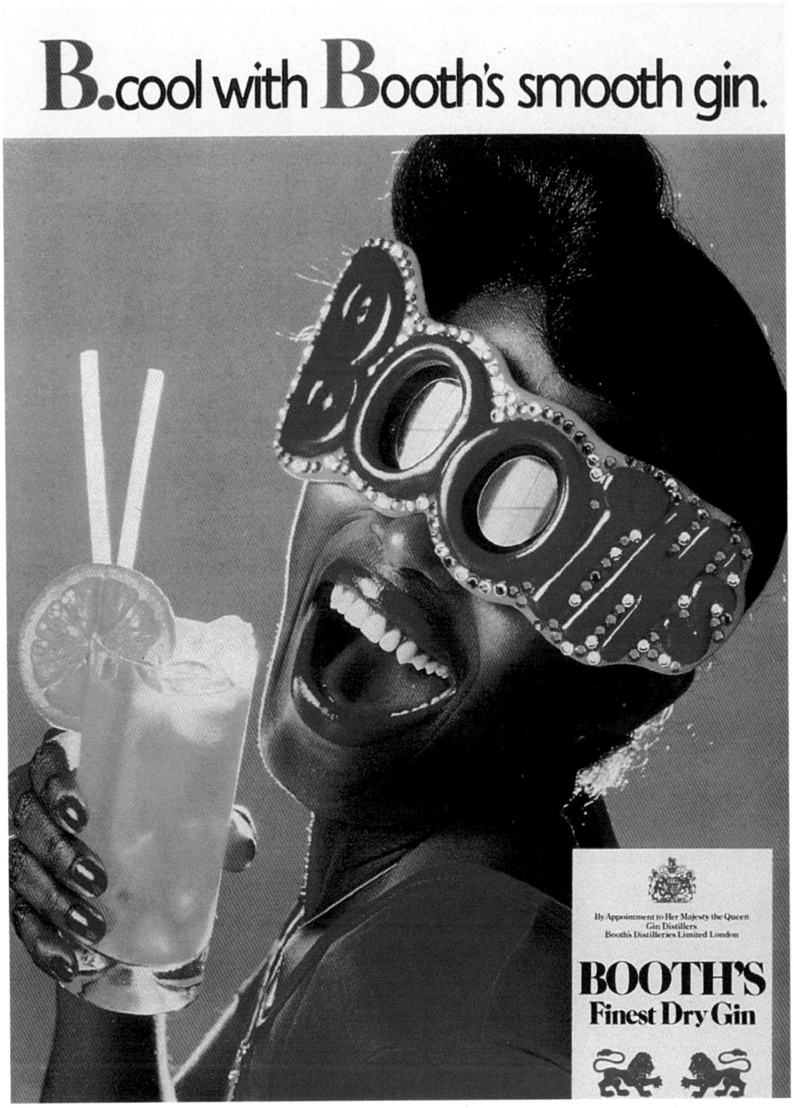
B.cool with Booth's smooth gin.
By Appointment to Her Majesty the Queen Gin Distillers Booth's Distilleries Limited London
BOOTH'S
Finest Dry Gin

THINGS LOOK DIFFERENT AFTER A GIN

imposed during the Second World War in a remarkably fit state. While whisky distilleries had been closed and little stock had been laid down, it was relatively easy for gin distillers to get up and running again. The boom continued through the 1950s, but gin was beginning to run out of steam, and by the 1970s it had become saddled with an old-fashioned image – the sort of drink consumed only by retired brigadiers. Vodka, which had started eating into gin's share of the US market in the 1940s, became the white spirit of choice in the UK as well.

The gin producers didn't know how to react. Just like blended whisky makers, they had assumed everything would remain rosy, that people would come to their senses and "mature" into gin. No chance. Cocktails were passé, gin and tonic was old hat (and badly served) and the firms searched in vain for a way to market themselves out of a crisis.

The return of flavour

In the United States of America, Michel Roux invented Bombay Sapphire, a new style of high-strength premium gin in stunning packaging. In the UK they went a slightly different way. Roux had already made his name with Absolut vodka, where he tapped into the new, design conscious drinkers and gave them a brand that not only tasted good, but looked good as well.

He felt that he could do the same with gin and took the rather tired Bombay brand, put it in a sapphire-blue bottle, emphasised the use of exotic botanicals and the delicacy of flavour and watched it take off. Sapphire was proof that not only could gin be made hip once more, but was evidence that drinkers were also beginning to think more seriously about their drinks.

In the UK they went a slightly different way. Someone at Gordon's realized that if they cut the strength from 40 per cent abv to 37.5 per cent abv, they would save money on excise duty which could be reinvested in promotion. You can understand the logic and, to be fair, Gordon's has remained the only British gin with a high profile during the recent slump in gin's fortunes. The trouble was that the cut in strength (which was followed by virtually every other brand with the exceptions of Tanqueray and Beefeater) had a direct effect on flavour. But more of that later.

Gin's crisis of confidence has been shared by all the "old" spirit categories as the youth market has turned to something that their parents didn't drink. But there's a glimmer on the horizon. Premium spirits are in vogue, as are cocktails. The most significant shift is in the new passion for flavour, and if the demand is for clean spirit with complex flavours, then what's better than gin? In recent years, just as with top-quality vodka, few people in the West have taken it seriously. Perhaps its time is due again.

How it's made

There are two main ways in which to make gin: redistilling a neutral spirit which has had natural flavouring ingredients (botanicals) added to it; or adding essences of the flavouring agents and stirring them into the spirit.

This latter method, known as cold compounding, has the advantage of being cheap, but the poor-quality gin it produces is not worth the money in the first place. Most (although not all) supermarket own-label gins are made by this technique. Avoid them. Stick with a gin that is labelled "Distilled Gin".

Needless to say, each distiller has its own slight variation on the gin-making process, which starts with the spirit itself. Neutral spirit is alcohol which has undergone rectification to bring it up to around 96 per cent abv, which is about as pure as you can go. That isn't to say that the spirit is neutral on the nose, or that it doesn't matter from which base the distillate was made. Most quality gin producers insist on (more expensive) grain spirit rather than cane (molasses), which can give a slight sweet note. Although distillers agree that the quality of cane spirit has improved, they still prefer to use the more delicate grain. Since the majority of the gin producers also own grain whisky plants, supply is not a problem, but even then the supply has to be constantly monitored to make sure that it remains consistent, not just in quality but in aroma.

For some reason though, no British gin distiller is allowed to produce its own neutral spirit on site, so it all has to be trucked in. This means that gin distilleries are strangely peaceful places to visit, even when they are distilling.

There are no clouds of steam from mash tuns, no bubbling fermenters; just the quiet hiss of steam heating the large pot stills and the steady flow of clear, new spirit into the sight glass – and the aroma. Gordon's has recently run an advertisement which shows a man being shot into a glass of gin and tonic (a nice idea, but probably a rather sticky experience). A gin distillery intensifies that image. The smell of juniper berries is all-pervading, then you notice other subtle smells which swirl around your head, just as the spirit vapour rises in the still, capturing the flavour compounds from the botanicals, stripping them, clutching and entwining them to itself.

The stills are copper pot stills, usually with high necks, which help extract only the higher, more fragrant alcohols – the stills at Glenmorangie, which produces a delicate malt whisky, are former gin stills. The gin still at Plymouth distillery, though, has a more unconventional shape, with a relatively short neck and an exaggerated curve on the lie pipe. This could account for Plymouth's characteristic richness of body – although that distillery also makes great play of the fact that it uses spring water which has run through granite and peat to first dilute the spirit in the still. Other distilleries have to clean their water before use. (The dilution, by the way, is necessary otherwise the still would be in danger of blowing up.)

Secret recipes

But what happens inside? This is where distilleries differ widely. All have a secret recipe of botanicals; how they put them in the still also varies. Some, such as Gordon's and Plymouth, put the botanicals in only a short time before the steam is turned on and redistillation starts. Beefeater, on the other hand, steeps them for 24 hours before distilling, while Bombay Sapphire uses a Carterhead still which contains a basket holding the botanicals. The vapour passes through the basket, stripping the flavours from the botanicals.

Of course, each distiller thinks that its approach is the correct one. Sapphire points to the delicate manner of the extraction, which gives a delicate gin (although, as we'll see, there are inherent problems with this technique). Beefeater feels that steeping gives a gentler extraction, but builds in complexity, as it fixes the aromas in the spirit before distillation, while

Plymouth counters that steeping can give harder flavours and allow certain ones to dominate.

A matter of aromatics

Distilling "fixes" the botanical flavours in the gin. But, as ever, distillation needs to be a careful process. For one thing, not all botanical aromas appear at the same time; they queue up in the still, waiting their turn to rise, mingle and be turned into flavoured spirit. After a quick foreshots run, the volatile citrus notes appear, then come juniper and coriander, then the roots such as orris, angelica and liquorice. That's not to say that one appears for a while, stops and then the next one starts; rather they blur into each other, each peaking at a different time. If you nose a distillation at regular intervals, you'll find the aromas changing continually, albeit subtly.

The speed at which the still is run is therefore of tremendous importance to the final quality of the gin. Run a still too hot and too fast, and all the botanical aromas will be pushed over at the same time, along with unwanted heavier alcohols from the end of the run. Equally, each distillery will stop collecting spirit at a slightly different strength. Although this is also a closely guarded secret, it would be fair to assume that the richest and heaviest gins, with greater evidence of rooty aromas, will have been allowed to run for longer than ones with more lifted, citric notes. Since Beefeater relies on having a light, citric aroma, it is likely to cut at a higher strength.

But, inevitably, it's not quite as simple as that. Each distiller has his own recipe, and each handles the botanicals in a slightly different way to attain a different effect. In Bombay Sapphire's case, this involves suspending the botanicals over the rising vapour. The gin makes great play of the sheer number of botanicals it uses – including oddities like cubeb berries and grains of paradise. The problem is that the technique seems to give *too* subtle an effect. The aromas don't appear to be fixed as firmly as they would if the botanicals had been placed directly into the still. Each nosing of Sapphire will

THE CALM ATMOSPHERE OF THE TANQUERAY & GORDON STILL HOUSE

give you a different aroma – perhaps that's a style you like, but at times it seems too ethereal. The aroma could also be the effect of the alcoholic strength of the gin. This may seem strange, but since different aromas come off the still at different times (i.e. at different strengths), so they are held in the gin at different points. There are bands of flavour compounds within the gin. When you reduce the gin, initially by water to get it to bottled strength and then with, say, a mixer like tonic, there's a series of little flavour explosions as these trigger points are hit. Citric notes, since they are the most volatile, are the first ones to be released.

When Gordon's made its decision to lower the strength in the UK from 40 per cent abv to 37.5 per cent, it saved money, but it also changed the aroma and flavour of the gin. The trigger point for the volatile citric aromas would appear to be around 40 per cent. Dilute to below that strength, and you'll kill them completely. The result is a flatter, more overtly junipery aroma and a flavour which doesn't carry all the way through on the palate. "There is clear correlation between alcoholic strength and the ability to hold botanicals," says Sean Harris, distiller at Plymouth Gin. "You can't hold light citrus flavours at low strength, which is why when you go below 40 per cent you lose them." If this just sounds like ungentlemanly criticism of a rival brand, remember he is talking from experience. Plymouth's previous owner reduced its strength – and quality and aroma suffered. It's worth trying out Gordon's at 37.5 per cent and comparing it to the same gin at "export strength" (which is how the rest of the world buys it). The fact that most UK gins followed the lead set by Gordon's meant that most gins in Britain suddenly lost flavour at the very time they were trying to attract new drinkers by saying that gin is full of flavour.

"Ultimately what you are doing in distilling is turning a science into an art," says Harris. "If that still was a nuclear submarine, it would be covered with dials telling us what to do. Distilling is knowing what to do intuitively and creating the spirit, not manufacturing it."

The use of BOTANICALS

The defining element in gin is the use of botanicals – with juniper as the main one. Without them you have a type of vodka. It may strike us as unusual that the early distillers would have used such exotic ingredients, but you have to remember that these early gin-makers were living and working in a society where the use of spices was the norm. According to Elizabeth David in her masterly *Spices, Salts and Aromatics in the English Kitchen*, Europe from the fifteenth century onward used "lavish" amounts of spices in its cooking – particularly in the great houses of the day. "In Europe, spices were the jewels and brocades of the kitchen and the still-room", she writes.

By the time that Dr Sylvius was making his first Genever, Holland was beginning to exert control over the Western world's spice trade. By the end of the seventeenth century it had a virtual monopoly of the business and, through the trade done by the all-powerful Dutch East India Company and its British equivalent, spices flooded into the two countries and flavoured drinks became a craze. This is another reason why gin became the preferred tipple of the English – it was tapping into an existing fashion. While the poor added herbs to their drinks, the rich explored the effects of different combinations of spices and aromatics in their alchemical researches. David singles out Sir Kenelm Digby, whose recipes for the then-popular honey-based drinks meath, metheglin and hydromel were published posthumously in 1669. One of them gives precise details on making a hydromel of crushed juniper.

Not only were spices coming into the country from distant lands, but others which seem unusual today were

being cultivated in England. Saffron was extensively grown in Suffolk and Cambridgeshire, while coriander – traditionally the second most heavily used gin botanical – was grown commercially in Southern England (and, in particular, Sussex).

In other words, Lucas Bols and the English alchemists/distillers who belonged to the Worshipful Company of Distillers would have had experience of using a vast range of flavouring agents in their spirits. Certainly, their gins would have borne little resemblance to today's London Dry (or Plymouth), although they do share similarities with some of the old-style gins produced in Holland and Belgium. Made in pot stills, these gins would have used juniper for two reasons: its aromas were preserved by the alcohol, but they also hid the off-notes in the alcohol. Better production meant that the botanical flavours were used as an attribute rather than as a masking agent, but it wasn't until the dry gins came off the continuous stills that the lighter citric flavours began to emerge.

Botanicals remain the single most important element in making gin, and each brand's recipe is known to only a few people. "You could use 120 different herbs, spices and aromatics", says Hugh Williams at Gordon's, "though most use no more than ten. Only 12 people know the Gordon's recipe and, even if you did know it, you couldn't replicate the gin."

All brands use juniper and coriander, but Gordon's also uses ginger, cassia oil and nutmeg; Beefeater uses bitter orange as well as angelica root and seed; Plymouth's seven botanicals include sweet (rather than bitter) orange and cardamom; while Sapphire uses cubeb berries, cassia bark and grains of

paradise. The aim is to produce a balanced, complex aroma – which doesn't necessarily mean the more botanicals, the more complex the smell. As any cook knows, flavours can end up cancelling each other out.

The combination of botanicals is also important. The roots not only give a dry, almost earthy, character but, according to Desmond Payne, distiller at Beefeater, angelica also helps to hold in the volatile orange and lemon aromas.

The distillers use some of the most exotic aromas in the world in their gins. Juniper, with its hints of heather, lavender and camphor, is from Italy and southern Germany; coriander seed, with its lemon balm notes, will come either from Eastern Europe – or, in Sapphire's case, where a peppery quality is wanted – Morocco. Musky, dry angelica comes from Saxony; orange peel comes from Spain; earthy orris root, with its hint of violet, from Italy; cinnamon and cassia bark from India; ginger from the Far East; nutmeg from Grenada; Javanese cubeb berries; and grains of paradise from West Africa.

It all starts with the juniper berries, which are hand-picked from October to March. Spice merchants either send distillers samples after the October harvest, or distillers will go to seek out

their supply. Then comes a long period of assessing the quality. Each vintage will give a slightly different crop and each merchant will also have slightly different berries. The quality-conscious distillers will extract the essential oil from each of the samples, put it in neutral alcohol and then nose all the samples – perhaps up to 200 – blind. Only then will they pick the supplier(s) they wish to use. A large concern like Gordon's will choose up to 20, Beefeater perhaps four or five; a smaller producer like Plymouth picks just one. Although all the berries will also be examined for oil content, that isn't the sole criterion. What the distiller is looking for is a berry that has the same character as their gin, and which will give consistency of style.

The same system is carried out with all the botanicals, and distillers will put together a blend of the ingredients to check if the style is consistent. The recipe remains the same in principle, but it may have to be tweaked given that each of the botanicals changes each year. The aroma isn't just from the botanicals themselves, but the relation between them.

At the end of the day, the botanicals supply the fingerprint for each brand. They are what ensures that every gin is different.

The brands

The start of gin's climb to respectabilty was partly down to improved production, but was also as a result of the efforts of the gentlemen distiller of London (and Plymouth) who elevated the spirit from one drunk in the slums to the preferred choice of the bourgeoisie. This is their story...

Gordon's

Alexander Gordon established his distillery in Southwark in 1769, although it moved premises to Clerkenwell in 1786. By the end of the nineteenth century Gordon's gin was widely exported, and was one of the gins "distributed" by the Navy. The firm recalls the tale that one of the first export orders came from Australian miners who sent payment, in advance, in gold dust. By that time it had merged with Tanqueray, and both firms came under the wing of DCL (now UDU) in 1922. Throughout Prohibition Gordon's planned how to attack the US market when it re-opened, and almost as soon as Repeal arrived it established two distilleries in the United States of America, stealing a march on its rivals and helping to make it still the best-selling gin in the world. Controversially, it cut its strength in the UK which freed up money for promotion but, as repeated blind tastings show, this damaged its quality. In its favour, though, the money has been used to build not only the brand, but also gin as a category

Beefeater

James Burrough was a pharmacist who started distilling gin in Chelsea in 1863, on the back of gin's rise to respectability. His sons had to shift production to a new distillery in Vauxhall in 1908, and then moved to the current site in 1958. The fact that the distillery is only a well-struck "six" away from the Oval

BEEFEATER: THE ONLY GIN STILL DISTILLED IN LONDON

cricket ground means that two (in recent times, rather shaky) pillars of English identity now sit cheek by jowl.

Long one of the most active gins on the export markets – particularly in North America – it became part of Whitbread's brief (and disastrous) foray into spirits in the late 1980s, before being bought by Allied Distillers in 1991. Recently, a new high-strength (50 per cent abv) brand, Crown Jewel, has been launched in the duty-free market. This, though true to the Beefeater citric style, is an elegant refined gin which carries its high alcohol content lightly. Beefeater remains the only gin distilled

in London – and one of the few British gins to stick at 40 per cent abv.

Tanqueray

The Tanqueray family were French in origin, arriving in England at the beginning of the eighteenth century. Although the family were originally silversmiths, they turned to the Church, with three successive Tanquerays becoming rector of Tingrith, Bedfordshire. Alcohol entered the equation only in 1828 when Charles Tanqueray followed the successful examples of Felix Booth and Alexander Gordon and built his distillery in Finsbury – a part of London noted in those days for its spa water. Tanqueray

TANQUERAY: THE PREMIUM GIN PAR EXCELLENCE

has always been a premium style; even in its early days it attracted a small, prestigious clientele, and was exporting to the rich sugar planters in Jamaica by the middle of the nineteenth century.

It joined forces with Gordon's in 1898 and the two firms split the world between them, with Tanqueray taking the road to America and the Far East. It is still the most widely distributed strong gin and the first to be recognized – not because of its strength, but its complex, rich flavour – as a premium brand. Badly affected after Prohibition (when DCL pushed Gordon's at the expense of its premium sister brand), it only re-established itself on the US market in the 1950s in its now-familiar

round bottle – modelled on the fire hydrants which pumped water to the original distillery. Recently it introduced a new brand, Tanqueray Malacca, a triple-distilled 40 per cent abv gin with a different botanical recipe.

Booth's

One of the oldest gin families was started by Philip Booth, who opened his distillery in 1740 in Clerkenwell, another water-rich area. By the end of the century control had passed to Philip's son, (Sir) Felix, who became the biggest gin distiller in Britain. At one point the distillery was threatened by the anti-Catholic rioters and the workers had to be armed with muskets.

Sir Felix eventually became the best-known distiller on the planet, thanks to his financing of Captain John Ross's 1829 expedition to find the North West Passage (Ross's crew, incidentally, were supplied with Booth's old muskets). It didn't find the elusive way through but did discover the magnetic North Pole, and the grateful Captain Ross named the Boothia Peninsula, Felix Harbour, Cape Felix and the Gulf of Boothia after his gin-making patron. As Stephen Bayley points out in his book *Gin*: "It's quaintly touching that one of the largest pieces of ice on the

planet should be named after one of the most distinguished gin distillers."

Booth's is famous for its "High & Dry" and "Dry" brands, the latter being a straw-coloured gin thanks to a period of maturation in oak casks. This was the

ABOVE: *BEEFEATER REVEALS A CITRIC CHARACTER*

LEFT: *BOOTH'S, UNUSUALLY FOR A BRITISH GIN, IS MATURED IN WOOD*

Tasting Notes

Beefeater *(40 per cent)*: Soft, fine, attractive nose; lime peel and orange notes dominant, with a delicate heathery/lavender juniper edge. Positive, with good weight on the palate and a mouth-watering zestiness.

Beefeater Crown Jewel *(50 per cent)*: Pleasant, not obviously alcoholic. Quite delicate and citric. When compared with Beefeater, the juniper is less in evidence and

lighter, delicate notes predominate.

Bombay Sapphire *(40 per cent)*: Delicate, exotic aromas which fade rather too quickly. Similar on the palate – delicate, with some juicy spiciness, but almost too fragile.

Gilbey's *(37.5 per cent)*: Light, dry and attractive, but slightly neutral.

Gordon's *(37.5 per cent)*: Rather flat and rooty/earthy, with a hint of sage and plenty of juniper.

Lacking in subtlety.

Gordon's *(40 per cent)*: Full juniper aromas with some orange notes and earthy hints. Clean, lifted and juicily rich.

Plymouth *(40 per cent)*: Intense, fragrant with angelica/juniper heatheriness surrounded by citrus blossom. A wonderful combination of smooth, rich texture with complex, delicate flavours

and a great sagey kick on the end.

Tanqueray *(47 per cent)*: Ripe, rich and pungent with plenty of coriander and juniper aromas coming across. Soft and rich on the palate with a firm, dry finish.

Plym gin's in!

the gin aristocracy. In 1857, after serving in the Crimean War, they set themselves up as fine wine merchants, specializing in wines "from the Colonies" in premises situated in Berwick Street, Soho. Soon they had 20,000 customers on their books – allowing them to move to a rather more salubrious site in Oxford Street in 1867.

By 1872, just as gin was becoming the drink to be seen with, they had built their own distillery in Camden and had begun to produce their London Dry Gin. By the 1920s, there were distilleries producing gin to the Gilbey's recipe in Australia and Canada. This latter distillery helped Gilbey's establish a foothold in the United States of America during Prohibition (during that period it was packaged in frosted bottles to avoid imitations). These days it claims to be the second-largest-selling gin in the world, with its biggest sales in the United States of America and the Philippines, although in the UK it has become a member of the 37.5 per cent gang. A premium brand, Antique, has recently been launched.

Plymouth

The Plymouth distillery was originally built as a monastery (although there are no records of distilling) and then was used as a meeting house; it was where the Pilgrim Fathers spent their last night in England before heading for the New World. In 1793 it was bought by the Coates family, and can therefore claim to be the oldest continually used gin distillery in England. Once the most widely distributed gin in the world, it can also

lay claim to be the gin recommended in the first recorded recipe for a dry Martini (published in Stewart's *Fancy Drinks and How To Mix Them*, 1896).

It was badly hit in the aftermath of the Second World War. A combination of poor-quality spirit lowered demand, then it changed ownership, first to Schenley, then to Whitbread (the British brewer) and then to Allied Distillers. The quality of spirit was downgraded, the strength was cut, the label cheapened. Now, thankfully, it's back in private hands and is growing. Back to its original strength, it is one of the world's great gin brands.

Bombay

Bombay Dry gin first appeared on the US market in the late 1950s, when Alan Subin saw an opportunity for a new premium gin aimed at competing with Tanqueray and Beefeater. He contacted the English distiller Greenalls and, after choosing a recipe dating from 1761, launched the brand in the United States of America. Bombay was handled by Carillon Importers and later went to IDV (Grand Metropolitan). In 1987, Michel Roux, the president of Carillon – and the man who broke Absolut on the US market – saw the potential for a new brand as a way of invigorating the depressed US market, and Bombay Sapphire was born. A triumph of striking packaging and excellent marketing (which makes great play on the use of a large number of botanicals and redistillation in a Carterhead still) has guaranteed it a place as one of the iconic brands of the late twentieth century.

result not of a cunning marketing ploy but, if legend is to be believed, an accident. At one point during last century there was a glut of Booth's, and it was laid for a short while in ex-sherry butts. The firm still has a cooperage, and its apprentice coopers still have to obey the rules laid down in the fourteenth century that they must not "contact matrimony" or "commit fornication" during their apprenticeship. Booth's, too, was cut in strength in the 1980s, to the detriment of its flavour.

Gilbey

Although their grandfather had been a publican, the brothers Gilbey, Walter and Alfred, were relative latecomers to

Dutch GIN

The original distillers in Holland had a ready market for their *genever*. While Sylvius produced *genever* purely for medicinal purposes, it wasn't long before the popularity of the spirit spread out to the local populace. Lucas Bols had a distillery up and running by 1575, only three years after Sylvius's alleged "discovery". Wenneker started in 1693, while de Kuyper was established in Rotterdam (Holland's spice capital) in 1675. By that time, Diderot had described the Dutch as "living alembics, distilling themselves". Right enough, spirits and the Dutch go hand in hand, and they are behind the growth of a host of the world's great spirits. As a mercantile nation the Dutch needed spirits to preserve wines so they could survive long sea voyages, and they had already helped to establish Cognac and Jerez as centres of brandy production. Spices were also being brought back from the East and West Indies, brandy was flooding in from France (most notably, Cognac) and Spain. But while brandy was popular, *genever* remained Holland's own drink, one of the great Northern European spirits from the grain belt.

One reason for its popularity was the fact that the Dutch excise department turned a blind eye to domestically produced spirits. So, while brandy was taxed, *genever* got off scot-free. Farmers began to produce their own *genevers* from excess grain and the market exploded. Every house would have had a jar (or stone crock bottle) of *genever* – and, as Gordon Brown recounts in his *Classic Spirits of the World*, distillers

had to employ jar sniffers to ensure that when people brought back the empty jars for refilling, they hadn't been using them for, well, other fluids.

While crock bottles continue to be used today, there's no need for jar sniffers and *genever* remains Holland's national spirit, retaining a central place in the Dutch drinking ritual, which it has singularly failed to do in the rest of the world. The reason is difficult to nail down, but one possible angle is *genever's* symbiotic relationship with the other main Dutch tipple: beer. That said, in recent years *genever* has become unfashionable with younger drinkers, prompting innovative firms like Bokma to introduce new, lighter styles. This has increased an already vast number of brands and styles from a host of large and small producers.

How it's made

There are three categories of *genever*: *Oude*, the old, straw-coloured, pun-

gently sweet style; *Jonge*, a newer style which appeared with the arrival of the continuous still, which is cleaner and more delicate; and *Korenwijn* (in Bols' case *Corenwyn*), which is a cask-aged product with a high percentage of malted spirit.

As ever, each distiller will have its own method of producing *genever* and, in general, *genever* differs from London Dry gin by being based on a heavier spirit. Traditionally this has been made from *moutwijn* (malt wine) which is a low-strength spirit made from a mash of wheat, rye and malted barley distilled in pot stills, but this will vary between distillers. The Schiedam-based firm Floryn, for example, uses pot still grain which gives a slightly lighter spirit, although one which is still more aromatic than the neutral grain spirit used by the majority of British gin distillers; while Hooghoudt produces a fine double-distilled pot-still *genever*. A distiller like Bokma, meanwhile, produces its top aged brand Vij Jahren (five years) in three component parts – a *moutwijn*, grain spirit and a botanical flavoured spirit – which are aged separately for the prescribed length of time before being blended. Its Volmout brand is a richer style, with a high *moutwijn* content.

It is often stated (wrongly) that *genever* uses only juniper. Other botanicals are used, but it's the way in which the Dutch distillers

CENTRE: SCHIEDAM REMAINS A CENTRE OF GENEVER PRODUCTION

MANY GENEVERS ARE STILL PACKAGED IN STONE CROCK BOTTLES

*A MODERN-STYLE
GENEVER PALACE IN
HOLLAND*

*GENEVER COMES IN MANY
DIFFERENT STYLES*

handle their flavouring ingredients which helps give *genever* its distinctive style. Bols, for example, passes the vapour in a fourth distillation over the juniper berries for its *Corenwyn*. Since triple distillation is common, juniper is normally introduced in the second distillation, with the other botanicals being added to the third (or sometimes fourth) distillation, although again this will vary between distilleries. In Schiedam, UTO's Notaris brand is first distilled, then part of it is redistilled with juniper, while a third blending component will be distilled with the other botanicals.

Newer-style brands include Bokma's Royal Dark – grain spirit aged in Limousin oak – while there are also some lower-strength flavoured *genevers* like Hooghoudt's blackcurrant, or Coebergh's *Bessenjenever* – the equivalent of a German or Austrian fruit schnapps, or an English sloe or damson gin.

The end result of combining a richer spirit and a higher percentage of juniper is a spirit which is more powerfully textured than London gin. Compare them by all means, but don't use "London" criteria to judge *genever*; just sit back with an ice-cold glass and sip contentedly.

Tasting Notes

Bols Corenwyn *(40 per cent):* Light gold in colour. Very rich and malty on the nose, with deep juniper aromas mixed with red fruits and almond.

de Kuyper Genever *(40 per cent):* Rich and malty with oily juniper undercurrent. Rich in texture, clean nutty finish.

Bokma Royal Dark *(40 per cent):* More delicate than most genevers, gently junipery with a subtle smooth character.

Bokma Volmout *(40 per cent):* Highly malted but with a crisp attack.

Bokma Vijf Jaren *(40 per cent):* Rich elegant with juniper oil well in evidence. Full unctuous feel and restrained wood.

Rest of the WORLD

PRODUCING BANANA GIN IN UGANDA

The *jenevers* (sic) from Belgium are as close as you'll get to the original gin – after all, it started in Flanders. Today there are around 20 small producers, many of them still farmhouse-style distillers like Filliers, which uses rye and malted barley for its base spirit. Production, however, is a mix between England and Holland, with a Coffey still used to produce the initial spirit, which is then redistilled once in a pot still with the botanicals and then given extended ageing (up to eight years). The closest you'll get to the original gin is Hoorbeke, which still makes a *jenever* which is distilled from juniper.

Gin is a hugely important spirit in Spain – volume-wise this isn't surprising. Anyone who has sat down and asked for a gin and tonic in a Spanish bar will confirm that the barman pours what seems to be a third of a bottle into the glass and, if there's any room, tops it up with tonic. The main brand is Larios which, despite the fact that it hails from Malaga, insists on calling itself a London Dry Gin, while its label pays homage to Gordon's. All of this rather takes away from the fact that Larios is a delicious, aromatic, off-dry gin.

If high strength is your bag, look out for the Lithuanian brand Nemunas which is 60 per cent abv and uses juniper, lime blossom, hops and honey as its flavouring agents. No matter where you are in the world, though, you'll find a spirit purporting to be gin. One friend brought me back a bottle of Filipino gin which didn't taste hugely junipery, but made a decent *caipirinha* (*see* pages 109 and 210). Then there are African gins, sometimes called banana gins, in which juniper is unknown. In Western Africa, these spirits are more often poured away as a sign of respect (and to drive away bad spirits).

Even today a Dutch brand, Steinhager, still sells massive amounts in Western Africa (*see* section on Schnapps – page 179) where it is used predominantly for ritual purposes. Gin is one of these categories you just know you'll never get to the end of. Scanning a feature on the war in Sudan, I read that someone had appeared "waving a bottle of Ethiopian gin". And so the search goes on.

How to make
A GIN AND TONIC

It would be wrong to leave gin without mentioning the gin and tonic. It may have recently taken on a rather staid image, but that's more to do with the utter inability of the vast majority of bartenders in the UK to make such a simple, but utterly refreshing drink. Gordon's, thankfully, is trying to redress the balance, but here's a small contribution to give its efforts a bit of extra shove. Incidentally, if you are ever stuck for something to drink with Thai food – or even mild- to medium-spiced curries – try a G&T!

COCKTAIL RECIPE

1

FIRST FILL A TALL (PREFERABLY CHILLED) GLASS TWO-THIRDS FULL WITH CLEAN ICE.
USE SPRING OR MINERAL WATER FOR THE ICE.
CUBES THAT HAVE BEEN MADE FROM CHLORINATED WATER WILL RENDER THE G&T UNDRINKABLE.
SQUEEZE SOME LIME ON THE ICE AND STIR.

2

CHOOSE YOUR GIN. GO FOR A BRAND THAT'S OVER 40 PER CENT ABV.
I PREFER BEEFEATER, PLYMOUTH, CROWN JEWEL OR BOMBAY SAPPHIRE.
POUR IN A GENEROUS SLUG.

3

TOP UP WITH FRESH, GOOD-QUALITY, BOTTLED TONIC WATER
(USUALLY TWICE AS MUCH TONIC AS GIN).
ONLY USE ONE-LITRE BOTTLES IF YOU INTEND
TO EMPTY THE BOTTLE ALMOST IMMEDIATELY.

4

ADD A WEDGE OF LIME AND STIR. YOU CAN ALSO
PASS THE LIME AROUND THE RIM OF THE GLASS.

Enjoy!

The Singapore SLING

Classic Cocktail

Barmen are naturally inquisitive people, always playing around with ingredients, seeing just what happens when another ingredient is added to a classic cocktail base. It was therefore inevitable that one of the oldest "simple" cocktails, the Gin Sling, would serve as the base for a whole range of outlandish experiments.

The Gin Sling itself is Tom Collins travelling under disguise and takes its name from the German *schlingen* (to swallow). So normal was this refreshing speciality of the English summer that no less a person than Mrs Beeton includes a recipe for one. It's the Victorian equivalent of Delia Smith telling you how to make a Martini.

Slings evolved into the Collins family (*see* Cocktails), but the name lives on in the Singapore Sling, which was allegedly created in 1915 by Ngiam Tong Boon, the bartender of that enduring symbol of British colonialism, Singapore's Raffles Hotel. Some gin experts (among them the doyen of gin writers John Doxat) disagree, claiming it dates from earlier. Certainly records show that there was a drink called a Straits Sling in existence before the Raffles recipe, which was another variant on the sling theme with Benedictine as a flavouring, but what we now know as the Singapore Sling does appear to have its origins in the Raffles' bar.

You can find some recipes for so-called Singapore Slings which still include Benedictine, just as you'll find some suggesting that you can replace the original lime juice with other, softer and sweeter, fruit juices. I even found one which fused (or froze) the classic Singapore Sling ingredients, (replacing Heering with kirsch) and added splashes of Benedictine and Cognac, plus maraschino cherries and their juice, then whizzed it all together with ice in a blender and topped it off with chilled ruby port. Try variants like this by all means – part of the fun of making cocktails is improvisation – but don't call the end result a Singapore Sling, call it a Phuket or Ko Samui Sling instead!

BARTENDER'S TIPS
There are seemingly infinite variations on this theme – start here and improvise your own take on this colonial classic.

THE SINGAPORE SLING

2 OZ BEEFEATER GIN

·

2 OZ FRESH LIME JUICE

·

2 TSP SUGAR

·

DASH OF ANGOSTURA BITTERS

·

POUR ON TO CRUSHED ICE IN A COLLINS GLASS. STIR.

·

TOP WITH SODA AND ADD 1/2 OZ COINTREAU AND 1/2 OZ PETER HEERING (REPLACE COINTREAU WITH BENEDICTINE FOR A STRAITS SLING).

Dry
M A R T I N I
Classic Cocktail

DRY MARTINI

3 OZ GIN

I TSP NOILLY PRAT

LEMON TWIST

PLACE VERMOUTH IN SHAKER WITH ICE. SHAKE AND STRAIN. ADD GIN. STIR AND STRAIN INTO PRE-CHILLED COCKTAIL GLASSES. ADD LEMON TWIST. YOU CAN VARY THE AMOUNT OF VERMOUTH TO TASTE, BUT THE PRINCIPLE REMAINS THE SAME.

Gin is the original cocktail spirit, and has provided the world with its most famous and most personal example of the barman's art – the Dry Martini. Arguments rage about every aspect of this most famous of all cocktails – even its birth is a matter of debate – although most serious students of the subject agree (more or less) that it first appeared in the bar of the Knickerbocker Hotel in New York in 1911, where head barman, Martini di Arma di Taggia, mixed a cocktail of half-and-half London gin, Noilly Prat vermouth and orange bitters.

Now, ingredient-wise this is, to all intents and purposes, a gin and French. Martini's twist on the recipe was that he stirred the ingredients with lots of ice and then strained them into a chilled glass. The olive, it is said, was an addition by Knickerbocker regulars. What is certain is that the cocktail swept all before it.

The confusion arises because there was already a sweet Martinez cocktail on the market, consisting of Old Tom gin, red vermouth, maraschino and orange bitters. Indeed, one of the first bottled pre-mixes was a Martinez made along these lines by the US drinks firm Heublein in 1892. Legend has it that this was a Californian product named after a hung-over travelling salesman who asked for a pick-me-up so he could make the journey from San Francisco to Martinez.

Although vermouth is an integral part of the cocktail, there is in fact no connection with Martini & Rossi – the firm wasn't even making vermouth when di Taggia made his great invention. Ironically, though, Martini & Rossi went on to buy Noilly Prat, the firm that produces the best vermouth for a Dry Martini.

GIN IS THE ORIGINAL COCKTAIL SPIRIT, AND HAS PROVIDED THE WORLD WITH ITS MOST FAMOUS AND MOST PERSONAL EXAMPLE OF THE BARTENDER'S ART – THE DRY MARTINI

Though the recipe is apparently simple, the Dry Martini is infuriatingly complex. Every Dry Martini lover has his or her own spin on it – every element is open to contention.

Luis Bunuel described the process of adding vermouth to the gin as being similar to the Immaculate Conception, as all that should happen was that a ray of sunlight should shine through the bottle of Noilly Prat before hitting the gin. Unbelievers would call that neat gin, but true aficionados would agree that it is in fact a Dry Martini.

Never has a cocktail had such a catalogue of obsessives – all of whom are on a personal search for some Holy Grail. These days that means as dry as you can get, although the fact is that, as it has aged, so the Martini has become drier. It started life as an equal mix between gin and vermouth; these days the ration is liable to be anywhere from 4:1 to 25:1.

The aim is to get a drink that has the illusion of purity, but which has complexity. It defines cocktails, yet it is barely a cocktail at all. There's little more than one spirit and an infinitesimal amount of flavouring, so why is mixing one so difficult? Because simplicity is the most difficult thing to achieve. Atomizer sprays, vermouth-flavoured ice cubes, vermouth-soaked olives – have been used to try and achieve that moment of satori when perfection is reached.

All the ingredients must be chilled – from glasses to gin. Only use the best-quality gin – that means Tanqueray, Beefeater, Crown Jewel or Plymouth. Be single-minded. Afterall, you are the only person who can make the perfect example.

These days the Martini is becoming the centre of a new cult as barmen find new twists on the old theme (*see* Cocktails for recipes). Some are post-modern classics, others are a mess. What is certain is that the Dry Martini will never die.

VERMOUTH

*F*or thousands of years, people have been flavouring wines and spirits with herbs and roots. It's the basis for many liqueurs, while aromatized fortified wines like Suze, with its flavour of gentian, or Dubonnet and St Raphael, with their high percentages of quinine, are still with us. However, vermouth continues to be the best-known of the breed.

It takes its name from the German for its main flavouring compound wormwood (wermut). The Latin name for this plant is artemisia absinthium, meaning that vermouth is a second cousin to Absinthe, the difference is that vermouth uses the flowers, while absinthe uses a distillate of the leaves.

There are three broad types of vermouth: Southern French (typified by Noilly Prat), Savoie (Chambery) and Italian (Martini & Rossi, Cinzano). Southern French vermouths (the best for the Dry Martini) are the most complex, being made from dry white wine that is lightly fortified with brandy and then left outdoors in open casks for two summers and two winters to "weather". After this, some casks are fortified to 50 per cent ABV, herbs are added and left to macerate. The remaining casks are flavoured with mistelle (wine prevented from fermenting by fortification). The final product (about 18 per cent ABV) is a blend of the two.

Savoie vermouths are more delicate, having not been weathered, while the Italian examples are made from spirit, infused with herbs, which is then blended with wine.

7 Vodka

VODKA HAS ENJOYED A RICH AND VARIED LIFE. IT'S BEEN DRUNK JUST ABOUT EVERYWHERE FROM THE GREAT HOUSES AND PALACES OF POLAND AND RUSSIA TO SHAMAN'S ALTARS IN SIBERIA, NOT TO MENTION EVERY BAR IN THE WESTERN WORLD. YET HOW MUCH DO WE KNOW ACTUALLY KNOW ABOUT THIS SPIRIT? VODKA MAY PLAY A PART IN THE DAILY RITUAL IN EASTERN EUROPE, BUT FEW IN THE WEST GIVE IT A SECOND THOUGHT.

VODKA HAS BEEN A PART OF FEASTING FOR CENTURIES

Vodka, you would think, is vodka. It has made its name by being the perfect partner for any mixer – flavourless, but with an alcoholic kick, undemanding and malleable. It's ideally suited to a lifestyle where easy choices are the norm, where you don't have to try too hard. Why grapple with the intricacies of Proust when you can be "entertained" by Jeffrey Archer? Vodka's been a bit like that.

But look again … things are changing. A few years ago, if you walked into a bar and wanted a vodka it would be poured out of the well; if you were lucky, you might have got Smirnoff Blue. Then Absolut arrived and the world was never quite the same again; it made vodka became hip, rather than just popular. It fitted the 1980s like a glove. It was clean, pristine, designed, the drinks world's equivalent of a Donna Karan suit.

But, despite the fact that Absolut has been superbly marketed (and is a fine vodka), its success was underpinned by the same principle that had taken vodka from foreign oddity to one of the world's most popular spirits –

namely, vodka tasted of, well, nothing. People were, and still are, being asked to pay large amounts of money for something that apparently claims to be flavourless. It's this paradox that lies at vodka's cool heart.

When you look at the subject, however, you find that true vodka is anything but tasteless; it has verve and subtlety. The best of the premium

vodkas make you look differently at spirits – their only equivalent is, perhaps, the new wave of grappas that are coming out of Italy. To get to grips with quality vodka requires you to open your mind to whispers of aroma, nuances of flavour. But this is miles from the image that most people have of this spirit. Only by looking at vodka's convoluted history are you able to get to grips with how this refined spirit has acquired this rather schizoid image.

Bill Samuels of Maker's Mark is fond of saying that bourbon died when Smirnoff started to be distilled in America and, to understand how vodka became the great mixable spirit, it's Smirnoff's story that you have to follow. What the brand did, brilliantly, was to take a drink redolent with negative imagery – hard drinking, strange ritual and, remember this is during the Cold War, – and make a household brand. Smirnoff's early US advertising claimed it was "the drink that leaves you breathless", and it certainly did that in the way that it quickly scaled the heights of the US market.

OPPOSITE: THE BRAND THAT BROKE AMERICA

Andy Warhol

ABSOLUT
Country of Sweden
VODKA®
This superb vodka

ABSOLUT WARHOL.

FOR GIFT DELIVERY ANYWHERE CALL 1-800-CHEER-UP (EXCEPT WHERE PROHIBITED BY LAW)
80 AND 100 PROOF/100% GRAIN NEUTRAL SPIRITS (ABSOLUT COUNTRY OF SWEDEN) © 1985 CARILLON IMPORTERS LTD., TEANECK, NJ.

Pierre Smirnoff & Fils, and started distilling in America in March 1934. It wasn't the runaway success he had hoped for. Vodka had been drunk during Prohibition, but it was one of many spirits which emerged from that period with a battered reputation – not surprisingly, since the bulk of the "vodka" that would have been sold was made in bathtubs in the back streets of Chicago and New York.

In fact in 1937, Kunett, close to bankruptcy, sold the Smirnoff licence to John Martin, president of Heublein, who nearly lost his job as a result. That's how poor an image vodka had. Heublein had to wait until after the Second World War for its troublesome new charge to prove its worth. Allied to some clever marketing, vodka became the spirit that the post-war market wanted. It mixed happily, it was light, it was undemanding. It was so versatile that barmen could create a huge number of new recipes for cocktails, but it was one of the first spirits that allowed you to make cocktails at home – add ginger beer and you had a Moscow Mule, a screwdriver was Smirnoff and orange juice. No matter what you threw at vodka, it accepted it quite happily. It even made Martinis!

Vodka was sophisticated, easy, fun – and it didn't make your breath smell. Within a brief time it had evolved into a different drink from the one which is still consumed in Eastern Europe.

Smirnoff began distilling in the UK, Canada, Australia, New Zealand and across America. Other vodkas followed in its wake – brands that were bland, neutral alcoholic bases for soft drinks and mixers.

By 1975, in terms of sales, vodka had become America's most popular spirit, and Smirnoff and Bacardi began

THE IMPECCABLE STYLE
OF ABSOLUT

Vladimir Smirnov (sic) had been fled his homeland after the Russian Revolution, and then tried to establish Smirnov distilleries in Constantinople, Lvov and Paris (*see* below). However, by the time he got to Paris, like so many other Russian emigrants, he was broke. Enter Rudolph Kukhesh, an ex-supplier of alcohol to

the Smirnovs who had moved to the USA, changed his name to Kunett and started working for Helena Rubenstein's cosmetics company. In Paris on business, he met Smirnov who, by now was down on his luck, gave him the rights and licence to sell the Smirnov portfolio in North America. Kunett changed the firm's name to

slugging it out as the world's biggest spirit brand. The triumph of the neutral white spirit was complete. Russia's "little water" (vodka's original meaning) had grown up.

But while Bacardi had become a category in itself (*see* Rum) Smirnoff, though a massive brand, couldn't do the same. Vodka was the winner, but rather than being tied to one particular brand remained rather anonymous. You may have got a Smirnoff in a bar, but you wouldn't have asked for it by name.

This the situation existed until Absolut swung into town with a marketing campaign that others have tried desperately to imitate but will never replicate. Absolut was right for its time. It tied itself to cutting-edge fashion and modern art. It was irreverent, weird, wacky, but it was never cheap. Rather, it was elitist and utterly, utterly hip. Absolut, thanks to its success in educating barmen and wooing design-conscious consumers, began to be asked for by name. The way was now open for people to look at vodka in a different light.

Absolut managed to bridge a gap that Finlandia and Stolichnaya had already been working on – though without much success. It was a vodka that could be used for cocktails (and push the price of the cocktail up), but it was also promoted to be drunk as a shooter – which was something that no one would ever have thought of doing with Smirnoff. New opportunities suddenly appeared for vodka.

Then, the Iron Curtain fell. Now, finally, there was a chance for Stolichnaya, Moskovskaya, Polish vodkas and the classic flavoured styles, which had been made for centuries, to make their mark in the world.

The simple reason that these vodkas are now the driving force in the market is that "premium" equates with "imported" – whether that is Polish, Russian, Finnish, Swedish or Danish. By hailing from a vodka-producing country, these brands appeal to the new consumer who wants to drink spirits that are somehow "authentic".

In the USA, this new image has now been widened to include domestic brands, which have cunningly put a different spin on the taste of nothing by emphasizing production and quality. These days you'll find pot-still vodka

from Texas, organic vodka from Kentucky, vodka from glacier water from the Tetons. So successful has this shift upmarket been that, to grab a slice of this lucrative sector, Smirnoff has gone back to Moscow and started to produce a vodka from pot stills.

These new premiums are drunk neat or contribute to the revival of the Martini (though being a bluff old traditionalist, I still believe a Martini is made from gin – no other spirit will do).

Just as with any quality spirit, the vodka drinker wants authenticity – although that term is a highly personal one. It means that "real" vodka has finally got the chance to show its true colours. But what is "real" vodka?

EVERYTHING ABOUT JAMES BOND EXUDES SOPHISTICATED CHIC INCLUDING HIS FAVOURITE DRINK

THE CHANGING FACE OF VODKA

The right stuff

It's impossible to wrap up vodka's history in one neat bundle because it has evolved differently in each of the countries where it is the national spirit. Vodka may be regarded as a commodity by the West, but in Poland, Russia and Scandinavia it is a very different beast.

POLISH *Vodka*

Trying to get to the bottom of Polish vodka alone is a Herculean task – with an estimated 1,000 brands available, it's a mission that would take a lifetime. Poland is the best place to start when looking at vodka's history. It may not please Russians or Swedes, but there is convincing evidence that the secret of distilling (wine initially) filtered into Poland from the West and spread from there into Russia and the Baltic States.

Peasants in the eighth century were making a crude alcoholic spirit by freezing wine, though the first written record of a spirit made from grain comes in 1405 – predating Russia. Precisely how distillation arrived in Poland is a matter of conjecture, but it is likely that the secret was brought to Poland by Italian monks (although some suggest they could have been Irish) who were, by then, well versed in the arcane subject of transforming a base material into another, far more potent, one.

As in every other country, these early spirits were initially used as med-

icines. In 1534, Stefan Falimirz devoted a chapter in his herbal book to distilling vodkas, but their usage was limited either to cures or: "for cleansing the chin after shaving [or] rubbed on after washing in the bath". Even in its earliest incarnation, vodka was being used as something rather stylish – an after-shave or cologne. Falimirz, however, claimed that not only did vodka make people smell nicer, but it also could be used "to increase fertility and awaken lust". Right enough, perfumes these days still allude to that latter quality.

These early vodkas wouldn't have been the clear, neat spirit we know today. They would have been spiced up with infusions of herbs, roots, spices and exotica like marzipan, almonds and sugar. The result was that, according to Marian Hanik's *History of Vodka* in Poland, the Polish pharmacies of their time were more like cafes, where people came to take their medicine and have a chat.

Vodka was given a significant boost when, in 1546, King Jan Olbracht decreed that all Poles could make alcohol – which they gleefully did, even though they had to pay tax for the privilege. Although this decree was soon restricted to the gentry, they seized on the money-making opportunity.

By the end of the sixteenth century, Poland was producing vodka in suffi-

VODKA STARTED LIFE AS AN APOTHECARIES' POTION

cient commercial quantities to start exporting – a trade that would grow in importance over the following two centuries. Production initially centred round the then capital of Cracow, and by 1580 there were 500 distilleries in Poznan, while Gdansk had taken over as vodka's capital – its first distillery being started by a Dutchman called Ambrosius Vermoellen.

With production rights restricted to the upper class, distilleries were springing up across the country, in towns, monasteries and in country houses and estates. "Naked" vodka was still less common than the vast range of flavoured vodkas that had appeared on the back of this distilling fever – there were medicinal vodkas, country vodkas flavoured with wild herbs, sweet vodkas (like Krupnik) for winter. Faith & Wisniewski, in their *Classic Vodka*, recount that over 100 different flavoured varieties were being produced in this period, with the Baczewski distillery alone making 123 different styles. Vodka had become part and parcel of Poland's life. Everyone drank it and, despite the legal restrictions, everyone made it, though quality differed according to your wealth. Those who could afford it produced vodka from rye, while the peasants had to make do with anything else they could get their hands on.

Hanik gives a typical example of a Polish manor house distillery in the seventeenth century – it drew water from local springs, had a malt house, a mill, cooperage and smithy; an ice house for cooling the yeast and the mash; a still room and a barrel warehouse. It was a sophisticated operation, not some cobbled-together, moonshining unit. The spring water was filtered through charcoal, distillation was in copper stills

and redistillation was common (though not universal).

With the arrival of triple (and, on occasion, quadruple) distillation and charcoal filtering in the eighteenth century, came a new style of vodka that was stronger and cleaner. Polish vodka became the model for quality production across Eastern Europe with equipment (and techniques) being exported to Russia and Sweden.

Vodkas would have been made from the main Polish starch crops – rye, wheat, barley and oats were all used. Potatoes, although they had arrived as an exotic ingredient in the fifteenth century, only began to be used for vodka production in the middle of the eighteenth century, becoming a major raw material a hundred years later.

The style was still following the aim of the earliest distillers, to try to produce as clean and pure a spirit as possible. Vodka by now was not only a spirit that could be drunk on its own, but one that would also provide a base for the seemingly infinite number of flavourings that had become established as an integral part of Polish vodka's style (*see* below).

The next major step towards this goal of a pure spirit came at the start of the nineteenth century, when the first three-chambered Pistorius column still was installed at General Ludowik Pac's distillery. When steam was incorporated into the method in 1826, Polish

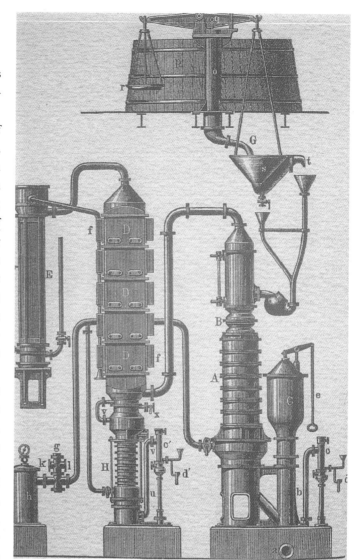

vodka production was ready to expand once more – with higher volumes of purer spirit flooding on to the market.

Although rectifying columns didn't make their first appearance until 1871, Pistorius equipment was a major breakthrough. From here on in purity was not only the aim, it was an achievable goal. As well as new technology appearing, as Faith & Wisniewski point out, the emergence of the first kosher vodkas in the 1830s also had a significant impact on improving distilling practice and making the production process as clean as possible.

The combination of this new technology and the planting of potatoes as a main crop meant that the beginning of

THE CONTINUOUS STILL IMPROVED QUALITY IMMEASURABLY

Tasting Notes

POLISH VODKA

Wyborowa Very clean and crisp. Light lime with good weight behind. Soft and full on the nose, with some creamy weight. Fine grip and a hot finish. A cracking vodka.

Zytnia Good rye zest on the very clean nose. Good crisp acidity on the palate. A dry aperitif vodka with white pepper on the finish.

Luksusowa If you need to be convinced that potatoes can make quality vodka, start here. Richly textured, almost sweet with a powerful, elegant finish. Drink neat.

VODKA HAS ALWAYS PLAYED A MAJOR PART IN POLISH SOCIAL LIFE

the nineteenth century saw a doubling of vodka consumption and an explosion in the number of distilleries. It wasn't to last long.

The potato blight (1843–51) crippled spirits production – as it did in Ireland – while increased taxation put paid to most of the smaller distilleries. By the end of the century, rural distillers could no longer compete in terms of volume or quality. Although they produced spirit, they were sending it off to the large plants for rectification. This spirit was either bottled or sold on once more to producers specializing in flavoured styles. These producers were using the new Henckmann equipment, which used alcohol vapour to strip flavours and speed up the process.

During the First World War, there was a further fall in the number of legal distilleries – much of it caused by a further rise in taxation, fuelling a rise in home distilling. In the 1930s, 4,000 illegal stills were confiscated every year. Vodka was too important to Polish life and culture to be given up without a fight. The industry, however, consolidated further and was brought under the control of a state monopoly after the

Second World War. In 1973, this body became Polmos.

Vodka remained the lifeblood of Polish society. During the shortages of the 1980s it was used as a form of currency to barter for goods, and those who wanted more than their ration made their own. Wisniewski highlights the sudden increase in the use of junior chemistry sets during this desperate time. With the arrival of democracy, the 25 distilleries controlled by Polmos were granted independent status, although they are still ostensibly government controlled.

This has produced an explosion of brands – there are an estimated 1,000 brands of Polish vodka available – with each distillery trying to find its own point of difference. It's only to the benefit of the spirits lover, as the newly liberated distilleries have gone for the top end of the market.

It's difficult to describe how important a role vodka plays in Polish and Russian culture. It's not just a neutral spirit to be diluted with a soft drink; it's a social event with its own rituals. Flavours aren't the recent invention that the West seems to think they are – they

all have their own use, their own ethos.

In Poland, drinking has long been seen as a social event, an act of generosity and hospitality. This means it's regarded in a very different light from how it is in the West (and, in particular, the USA). Hanik quotes Jedrzej Kitowicz, who wrote in 1850: "Among the Poles, nothing could be done without getting drunk... It was the host's greatest ... satisfaction when [the day after a party] he heard how none of his guests had left sober."

It was nothing new. "Among them [the Poles] getting drunk is a praiseworthy custom, certain proof of sincerity and good manners," wrote Fulvius Ruggeri to Pope Pius V in his 1568 description of distilling in Poland. The maxim was repeated 400 years later by the aristocrat Czartoryski, who wrote: "twice a year, one should get properly drunk".

It might seem reprehensible advice in these abstemious times, when the merest hint of a lack of sobriety is seen as a crime, but vodka remains a safety valve in Polish life, as well as an inherent part of the culture.

Poles, Russians and Swedes all treat vodka in the same way as the French treat wine. It's an aperitif, served with the snacks that appear before the meal, drunk as a liqueur after the meal. Children are weaned on to its charms at an early age – and end up more responsible drinkers as a result. My (half-Polish) brother-in-law remembers as a child being given a small glass of Wisniowka (a sweet, cherry vodka) on special occasions.

Polish vodka's inherent high quality and versatility demand to be examined more closely.

RUSSIAN *Vodka*

If Poland can lay claim to being the first vodka producer, its image is still associated with Russia. But until the mid-fifteenth century the Russian nobility were still sipping on mead and wines, while the people were drinking beer. Faith & Wisniewski argue that some distillation was taking place beforehand as an adjunct to producing pitch from pine. It's possible that alcohol was being distilled in log stills (the same thing happened in Kentucky), and it was the need to keep redistilling the alcohol to remove unwanted elements that, they argue, established vodka distillers' obsession with producing a pure spirit.

This proposition goes a long way to explaining why when other distillers across Europe were happy to retain flavouring compounds, those in Russia and Poland wanted to get rid of as many as possible. There is a further theory, but we'll come to that in a minute.

Russian vodka historian William Pokhelbin claims that vodka production was known from the mid-fifteenth century, citing the sudden degeneration of public morals and accounts of mass drunkenness and violence. This, he argues, points to a change in the type of alcohol consumed. Sadly, whether this wild depravity was caused by strong spirits or another wider social cause we cannot (yet) ascertain.

Though there is no evidence that vodka was at the root of this dissolute behaviour, records do show that a Russian delegation had visited Italian monasteries in 1430 where they were shown how to make *aqua vitae*. Given that their return coincided with a grain surplus, it is entirely possible that vodka distillation was in place by the middle of the century.

Virtually every country has tried to control spirits in some way or other. Taxation is the most common method. In Russia they went one step further. While Jan Olbrecht was allowing all Poles the right to distil, Ivan the Great had already established the world's first spirit monopoly. Ivan the Terrible took state control one stage further, decreeing that vodka could only be sold in official taverns and be produced from stills owned either by tavern owners or nobles. Vodka fitted in neatly with the age-old framework of Russian society – the landowners got rich and the poor got drunk.

Though Peter the Great (1672–1725) liberalized distillation – mainly to collect taxes – vodka production was a rich man's hobby. Peter himself invented a modified still to improve quality, and his recipe for vodka involved producing a triple-distilled spirit, flavouring it with anise and then redistilling it once more. The search for a pristine spirit was well advanced.

It could be argued that this was only to the benefit of vodka's quality. By the turn of the seventeenth century, four distillations were common, and exotic, complex flavoured vodkas were being drunk by the ruling classes. Filtering the spirit through charcoal to further clean it up arrived in the eighteenth century – at much the same time as in Poland – and is credited to Theodore Lowitz, who was working on the Tsar's request. There's every chance that it was a Russian or Polish émigré who took the art of charcoal filtration to America and into Tennessee. It certainly was known long before the 1880s, when Smirnoff claims to have invented the technique.

In the eighteenth century, a series of government bills restricted production still further. This effectively split production into two quality tiers. The nobility, who used their vast feudal power and wealth to make it to perfection; and the state distillers, who supplied base spirit for the poor. While the poor soaked up crude spirits to obliterate their misery, the top Russian vodkas began to acquire an international reputation. Catherine II sent vodka to the kings of Prussia and

*CATHERINE THE GREAT:
PROMOTER OF VODKA*

THE CREAM OF THE
RUSSIAN CROP

Sweden, to Voltaire and to her friend, the Swedish botanist Karl von Linne, who, suitably inspired, wrote a lengthy treatise on "vodka in the hands of a philosopher, physician and commoner".

By now, class divisions had created different vodkas for each stratum of society. The nobility drank rye and ele-

gantly flavoured vodkas, while the poor drank rank spirit made from potato, beet and nettles bought in at low prices from Poland, Germany and from illicit stills, rather than from the state distillers.

The state was forced to take control of production once more, cut the number of distilleries in half, introduced the continuous still and, under the controlling influence of the chemist Dr Mendeleyev, set quality control standards. By the time that Piotr Smirnov started to make his own vodka in 1861, the best Russian vodkas had become the elegant, clean spirit we know today.

Smirnov's rise was inexorable. The firm built a distillery in Moscow in 1868 and was granted a Royal Warrant in 1896 – an award which didn't go down too well with the Bolsheviks. By the turn of the century, the firm was producing 3,500,000 cases a year and had an annual income of US$2 million.

Vodka was very big business and distillers were pillars of the capitalist class. Little surprise that vodka was one of the first targets of the Bolshevik government – and that Vladimir Smirnov fled to Constantinople, Lvov and Paris in his unsuccessful attempt to start all over again.

The initial reaction of the Bolshevik government was to restrict vodka's strength to 20 per cent ABV to try to reduce drunkenness – but people just kept on making stronger stuff at home.

Things changed dramatically when Stalin took power. Faith & Wisniewski make a strong case that Stalin used vodka as a means of social control. By keeping the price artificially low and making it easily available, he ensured that the Soviet Union was in a state of endemic alcoholism. Vodka was a way of suppressing dissent and, in those dark days, the drinking wasn't heroic – it was desperate.

Stalin wasn't the first to use cheap alcohol as means of keeping people compliant. Rum was also used in this fashion in the Caribbean by planters who gave the spirit to their slaves. Brandy, too, was given to the black majority by white employers in apartheid South Africa.

Now with Communism (allegedly) overthrown, things have gone full circle, with Smirnoff now being produced in pot stills in Moscow once more. The market has opened up, allowing Stolichnaya to blast on to the world market. Then there are Moskovskaya, Kubanskaya and Ultraa from St Petersburg, and vodkas like Altai, a winter wheat vodka from Zmeinogorsk in Western Siberia. There may not be quite as many brands as there are in Poland, but the gates have been opened.

Vodka epitomises Russia. It has kept spirits buoyant in times of desperation and obliterated misery. In the wilds of the Altai and Tuva, it is used by shamans as a libation to the spirits. In Moscow it is sipped by the new bourgeoisie.

Although Russia's future is less than clear, one thing is for certain: empires may rise and fall, but vodka will always survive.

SCANDINAVIAN *Vodka*

Records suggest that distillation arrived in Sweden in the fourteenth century when *brannvin* (burnt wine) was being distilled from imported wine – and domestic grain.

This was initially used as a medicine (which has echoes in later years) and also in the development of gunpowder. It was first embraced by the aristocracy, and only began to spread to the rest of the population in the seventeenth century.

As soon as it did, though, distilling became endemic. By 1756, the country could boast 180,000 stills.

Home distillation was banned in 1860, the first of many attempts by the Swedish government to exert control over consumption, and large commercial plants equipped with Coffey stills began to exert control over the market – and produce more vodka. Less than 20 years later, Sweden's most famous distiller emerged on the scene.

Lars Olsson Smith started distilling young. Unbelievably, by the time he had reached his early teens he was producing an estimated one third of Sweden's

vodka. It was his creation of Sweden's first rectified spirit in 1879 that was to elevate his name to one of legend.

Smith was a stubborn individual with very fixed ideas about quality. He was so convinced that his new Absolut Rent Brannvin (Absolutely Pure Vodka) was the very best vodka on the market that he took on the might of the Stockholm monopoly.

His distillery was located in an elegant house situated on the small island of Reimersholme, conveniently just outside Stockholm's city boundaries. By providing a free ferry service to his customers he not only guaranteed high sales, but angered the other distillers to such an extent that shots were fired at the boats.

His Absolut vodka was an instant success and Smith soon needed more raw material for his new brand. Accordingly, he switched production to the far south of the country, to the wheat fields of Skåne. He went about buying up distilleries and ensured that his vodka was the best-distributed brand in the country – at one point even using the unions to boycott shops that were selling what he claimed were inferior brands.

By the end of the First World War, Sweden had a state monopoly, Vin & Spirit, in place to control the sales and production of all alcoholic beverages and immediately put up taxes to astronomical levels.

Who knows what would have happened to the fortunes of Smith's brand had it not fallen victim to Sweden's strict state control of drink?

Scandinavian governments (with the notable exception of Denmark) have long had a strange relationship with alcohol. The people drink a lot of

SPIRIT OF THE MOUNTAINS

THE EPITOME OF PURITY

it, but their rulers don't like them indulging and, until recently, have tried everything in their powers (Finland even tried a period of total prohibition) to make it impossible to enjoy a drink – though without any real success.

It only encouraged Swedes, Finns and Norwegians (who also have state monopolies) to go on massive drinking binges, either on the duty-free ferry routes between the countries, or in Denmark. Many people have also con- tinued to distil at home. Even the Swedish state monopoly will admit that more than 20 per cent of the vodka drunk in Sweden is distilled privately – though the true figure in fact could be a great deal higher.

Strangely, this tight control – which is part and parcel of the Swedish state's benign interpretation of socialism – created one of the world's biggest spirits brands. Absolut was forgotten until 1979 when V&S decided to hit the international vodka market.

The brand was distilled once more, repackaged in a replica of an old medicine bottle and went for the top end of the US market – the most competitive vodka market in the world. Carillon Importers' Michel Roux took it up and ran with it (he was later to do the same with Bombay Sapphire). It's now the seventh biggest brand in the world.

Absolut was following in the footsteps of Finlandia, which had hit the USA in 1970. Finnish vodka dates back to the sixteenth century, but it too was taken under the state's wing this century – when the distillery was closed down to make alcohol for Molotov cocktails.

Denmark traditionally has been better known for its akvavits (*see* Other Spirits), but has always produced fine quality vodkas. The father of these was Isidor Henius who, in the 1850s, installed the country's first rectification column at his Aalborg distillery.

This famous site is now owned by the giant producer Danisco, home to the new wave of Danish vodkas foremost among which is Danzka. To be strictly accurate, Danzka was originally produced by an independent distiller but, in the way of these things, was snapped up by the giant firm when it saw the potential for a high-quality brand on the export markets. The fine, ultra-clean grain vodka in its distinctively packaged silver metal bottles comes in a range of flavours, including Citron and Currant. They are fine and rather attractive. The firm also produces Fris, a vodka created to be served straight from the freezer.

Norway's contribution to the growing band of Scandinavian brands is the potato vodka Vikingfjord. It's a good example of the Nordic style, flirting with neutrality, but being saved by smooth mouthfeel and delicate flavour.

Finnish industry started in earnest in the 1950s and now has one of the most technically advanced distilleries in the world making the Finlandia a by-word for Scandinavian purity.

Rest of the WORLD

The rest of the world has always looked on vodka in a slightly different light to eastern Europe and Scandinavia. Although you can say that vodka akvavit, korn and gin are all white spirits from the northern European grain belt, they have evolved in subtly different ways.

In vodka the prime motivator was to produce as clean a spirit as possible. This could then either be drunk neat or subtly flavoured. While cleanliness of the base spirit was important for the rest of these white spirits, their aim was to still have a dominant powerful character – juniper for gin, caraway for akvavit.

It wasn't until America recreated vodka as a neutral, mixable spirit in the 1950s (*see* above) that vodka began to make inroads into Western European drinking culture. Vodka had been produced prior to this date – the Dutch firm Hooghoudt has been making vodka since the end of the last century – but it had never captured the public imagination. Now, with America reinforcing its role as the arbiter of global cultural taste, vodka became the latest in a chain of cultural signs like jazz, rock n' roll and the movies, which signified modernity – and "American-ness".

The vodka that Western Europe drank therefore wasn't a European creation but an American one, a drink where neutrality was the sole intent. But what's the difference between any of these commodity vodkas with their pseudo-Tsarist names and Moskovskaya, Luksusowa or Belvedere? The simple answer is that the quality brands have retained subtle traces of their raw material, they have grace and elegance – and they therefore retain your interest.

What you got with the Westernized versions was a spirit that, even neat, gave no offence, that was a bland, non-commital mixer. Vodka was dumbed down before the phrase was ever thought up.

It was also relatively easy to produce. Any distillery with a rectifying column can make it. Smirnoff is made across the globe, there's Suhoi from Italy, Zar from Bolivia. Things, however, are beginning to change and a new, more flavoursome premium sector is emerging. There's Skyyy and welcome innovations such as Tito's Texas Handmade and the organic Rain from the Ancient Age distillery in Kentucky, Fris and Danska from Denmark and the Dutch brands Ketel One and Royalty. The West is slowly beginning to pay attention and take note of what real vodka is all about.

How it's made

In technical terms, vodka is pure (usually rectified) spirit that has been diluted with water and filtered before bottling. The aim has always been to look for the purest spirit possible.

But why did Poland and Russia decide that a flavoursome grain spirit – akin to the early whiskies made in Scotland and Ireland – wasn't for them? One answer was the need to redistil the spirit from the early log stills *(see* above); another is down to the climate. Low-alcohol spirits freeze. If you were wanting to transport spirit during the bitter winters, it made sense to have as high strength a spirit as possible – and that meant redistillation.

In addition, it is worth remembering that even in the early days vodka was flavoured, and that while herbs were used as masking agents, they were also there to be tasted (the complexity of the recipes is evidence of this). The need, therefore, was for as light a spirit base as possible.

Neutral spirit can be made from anything that contains starch – in principle, vodka can be made from molasses, sugar beet, potatoes, rye, wheat, millet, maize, whey and even rectified wood alcohol.

Most basic commercial brands these days will use molasses, but premium vodkas, however, need to retain the finer qualities of their raw material – and the best are made from either grain or potato. "Vodka seems to be the simplest liquor," says Dr Boleslaw Skrzypczak, one of Poland's recognized vodka experts. "But this understanding only skims the surface. In reality a host of factors influence the quality of vodka – proper raw material and technology for producing raw spirit, the effectiveness of spirit purification and water quality."

Raw materials

The early distillers made their spirit from the most widely available source of starch. That meant wheat in Sweden, rye and potatoes in Poland, rye and wheat in Russia. Already you are looking at different styles. Of the widely available premium vodkas today, Absolut and Altai are made from winter wheat, Moskovskaya is a classic Moscow rye (although Stolichnaya also uses wheat), while Luksusowa and Chopin are potato spirits. Rye gives bite and weight, wheat a delicacy, while potato gives a distinctive creaminess to the spirit.

The mention of the last ingredient is always liable to produce a strange reaction from Westerners. Potatoes are seen as a sign of an inferior spirit, something rustic and crude. You use potatoes to make hooch in prison, not in a distillery. While golden fields of grain are infinitely more alluring (and photograph better), a vodka like Luksusowa proves that potatoes can result in a beautifully rich, creamy spirit that's more than a match for grain vodka. In Poland, only special high-starch varieties grown along the Vistula river and on the Baltic

POTATOES MAKE WONDER-FULLY SOFT VODKA

coast are used for vodka production – and although they give less alcohol than wheat, they are still preferred for the distinctive character of the final spirit. Dr Skrzypczak also claims that, since potatoes have fewer aromatic compounds, they are better for producing neutral rectified spirits

Water

One distiller claims that 60 per cent of vodka's quality is down to the water used – although quite how this figure is quantified isn't specified. Water, however, is of vital importance to any spirit, and vodka is no exception. Expert tasters agree that Moscow vodka's quality suffered when the water supply changed. Finlandia, rightly, can point to its pure water source as one of the major contributory factors in its natural clean taste, as can the Siberian brand Altai, while Absolut has its own well.

Water is used twice – once for mashing, and then again at the end of the process when the spirit is diluted prior to filtration. While some distilleries can use pure spring water at this stage, others have to soften and demineralize the water in order to prevent any clouding of the spirit. Distilled water was widely used, but it's agreed that it gives a flat flavour to the spirit and, for quality brands at least, is not used. Nothing must get in the way of the pure flavour.

Distillation

That purity has been achieved by a highly controlled distillation process. Vodka distillers will point out that after ferment they have a mash that contains hundreds of flavouring compounds and different alcohols. No different from a Scotch distiller. The difference is that vodka distillers will talk of congeners as "harmful" compounds, which must be eliminated. For whisky, rum and brandy producers, they are the very things that they want to retain to give their spirit its personality.

To get to that stage of cleanliness a vodka will be distilled two, three, four or more times. While some vodkas are produced in pot stills (for example, Smirnoff Black and Ketel One), the majority are made in continuous stills with a rectification column (or columns) to remove the unwanted byproducts. The difference between premium vodkas comes in the manner in which they are rectified and, later, filtered.

In the Absolut distillery, for example, the spirit passes through a number of columns, each designed to extract a different set of "impurities". One takes out solvents, another fusel oils, another methanol, while the fourth concentrates the spirit to 96 per cent ABV. Go to the Absolut lab and they'll point proudly to the chemical readouts and show that it's as close to ethanol as you'll get.

Here's the dilemma: distillation and rectification are so efficient that they have also removed the trace elements that give premium vodka its character. Absolut at this stage is indeed absolutely pure – so pure, in fact, that it

*WOOD MATURATION IS
USED FOR SOME VODKAS*

the spirit. Other distillers take the Absolut route (though few are willing to share in any aspect of production) to ensure that character and personality are evident in the final product.

Filtration

The final stage for any vodka is filtration, the aim of which is to remove the spirit's raw, aggressive edge and replace it with a mild, mellow, often sweet taste. In many ways, filtration replaces wood ageing as a method of getting smoothness to the spirit.

It's a process that distillers guard jealously – there are as many secret methods of filtration as there are of distillation. The most common method involves passing the spirit through activated charcoal. What the charcoal is made from will have an impact on the spirit – most agree that alder and birch are best – though some distillers use synthetic or bone charcoal, but the results aren't as good. Some have a more complex fil-

tration system. Stolichnaya and Altai, for example, are repeatedly filtered over silver-birch charcoal and pure quartz sand; Suhoi, allegedly, is filtered through diamonds, while Smirnoff is passed through seven columns packed with charcoal. Distillers can then add compounds to round out the mouthfeel.

Technical though this undoubtedly is, at the end of the day the best vodkas are only approved if they are passed by a tasting panel. Any professional spirits taster possesses a rare ability for smell. In vodka they are detecting minuscule differences. "There are people with extraordinarily refined sensitivity," says Dr Skrzypczak. "Before World War Two, there was a Mrs Wasikowa working at the State Spirits Monopoly Central Laboratory. Just by tasting, she could say which of the 50 or so rectification apparatuses then operating in Poland had produced a given sample, and what kind of defect the apparatus had. Another specialist was in the habit of having stiff shots of the tested beverages before starting the tasting proper." You bow in awe.

tastes of nothing. What they have to do is put flavour back in by blending in a spirit that's been distilled at a lower strength, along with some vodka that has been aged in wood. That isn't to say that these top vodkas will blow you away with a massive whack of the original raw material, but it will be there and you can differentiate between them.

Though most vodka producers aim for a neutral rectified spirit, Polish distillers rectify to a lower degree and attempt to retain some elements of the base material, while still achieving purity of flavour and character.

Some distillers are quite happy producing nothing more than ethyl alcohol. These vodkas are stateless drifters that have no connection with the place of their birth – but they have their uses if you are wanting to make a long drink that tastes of the mixer, not

THE PERSONAL TOUCH

FLAVOURED *Vodka*

THE NEW WAVE OF
STYLISH BRANDS

After filtering, the vodka is either reduced and bottled or passes to another stage – flavouring. Most people these days think that flavoured vodkas are some new phenomenon. Bars have gone flavouring crazy – although they almost inevitably end up with vile home-made examples. Some lower-end brands have also jumped on the bandwagon by adding flavour extracts to the vodka, but these clumsy attempts to replicate the classic old styles are immediately exposed when you taste them side by side. Sadly, though, not everyone has the chance to do this experiment, and these new gimmicky flavours could end up destroying one of vodka's forgotten styles.

While flavours were originally either medicinal herbs or sweetening agents used to disguise off-notes in the distillate, the intricacy of the old Polish and Russian recipes implies that flavour for its own end was an aim at an early stage in vodka's evolution. These classic flavoured vodkas give a window into the past, lighting up the woods and fields that surrounded the early distillers.

Flavouring is added not by redistillation – like gin or akvavit – but by maceration, leaching or, in some cases, by blending in distillates of flavourings or wine. The cheapest option (which also gives the clumsiest examples) is cold compounding, where flavourings are poured into the vodka. To achieve better results you have to macerate the ingredients in the spirit for a lengthy period at room temperature. The time will vary according to the ingredients, and some of the more complex recipes will have different ingredients added at different points.

A newer method, outlined by Faith & Wisniewski, is the circulation process, which is used for styles such as Zubrowka. Here, the flavouring agents are placed on a rack inside the tank and the alcohol is passed through them at regular intervals to get an even, quick extraction. Ricard uses a similar technique for making pastis.

The end result is a vast range of flavours with extraordinary tastes – and a history that dates right back 500 years to vodka's origins. In those days the distillers would have used the ingredients around them – like Tatra vodka

FREEDOM OF VODKA

STOLICHNAYA OHRANJ

flavoured with the herbs from the mountains, while others give a clue to their aristocratic heritage by using the essences and contents of the manor house's spice room.

You'll find vodkas like the Polish winter warmer Krupnik, which is flavoured with honey (the oldest of all fermented drinks) and 30 other herbs and spices, including cinnamon, nutmeg and ginger; or the Russian hunter's vodka, Okhotnichaya, which combines 10 spices and herbs, including ginger, clove, juniper, anise, orange peel and port.

There are echoes of the age-old rural custom of using wild autumn fruits in Jarzebiak, made with rowan berries, or the heady languorous sweetness of wild cherry in Wisniowka. Then there are vodkas which must have originally been the preserve of the rich – lifted, effervescent Cytrynowka (using lemon peel and leaves in Poland) or Russia's equivalent Limmonaya (which only uses peel) and, most expensive of all, the rare, delicate Rose Petal.

You name the flavour, it's there. Bloody Mary aficionados can choose between crisp Pieprzowka; the softer Wyborowa pepper; the dry Absolut Peppar; or the powerful Stolichnaya

Tasting Notes

FLAVOURED VODKA

Smirnoff Citrus Twist Confected lemon sherbet bon-bons laid on top of neutral spirit.
Cytrynowka (Polish lemon) Delicate nose that's a little spirity. Attractive, light and clean on the palate, it's a little short.
Goldwasser Bitter nose with anise and caraway dominant. Very sweet, but with a bitter lime marmalade peel drive keeping it fresh.
Absolut Kurant Intense aromas which seem artificial. Clean, dry spirit behind. Very light.

Pieprzowka (Polish pepper) Fragrant and surprisingly sweet on the nose with a mix of thyme, rosemary, cloves, cinnamon and dry pepper behind,. Bone dry with a crackling mix of black pepper and chilli on the palate.
Absolut Peppar Green jalapeño/fresh dill nose. The pepper carries through with chilli seed heat burning on the finish. Tremendous, it goes for the throat with fangs bared.
Zubrowka A haunting aroma of cut grass and blossom, like a meadow after a rain-

storm, the air doused with the ever-changing fragrance of herbs, grass and lavender. Very soft with a hint of sweetness and spice Crisp clean finish. A classic.
Krupnik A little spirity on the nose, with rounded wild herbs. On the palate it's lightly sweet with some baked apple, herbs and a lightly vegetal edge. Lovely.

Pertsovka. To put a different spin on things, there is even oak-aged vodka, Starka. In Poland this is made from a 50 per cent ABV rye spirit that is aged in Tokaji wine barrels or large vats, sometimes with a touch of Malaga fortified wine to sweeten it. Originally, this was a feast vodka, which was made by pouring the spirit over the lees in a wine barrel and then burying it for three to four years. Starka is pretty rare, but those keen to explore them should investigate the range from Szczecin distillery – Specjalna (12-year-old), Jubileuszowa (15-year-old), Piastowska (20-year-old) and Banquet (30-year-old).

Russian Starka has apple and pear leaves, as well as a fortification of brandy and port. Unusual though it may seem to those of us brought up on naked vodka, adding wine and other distillates

is common practice. In Poland the marvellous Zytnia is a strong rye vodka which has had apple and plum wine blended in.

If that leaves your mind reeling, unsure of where to start, then go straight to the top of the tree, however, and search out Zubrowka (spelt with a 'v' in Russian).

Hailing from the Bialowieska forest on the Polish/Belarus border, Zubrowka was originally a seventeenth-century regional speciality, and a particular favourite of the Polish royal family on their hunting visits to the forest. Each bottle of Zubrowka has a blade of bison grass (*hierochloe odorata*) in it. This plant is the favourite grazing of the European bison, which still roam wild in the forest – in fact, legend has it that only grass that's been urinated on by one of

LEMON APPEAL

the beasts can be used in the vodka. The grass itself is high in fragrant components which impart an evocative, green scent to the vodka with a delicate vanilla touch (coming from the coumarin ester in the grass). A glorious drink.

Today's MARKET

Vodka will endure, of that there's little doubt. The question is whether it can break free of its commodity image and be recognized as the classy spirit it is. There are a number of different factors at play in today's market. Almost inevitably, there has been a raft of brands that have entered the market hanging on to Absolut's coat-tails. Here style is considerably more important than content. Fancy bottles and huge price tags can't hide the fact that there are a large number of premium vodkas on the market that are not worth the money, and hopefully someone is soon going to notice that these Emperors (or Tsars) have no clothes.

At the same time, though, there are "new" brands from Poland and Russia

that deserve wider attention. Vodka lovers already appreciate the herbal lift of Stolichnaya (and its richer big brother, Cristal), Absolut's clarity and Finlandia's light dryness.

But don't pass over the lime oil richness of Wyborowa; Moskovskaya's full, elegant, rye weight; and the creamy, soft Luksusowa – or dismiss Smirnoff Black. Poland can also weigh in with the premium potato vodkas Baltic and Chopin, or the rye crunch of Belvedere. Also try and find the kosher vodkas made at the Nissebaum's plant in Bielsko-Biala or at Lancut – it's worth it.

Elsewhere you can browse among Holland's pot-still Ketel One, or Royalty, Denmark's Fris and Danska

and, from the States, Rain and Tito's Texas Handmade. Though these may all be seen as esoteric brands at the moment, they are providing the impetus for vodka's future long-term success as a serious spirit.

This shift upmarket is much needed, as the category has become increasingly bogged down with inferior, cheap products and a rather peculiar image. Vodka isn't seen as a bad spirit, but few consumers in recent years have bothered giving it a second thought. This in itself isn't surprising as, since the 1950s, the whole category has been sold on the premise that it tastes of nothing.

Well, as we have seen, times are changing and vodka is most definitely making a comeback.

The MOSCOW MULE
Classic Cocktail

BARTENDER'S TIPS
Use fresh lime juice rather than lime cordial to avoid this drink becoming too sweet.

MOSCOW MULE

2 OZ VODKA

GINGER BEER

SQUEEZE OF LIME JUICE

WEDGE OF LIME

POUR VODKA OVER ICE IN A COLLINS GLASS. ADD OTHER INGREDIENTS. STIR.

Back in the 1940s when America hadn't woken up to vodka, John Martin of Heublein met in New York with Jack Morgan, the owner of the Cock 'n Bull restaurant in Hollywood. Morgan had landed himself with a surplus of ginger beer, which was proving difficult to shift. Martin wanted to get rid of the equally slow-moving Smirnoff.

They put their heads – and their products – together, added a splosh of lime juice and created the Moscow Mule. Martin and Morgan then went a step further and ordered

THE DRINK THAT MADE SMIRNOFF A HOUSE-HOLD NAME IN AMERICA – AND THE ORIGINAL COCK 'N' BULL STORY

500 copper mugs to be engraved with a kicking mule – now highly prized by mixologists – and marketed the items to bars.

On the back of the mule, Smirnoff's sales tripled between 1947 and 1950, and then doubled again the year after. America would never be the same again.

The Bloody MARY
Classic Cocktail

BLOODY MARY

2 OZ ABSOLUT PEPPAR VODKA
·
POUR OVER ICE IN COLLINS GLASS.

IN A JUG, COMBINE:
TOMATO JUICE
WORCESTERSHIRE SAUCE
WHITE PEPPER
SALT
DASH OF CELERY SALT
SPLASH OF FINO SHERRY
SPLASH OF ORANGE JUICE
TABASCO SAUCE TO TASTE
·
ADD MIX TO VODKA AND ICE.

As vodka started its rise to become America's favourite spirit, so it began stealing cocktails away from gin. It muscled in on the Martini action and wrestled away the Bloody Mary. Actually, it's a bit more complicated than that. The Bloody Mary started life in the 1920s in Harry's New York Bar in Paris, where a barman called Fernand Petiot mixed vodka (available in Europe) with tomato juice and called his creation "The Bucket of Blood". It wasn't a hit.

Petiot decided to try his luck in the States after Repeal and took his recipe with him. However, because he couldn't guarantee a supply of vodka, he used gin instead and re-christened his drink "The Red Snapper", which later got changed to "The Bloody Mary". Who Mary was, nobody really knows.

It was sold as a hangover cure from the start – and quite right too. It's one of the great restorative drinks, the only remedy when the world is a little too noisy, colours are too bright and all

THE WORLD'S FAVOURITE HANGOVER CURE – AND IT WORKS!

you want to do is sit and groan. It gives enough of a kick of alcohol to get you started again, but enough flavour and liquid to build you up without having to face a full cooked breakfast.

As ever, no two people can agree on what should and shouldn't go into a Bloody Mary – OK, other than vodka, tomato juice and Worcestershire sauce. The recipe here works for me, simply because it isn't too soupy. It also omits those irritating celery stalks that just end up disappearing up your nose or poking you in the eye. You are fragile enough – the last thing you need is a belligerent vegetable.

In Canada, they give the recipe a brilliant spin by substituting Clamato juice for tomato, adding horseradish sauce and celery salt and calling the result a Caesar. It's a great alternative – unlike the Bullshot, which uses beef bouillon (not consommé). Steer clear of mad cows.

8 Tequila

FEW CONTEMPORARY SPIRITS TAP INTO THE MYTHIC PAST QUITE LIKE MEZCAL (OF WHICH TEQUILA IS A REGIONAL SPECIALITY). THOUGH BECOMING INCREASINGLY SOPHISTICATED – SOME WOULD SAY, GENTRIFIED – AT ITS HEART THIS MEXICAN SPIRIT, DISTILLED FROM AGAVE (NOT CACTUS!), HAS RETAINED ITS MYSTERY, AND STILL EMBRACES THE ANCIENT NOTION OF ALCOHOL AS A GIFT FROM THE GODS.

TEQUILA AND MEZCAL REMAIN SPIRITS OF THE PEOPLE

Although distillation didn't arrive in Mexico until the invasion of the Spanish Conquistadors, if you want to get to the "why" of mezcal you have to examine how its fermented equivalent, pulque, was used by the indigenous inhabitants of this vast, mysterious country. According to mythology the agave plant is the incarnation of the goddess Mayahuel; the honey-like sap (aguamiel) is her blood. The secret of fermenting pulque was given to man by the trickster figure (and the first drunk) Tlacuache. It's said he still shows producers when the agave is ready to be harvested, although these days José Cuervo prefers to rely on satellite imaging.

Pulque had a dual significance. By getting drunk on pulque, the god-king Quetzalcoatl committed the sin that precipitated his leaving earth and ascending into the heavens. At the same time, though, pulque had acquired a ritual importance, with its own god (Tetzcatzoncatl) and his symbolic entourage of 400 rabbits who represented the different forms of intoxication.

Unlike in North America, the otherworldly experience induced by intoxication (either of pulque or hallucinogens) was of fundamental importance to religious ritual and culture. The agave was seen as a cosmic plant that received and dispensed energy, so pulque eventually became a powerful symbol of nature's rebirth, and was used ceremonially after the harvest to guarantee a good crop the following year. The same ritual was performed with fermented drinks across the world, from Celtic Europe to Indonesia and Crete.

In Mexico there is an established culture of producing alcoholic brews from wild ferments. Corn was used to make chicha and tesguino; wild plums were used to make obo mezcal; honey was fermented with bark to produce balche, but these were local specialities. The agave, however, grows wild in every region of Mexico, so pulque became the "national" drink, hugely important socially, economically and religiously. Myths, legends and ritual sprang up around its usage – and even today there's no other drink that has so many rituals as mezcal and tequila.

When distillation arrived, many of pulque's ancient usages were simply transferred to tequila and mezcal. The spirits are used in traditional medicine, to bless fields and new buildings and, running true to the Mexican fashion of melding Christianity with a pre-Columbian belief system, even for blessing crosses. In Oaxaca on the Day of the Dead, the last glass of mezcal in the bottle is sprinkled over the deceased relative's grave. Though for long a social drink, the spirit has stubbornly

LOOKING FOR THE PERFECT BALANCE

*BLUE AGAVE IS NOW
FLAGGED ON LABELS*

*BECOMING ONE WITH
THE GODS*

refused to relinquish its symbolic power.

"It's a special, sacred event when you take mezcal", says Ron Cooper of mezcal specialist del Maguey. "Originally, the people could only drink it on feast days – but you could consume it until you were smashed because then you were considered to be 'with the gods'."

Sources suggest that mezcal wasn't the first spirit to be produced after the Conquest in the sixteenth century. There is circumstantial evidence that aguardiente (or chinguirito) was illegally made by slaves on the Caribbean coast from molasses and sugar cane. In spite of the Conquistadors clearly being aware of pulque, they mainly drank wine or brandy, which was imported from the home country. So why didn't they make brandy in Mexico? There are three reasons. The first is that grapes cannot be grown throughout the whole of the country. The second is that distillation was, technically, not allowed – everything had to come from Spain. Thirdly, even if brandy production had been permitted, the lack of a good communications network meant that transportation was well-nigh impossible. So they, like the indigenous people

before them, turned to the most ready source of fermentable sugars – the agave.

It's likely that crude distillation took place in the seventeenth century (or even before), but it wasn't until 1758 that today's industry began to emerge around the town of Tequila. The town was an important centre of the New Kingdom of Galicia, and it was near there that Don José Antonio Cuervo was granted land by the King of Spain to farm agave in Jalisco province. This was the first time that permission had been granted to plant crops (other than grapes) that could be turned into alcohol. It was also the first time that producers of pulque or its distilled relative had used cultivated, rather than wild, plants.

In 1795, Don José's son (José Maria Guadeloupe Cuervo) was granted a licence to produce "mezcal wine" in his La Rojena distillery, which is still used by the firm. Agave plantations soon spread across the region and other distilleries appeared – such as Sauza's La Perseverancia, which was founded in 1873. The market expanded further when the railway arrived – an initiative by General Manuel Gonzalez, whose great-grandson went on to found the tequila producer Chinaco.

It wasn't until after the Second World War, though, that tequila began to build up a head of steam on the export markets. By that time, Mexico had acquired a heady exoticism for young Americans – writers like Jack Kerouac and William Burroughs were attracted to its image of being somehow a "lost" America. It had a frontier spirit – there was a sense of recklessness about it, an

element of danger (more wishful than real), and if it got too much you could scuttle back across the border. Tequila came back with these travellers and brought with it the essence of this heady, decadent, weird Mexican experience.

Matters improved further with the creation of the Margarita in the late 1950s and, with increased tourism and a more liberal attitude to life in the 1960s, tequila became the counter-culture drink. New rituals started up – slamming it, and drinking it with lime and salt. Tequila fuelled youth culture. Then people grew up and forgot about the joy of a well-made Margarita. Tequila remained a youthful kick, or a morally dissolute drink.

Tequila comes of age

It was all right pretending to be like Geoffrey Firmin in Lowry's *Under the Volcano* in the 1960s. In the reactionary backlash of the late 1980s, two-fisted drinking just wasn't the thing to be seen doing. But then, just as with malt whisky and Bourbon, the pendulum began to swing back. There are various theories as to where it started, or who started it, but what is certain is that in the past five years or so, younger drinkers have been looking at tequila in a new light, and distilleries have responded. Many believe it started in Mexico with young, middle-class drinkers turning their backs on the white spirit that happened to be tequila and wanting something better – something that could be sipped.

Sipping tequila? That seems like a contradiction in terms. Or it did until aged tequilas from Porfidio, Herradura, el Tesoro, Tres Magueyes, Chinaco and the top brands from Cuervo and Sauza hit the scene. Martin Grassl of Porfidio recalls that when, in 1990, he decided to produce a top-quality tequila, the top

product in the category was selling for $20. These days tequila aficionados don't blink at $100-plus.

The difference lay in production. In the past tequila was made to satisfy the slammin', shootin' market. To make matters worse, in the 1970s the Mexican government allowed tequila to include 49 per cent of "other fermentable sugars" (in other words, neutral cane spirit), which suited the large firms perfectly. Gold tequilas were not necessarily aged; they were usually just sweetened versions of silver.

What the new wave did was to get back to basics. The new sipping tequilas are (by and large) made from 100 per cent blue agave; they are given either a short time in wood (reposado) or aged in small barrels (anejo). As a result the full character of the spirit is finally being revealed in its subtle, often elegant, glory. Part of tequila's easy charm is down to the fact that it tastes like an overripe exotic fruit punch, with a seductive sweetness that borders on decay. These new tequilas give that quality an extra layer of complexity.

This fits in neatly with the changing American palate, which is demanding richer, fuller flavours; which is looking for genuine native cuisine – and that means south-western food, not Taco Bell; and which believes that small is beautiful.

Tighter controls are in place. Each label must carry a registered NOM number, blue agave being mentioned on the front label, while the European Community has banned the production of ersatz tequila from sugar beet in Spain and Greece. Tequila has come of age.

AT THE TOP END

How tequila is MADE

THE TRUE TREASURE OF THE SIERRA MADRE

Tequila is a distillate of the blue agave (*agave azul tequilana weber*), one of over 200 strains of this family of desert lilies which grow across Mexico. Half the size and quicker-maturing than the giant agave that produces pulque, the blue agave is the true treasure of the Sierra Madre – that high, dry, mineral-rich volcanic plain to the north-west of Guadalajara. Weighing in at between 40 and 70 kilograms when harvested, each plant has a hard, caustic centre of pure starch which, when distilled, will give roughly two-and-a-half litres of tequila.

To qualify as tequila, the blue agave must be grown in one of five designated regions – the whole of Jalisco, parts of Nayarit, Michoacan, Guanajuato and, thanks to the efforts of Chinaco's Guillermo Gonzalez, parts of Tamaulipas. Only here is the terroir correct for it to grow and thrive.

Agave hijuelos (babies) are collected from mother plants, and are

Tasting Notes

GOLD/REPOSADO

Tres Magueyes Reposado
Vanilla ice and light lime leaf.
Real Hacienda Reposado
Floral nose with hint of peppermint. A sipping tequila.
Porfidio Reposado Fragrant
ripe fruits. Elegant, restrained.
Chinaco Reposado Waft of
citric juiciness backed with
ripe agave.

ANEJO

Jose Cuervo 1800 Pulpy
fruit with a slightly sugared
quality. Clean and smooth.
Sauza Comemorativo
Chocolatey aroma with
positive agave character.
Tres Magueyes Don Julio
Ripe pears with soft orange
blossom. Gentle in the mouth.
El Tesoro Anejo Spicy, rich
and profound. Subtle with
exotic fruitiness. Classy.
Real Hacienda Fragrant
lemon/lime zestiness mixed
with white chocolate.
Porfidio 5yo Rich with
assertive ripe agave nose
with nutty fruit on the finish.

*SMALL-SCALE HANDS-ON
PRODUCTION*

transplanted in the rainy season (June–October) to prepared fields in the plantations. It takes eight to 10 years for the plant to reach maturity, during which time the grower will feed it, fertilize it, prune back the leaves to retain the plant's energy in its core and remove the sharp, spiny tips from the leaves. Once the agave is ripe, its lower leaves begin to turn brown and a flower spike starts to sprout. This and the leaves are macheted off, exposing the central core which, because of its appearance, is called a pina (pineapple). An experienced worker will be able to harvest between 130 and 150 pinas a day – three to five tons of agave. The leaves are ploughed back into the field, which will lie fallow for a year before being replanted.

Once in the distillery, the rock-hard pinas are cooked to convert their starches into sugar. There are two ways of doing this. The traditional fashion is to leave them in massive ovens at around 95°C for 36 hours. But producers such as Sauza are increasingly using pressure-cooking, which means they can complete the process in less than half the time. The end result is the same. The great, solid ball of starch has been turned into a gloopy mass of sweet, brownish sugar.

This then needs to be crushed and the juice drained off. Traditional producers (like el Tesoro) still place the cooked pinas in a pit and crush them with a stone wheel, while Cuervo and Sauza feed the mass into shredders and pass running water through.

The liquid (aguamiel) is then put into large fermenting vats made of either wood or stainless steel. Once again there's a split in production techniques, with the firms who crush traditionally putting both liquid and fibres into the vat (and ultimately into the first distillation). This, they argue, gives a richer flavour. Some firms (such as Cuervo) add their own strains of yeast to the fermenters, others add a little sugar, while it's also common for firms to add chemicals in order to produce a standardized ferment which can be whizzed through in a matter of a few hours.

The traditionalists however still rely on wild yeasts to trigger the ferment. Porfidio occupies a half-way house in that its new distillery is equipped with closed fermenters, but the ferment is allowed to run for up to four days.

All tequila is double-distilled in either copper or stainless steel pot stills. Once again, the exception is Porfidio whose new stills are adapted from the schnapps stills that Austrian-born owner Martin Grassl was trained on. These consist of a pot with two linked columns to concentrate and refine the distillate.

Many firms distil to a high strength and dilute immediately after, but others, such as el Tesoro and Sauza, distil to a lower strength – and the results are more pungent spirits which have retained the rich fruitiness of the agave. Sauza also claims to use a smaller central cut for its 100 per cent blue agave brands.

Silver tequila can be released after a brief period of marrying, while gold usually has some caramel added to it. However, it's the wood-aged styles – reposado (aged for between two and 11 months) and anejo (one year and over) which are turning the market around. The quality-conscious firms are experimenting with different sizes of cask and also with different woods. Traditionally ex-Bourbon barrels have been used, but sherry butts are also appearing, as are ex-Cognac barrels and, in the case of Cuervo's Reserva de la Familia, new French oak and, for Porfidio, new US oak for its Cactus brand. It gives blenders more building blocks to work with – different ages, different barrel types – to assemble these new premium brands.

Traditionally, tequila has never been aged for much over five years. In essence it is a fragile spirit, and after a lengthy period in wood that character begins to disappear (some distillers believe it actually degrades) while the wood takes over. Sauza has recently tried to prove the point that tequila can cope with extended ageing by releasing Tres Generaciones which, at eight years, is claimed to be the oldest brand on the market. Fine spirit though it may be, you're hard pressed to find true blue agave character in there. Still, it is evidence of the new-found spirit of quality that's taken over the industry.

How Mezcal is MADE

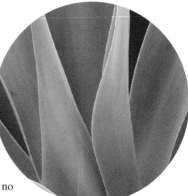

AGAVE UP CLOSE

There are many myths about Mexican spirits. Tequila being made from cactus is one of them, Mezcal making you "trip" is another. Both are untrue. Like tequila, mezcal is made from agave. In fact, technically speaking, tequila is a mezcal from a designated area. Wherever agave grows, mezcal will not be far behind – although most is from Oaxaca, it's produced across the central plains to the Chihuahuan desert, the Pacific coast and Chiapas. Each remote village will have its palenquero, or distiller.

What makes mezcal different is the result of a number of factors. The *terroir* of the region will have an effect, as will the type of agave used. While tequila can only be made from blue agave, mezcal can be produced from a host of different strains, including the giant agave, the wild silvestre, the rare but highly prized tobala, sotol and, most commonly, espadin.

The production, with a few exceptions, remains resolutely rural and rustic. The pinas are harvested at around eight years old, although this will vary between species and the richness of the soil. The sotol agave, for example, is smaller than the blue agave, takes longer to mature – and requires twice as many pinas to make a litre of spirit.

The process is subtly different from tequila. Whereas blue agave is baked or steamed, the pinas for mezcal are slow-roasted for three days, either over a fire in adobe or gas-fired ovens or in a deep rock-lined pit that's sealed with leaves and earth. As the pinas roast, so they absorb the smoke, which gives mezcal its distinctive earthy, rich pungency.

This roasting activates the wild yeasts in the pina and the cooked hearts are left to start fermenting naturally before being placed in a stone ring and crushed by a horse-drawn millstone. The fibrous juice is put into open-topped fermenters with a little water and left to ferment naturally.

Once the ferment is deemed to have finished – it can take between four and 30 days – the entire contents of the vat are transferred to the pot still. These are usually copper, but can be clay, like the one used for del Maguey's single village brand Minero. After the first distillation, the fibres are cleared out of the still and the second run takes place.

In del Maguey's case, the second distillation will contain the head and heart of the first distillation with a small percentage of the tail to increase the flavour. There aren't any hydrometers in these remote villages. The palenquero (distiller) will judge when to start and stop collecting spirit by sucking up the mezcal in a bamboo pipette and spraying the liquid into a gourd. The size and density of the bubbles on the surface tell him the strength and purity of the spirit. It's distillation as it has been done for hundreds of years, by people using nothing more than local resources, intuition and soul.

Mezcal remains the drink of the rural communities. You'll find some that's been sweetened, flavoured with herbs and bark and fruit; some that's fermented in leather and distilled once. The most unusual (and expensive) is the rarely seen Pechuga, a double-distilled mezcal which is redistilled with the addition of wild plantain, mountain apple, pineapple, plum, fruits, nuts, rice and sugar. To complete the melange of flavours a chicken breast is suspended over the alcoholic vapour.

These hand-crafted spirits are normally consumed not far from where they are made. Some are no more than crude moonshine, others are made with care and love. The few firms that do export (the most notable in quality terms being Hacienda Sotol and del Maguey) have then to try and convince people that mezcal can be as serious a drink as one of the "new" sipping tequilas. The complex range of hand-crafted organic, single village mezcals from del Maguey are a resounding demonstration of the heights that this spirit can reach. Untainted by commercial demands they remain the few spirits in the world which have a direct link to the past.

The trouble is that if tequila has long suffered under the image of slamming, then mezcal has to live with the legacy of the gusano worm, which some brands pop into their bottled product. In legend, because these moth larvae live in the agave, they have ingested some of its power. Therefore, the person who eats the gusano also acquires some of the spirit of the plant. That's one story. Another is that they add flavour to the drink – which is possible, but unlikely. Yet another claims that it "proves" that the mezcal is made from agave – which is a strange way to get an appellation. The most common story is that eating the worm makes you hallucinate. This comes from a basic confusion between mezcal and the unrelated psychedelic drug mescalin.

At the end of the day, the addition of the gusano worm is nothing more than a gimmick, and it's one which hasn't done mezcal any favours.

The MARGARITA
Classic Cocktail

The Margarita has been rather overlooked in the brave new world of the post-modern cocktail. This is partly because it was abused by unfeeling and uncaring barmen during the 1970s and 1980s, who turned it from a cracking aperitif that cleared your head and made your eyes gleam, into a glorified slush puppy.

The cocktail, in fact, has a pretty refined history before the madmen with their blenders got hold of it. Legend recounts that it was created though, as soon as the blenders began to be wielded with reckless abandon, so fruit began to be whizzed into the mix. To be fair, some are good – strawberry is a common variant, although the best I ever tasted was a blueberry one at London's Cactus Blue.

In principle there's nothing to making a Margarita. A good one doesn't mean a drink that will blow your socks off. Being too aware of the alcohol is the opposite of what you want to achieve. The aim is to

THE MARGARITA STARTED LIFE AS A SOCIALITE'S DRINK AND HAS SPAWNED A MASS OF VARIANTS FROM HIDEOUS TO SUPERB

for (or invented by) Margarita Sames, an American socialite of the 1940s, who used to serve it at parties in Acapulco. To be honest, there are rumours aplenty that a similar drink was already popular in Mexico before Margarita graciously allowed her name to be attached to it. What's certain, though, is that it was the first tequila cocktail, and a great one at that.

As so often, it's probably best to get back to basics. The first Margarita was a mix of tequila, Cointreau and lime juice. The best Margaritas still follow this basic recipe (*see* left). As with Daiquiris, intoxicate subtly.

First, use a good tequila, made from 100 per cent blue agave, such as abasic silver or reposado. Don't waste an expensive anejo brand on a Margarita. Cointreau is the best triple sec. Use fresh limes for the juice. If the drink seems too sour, don't reduce the lime, simply add some more caster sugar.

The best Margaritas are either shaken or stirred on the rocks – blending with ice may make them good and chilled, but you run the risk of diluting the mix – and just as you don't want too much alcohol, nor do you want too little!

TEQUILA

Ritual and tequila are so interlinked its often difficult to separate fact from fiction. At one time slamming was regarded as the real way to drink tequila, before then it was the salt and lime ritual.

Slamming was often the best way to drink some of the dodgier brands on the market, while the salt and lime way is basically just a lazy Margarita – the underlying principle in both methods was to get the alcohol down your neck quick.

In these days of sipping tequilas and mezcals a new ritual is needed. So welcome a truly Mexican way of enjoying tequila or mezcal – drinking with Sangrita.

This tomato-based fruit juice with its chilli kick is served chilled in shot glasses. A sip of tequila, a sip of Sangrita. You can buy it pre-mixed or make your own. In principle, it's a Mexican Bloody Mary mix.

As always, using fresh ingredients makes all the difference. Blend together 2lb of tomatoes, the juice of three oranges and a couple of limes, some onion and fresh chillis. Some recipes add hot pepper sauce (a Caribbean one is better than Tabasco) and use sugar, although if you need to sweeten the mix, then a splash of sherry is best. A true taste of Mexico is the result.

9 Anise

ONE OF THE WORLD'S OLDEST MEDICINAL HERBS, ANISE, (FIRST CULTIVATED BY THE EGYPTIANS) AND STAR ANISE (THE FRUIT OF A TREE ORIGINALLY GROWN IN THE FAR EAST) HAVE BEEN USED AS INGREDIENTS IN ALCOHOL SINCE THE DAWN OF DISTILLATION. WITH CLAIMS THAT ANISE CAN CURE STOMACH CONTRACTIONS, AID CIRCULATION AND BREATHING, AND ACT AS A STIMULANT AND A DIURETIC, THE TRADE IN ANISE WAS ALREADY WELL ESTABLISHED IN ROMAN TIMES.

ABSINTHE LURKED IN THE SHADOWS OF 19TH-CENTURY FRANCE

Pastis, anise and absinthe: the history

An important ingredient in the medicines produced in Egypt, Mesopotamia, and Ancient Greece – the key centres of the first experiments in distillation – anise lives on in the national drinks of these and other Mediterranean countries.

As an ingredient it is best-known as the main flavour compound in such brands as Pernod and Ricard, but it's also used in ouzo, raki, sambuca and the huge range of Spanish anise-based aperitifs and liqueurs. Peter the Great used anise as the sole flavouring for his own personal vodka (*see* Vodka), and it is still used in some flavoured vodka recipes, such as the Russian hunter's vodka, Okhotnichaya.

Anise only sloughed off its medicinal image in the sixteenth century, when it began to be used as a part of spirits such as the Italian liqueur Popula – which was made from water, *eaux-de-vie*, anise essence, cinnamon, musk and amber. It was also added to vinegars and soft drinks like early lemonades.

OPPOSITE:

THE STAR OF THE SHOW

These days it remains the most widely drunk style of spirit in all the countries that border the Mediterranean. From Lebanon to Morocco, Greece to Italy, France and Spain, every culture has its own variant on this most ancient of drinks.

The Green fairy

These days the drinks flavoured with anise are cosmopolitan aperitifs, cloudy, light green, yellow or white,

sipped in the shady squares of the Mediterranean. But the precursor of today's Pernod, Ricard and ouzo was a drink that scandalized Europe in the late nineteenth century – absinthe.

This notorious spirit first appeared in the late eighteenth century when a Dr Pierre Ordinaire fled revolutionary France and set up as a travelling physician in the area around the Swiss town of Covet. There he began peddling an elixir that was produced by the two Henriot sisters in a tiny still that sat on top of their kitchen stove. The sisters, carrying on the old tradition of "wise women", had concocted a recipe which involved infusing star anise, fennel, hyssop, melissa, parsley, camomile, coriander, veronica, spinach and, most importantly, wormwood, in alcohol.

Wormwood (*artemisia absinthium*) itself is an ancient ingredient, and is mentioned in John French's 1651 treatise *Art of Distillation* as one of the vast number of herbs, spices and roots that went into Aqua Celestis. French also recommended adding a few drops of the

essential oil of wormwood to a glass of "Rheinish" wine to make a "wormwood wine". The name, wormwood, comes from the German, wermut, meaning "preserver of the mind".

Dr Ordinaire's medicine became known as absinthe after this ingredient, and soon became a local speciality drink rather than just a cure-all. In 1787, the Henriot sisters sold their secret recipe to one Major Henri Dubeid, who promptly established his own distillery dedicated to commercial-scale production of the drink – which by now was building itself a reputation in Switzerland and the bordering regions of France. Spurred on by the success of absinthe, Dubeid's son-in-law, Henri-Louis Pernod, opened a larger distillery in Covet; eight years later he moved production back to France at Pontarlier, and his

BEFORE THE FALL FROM GRACE

absinthe – now known as Pernod – began to take France by storm.

The French aperitif market offered a pretty limited choice in those days, with people having to choose between wine and one of the bitter quinine-based tonics. The arrival of this strong (between 65 and 75 per cent ABV), dry, refreshing, scented drink was the fillip the market needed.

Absinthe received its biggest boost in the 1830s when soldiers from the African Battalion returned from the continent with tales of how diluting their drinking water with absinthe had saved them from a whole host of tropical diseases like malaria. On their return home they continued to drink absinthe and, in the way people do, smart society followed. Absinthe had become the hero's drink.

With this acceptance by bourgeois society, La Fée Verte (the green fairy, so called because of the green colour it went after water was added) became France's chosen spirit. Ironically, by the 1850s, when Cognac was making its mark on the world, the French were drinking more absinthe than brandy.

Production increased. Four more distilleries opened in Pontarlier and others were started in Doubs, Haute-Savoie, Jura, the Midi and Paris, although the best absinthe was still regarded as being from Pernod's original distilleries close to the Swiss border.

By the middle of the century, absinthe drinking took another twist when it was embraced by the radical artists, writers and poets – Baudelaire, Verlaine, Huysmans and Rimbaud – who were scandalizing polite society with their flouting of morals and their radical, visionary approach to writing and painting. As well as experimenting with hashish and opium, they saw absinthe

not just as a drink, but as a stimulus to creativity. In 20 years absinthe had gone from being the saviour of heroic soldiers to the equivalent of LSD. "The most delicate, the most precarious adornment, to be drunk of the magic of that herb from the glaciers, absumphe!" wrote Rimbaud in 1872.

Almost inevitably, it came under the scrutiny of the self-appointed guardians of the nation's morals, and from the late 1870s on absinthe began its rapid fall from the height of fashionability and cafe society to become the tipple of madmen and degenerates.

By the start of this century, absinthe was being blamed for all of French society's ills (a bit like the English middle classes had done with gin). Dementia, crime, TB ... you name it, absinthe took the rap.

Scientists claimed to have discovered a new mental disease called "absinthism", which could be passed on from mother to child. In *The Hyperreal Drug Archives*, Matthew Baggott relates that absinthism was allegedly "characterized by addiction, hyperexcitability, tremors, convulsions and hallucinations".

Politicians railed against the evil grip that the Green Fairy was exerting on the nation, as did the protectors of "family values" and the Press. Winemakers, seeing an opportunity to get sales moving again after *phylloxera*, joined in the free-for-all, rallying support around the less-than-catchy, but effective, slogan of "Up With Wine, Down With Absinthe". On January 7, 1915, production of absinthe was banned.

Over 80 years on, absinthe still has a sinister reputation. Even today you will hear people claiming that artists such as Toulouse-Lautrec were killed by their addiction to absinthe –

although syphilis and laudanum were probably more to blame.

There is no doubt that absinthe ruined many lives, but this was more a result of its extremely high alcoholic strength, than of any weird, addictive, mind-bending poison that lurked in its opalescent depths.

It might seem strange to devote all this space to a drink that barely exists today, but absinthe still captures the imagination of all spirit lovers. It mirrors the change in Western society's attitude to spirits that emerged in the twentieth century – it also carries with it echoes of the primal spirits, the mind-altering shamanic drugs that elevate you to a different plane of reality.

But was absinthe itself addictive? Yes and no. Pernod's absinthe was 75 per cent ABV. Drink a lot of that on a regular basis, and you are liable to be flirting with alcoholism, which has remarkably similar symptoms to "absinthism". The drink was cheap, it was strong, it was widely available and it was often poorly made. There are records of unscrupulous producers

making "absinthe" from a base of wood alcohol with copper sulphate being added for colour, and (the highly toxic) antimony to make it go cloudy. No great surprise, then, that it produced rather bizarre effects.

That doesn't quite address the fact that absinthe intoxication is unlike any other. In my experience the closest is achieved with Chartreuse and Calisay (*see* Liqueurs), but while they both give a certain detached, contemplative effect, absinthe is an altogether more intense experience – an absinthe-induced hangover feels as if your brain stem has been severed. This could be entirely down to the alcoholic strength, but, intriguingly, as Baggott points out, wormwood contains thujone, part of the same chemical group that includes THC, the active ingredient in cannabis that induces hallucinations. Records also show that some absinthe producers used the mildly psychoactive calamus and nutmeg in their recipes. Perhaps there's something to it after all.

Absinthe remains banned in most of Europe, although it can be bought in Andorra, Spain, Portugal, Denmark and

the Czech Republic. Sadly, given today's timid attitude to alcohol, it would seem unlikely that many spirits lovers will be able to join in Rimbaud's toast: "Long live the Absinthe Academy!"

What happened next ...

Pernod's Pontarlier distillery was closed by the ban on absinthe and France had to wait until after the First World War before a new, acceptable variant was allowed to be made.

In 1920, the various firms that had been set up by Pernod and his sons joined forces, and in 1928 the firm launched its new eponymous anise drink, sweeter, lower in alcohol and without wormwood. The French, deprived of their favourite aperitif, took to it immediately and the absinthe that had fuelled the fantastical writings of Baudelaire, Poe and Apollinaire became the more civilized Pernod, once more sipped by cafe society.

This time, though, Pernod wasn't to have the market all to itself. In 1932, 23-year-old Paul Ricard discovered a formula for an anise-based pastis, while other small producers, based in the south of the country, also started up. Ricard took Pernod on before eventually reaching an amicable agreement in 1975, when the two firms merged. By 1984, one billion bottles of Ricard had been sold. The Green Fairy had gone like the Wicked Witch of the West; the world was ready for anise once more.

ABSINTHE REPLACES THE TEARS OF A CLOWN WITH A PERMANENT GRIN

A NEW STYLE LED TO A NEW RESPECTABILITY

How it's made

From elixir to fashionable drink to scourge of scoiety and, now, once again, a distinctly classic and individual aperitif, anise-based spirits have a long, varied and colourful history in all the countries that border the Mediterranean.

Absinthe

All anise (and wormwood) drinks would have started their days as medicinal extracts obtained by either distilling or macerating herbs in alcohol. The absinthe prescribed by Dr Ordinaire was a complex infusion of 15 herbs – the main ingredients being star anise, fennel and wormwood left to steep in alcohol and bottled at around 80 per cent ABV. Though unusual these days, this high strength was quite common for medicinal extracts. Chartreuse Elixir (*see* Liqueurs) is 71 per cent ABV, and the standard Green Chartreuse is 50 per cent.

Pernod built in greater complexity to his absinthe recipe by not only adding other ingredients – hyssop, lemon balm, angelica, dittany, juniper, nutmeg and veronica – but then distilling the macerated alcohol (made from wine spirit rather than the more widely available maize or beet) and then adding more dried herbs, including an extra dose of wormwood, before diluting the mixture to the desired strength of 75 per cent ABV.

Pernod

When the firm was allowed to produce anise-based spirit again, it revamped its production methods and some of the ingredients. Until recently, all of Pernod's aniseed flavour was derived from Chinese star anise, although since 1982 the firm has also been using fennel.

Pernod is built up in three main blocks. The star anise and fennel are distilled and rectified to produce an essential oil called anethol. This is then blended with neutral alcohol and the distillates of a number of aromatic plants. The firm keeps the number and nature of these a closely guarded secret. Meanwhile liquorice is macerated in alcohol and blended with another distillate of flavouring herbs. These component parts are then blended together with neutral alcohol, softened water, glucose syrup and colouring agents before being filtered, stored and bottled.

You'll find Pernod's recipe varies slightly between countries – some get a spirit that's been sweetened with saccharose rather than glucose syrup, while the addition of synthetic colouring is not permitted in some countries. The strength will vary between 40 and 45 per cent ABV. If you get the choice, go for the higher strength.

Pastis is made in a significantly different fashion. While Pernod uses distillation, pastis is made solely by macerating the flavour compounds in spirit. The aniseed flavour is also obtained in a different fashion – while the colour is different.

Ricard is made in a four-step process. It, too, uses anethol, produced by rectifying star anise and fennel, but it also uses alcohol flavoured with liquorice root. The roots are crushed and placed on a screen inside a closed-circuit system through which water and neutral alcohol is forced, thereby extracting the aromatic juices, (a similar process is used to produce Zubrowka vodka). It's this particular method of extraction that gives Ricard its amber colour.

These two aromatic bases are then shipped to all of Ricard's production centres in France and abroad. There the secret collection of other dried aromatic ingredients native to Provence are mixed together. These are then placed in a mix of neutral spirit (most commonly from sugar beet), water and the two aromatic concentrates. The mix is adjusted with sugar and caramel and left to macerate for a minimum of 24 hours and a maximum of 72 hours.

The product is filtered three times and then bottled at a higher strength than Pernod, as Ricard claims that pastis has to be at a minimum of 45 per cent ABV in order to fully dissolve the anethol and make the product stable.

A smaller pastis producer, Janot, claims to use a more traditional method. For its standard pastis, the Provençal ingredients are left to macerate in neutral alcohol for a minimum of three weeks before being filtered and then bottled.

Janot's top pastis, Grand Pastis Lou Garagai, is one of the most complex on the market – having a wider selection of flavouring ingredients (including wormwood flowers), which are left to steep in higher-grade spirit for 12 weeks. The firm claims it is the only one to use this old, long maceration technique.

PASTIS – THE PROVENÇAL CLASSIC

The TASTE

Absinthe makes the heart grow fonder

My first meeting with absinthe was in a duty-free shop in Andorra where a bottle was bought partly for academic interest – and partly to scare my mother-in-law. It's difficult to separate fact from fiction when it comes to this spirit. Absinthe has been an unknown quantity for so long that no one quite knows what it should taste like. The initial reaction is that it is simply a more intense pastis, but there's a depth to it – partly from the alcohol.

Then there's its extraordinary colour. All anise-based drinks go cloudy when water is added because anethol forms an emulsion when it's diluted, but while Pernod turns a gentle green and pastis goes yellow, absinthe turns the colour of opal and seems to glow in the glass.

If you experience difficulty in finding a bottle, look at Degas's *The Absinthe Drinker*. Not only does the painting capture the lifeless slouch of an alcoholic, but the colour of the drink is exactly correct.

These days absinthe is also sold in the Czech Republic. It was one of the spirits that eluded me in my global trawl, but a friend who visited Prague agreed to act as guinea-pig. His tasting note is worth repeating in full. "...As per your recommendation I tried the absinthe – Bloody Hell!! What is that stuff? It seemed to metamorphose in the mouth into some weird, hot substance reminiscent of something used to aid aircraft propulsion. Mind you, its blue colour was rather reminiscent of paraffin. It seemed to change to a "hot" liquid in the mouth. Not "hot" in the usual alcoholic "nippy" way, but hot as in temperature, and weird in texture, slimy?! I have tried many unusual drinks in my time, but I have to say I think this one beats them all." Quite what this blue spirit was made from is not worth investigating.

Although pastis and Pernod can be

mixed with various soft drinks and cordials, the best way to sip them is to dilute them with five parts of water, see the drink change from clear to cloudy and allow the rich aniseed and liquorice aromas to rise from the glass. While Pernod smells of aniseed twists and sweet shops, pastis is refreshing, delicate and dry. Ricard is the benchmark style, but Pernod's 51 is a crisp alternative, while Janot's rich, clean mix of liquorice and wild herbs is the perfect refreshing drink for a hot, dusty climate.

Indeed the best place to drink them is in pastis's home territory, the south of France. It could be the scent of herbs in the air or just the general ambience: on ariving in Provence you'll automatically start drinking pastis. Whether you are in the midst of Marseille's chaotic anarchy or a tiny cafe in the hills, it's simply the thing to do. Pastis makes the south of France suddenly make sense.

DEGAS' DEFINITIVE STUDY OF THE DESPAIR OF ABSINTHISM

Other Anise-based DRINKS

ENJOYING A REVIVAL

Ouzo and raki

Anise-flavoured spirits have been the national spirit of the Eastern Mediterranean since the days of the Byzantine Empire, when the distillers of Greece and Smyrna were recognized as being masters of their craft. These rakitzides used copper stills produced for them by Armenian coppersmiths, and distilled spirits from the dried pomace (raki) of grapes, although occasionally figs would be used. This was then flavoured with aniseed, fennel, aromatic herbs and mastic – the aromatic resin from an evergreen tree.

The drink's height of popularity came during the Ottoman Empire; in

fact, so much raki was being drunk that alcohol had to be imported from Russia and France to cope with demand.

When the Greeks were kicked out of Asia Minor in 1922, the rakitzides moved to Macedonia, by then the centre for production of Greek spirits. Rapid commercial success followed, with production and consumption growing at an extraordinary rate. The drink by now was called ouzo – allegedly after the inscription *uso Massalia* that was put on casks of the spirit that were bound for Marseille. The French, it would seem, had looked east during the dearth of home-produced anise spirits.

The arrival of mass production resulted in a drop in quality, although ouzo experts now agree that things are improving once more, with greater care being taken over distillation, and many producers reviving the old ways of producing their native spirit.

There is a variety of ways to make ouzo and its relatives. Some producers use pot stills to redistil aniseed and other flavouring agents with molasses spirit. Others, such as Mavromatis, distil anise and fennel seeds and blend it with alcohol. In general, ouzo is used to describe molasses-based alcohol with aniseed flavouring, while tsipouro and raki are made from pomace and flavoured with aniseed (although to be strictly accurate not all tsipouro are aniseedy). It's complicated.

In general ouzo is drier and more delicate than pastis, and goes a pale, milky colour when diluted. Although the standard brands – such as the top-selling <12> – tend to be at 40 per cent ABV, the best examples are stronger, confirming Ricard's belief that you need to have a strength of 45 per cent ABV or more to achieve a balanced anise drink.

Typically ouzo producers are now making in a different number of styles and strengths. The EPOM group, based in Mytilene on the island of Lesvos, make three styles – Mini (40 per cent ABV), the more delicately flavoured Fimi (42 per cent ABV) and the old-style double-distilled Lesvos (46 per cent ABV).

Raki remains an important spirit in Levantine countries like Lebanon. Although the country produces world-class wines, raki remains the drink most commonly seen on the table in restaurants – and top wine producers such as Chateau Musar and Kefraya both make excellent, delicate examples.

Every Mediterranean country has an anise-based spirit, often bridging different categories. Italy has sambuca (*see* Liqueurs), while Spain has a vast range of liqueurs and aperitifs based on anise, from the Basque speciality Pacharan (*see* Other Spirits) to Chinchon (Liqueurs) and the most widely distributed straight anise, Anis del Mono. This is made by redistilling anethol with neutral spirit, and is sold in two styles – Dulce (sweet) which has a red label, or Seco (dry) which has a green one. It is a classic Spanish anise, light and fragrant and a design classic, not just thanks to its ornate bottle – based, legend has it, on a perfume bottle that was owned by the owner's wife – but to the story attached to its bizarre label.

The firm was founded at the end of the nineteenth century by Vicente Bosch, who had gone into business with his brother, but they fell out. In fact, they fell out so acrimoniously that Bosch replaced the face of the monkey on the label with a caricature of his brother. The label features this hideous, man-faced creature to this day. Somehow such a bizarre story seems only appropriate for this age-old drink.

THE PERFECT ACCOMPANIMENT TO MEZE

10 Other *spirits of the* World

THESE DAYS INTERNATIONAL BRANDS RUN INTO HIGH NUMBERS, YET DESPITE THE INCREASINGLY HOMOGENOUS RANGE OF DRINKS THAT ARE AVAILABLE, THE TRUE SPIRITS HOUND CAN ROOT OUT THE LESSER-KNOWN (BUT IN NO WAY INFERIOR) STYLES OF SPIRITS. HERE ARE SOME TO LOOK OUT FOR.

Other brandies

YOU NAME IT – IT CAN BE TURNED INTO A SPIRIT

Every wine-producing country has a brandy industry attached, yet few reach the quality standards set in Cognac, Armagnac and Jerez. In Germany, for example, huge volumes of brandy are drunk, but the product – though pleasant enough – hardly gets your pulse racing. One reason for this is that German brandy producers have traditionally distilled from grapes sourced in the hotter south of Europe for their spirit – although some, such as Asbach, also import wine from Cognac and Armagnac.

A warm climate means that it's difficult to produce grapes that have the right balance between ripeness and acidity that's needed for brandy production. A high-sugar, low-acidity grape is deadly for quality brandy (*see* Cognac, pages 70–78), producing a fat spirit that lacks definition.

OPPOSITE:

AN ACQUIRED TASTE – BUT ONE WORTH GETTING

German brandy can be distilled in either column or pot stills, and additions such as caramel, boise and other flavouring agents (such as prune juice) are permitted. A brandy must spend a minimum of six months in oak before being released. Any longer than a year in cask, and it can be designated as either Uralt or Alter. The top brand is Asbach, a tasty, undemanding product – not far removed from standard VS Cognac in style.

Although Italy claims to have invented the term "brandy" (*branda* in the Piemontese dialect meant *aqua vitae*), it has never been recognized as a top-class producer. Like the German product, the style is decent enough – produced from a mix of varieties, distilled in column and pot stills, and aged in large vats and small barrels. Generally they are rather light and delicate, with Carpene Malvolti and the top-end selection from Buton (sold as Vecchia Romagna) being the finest examples. Good though they are, if you want to discover Italy's true spirit, look at grappa (*see* pages 87–89).

The further south you go in Europe, the hotter it gets. Therefore by the time you hit Greece you know that you won't be getting grapes with low ripeness and high acidity. The Greeks have got round the problem of super-ripe raw material by turning their brandies into a cross between a brandy and a liqueur. Brands such as Metaxa

have herbal additives and sweetening agents blended into them. Metaxa is drunk in huge volumes by holidaymakers, but tends to be one of those bottles that sits in the back of the cupboard when you get home.

The top brandies from Eastern Europe have long been recognized as coming from Armenia. Since this country can lay claim to being one of the cradles of winemaking, there's little surprise that it has a heritage of distillation. The top examples hail from the Ararat distillery, which uses Charentais stills and ages in barrels made at the distillery's own cooperage. The finest ones, sold under the Noyac label, are world-class.

These brandies were rarely seen outside the Soviet Union during the Communist era – although they were great favourites of the Politburo and were praised by visiting brandy-loving dignitarie, including Winston Churchill.

When the Iron Curtain came down, they made an all-too-brief appearance in the West, before war disrupted the joint ventures that were aiming to secure them long-term distribution.

American brandies have been saddled with an image problem. For years the industry was quite happy churning out basic, bottom-end stuff, predominantly from the massive plantings of Thompson Seedless grapes in California's (hot) Central Valley. Gallo – now better known for its table wines – is the biggest producer, followed by such names as Paul Masson, Korbel and Christian Brothers, however the brandies are not anything to write home about.

There is a ray of hope, however, with the emergence of a new top-quality tier. These brandies are being produced by firms who have gone to the cooler regions of the state, and using Charentais stills. They have planted the top Cognac and Armagnac varieties – although some also use Pinot Noir and Gamay. These firms, such as Germain-Robin (also known as Alambic), Jepson and RMS, all produce high-quality, Cognac-aligned brandies that can hold their own with VSOP and XO brands.

Perhaps surprisingly, Mexico is home to the world's biggest-selling brandy – Presidente. Made by Domecq from its own vineyards and aged in solera, it's light, slightly sweet, and best drunk long and mixed.

South Africa has a long history of brandy production, with distilling starting immediately after the Dutch planted vines in the Cape in the seventeenth century. The early spirit, however, was noted only for its hideous quality – and its ability to disinfect snake bites. You have to wait until the end of last century for quality production to start, with the arrival of a French distiller, René Santhagan.

Today most of South Africa's brandy is made from Chenin, Colombard and Folle Blanche grapes although, with growers being encouraged to push yields up to the maximum and not picking when the grapes are high in acidity, the base material is not always ideal.

Light-flavoured, mixable blends made from column and pot stills make up the bulk of production, but there are some good-quality pot still brands on the market that have been aged in Limousin oak.

Production has been dominated by the massive KWV co-op, whose top-end range of pot-still distillates is underestimated. Smaller producers such as Backsberg are producing fine, high-quality brands on a small scale by rigorously following the same principles as Cognac, while the highly eccentric Carel Nel manages to make good stuff on his Boplaas estate in the torrid heat of the Klein Karroo.

The style of PISCO

A FITTINGLY SPECTACULAR SETTING FOR A SUPERB BRANDY

This South American brandy deserves an entry to itself. Pisco is best known these days as a Chilean speciality – although Peru claims it was the first to make the drink, pointing out that the town of Pisco is Peruvian and took its name from the local tribe who manufactured the clay pots in which the brandy was first stored. The drink's origins date back to the early seventeenth century when Spanish settlers, having already established vineyards, started to distil the wine. These days Pisco is a major industry in Chile, Peru and Bolivia – although it is predominantly thought of as a Chilean product.

Chilean Pisco is made from three strains of Muscat along with small amounts of other aromatic varieties like Torrontel, Moscatel de Alexandria and Pedro Ximenez. Producers often give the wine a short period of skin contact to increase aromatics. The grapes are grown in the north of the country, the best region being recognized as the Elqui valley. Although daytime temperatures are high, Chile's clear night skies means the temperature drops dramatically at night, which allows the grapes to retain acidity.

Contrary to popular belief, Pisco is not made from grape pomace but from "potable" wine distilled in pot stills. After distillation, the producer can choose between four legal designations. In ascending order these are Seleccion (30 per cent ABV); Especial (35 per cent); Reservado (40 per cent); and the top designation, Gran Pisco. Seleccion is usually kept in stainless-steel tanks for a short period before being reduced and bottled, while the others are given progressively long periods of ageing in large used barrels traditionally made from the local rauli wood, which imparts a very pale lemon/pink hue to the top brands. The most notable two brands are Capel and Control, but La Serra, RRR, de Guarda and Mistral are worth searching out.

In Peru, the different designations apply to the grapes used. You can therefore pick from single varietal Pisco Fur or Pisco Ciuvre (made from Quebranta, Quebranta Mollar or Negra Corriente), the more fragrant Aromatico (from Moscatel, Torrontel and Albilla) and the unusual Pisco Verde, which is made from partially fermented grapes. Top producers include the classy Ocucaje

GRAN PISCO IS THE TOP DESIGNATION

and Rosario de Yaura. The latter also produces a Pisco Crema, made by blending pisco with sugar, fruit concentrate and cream.

Bolivians know the drink as Singani, which is predominantly made from a distillate of Muscat of Alexandria. San Pedro is the best-known producer, and its San Pedro de Oro Monolito is rightly regarded as the premium brand on the market.

Pisco, like all South American and Mexican spirits, has long been sneered at by Western markets, who see them all as crude firewater. This couldn't be further from the truth. Good pisco is an excellent spirit, headily aromatic, mellow in the mouth. It's mixable and a useful cocktail base – responsible for one of the great summer cocktails, the Pisco Sour (*see* Brandy, page 90).

The higher up the scale you go, however, the more complex the aromas are and the drier the drink becomes, allowing the best Gran Pisco brands to be enjoyed in much the same way as a good grappa.

The other SPIRITS

Calvados

This apple brandy is the pride of Normandy, and is proof once more of the ability of artisanal distillers to use their skill on any ingredient that was readily to hand. The first record of Calvados production was in 1533, although as usual there is circumstantial evidence that it had been going on for some time before. Initially, Calvados producers would have used glass stills, like their Flemish colleagues (*see* Gin, pages 125–6), but copper pot stills soon took over. These days pots similar to those of Cognac, and small column stills like those used in Armagnac, are both used.

This being France, it's inevitable that Calvados has its own *appellation* (in this case, "apple-ation") rules, which govern permitted varieties, nature of distillation and ageing. Over 40 varieties of apple and pear are allowed to be used, and these are further divided into different classifications: sweet, bitter, bitter-sweet (the largest grouping) and acid.

The apples are picked (no fallen apples are used) and each distiller will have his own recipe of how to combine and blend the juices of different varieties to make his wash. Some will

APPLE-ATION CONTROLEE IN CALVADOS

include pears to give a jab of acidity. The juice is fermented, usually using only natural yeasts, and then distilled. In the top region of Pays d'Auge (which has its own AOC) only pot-still distillation can be used, while the rest of the region predominantly uses column stills. In general, Pays d'Auge Calvados is also aged for longer.

Ageing usually takes place in used oak barrels or large vats, and the maturing period can last as long as 40 years. Most Calvados, however, will hit the market as a 3-Star, (a minimum of two years old), but there are a number of other age descriptors. To qualify as Vieux/Reserve the Calvados has to be three years old, and VSOP/Vieux Reserve a year older. Older brands, often called Hors d'Age or Age Inconnu, are just that – old. There are also some smaller producers who release age-designated brands, and some vintages are also on the market. In other words, there's a lot to choose from – probably more than you thought.

As Calvados matures it loses its initially rather aggressive, sharp apple character and begins to mellow, picking up some character from the wood and softening into an evocative mix that brings to mind hot apple pie with hints of cinnamon, sugar and cloves.

Just as in every French region, production is dominated by the large *négociant* houses – like Busnel, which produces a well-rounded style; Père Magloire, whose brands tend to be younger and racier; and the excellent Camut, which has a house style that emphasizes richness of fruit.

The real delights, however, are to be found in the small artisan producers who distil from their own orchards. Top among these is Berneroy, whose brands are proof of how dazzling the complexity of top Calvados can be.

They are delicious, multi-layered, mouth-watering spirits. If you are lucky, you may even find venerable ones from producers like Isidore Lemorton, whose pear-dominant vintage releases go back to 1926.

Rest of the world

Apple brandy, or applejack, actually predates rum as America's first native spirit. Initially made by leaving cider outside to freeze, it was a viciously strong liquor. These days, brands like Laird's or Yukon Jack are made by double distillation and aged in wood, but they haven't lost the bracing quality that those early pioneers needed to keep them going.

In England, the flag for apple bandy has been defiantly flown by Julian Temperley's Somerset Royal brand. Temperley had to fight long and hard – first to get permission to distil, and then to call his product brandy! It was worth the battle. His brandies are a match for many Calvados and, with this being a new venture and with brandies maturing

quietly away, the future looks as rosy as a Cox's Pippin.

At their best these apple brandies demonstrate that what matters most in distillation is the care and attention that only a true master distiller can devote to turning any fruit into a marvellously complex drink. They also refute the idea that grapes are somehow automatically a superior raw material.

Other fruit brandies

The production of pure fruit distillates (*eaux-de-vie*) is a tradition that runs across a band of Europe stretching from Alsace through Southern Germany, Switzerland and into Austria – although, these days Spain also produces huge amounts. They appear to have been relatively late arrivals in the European world of spirits, although if Calvados was being produced in the century before, it seems unlikely that no small production was being carried out – especially since they share their heartland with some of the oldest monastic distilleries.

That aside, it wasn't until the middle of the eighteenth century that *eaux-de-vie* began to be produced in what could be called commercial quantities in this part of Europe. One reason is that distillers were spoiled for choice. They had an abundance of wild and cultivated fruits – soft berries from the forests, pears and plums from the orchards – on their doorsteps. The style of the spirit gives another clue. *Eaux-de-vie*, with an emphasis on clean, pure, natural flavours and an avoidance of wood ageing, can be seen as an extension of the northern white spirits – vodka, gin and akvavit.

Although there are some large concerns, the bulk of *eaux-de-vie* is produced by small, family-owned producers from their own stills. It may be a

cottage industry compared with gin or vodka, but the aim has always been high.

Production differs slightly for stone and soft fruits. Stone fruits (pears, cherries and plums) are lightly crushed, but, in general, the stones are not cracked as they are in liqueur production. Fermentation is usually left to nature, and so lasts as long as it takes. The more sugar, the longer the ferment, but the resulting "wine" is rarely above 5 per cent ABV, fairly low for spirits production.

Soft fruits are even lower in sugar, meaning that their "wine" wouldn't be sufficiently strong to be able to be distilled. To get round this problem, the fruit is macerated in alcohol before it's given a single distillation in order to concentrate the flavoured spirit.

Traditionally, double distillation in small pot stills is used for stone fruits. These are often equipped with an inner chamber to prevent the fermented fruit coming into direct contact with the outside wall of the still. Some firms have also refined this by adding a column to the pot. A number of top grappa producers in Trentino have adopted both these techniques.

The spirit is then allowed to rest and mellow in glass jars. Wood is rarely used, but when it is, old ash barrels that won't impart colour will be used.

Name the fruit and you'll find an *eau-de-vie* to match. Kirsch is probably the best known, and the top examples – usually from Germany – are elegant, rich distillates. The cherry stones are often lightly crushed, giving the spirit a delicate hint of almond. Don't confuse true kirsch with cooking stuff, which is made from kirsch essence and neutral

ALL OF THESE – AND MORE – CAN BE TURNED INTO EAUX-DE-VIE

BRITAIN'S TOP APPLE BRANDY

LA MIRABELLE DE METZ

Le retour de Rabelais

Du 25 août
au 2 septembre 1984

*A PLUM CHOICE FOR A
DIGESTIF*

alcohol. In fact, don't even cook with it.

Also widely seen is Poire William, although pears are noted for being difficult to get to ferment naturally and tend to be low in sugar, giving a weak "wine". This lack of guts often carries through to the spirit, which tends to be aromatic but lifeless.

A better bet is Mirabelle, a type of yellow plum which gives a charming floral *eau-de-vie*; Quetsch is from a larger mauve-coloured plum and, while not as delicate as Mirabelle, makes up with fruity weight.

The Eastern European speciality, Slivovitz, is another plum distillate. Its heartland was Yugoslavia, but you'll find Slivovitz across Central Europe – there's a proud tradition of illegal distillation of plums in Poland. The best variety for Slivovitz is considered to be Madjarka, and many brands spend a period in wood, which helps to mellow the spirit and give it an attractive, delicate colour.

The list is endless. There are *eaux-de-vie* made from cultivated fruit like raspberry, apricot, apple and quince (the last giving a robust, punchy spirit), but the most intriguing are those that use wild fruits as their base. In addition to well-known fruits like Mure (blackberry) and Myrtille (bilberry), you can find Houx, made from holly berries. It's frighteningly expensive, but has a wonderfully complex woodland aroma. Equally obscure is the piquant Gratte-Cul (it means "kiss my arse" ...) made from wild rose hips. It's a more polite drink than the name suggests.

While most of the world knows the *eaux-de-vie* from Alsace and Germany, those from Austria are unknown quantities – mainly because the Austrians drink them all. Here, under the name schnapps, they are part and parcel of civilized life, and the best schnapps are sipped neat in small glasses as a digestif. With the exception of the most rustic style, Obstler, which is made

from windfall apples and pears, they are beautifully poised, pure distillates. The most intriguing include Juniper, which manages to be delicate and elegant (a tricky feat with such a pungent ingredient); Ringlottenbrand, a zesty schnapps made from greengages; while Rowan is as hard to find as Houx berry, but is regarded as one of the finest.

The most exciting aspect of *eau-de-vie* is the often bizarre and obscure raw materials that are used. Right enough, not all are particularly pleasant – I'd steer clear of *eau-de-vie* made from gentian root – but you can chance upon some of the spirits world's weirder creations. It's a field made for the spirits hound.

Take Alsace distiller, J. Bertrand's Fleur de Bière. This is made by allowing an Alsace Pilsner-style beer to oxidize. The top part is then skimmed off and double distilled, and produces an astounding *eau-de-vie* with an intense perfumed aroma, with notes of cloves, orange, ginger and cinnamon and just a hint of hop flower.

If obscurity is your bag, try and find a bottle of Adlitzbeere/Elsbeer, an Austrian speciality that can lay claim to being the rarest spirit in the world. It's made from the fruit of the wild service tree, which is noted for its wood, but only Austrians value its fruit (the last recorded use of it in the UK was in the fifteenth century). The trouble is that the tree only comes into fruit when it is 15 years old, and when it does it produces a minuscule crop high up on its brittle branches. All of this adds up to a correspondingly high price (be prepared to pay over £100 for a bottle). Those who have tasted it claim it has an evocative scent reminiscent of marzipan.

At the other end of the scale is the old "scare the tourist" trick, Vipre, which contains a snake inside a bottle.

Thankfully the snake doesn't seem to impart any flavour (or poison) to the spirit, but it is an alarming sight that usually induces screams and fainting fits at the table when it's brought out by the grinning patron. There is a Polish vodka variant of this, called Zminowka.

Pacharan

This Spanish Basque speciality is one of those spirits that straddles two camps – a trick that Spain seems to perform more often than any other country. Is it a liqueur, an anise, or something else?

Pacharan is made by blending together alcohol that has had sloe (blackthorn) berries macerating in it, sugar syrup, anisette and small quantities of other supporting fragrances such as vanilla or peach. Each firm will put its own spin on production. For example, Destilerias la Navarra (which makes Etxeko and La Navarra) uses *eau-de-vie* distilled from the previous year's spent sloes as the macerating alcohol, rather than the more common neutral alcohol. The month-long maceration cycle takes place in rotating vats filled with nitrogen to prevent any oxidation of the fruit.

To make matters more confusing, Pacharan comes in varying degrees of sweetness and dryness, and a range of different hues from shocking pink to dark brooding cherry. Zoco, the most widely distributed brand, is the sweetest – in fact it's sweet to the point of being confected. Pacharan aficionados rightly dismiss the brand, preferring more traditional brands like Etxeko or La Navarra. The latter is light in colour, very fragrant and medium sweet, and packed with fruit. Etxeko is an altogether more serious proposition. Deeper in colour, it has a rich,

dry, powerful flavour in which the anise is muted, allowing the heady scent of sloes to be given its fullest expression. The extra effort that goes into production pays off.

Pacharan's origins are in the farmhouse kitchen, where it would have been made like sloe gin is in the UK, although in barrels rather than bottles. You can

still find "rustic" restaurants across the Basque region with barrels of homemade Pacharan in their bar. Try them. One of the finest pacharans I have ever had was one of these. Relatively low in alcohol, Pacharan is a style that fits in perfectly with the laid-back approach to life and eating that personifies Spain – although it's so easy to drink, that it can become a dangerous addiction.

Bitters

Originally spirits were there for your health. Any thoughts of pleasure could be forgotten. While most have managed to extricate themselves from this original purpose, there is one group – bitters – that remains firmly rooted in this ancient purpose. Because of this "drink it, it will do you good" aspect (and their often alarming bitterness), they are usually regarded as an acquired taste, and are not hugely popular in the UK and the USA, where the thought of drinking something to aid digestion is a

bizarre concept. While there are some brands that are so bitter that little pleasure can be got from drinking a glass, there are some cracking examples that can be drunk as aperitifs, digestifs, or used as highly effective hangover cures.

Bitters date back to the days of apothecaries, alchemists and distiller monks, and use secret amalgamations of roots, barks, herbs and peel to work their magic on your internal organs. Although you can find examples from Germany, Denmark, France, Spain and Trinidad, the country with the largest number is where it all started – Italy, where they go under the catch-all term of Amaro.

The notion of drinking something bitter to get the gastric juices going dates back to Ancient Greece – Hippocrates drank an amaro-style tonic, and there are records of a Roman patent medicine that is basically the same as a modern amaro, but without the spirit. One brand, Cinha, is still promoted as an effective laxative, which rather rules it out as a session drink.

Such was the success of amari that several Italian monasteries grew herbs purely for the drink. In time their cultivation was taken care of by a specific order of the Fatebene (do-wells) – one of whom was eventually canonized, thereby making amaro the only spirit with its own patron saint.

The bitterness is always derived from some vegetal ingredient, and brands usually include one (or more) of the following bitter substances: quinine, angelica, gentian, bitter orange, rue, nux vomica, artichokes, wormwood, bitter aloes and rhubarb root. The potion is given an aromatic lift by botanicals like vanilla, cloves, coriander, nutmeg, lavender and ginger,

ANGELICA IS ONE OF THE MAIN BOTANICALS IN BITTERS

ZOCO, THE TOP-SELLING AND SWEETEST PACHARAN

THE PERSONIFICATION OF
ITALIAN STYLE

... AND FRENCH

flavour is all bitter orange peel, liquorice and cloves backed up with a hefty alcoholic kick. It's not advisable to drink it in large quantities.

Averna and Montenegro are slightly less bitter thanks to the addition of sweetened wine, while Cynar is lighter and more subtle. This last brand is produced by redistilling its secret mix of alcohol and herbs before it is reduced to a gentle 16.5 per cent ABV. Rhubarb root, bitter and sweet orange peel are used, but Cynar is defiantly proud of its main bitter component – artichokes, so much so that one is on the label. It doesn't help sales in export markets.

The best-known Italian bitters is the aperitif Campari which was created by Gaspare Campari in his Milan cafe in the 1860s. There's no middle ground with Campari. It's one of those drinks that you either love or hate. It's the spirits world's equivalent of Marmite. Speaking personally, I love it. The affair started in my teenage years when I realized that it was the only bottle that was ever left unopened at parties. I weaned myself on to it and never looked back.

True Campari lovers have it ice-cold, neat with ice or with soda, but it is equally good with orange juice – orange peel being a main ingredient in the (secret) recipe. It's a brilliant drink that refreshes you and stimulates your appetite. It even looks good!

Martini makes a good Campari-style bitters which is slightly sweeter, Aperol is lighter, while Punt e Mes is sweeter again – in much the same frame as France's elegant aperitif Dubonnet, and great as a long drink.

Suze, France's top bitters brand, is more in line with Campari, being mainly served as an aperitif drink. Its bitterness is obtained from gentian roots, which are either distilled to get an essential oil

or macerated in alcohol before being blended with other ingredients and fortified wine. Gentian, though prized for its medicinal properties, produces a very earthy, essential oil as dry and dusty as a gnome's cave. The fact that Suze is an elegant, mouth-watering drink that shows none of this character is proof of a very skilful recipe.

Germany, however, remains firmly in the "this is good for you" camp, and the country is home to two of the most uncompromising brand of bitters – Jagermeister and Underberg. Jagermeister, whose recipe includes anise, poppy seed, juniper and ginseng, is currently attempting to relaunch itself as a versatile drink for today's clubbing generation, and is trying to get people to drink it mixed and long. In actuality, most seem to be treating it as the 1990s equivalent of the tequila slammer. Needless to say, because of Jager's relatively high alcohol content, it produces a quick hit soon followed by oblivion.

This potency is also the reason that people turn to Underberg, which is packaged in tiny bottles wrapped in brown paper. Underberg is meant to be a digestif, but it is most commonly used as a last resort by people suffering from a crippling hangover. It works – mainly because it tops up the alcohol levels in an instant, although the firm claims that it is low in histamines and biogenic amines, which cause headaches after too much alcohol. There might be something in it after all. Strangely enough, Campari and orange has a similarly efficacious effect on hangovers.

The two most famous Eastern European bitters, Hungary's Unicum and Melnais Balzans from Latvia, are more agreeable in style. Unicum, created in 1790, uses 40 botanicals and is gently sweet with a pleasant bitter-

although each brand will keep the percentages and ingredients a closely guarded secret.

The best-known traditional Italian brand is Fernet Branca. The brand, which started life as a chemist's potion at the beginning of the nineteenth century, uses over 30 herbs and spices (things are always vague in bitters), including rhubarb, liquorice and agarico bianco (mushroom), for bitterness, and angelica, anise, lemon peel and peppermint for aroma. The ingredients are either cold-steeped (macerated) or infused (gently heated) in alcohol before being combined and aged in large vats.

One of the most bitter of the amari, Fernet Branca is a digestif in the classic mould. Powerful, explosive even, you can sense the peppermint, but the

ness. Melnais Balzans is an altogether denser proposition that uses secret resins as part of its recipe – honey, mint and wormwood are also included. A richly complex mix of bitterness and dark mysterious aromas, it's an unforgettable experience.

One of the most recent bitters to appear is Denmark's Gammeldansk Bitter Dram which was launched in 1964. It's a blend of 30 different herbs, berries and essential oils – including cinnamon, star anise, rowan berries and cloves. Tawny/gold in colour, it's a soft, approachable drink, mildly herbal, slightly sweet and with only the merest bitter twang. A great introductory brand.

Altogether weirder is Catalonia's native bitters, Calisay, which is one of the bitterest of Spain's vinos quinados. These take their name from their main flavouring ingredient, quinine-rich bark from the chinchon tree. Calisay, specifically, uses bark from one particular type of chinchon – called, not surprisingly, calisaya – which grows only in Ecuador. A large amount of bitter orange peel is also added, along with other herbal components. They are all macerated in sweetened fortified white wine before being aged in oak. It has a bitters' signature intensity, but this is balanced with a liquorice herbal sweetness, making it seem almost like a liqueur. Like Chartreuse and absinthe, it produces a peculiarly floaty state of intoxication.

The most widely seen vino quinado is Chinchon, which is halfway between a bitters, an anise and a liqueur, and shares ingredients and techniques with all three styles – bitterness from the chinchon bark, anise extract and lots of sugar syrup. The legend has it that Chinchon was first produced by the seventeenth-century Marquesa de Chinchon, the wife of a governor of Peru who, when she was in South America, "discovered" the medicinal properties of quinine and gave her name to the tree from whose bark it is extracted.

South America was the original home of one of the most widely used bitters – Angostura. This powerful, aromatic brand was created by Dr Siegert, Simon Bolivar's German doctor who named it after a small town in Venezuela. It is still made to the same secret recipe, but is now produced in Trinidad. The company is fiercely protective of the recipe; all that is known is that it uses strong rum as a base and gentian root as the main bitter agent.

Angostura is such a powerful concoction that it is only used in miniscule quantities. Originally a medicine for malaria, it is now one of the most essential and versatile items behind any bar. It makes a pink gin pink, balances a Manhattan and, mixed with Campari and gin produces the Negroni. More difficult to find, but an equally useful mixer, is Peychaud's Bitters.

BUILDING A GOOD REPUTATION

Pimm's

Although bitters are not a British tradition, one of the most quintessentially English drinks comes from this field. James Pimm was the owner of an oyster bar in the City of London in the 1820s. It was the custom for these places, the fast-food joints of their day, to serve their customers either pints of stout or the same quantity of "the house cup" – a variant of the rum punches of the century before – with their oysters. Pimm's cup, which was based on the newly acceptable gin along with a secret collection of fruit extracts,

How to make a CLASSIC PIMM'S

Pimm's is a drink made to be diluted and drunk by the pint (preferably in a silver mug).

CUT A CUCUMBER RIND INTO STRIPS, SLICE AN ORANGE, APPLE, LEMON AND LIME.

•

FILL A TALL GLASS WITH ICE.

•

ADD A FEW DROPS OF ANGOSTURA.

•

1 LARGE MEASURE OF PIMM'S.

•

1 LARGE MEASURE OF GORDON'S/TANQUERAY.

•

TOP UP WITH 3 MEASURES OF LEMONADE OR SODA.

•

GARNISH WITH MINT OR BORAGE AND THE FRUIT AND CUCUMBER DECORATION.

liqueurs and bitter herbs, soon became noted as the finest. Even today, only six people know the recipe, and the purchases of ingredients are staggered so no one can know the exact proportions.

By the end of the century Pimm's was being exported to officers and gentlemen in the colonies, and it has never quite relinquished this rather snooty image – in fact, it has benefited from it.

Earlier this century, Pimm's was made in six styles, each with a different spirit base. No. 1 was gin; No. 2 whisky; No. 3 brandy; No. 4 rum; No. 5 rye; and No. 6 vodka. These days, only Nos 1 and 6 are available, after an all-too-brief attempt to relaunch the full range. There are Pimm's lovers in England who occasionally unearth a cache of one of the discontinued styles mouldering in the cellar of a country house. Contact your local wine merchant to see if they have recently liberated any.

Akvavit/schnapps

Akvavit is a Scandinavian variant of flavoured vodka, and is one of the great northern white spirits that are pure and delicate in aroma but still pack a decided punch. Its home is Denmark, where distillation started in the fifteenth century, but Norway also produces some excellent brands.

Like vodka, it's produced from a rectified spirit – most commonly made from potatoes. The difference between akvavit and flavoured vodka is that, while flavoured vodkas have their flavouring agents steeped or infused in them, in akvavit they are added and the mixture is redistilled à la gin.

The main flavouring is caraway seeds, but you'll find brands that also use fennel, dill, cumin and bitter orange peel. These are either macerated in alcohol and redistilled, or distilled to obtain

essential oils before being blended together, diluted and allowed to marry.

Slightly confusingly, although the labels will say Akvavit (Danish), or Aquavit (Norway), people refer to it as schnapps – the word coming from the Old Norse *snappen*, meaning to snatch, or gulp. That indicates how it should be drunk: ice-cold in small shot glasses as part of a meal. In Denmark it's traditional for each person on the table to stand up in turn and shout a toast (*skål*), after which everyone drinks the schnapps down in one. It makes dining out a highly entertaining, if hazardous event.

The most widely seen brand is Aalborg Akvavit, a style which was invented by Isidore Henius, a young distiller with very fixed ideas about quality (similar, in fact, to Sweden's Lars Olsson Smith – *see* Vodka, page 141). With caraway as its flavouring agent and bottled at 45 per cent ABV, Aalborg remains the benchmark style, whistle-clean but with an intriguing, delicately flavoursome bite.

The premium Aalborg line, Jubilaeums, is lower in strength and has dill and coriander in addition to caraway as flavouring. It is also aged for a short period in wood, giving it a pale gold colour.

Norway's top aquavits are Lysholm Linie and Loiten Export. Both are potato-based spirits with caraway and other flavourings added. So far, so good. What makes them stand apart from any other spirit in the world is their strange ageing process. Both brands must have been aged in casks that have travelled around the world in the cargo-hold of a ship. Strange ... but true. They are softer than their Danish counterparts, but equally clean.

Akvavit should be treated exactly the same as a premium vodka: drunk neat,

Arak started life in the back roads of the Far East

with food – it's particularly good with seafood and dill-flavoured sauces, or as a base for cocktails that call for vodka.

Korn

Although most people know Germany's main white spirit style as "schnapps", German distillers dislike the term, feeling it signifies a cheap, rough spirit. They prefer to use the term Korn, which is a more accurate descriptor, as the spirit is predominantly made from grain, although potatoes are also used.

The classification is further divided into two designations: the lower-strength Korn, usually used as the base for mixed drinks; and the stronger Doppelkorn, a double distillation of corn/grain – an easy-drinking spirit akin to a lightly malty vodka. Kornelius is a good example. The category's leading producer, Berentzen, has a premium brand, Edelkorn vom alten fass, which has been aged for three years in Limousin oak.

Recently, the market has been given a boost by the arrival of flavoured Korn, spearheaded by Berentzen's Apfelkorn. Low in strength, the Berentzen range blends the juice from fresh fruits with reduced-strength Korn. The selection now includes Saurer Apfel and peach. This last flavour is used in the British brand Archer's – a mild, dry spirit that's a versatile ingredient in cocktails.

It's unlikely that Henkes Aromatic Schnapps is much used by mixologists. A Dutch malted white spirit which, contrary to its name, has no flavourings, its main market is West Africa, where it has acquired ritual significance – in Ghana and Nigeria it is sprinkled on the ground in ceremonies associated with birth, death and marriage.

Arak

The last spirit category in this book could well have been the first one of all. Arak, after all, is claimed to have been distilled in India in 800 BC. Palm wine and fermented sugar-cane drinks were being made around this time, but sadly there is no documentary evidence that distillation was ever done.

Arak is a catch-all term that covers a multitude of spirits hailing from the East Indies, India, the Middle East and North Africa. To make matters more complicated, each country makes it in a slightly different fashion – often using completely different raw materials. In the East Indies it's produced from sugar cane and rice. In India, the name is used for a distillate of the sap of palm trees.

The name is originally Arabic (*araq*, meaning juice or sap), and it's worth speculating if the secret of distillation and the making of araq came from the East along the spice roads to the Arab seats of learning, or if the term and the secret was an Arab invention that was carried back to India and beyond.

In North Africa, Arak is made by distilling fermented figs or dates – Tunisia's Boukha is a good, if rather pungent, example of a fig-based Arak with a certain aggressive charm. The name is often confused with raki, which is an anise-flavoured spirit (*see* Pastis, pages 160–166) made from molasses or wine skins.

''Liqueurs

ALTHOUGH LIQUEURS CAN LAY CLAIM TO BE AMONG THE EARLIEST OF ALL SPIRITS, THESE DAYS THEY REMAIN A STRANGE, RATHER DISPARATE, GROUPING. THEY RANGE FROM THE CLASSICS LIKE CHARTREUSE, GRAND MARNIER AND DRAMBUIE TO MODERN BEST-SELLERS LIKE BAILEYS AND MALIBU. EVEN THOUGH YOU WOULD NEVER MISTAKE ONE FOR THE OTHER, THEY ARE ALL LIQUEURS.

THE MONASTERY OF GRAND CHARTREUSE – HOME TO THE FINEST LIQUEUR OF ALL

They come in all colours, from clear to Day-Glo, they are nearly always packaged in strangely shaped bottles, and almost inevitably have a fantastical story attached to their origins. They can be used as cocktail bases or be drunk on their own. They are made from a vast range of natural products gathered from across the globe and usually assembled in a secret recipe. You'll find liqueurs made from the skins, seeds, stones, flowers, leaves and pips of fruit, vegetables, spices and herbs. Every brand has a different story to tell – and many of them don't want to tell it.

So what are liqueurs? That's a tricky question, but for simplicity's sake we'll define them as being spirits-based drinks that have been flavoured and perfumed by natural ingredients and then sweetened. After all, they get their name from the Latin *liquefacere* – meaning to melt or dissolve – and it's this liquefying of ingredients, rather than the flavours of base spirit and wood used by other categories, that liqueurs rely on for their character.

Alchemists, apothecaries and abbots

Nowhere is the alchemist's hand seen as clearly as in liqueurs. When the art of distillation changed from producing perfume to producing medicine, the research involved making spirits and adding various beneficial plants, herbs and spices to it. Some were there solely for their medicinal effects, while others were added for more mystical reasons. The original recipe for Chartreuse – old, even when it was given to the monks in 1603 – doesn't just specify what ingredients were to be used to make the elixir, but where they were to be picked and during what phase of the moon.

This element of legend and mystery is still retained by these old liqueurs. Nowhere else will you find such a wall of silence when you ask how a brand is made.

The Middle Age alchemists and monks were looking for similar things, and their early results included a huge range of magical elixirs. It was a long process of trial and error that drew on folk wisdom, then-modern science and a fair amount of intuition.

The flavouring agents they used in their potions played a dual role. Not only did they mask the crude spirit (which itself was seen as a curative), but they had their own medicinal uses.

These early laboratory/distilleries were usually in monasteries (the art is generally agreed to have started in Salerno), and even today there is a religious connection with many of the most venerable liqueurs. The herbs, spices and fruit would originally have been sourced locally, either from the countryside or cultivated in the orchards and physic gardens, but as

OPPOSITE:

A MULTI COLOURED, MULTI-FLAVOURED CATEGORY

trade routes opened up between Europe and the East so more exotic ingredients began to be included in the recipes.

As the knowledge of distilling spread out from behind monastery walls, so the other guardians of folk medicine – wise women and healers – became involved. The name Strega comes from a local legend that women used to dress up as witches and make secret potions. The Henriot sisters, who made the first absinthe, were descendants of this tradition, while the secret essence that is used in Drambuie has always been made only by the women of the Mackinnon family. The past continues to live on.

Distillation was also taken up in grand houses that had huge inventories of flavouring agents in their kitchens and still-houses. They were distilling essential oils to make perfumes as well as medicinal tonics. Inevitably, there would have been some cross-experiments going on. You can imagine the woman in charge of the still-house wondering what would happen if she added rose oil to the distillate of fruits and herbs that was meant to calm her master's stomach.

In fact, stomachs play a large part in the history of liqueurs. The first recorded commercial liqueur – Lucas Bols's recipe for kümmel in 1575 – was made to aid digestion, not as a social drink. By this time, making liqueurs had spread from its Italian heartland, thanks partly to the marriage of Catherine de Medici to Henri II, which brought Italian Renaissance culture to France, and ushered in a different approach to liqueurs. From here on, alchemists continued their researches into the mysteries of existence, apothecaries and monks made medicines and elixirs, while home distillation brought sweet, flavoured spirits to the banqueting halls.

The compounds ranged from the simple to the complex. Alchemist John French listed 64 ingredients that went into his seventeenth-century creation Aqua Celestis, including roots, seeds, flowers and fruit, amber, honey and crushed pearls.

His recipes, published in *Art of Distillation* (1651), includes "cures" for 150 ailments, from fainting to baldness to impotence, with ingredients that not only ran through the usual aromatics but included human brains, swans, snakes and horse manure. Clearly, we're not talking of an elegant, after-dinner tipple here.

While social drinking of spirits was happening, it was only when sugar began to be brought to Europe from the Caribbean colonies that widespread commercial-scale production could start, and liqueurs' image begin to change. While there were still bitters and liqueurs used purely as aids to digestion, newer drinks were emerging that were simply there to be enjoyed – yet which retained the fruits of centuries of learning.

It wasn't just sugar that was arriving in Europe. Botanical ingredients were also flooding into Europe thanks to the Dutch spice trade. It was a godsend to liqueur and gin specialists like Bols and de Kuyper. The two firms – along with the French giant Cusenier – produced masses of brands from every exotic ingredient you could imagine: cinnamon, citrus fruit, cloves, vanilla, rose oil and coffee.

While they have rationalized their ranges in recent years, these firms can still boast ranges of drinks that look like an explosion in a tie-dye factory, and which are made from a huge range of flavourings. Their portfolios are a godsend to the world's barmen.

By the early to mid-nineteenth century liqueurs had got into their swing, and many of the most famous names – Cointreau, Grand Marnier, Benedictine, Amaretto Disaronno – were founded around this time. There was also a rash of strange brands, with long-forgotten names like Rose without Thorns, Illicit Love and Up Your Nightshirt, underlining the fact that they were the sweet potions that were plied on unsuspecting ladies by unscrupulous suitors.

This increase in brands was helped by the invention of the column still, which finally allowed distillers not only to produce in volume, but provided them with a neutral spirit base – which, in turn, allowed the flavours to express themselves more fully.

Liqueurs were still being sipped gingerly from small glasses by women at the end of a meal. Then the Americans got in on the scene and the market for liqueurs was turned on its head. Barmen, on the search for new potions in the first great cocktail age, discovered a database of flavours and colours that acted as brilliant boosters to the standard spirit bases of gin and vodka. They jazzed up drinks in the jazz age, giving them extra pizzazz, sweetness and personality.

In recent times, though, liqueurs have become rather *passé*. They are still drunk, but they have lost their lustre and appeal. There are only so many times you can tell the same story; they don't have a premium sector. Furthermore, there are very few brands (Chartreuse and Grand Marnier being exceptions) that have premium versions.

The market was given a new lease of life by the arrival of Bailey's Irish Cream, which introduced a whole new category to the world, but although cream liqueurs may make the figures for the liqueur market look healthy, liqueurs are very different from, say, malt whisky or vodka. If you drink a new malt or premium vodka, you're more than likely to try another brand the next time. If you like Bailey's, however, you won't necessarily become an instant convert to every single liqueur on the market.

It seemed as if they would just tick over nicely, until ... cocktails started up once more. Suddenly things are beginning to look brighter for these ancient brands. They may no longer be cure-alls or give insights into the workings of the universe, but they certainly make a cocktail taste good.

ORIGINALLY MADE BY WISE WOMEN

How they're made

It is virtually impossible to describe exactly how liqueurs are created because not only does each brand have its own technique, but many of them won't let you know how they are made anyway! Part of a liqueur's mystique, after all, is its secret recipe.

Although the possible combinations of ingredients are infinite, broad techniques are used to produce a liqueur – maceration/infusion, distillation and adding concentrates before finishing.

Maceration/infusion

Maceration is a simple enough principle. The ingredients – be they fruit, peel and/or roots – are placed in the spirit base (usually a neutral spirit) for a long period to allow their flavours to be leached out. This can take weeks or even months, depending on what the raw material.

Some brands will macerate different collections of ingredients in batches, while some will continue to add ingredients throughout the macerating period – just as a chef will add spices and herbs at different points when creating a dish. These days, some producers force the alcohol through the aromatics, while others use gentle heating (infusion) to break down the flavour compounds in the ingredients. The end result is the same: you have a flavoured base spirit.

Distillation

In broad terms, soft fruits such as raspberries, strawberries and blackberries will be left to sit in the spirit, which will be adjusted and bottled. Other brands will keep a macerated component as part of the final blend.

Seeds and nuts, peel, roots and leaves, however, have to be redistilled after their period of maceration in order to release their full flavour and to fix it in the spirit (*see* Gin).

The bulk of the top liqueurs will use redistillation for all, or part, of their product, although it's up to each distiller how he or she approaches this process. Some distillers will keep their different batches of botanicals separate and distil them on their own before blending at a later stage, while others will combine them and redistil the whole lot.

Occasionally the distiller will take some of the major aromatic ingredients and distil them with some water in order to release their essential oils, which can then be used as a powerfully scented blending component. Crème de menthe, for example, is made by combining the essential oil from mint with neutral spirit.

Concentrates

These are industrially produced additives that can be added to a base spirit, bypassing the need for maceration or redistillation.

Base spirit

The most commonly used spirit is a neutral (or high-strength) alcohol made from molasses, grain or grape. This allows the distiller to be able to show the complex way in which the flavouring agents mix and marry. There are some distillers, however, that also use a flavoured, aged spirit – for example, Grand Marnier uses Fine Champagne Cognac when assembling its blend, while Drambuie uses a blend of aged grain and malt whisky.

Finishing

It's common practice for the top brands to then age the finished blend – usually this takes place in large, used wooden vats which will mellow the spirit and allow the flavours to marry, but which won't impart woodiness or colour. Glass or stainless-steel tanks are also used.

After the ageing process, the liqueur is sweetened – mainly with sugar syrup, but occasionally with honey – and adjusted for colour. Some brands use caramel; others, such as Sambuca, use saffron; while others use turmeric, carrot or vegetable dyes. Then the liqueur is filtered, cold stabilized and bottled. It couldn't be simpler!

SECRET INGREDIENTS GALORE

The styles

Liqueurs are a minefield of different ingredients, techniques and flavours, but for simplicity's sake, I have divided them into eight broad camps: Herbal, Seed, Fruit, Nut, Crème, Whisk(e)y, Emulsion and Cream.

Some brands straddle two or more camps, and others seem to exist in a space all of their own, but hopefully this is a manageable way of looking at this diverse band of spirits. It will soon become clear that more legends and tall tales are involved in this family of spirits than anywhere else. Forgotten recipes, heroic acts, the hand of God, artists' models, witches – all will make an appearance. Many of the stories have to be taken with a pinch of salt, but which ones?

Herbal

This group includes some of the oldest spirits known to man and touch on ancient wisdom and arcane knowledge. They were initially created not to bring joy, but to cure illness. The only brand that has retained this link is the high strength Elixir de Chartreuse (*see* below) the most concentrated "liqueur" of all.

Thankfully for today's social drinker, the herbal brands are now lower in strength and not only serve as elegant after-dinner drinks but also make marvellous cocktail bases. It's impossible to list all the ingredients of all the brands, but enough can be winkled out of the producers to say with a certain degree of confidence that they will contain botanicals, such as angelica, hyssop,

mint, cloves, vanilla, nutmeg, saffron, thyme, wormwood, anise, aloes, orange and lemon peel, honey, gentian, quinine, caraway, cumin and almond. Some, such as Izarra, Fior d' Alpe, Argentarium and Millefiori, still only use local ingredients, but the majority will draw from the four corners of the globe for their flavourings.

Chartreuse

The story of the greatest of all liqueurs begins in the 17th century when the Marechal d' Estrees handed the monks in the Monastery of the Grand Chartreuse an already ancient manuscript which claimed to contain the

secret formula of an elixir bestowing long life.

This drink made from this concoction of flowers, herbs roots and spices was originally used by local people as a medicine, but as its fame spread, so the monks adapted the recipe to produce a more palatable drink for everyday drinking – and so, in 1745, Green Chartreuse was born, followed in 1840 by Yellow.

A visit to the Chartreuse distillery in Voiron is one of the stranger experiences for the spirit hound. For starters, there appears to be no-one working there and when you ask for details on how the liqueur is produced, the answer is always: "Only the Monks know the answer to that". The reason why no-one is around is that most of the day-to-day running of the distillery is done by a computer link between it and the monastery, 30km away. This means that two monks involved in producing every bottle of Chartreuse need only visit the distillery occasionally, leaving more time for prayer.

It is unlikely that any of Chartreuse's secrets will ever slip out. Only three monks know the recipe and they are only allowed to talk (to each other) once a week.

All we know is that the liqueurs are natural, their extraordinary colour coming from their ingredients and not

THE MYSTERIOUS STILL ROOM OF CHARTREUSE

DIVINE INSPIRATION?

through artificial colouring. A total of 130 are named in the complex formula, which advises where each ingredient should be harvested and when they should be picked.

As for production, all that is known is that the ingredients are macerated in alcohol in different combinations before being distilled.

The Elixir still adheres to the original recipe and is the most extraordinary flavour – and at 71 per cent ABV is best taken as a drop on a sugar cube, or diluted in warm water. Green (55 per cent ABV) and sweeter Yellow (40 per cent ABV) both have distilled honey added, before being aged, like the Elixir, in casks for up to eight years. The liqueurs which have been kept in casks for longer are designated as Chartreuse VEP.

No other spirit comes close to Chartreuse's intense complexity and, Green VEP in particular, is a taste that's never forgotten, an extraordinary explosion of wild flowers, honey and fruit that mixes sweetness with herbal power. All other liqueurs – and many other spirits – pale into insignificance beside it.

If legend is to be believed, the recipe for Benedictine was created in 1510 by Don Bernardo Vinvelli, a monk at the order's abbey at Fecamp in northern France. He was so delighted with his creation that he cried out "Deo Optimo Maximo!" (Praise be to God, most good, most

great!) a religious equivalent of "Eureka!". Given that Vinvelli isn't a particularly French name, it's possible that the brother had learned distillation in Italy.

The monks continued to produce the cordial until 1789, when the Revolutionary Government dissolved the monasteries and forced all religious orders into exile and the spirit disappeared for almost 100 years.

It was only revived when one of the monastery's lawyers, Alexandre le Grande, chanced upon the recipe. Liqueurs were enjoying an unprecedented boom at the time and, knowing

a good thing when he saw one, he went into production in Fecamp, in the process building one of the world's most bizarre-looking distilleries – a high-camp collision between Renaissance and Gothic styles, but with more gold.

The exact recipe is a secret, but Benedictine is constructed by first assembling five separate batches of 27 botanicals (among them juniper, myrrh, angelica, cloves, cardamom, cinnamon, vanilla and tea). These are either distilled to release essential oils or macerated in neutral spirit and redistilled. The batches are then aged

separately for a short period, blended together and aged again before being sweetened with honey and c a r a m e l , coloured with saffron, filtered and bottled.

It's a classic old liqueur, softly sweet without being cloying, filled with spice, some vanilla and scents of wild remote places.

Izarra

This Basque liqueur doesn't have such religious overtones. It is produced in green and yellow styles in a small distillery in Bayonne, and dates back to the 17th century. It's emergence coincided with the banishment of the Carthusians and was a sensible commercial attempt to steal Chartreuse's market.

The brands are rarely found outside their Basque heartland, but within it locals will go as far as protesting that Izarra is not only better than, but pre-dates Chartreuse. It's advisable not to argue with them.

Izarra is produced from a melange of 48 ingredients, including herbs, flowers and roots, sourced from the Pyrenees. Some of these are distilled to extract essential oils, while the rest are macerated in sugar beet spirit which has had a little Armagnac added to it, before being redistilled in a

pot still. The two components are blended, adjusted with more Armagnac and aged in large wooden vats. The yellow version is then sweetened and coloured with honey.

Though it sets itself up as the Basque Chartreuse, it doesn't have that drink's magnificent complexity – but is a pleasant, fairly sweet, lightly herbal drink which can be drunk either on its own or mixed.

The roots of the herbal liqueurs lie in Italian monasteries, but today the flag is flown by two relatively recent arrivals on the scene. Like most Italian herbal brands, these are sweeter and have more obvious anise components than their French counterparts and are coloured a fairly alarming yellow.

That said, Strega is obviously from the same camp as the oldest French herbal brands. The liqueur was invented in the southern Italian town of Benevento in 1860 by the Alberti family. It remained in small-scale production as the family was doing very nicely out of its main business, which was the export of wine to the north of the country and into France. However, when the wine business collapsed the family turned to liqueur production, and produced a drink called Strega (witch) after a local legend of women concocting secret potions in the hills.

The liqueur is made from no fewer than 70 botanicals which are macerated in grain spirit, redistilled in small steel pot stills, and then aged in large oak and ash vats before being

coloured by saffron. As a result, Strega has a gentle lifted aroma, where mint mixes with fennel leaf.

Italy's other famous herbal liqueur shares its name with the finest designer in the world and an acid jazz band. It has one of the drinks world's most distinctive bottles. Galliano was created by Arturo Vaccari, a Tuscan distiller who named his brand after a Major Guiseppe Galliano, an Italian military hero who in 1896 was placed under siege in the Abyssinian fort of Enda Jesus, a picture of which is on the label.

It's an amalgamation of over 40 Alpine herbs, roots, berries and flowers as well as fennel, star anise and vanilla, which are divided into seven component parts and distilled. The distillates are kept separate for three months in a tank before being blended, adjusted with alcohol, sugar syrup and colouring and given a second period of marrying.

Sweet with rich aromas of anise and vanilla, Galliano is too much to drink on its own but is a great cocktail ingredient – in fact it was the component which turned the Screwdriver into the Harvey Wallbanger – and made Harvey, a Californian surfer, hit the wall in the first place.

The final major European herbal liqueur is Spain's Cuarenta y Tres which, as the name suggests contains 43 herbs in it secret recipe. Oranges, cloves and anise are the dominant aromas in what is a rather sticky experience if drunk neat.

NOW THE FENNEL START ...

COMMEMORATING A FAMOUS HERO

The use of FRUIT

If the herbal liqueurs are direct descendants of the old medicines and elixirs prepared by monks and alchemists, the arrival of fruit liqueurs marks the change in drinking patterns, from the drinks that were good for you to those which were made for the drinker's enjoyment. That doesn't mean that they're simple concoctions – the best share a complexity with the finest herbal liqueurs.

Oranges…

Liqueurs can be flavoured with any ingredient that comes to hand – so the range of fruit-based examples is massive. The largest and most interesting section, however, consists of those that use dried orange peel. Although most fruit-based liqueurs only arrived in the flush of new brands that first emerged in the mid- to late-nineteenth century, orange peel was first used much earlier.

Dutch firms started using it in the seventeenth century, when the merchant fleet brought back bitter oranges from the new colonies in the Caribbean and the West Indies. It is a Dutch-owned island which has become inextricably linked with this style – Curaçao.

The liqueur trade became a larger commercial enterprise around the height of the Dutch East India Company, and de Kuyper – the important liqueur and gin producer – was founded at this time. One of its most famous brands remains the liqueur that takes its name from the bitter orange peel from Curaçao.

The method of making curaçao remains the same. Bitter oranges from Curaçao, Haiti and Seville and smaller percentages of other citrus fruits, blossoms, leaves and roots are soaked in a water and alcohol mixture and redistilled to release their essential oils. This will then be blended with either neutral spirit or brandy – and often coloured. They are subtly different from triple secs, which traditionally also use some sweet orange peel. Despite their name, triple secs aren't three times as dry, but they tend to be slightly more complex.

The best-known orange-based brand is Cointreau. It was invented in 1849 by Edouard Cointreau, the son of a liqueur producer based in Angers. He had arrived at Curaçao – quite probably to find out what the Dutch liqueur firms were going on about – and immediately started shipping back peel to the family distillery. He was a quick worker, as the first bottle of Cointreau hit the market in the 1870s.

Initially it was sold as a triple sec white curaçao, but such was the success of the brand – and so many other firms put out copy-cat products – that the name was switched to Cointreau. These days it's also produced in Spain and the USA.

Cointreau is made from a blend of bitter oranges from Haiti, Brazil and Spain, sweet oranges from the south of France and other citrus ingredients. These are macerated in neutral alcohol and double distilled in pot stills, before being adjusted with refined sugar and water. Light and delicately fragranced, with a whole range of citrus aromas – there's plenty of leaf and blossom evident – it was the liqueur used in the original Margarita (see Tequila).

Less well-known, but well worth searching out, is Ponche, Jerez's own liqueur. It is a classic example of how producers use local ingredients – in this case, oranges, sherry and brandy. The style was first made commercially by sherry producer José de Soto who distilled local bitter oranges, almonds, vanilla and herbs, then blended the concentrate with a blend of old amontillado sherry and Brandy de Jerez. Other Ponche producers, such as Caballero and Ruiz, have their own subtle variations.

One of the most distinctive-looking brands in the world, Ponche traditionally comes packaged in an eye-catching 75cl silver bottle and remains a classic digestif – delicate, aromatic and with a refreshingly bitter finish.

Although every bar in Spain will have a bottle on the back shelf, it's one of those drinks that has found it difficult to go beyond its domestic borders. It deserves wider attention.

The same could be said for Estonia's Vana Talinn. This is one of a range of high-quality spirits, made in the Baltic States that, sadly, are rarely seen out of their homeland. Hopefully, now that independence has been restored, they'll start to find their way on to a wider market. The liqueur is a blend of the essential oils of orange and lemon peel, with a macerated extract of cinnamon and vanilla. The mixture is then blended with some high ester Jamaican rum (*see* Rum).

Every country appears to have its own variation on the orange-peel theme. In South Africa it's called Van der Hum. This uses tangerine as well as orange peel, and macerates the two ingredients (and some nutmeg and other spices) in brandy before redistilling. It's a finely fragranced, well balanced example of the style.

Grand Marnier, however, is something else again. The brand is owned by the Lapostolle family, a famous nineteenth-century liqueur producer who also owned the Château de Bourg in Cognac. In 1880, Louis-Alexandre Marnier-Lapostolle, like M. Cointreau before him, was in the Caribbean looking for ingredients. He came across Haiti's bitter oranges and, once home,

started to create a recipe for a liqueur based on the fruit and the firm's Cognac.

What Marnier-Lapostolle did was to take basic triple sec/curaçao one step further. Most liqueurs would originally have used the local spirit as the base ingredient but, with the arrival of the continuous still, most were using neutral spirit. He reverted to the original technique and, as a result, built in

another layer of flavour and complexity to his liqueur.

Bitter orange peel (no sweet oranges are used) is given a long maceration in young, high-strength brandy and then redistilled at the Château de Bourg. This then is blended with aged Fine Champagne Cognac, sugar syrup and the inevitable secret herbs, and aged for another period in cask at the firm's cellars in Neauphle-le-Château.

The firm still makes a range of brands – including Cherry Marnier, Crème de Grand Marnier and Cordon Jaune (which uses grape brandy rather than Cognac) – but Grand Marnier Cordon Rouge remains its highlight.

It's a sophisticated, aristocratic liqueur that exudes orange richness with a complex mix of spice behind. The deluxe version, Cuvée de Centenaire, uses 10-year-old Fine Champagne Cognac in the blend.

The closest orange liqueur to Grand Marnier in terms of complexity is Italy's Aurum. Invented by distiller Amadeo Pomilio, it was named by the famous Italian poet Gabriel d'Annunzio. There are entirely plausible claims that it is based on an ancient recipe that originally involved the addition of flakes of gold.

It is made by a complicated procedure. Orange peel and flesh (from a local strain grown in the Abruzzi mountains) are macerated in brandy and then triple distilled. This is then blended with 10-year-old brandy, also produced by the firm, and aged again before being sweetened and coloured with saffron. Packaged in a bottle based on a flask found in Pompeii, this is a delicately coloured, complex liqueur.

The final classic peel liqueur, Mandarine Napoleon, actually uses tangerines rather than oranges. It was invented by Antoine-François de Fourcroy, and was allegedly the drink used by Napoleon in his attempt to seduce the actress Madame Mars. Records do not reveal his success.

The recipe was revived in 1892 by the Belgian distiller Louis Schmidt, and uses the essential oils of Sicilian tangerine peel blended with aged Cognac, which is then aged and sweetened. It's a fragrant, polished drink. A premium version, Millennium, packaged in a decanter, is occasionally seen.

SEDUCTIVE POTION

ARISTOCRATIC CLASS OOZES OUT

… and lemons

These days, a citrus-peel liqueur can claim to be Italy's top-selling style. Limoncello is, quite simply, the trendiest drink to be seen with. Originally a home-made liqueur, it has its roots in the Amalfi coast. The peel from local lemons would be macerated in alcohol for around a month to extract colour and flavour, before being decanted and sweetened with sugar syrup, left to settle and bottled.

The first time I tried it was on my honeymoon, at lunchtime in a deserted restaurant in Ravello, high in the hills above Sorrento. Nuns were playing football outside. The home-made liqueur was ice cold, the moment perfect.

Limoncello is the perfect palate cleanser, acting a bit like an alcoholic sorbet. In fact, originally it was created to be drunk, almost frozen, after a fish course, the equivalent of drinking the finger bowl. It's vibrant, brightly coloured and utterly refreshing. Sadly, as its popularity has grown, so has the number of brands on the market, some of which are a touch confected. If you can't find the real stuff, try making it at home with a good vodka, lemon peel and sugar.

Strangely enough, lemons also make up the main flavouring ingredient in the lurid purple concoction, Parfait d'Amour. An old eighteenth-century style, this is an amalgamation of macerated and distilled lemon (and other citrus fruits) with aromatic elements such as cloves, cinnamon and the all-important violet – although this doesn't give the drink its colour, that is achieved by vegetable dye.

Other fruit liqueurs and fruit brandies

The Italians also have a monopoly on high-quality cherry-based liqueurs. There are as many styles as there are types of cherry, but at the pinnacle is maraschino. Cherry liqueurs are not the same as cherry *eaux-de-vie* (*see* Other Spirits), but they are, by and large, made by macerating skin, pulp and stones in grape spirit.

Luxardo, which has its own marasca cherry orchard, takes this simple technique to extreme lengths. The process starts with the removal and distillation of the cherry stones to capture their almost almond-flavoured essential oil. The remaining flesh of the cherries (and some elderberries) is then fermented before the ferment is arrested by the addition of alcohol. This lightly fortified spirit is only used for cherry brandy – what the maraschino producer wants is the skins, stems and yeast that are left at the bottom of the tank. This is added to the stone concentrate and left to infuse for a number of months, before being triple distilled and then aged once more – this time for three years in ash vats. It's then sweetened and bottled.

Luxardo's maraschino ends up a marvellously concentrated sweet-and-sour mix with pungent cherry notes, mixed with a refreshingly bitter twang on the finish. It can be drunk on its own, but most people find it a bit too much solo. Best to use it judiciously in cocktails – try a tiny splash in a Manhattan.

Other cherry-based liqueurs may not have maraschino's intensity, but there are some soft and rather elegant examples – such as France's Cherry Rocher, or Denmark's Heering. Originally created in 1818 by Peter Heering, a Copenhagen grocer, Heering uses Sevn cherries from its own orchards. The fruit and the stones are crushed and, along with other botanicals, are macerated in wooden vats for months, during which time they are pro

gressively blended in a form of *solera* (*see* Brandy de Jerez). Heering's mix of intense cherry fruit with a light body has made it the integral liqueur brand used in a Singapore Sling.

Every fruit in the world can be turned either into an *eau-de-vie* or into the rather misleadingly titled fruit brandy. These aren't clear, pure fruit distillates, but are crushed fruits (often complete with their bitter stones) that have been steeped in grape spirit and sweetened. Some are wood aged, but that's uncommon, while many firms use fruit concentrate. Bols, de Kuyper and Cusenier all make good-quality, if rather simple, fruit brandies – the most commonly seen being cherry, apricot and peach, although in the 1980s, Suntory weighed in with its melon liqueur Midori.

Just to add to the confusion, you can find Poire William liqueur as well as the *eau-de-vie*. The liqueur is made by infusion rather than distillation, and is sweet and concentrated. Don't get them confused; they are quite different beasts.

The advantage with soft fruits is that you can do what people have done for centuries and make your own at home – though it's advisable not to distil your own spirit! Any soft fruit or citrus peel left in alcohol for a period will release its colour and flavour. Vodka is a good neutral base, but gin is a brilliant medium – seen in that English classic, sloe gin. This is made quite simply by steeping sloes in the gin for a few months in the dark. Sugar can be added during the maceration or after, according to taste. It's important to remove the berries after a few months, otherwise they become unpleasantly bitter. Several commercial brands are available on the market – Gordon's, Hawker's and Plymouth all make a sloe gin (Plymouth also has a damson gin) – but it's more fun to do it yourself.

THE ALL-CONQUERING CHERRY

POIRE WILLIAM COMES IN TWO STYLES

The use of SEEDS AND NUTS

A COTTAGE INDUSTRY

INTERNATIONAL FAVOURITE

Gdansk were producing caraway-accented Goldwasser from the sixteenth century onward (*see* below).

Whoever was first, kümmel remains a northern classic that's made by rectifying caraway seed and then blending the infusion with neutral alcohol and other flavouring ingredients (although cumin seed is not used, as is widely believed), and then sweetening the mixture. Mentzendorff includes aniseed and violet roots among its secret botanicals.

Mildly dry and slightly bitter, kümmel has moved a long way since its invention as a cure for flatulence. For some reason, it's highly regarded by senior members of English golf clubs... whether there is a connection between the two, I know not.

As well as being a main ingredient in akvavit (*see* Other Spirits), caraway crops up in the ancient Gdansk speciality vodka, Goldwasser. First made in 1598, Goldwasser contains infusions of aniseed, caraway, citrus peel, other botanicals and, most importantly, flakes of gold. The gold may originally have had a medicinal reason for its inclusion, but it's more than likely that it was used as an ostentatious way of showing that the owner of the bottle was very rich indeed.

If the northern sea ports' speciality was caraway-flavoured liquors, then their equivalents in the Mediterranean were doing the same with anise. Although the majority of these are dry to medium-dry, there are a number of liqueurs that have evolved out of this tradition – the most visible being Sambuca. Originally a Roman speciality, Sambuca is produced from

The production of liqueurs from spice seed is a natural spin-off from the ancient herbal elixirs. Rather than relying on the impact of a large number of ingredients, these liqueurs were usually made from relatively few ingredients and dominated by one particular flavour. They heralded a change in the apothecaries' art as, rather than being cure-all cordials and tonics, they were distillates of one beneficial herb for one specific purpose.

The oldest commercial liqueur, kümmel, is a member of this small grouping, as is anisette – the liqueur equivalent of anise.

The use of caraway seeds, the main ingredient in kümmel, is a peculiarity of countries that border the North Sea and the Baltic. Quite why this particular flavouring was used is lost in time –

caraway certainly wasn't an indigenous plant, although some producers like Blanckenhagen began cultivating it purely for liqueur production.

Where it originated is also open to debate. In 1575 Lucas Bols produced the first commercially produced kümmel, although Mentzendorff, the London-based fine wine importer, claims that its Latvian brand (sold as Mentzendorff or Blanckenhagen-Allasch) was the original brand, first made by the aristocratic Blanckenhagen family on their estate near Riga.

According to legend it remained a Dutch and Northern German speciality until Peter the Great arrived in Holland in the late-seventeenth century. A noted distiller (*see* Vodka), he is credited with taking the recipe back to Russia. It seems unlikely. For a start, distillers in

infusions of elderberries, anise and other herbal flavourings. Lighter and more fragrant than anisette, it was one of the fashionable drinks of the disco era, drunk according to traditional ritual with two or three flaming coffee beans floating on its surface – a remarkably dangerous practice if tried when you were less than coherent.

Anisette remains the main brand in the Marie Brizard range. It is produced by macerating a concoction of 16 seeds, plants and citrus peel, and then blending in anethol and huge amounts of sugar syrup. It is chill-filtered to stop any clouding. One for people with a sweet tooth.

Nuts

The infusion of fruits, seeds and nuts in alcohol is an old rural tradition – even today in Umbria, green walnuts are gathered, taken home, quartered and placed in large jars full of either grape spirit or a simple water-and-sugar mix. It is this tradition that could well have been the origin of one of the most famous liqueur brands in the world – Amaretto Disaronno.

Legend has it that the sixteenth-century artist, Bernardino Luini, was given the recipe for Amaretto by an innkeeper's wife, whom he was using as a model for the Virgin in his fresco in the convent of Sta Maria delle Grazie in Saronno. The story goes that, overwhelmed with gratitude (this is a familiar motif in the folk tales surrounding liqueurs), she whipped up a bottle of the liqueur from the fruit of the almond trees growing in her garden. Probably she'd have had a bottle already sitting from the previous year's harvest.

Whatever the truth, it wasn't until the late eighteenth century before it was commercially produced, first by an apothecary called Reina in his store in Saronno.

Although there are a number of brands on the market, the first (and best) is the Amaretto from the Reina-owned firm Illva that's packaged in a thick rectangular bottle. A total of 17 flavouring ingredients go into this brand, the most important of which are an infusion of bitter almond oil and crushed apricot pits macerated in neutral alcohol. These combine to give the drink its distinctive, rich, marzipan aroma.

Walnuts are the main ingredient in a speciality from Madrid called Madrono. The liqueur, made by blending the essential oil from madrono nuts with alcohol, had been forgotten until the early 1980s, when a small patisserie in the working-class district of La Vapies began to use the madrono nuts in its cakes. When the cakes began to acquire a cult following with the students who lived in the area, the couple who ran the patisserie decided to revive the liqueur, and for years it was only available by the glass in this tiny shop.

The cult continued to grow, and the firm has now switched to full commercial production – and larger premises. It tastes like walnut whip concentrate with a slight bitter edge. Italy's equivalent is the richer, heavier, more serious Nocino.

Good though it is, Madrono will never be able to compete in volume terms with Malibu, one of the most successful new brands launched in the 1980s when people, mistakenly, thought cocktails were making a comeback. A blend of rectified rum and an extract made from coconut pulp and milk, Malibu has a strangely thick texture, and how much you like it depends purely on how much you like coconut and how sweet your tooth is. The Brazilian equivalent, Batida de Coco, isn't quite as fat.

Personally, if you have to drink a coconut drink, I'd recommend sticking to a flavoured rum, like Wray & Nephew's Koko Kanu or Cruzan's Coconut, both of which are lighter and less cloying.

The French and Italians make a huge range of liqueurs from other nuts, such as Noisette, Crème de noix (hazelnut and walnut, respectively) and Crème de noyau (a mix of cherry, peach and plum stones).

The principle is the same for all the styles. The nuts are chopped up and steeped in neutral or grape spirit, filtered, sweetened and sometimes coloured. The most famous Italian nut brand is Frangelico, a sticky mix of hazelnut and herbs.

ONE FOR FLAMING LIPS

WALNUT SELLERS
IN ITALY

The use of CRÈMES

Although closely related to fruit brandies (*see* above), crème liqueurs form their own select club. The main difference is that they don't use the stones of the fruit, and are often produced with concentrates rather than by macerating the fruit, although some brands – crème de menthe, Himbergeest and Kroatzbeere – will also use essential oils. They are also considerably sweeter, lower in alcohol and more brightly coloured than fruit brandies. Fundamentally, they are sweetened alcoholic essences of a single fruit, herb or pod. They might not be complex, but where would the cocktail barman be without them?

The three huge liqueur firms of Bols, de Kuyper and Cusenier dominate this market with vast ranges of multi-coloured potions, but it's worth searching out the wild fruit crèmes from smaller liqueur producers such as Chartreuse and Izarra. Both these firms produce astonishingly concentrated examples that are hugely versatile, both in making cocktails and in cooking. Once you have tasted examples like their cassis or mure, life will never quite be the same again.

By and large, crèmes aren't intended to be drunk on their own. There are, however, two international crème brands that can quite happily be sipped with nothing more than a lump or two of ice – Kahlua and Tia Maria. These two coffee-based brands have taken the market away from the older, sweeter crème de cacaos made by Bols and de Kuyper.

Kahlua claims to hail originally from Mexico, although as ever there's

What do you do when you want to let things slide?

DO A KAHLÚA
Mudslide

It's get down good.

Over ice: 1/2 oz. Kahlúa,

1/2 oz. Irish Cream,

1/2 oz. vodka, 1 oz. cream.

Ohhhh yeahhh.

some debate over the accuracy of the statement. Some feel that the brand originated in Turkey, pointing to the turban-clad figure that appeared on the original label and the continued use of a distinctly Arabic archway – although both of these might be nothing more than Andalucian nostalgia.

A rich, flavoursome blend of cane spirit, Mexican coffee and vanilla, Kahlua was one of the brands that stormed into America after Repeal and immediately made its mark with the Kahlua Sombrero, and its inclusion is essential in the making of a good

Black Russian.

These days it claims to be the world's second biggest-selling liqueur brand, and is produced under licence in Mexico, Denmark and Scotland.

Its only rival in the coffee-crème market is Tia Maria (which is also owned by Allied Domecq). The story of the recipe dates back to the seventeenth century, when Jamaica was caught up in the colonial wars that raged across the Caribbean. When one estate was attacked the owners had to flee, and the young daughter and her maidservant Maria got separated from the rest of the

family. Maria managed to collect her mistress's possessions, along with a box containing (wait for it) the secret recipe for the family's coffee liqueur. Years later the girl gave the recipe to her daughter, who named the liqueur Tia Maria (Aunty Mary) after the servant.

The liqueur is a blend of Blue Mountain coffee beans and spices (including vanilla), which are infused in Jamaican cane spirit. A touch of chocolate is added before bottling. Tia Maria is sweeter than Kahlua, but lacks the former's body, allowing the spirit to show a little too much. It's a versatile mixer though.

This small but select band has recently been joined by Touissant, named after the black Jacobin revolutionary who liberated Haiti from the French. It is made by a Trinidadian in Flensburg, Germany. Life can get pretty complicated in the world of liqueurs!

It's a great alternative to Kahlua and Tia Maria with far more coffee (and a touch of bitter chocolate) on show on the nose. It's much drier than its rivals, making it easier to drink on its own or on the rocks. Worth looking out for.

Don't get confused between crème liqueurs and cream liqueurs, such as Bailey's. They are different creations.

The use of WHISK(E)Y

The vast majority of liqueurs use a neutral spirit base – Grand Marnier and Aurum are notable exceptions, as are the whisk(e)y-based specialities that include Drambuie, Glayva and Southern Comfort.

Drambuie harks back to the old herbal infusions that were made when whisky was first distilled in Scotland. In those days it was common practice for the Highland distillers to throw in heather and other aromatic plants to their *uisce beatha* and sweeten the result with heather or clover honey. Smith's 1729 work *The Compleat Book of Distilling* lists mace, cloves, nuts, cinnamon, coriander, ginger, cubeb berries and English saffron as being integral ingredients in making "Fine Usquebaugh".

It comes as no great surprise, then, that Drambuie is an ancient recipe, although the story of how the recipe came into the hands of the Mackinnon family of Skye is one of the more fanci-

ful that litter the history of liqueurs.

According to the tale, the recipe was given by a grateful Bonnie Prince Charlie to Captain Mackinnon as a token of his gratitude for saving him from the Duke of Cumberland's troops after Culloden.

Now quite how the Prince would have had the time or the inclination to do this when his life was in danger, the legend doesn't say. It's pretty unlikely that he would have carried a recipe about his person on a long military campaign in case it came in useful. In fact, the Prince spent very little of his life in Scotland, and had virtually no experience of whisky.

What's more plausible is that the Mackinnons were already making their liqueur, and gave it to the Prince before he sailed off to exile in France.

Whatever the truth, Drambuie is a cracking liqueur. The family kept the recipe to themselves for over 150 years until, in 1906, Malcolm Mackinnon

moved from Skye to join the Edinburgh wine trade and started to sell the occasional bottle. Very occasional, in fact. In the first year only 12 cases were sold.

These days Drambuie is still made by the family in their plant at Kirkliston, just outside Edinburgh. In accordance with family tradition that only the women can make the secret recipe, Mary Mackinnon assembles the

"...I hear normal folks milk cows..."

SOUTHERNERS HAVE THEIR OWN RULES

REBELLIOUS IMAGE AND
PEACHY FLAVOUR

essence and then seals it in locked containers. Another employee then blends it with aged grain and malt whiskies (the oldest malt is 17 years old) before it is sweetened with heather honey. Intense on the nose with touches of clove, nutmeg and wild herbs, it's a medium-sweet liqueur that's fresh in the mouth with a dry cinnamon-stick finish. Add one measure of Drambuie to two of a good blended Scotch, and you get the delicious (but dangerous) Rusty Nail.

Scotland's other main whisky liqueur, Glayva, was invented in the post-war period. It appears to be based on similar ingredients to Drambuie – heather honey, malt whisky and wild herbs – but it has a more pronounced sweet orange-peel aroma and is generally a sweeter drink. The name comes from the Gaelic Gle mhath! (very good!), the Scottish secular equivalent of Don Bernardo Vinvelli's "Deo Optimo Maximo!".

Scotland has seen a mini-explosion of whisky liqueurs in recent years. Stag's Breath (once memorably called "Baby's Breath" by my Glaswegian mother) is a blend of malt and fermented honey; Wallace is a clean, medium-dry mix of Deanston single malt, berries and "French" herbs – which appears to include some anise; while Hebridean is more malt-accented, with touches of cinnamon on the nose and a very light, almond-paste palate.

These are mere whippersnappers compared to Southern Comfort, America's greatest contribution to the world of liqueurs. The brand's origins are rooted in New Orleans where in the 1860s a barman called Heron allegedly tried to improve the taste of the barrels of red eye he was receiving from Bourbon County, by adding spices and fruit to them. His invention was such a success that he moved to St Louis and went into commercial production.

Southern Comfort still uses American whiskey as its base spirit, but it is not – as many people still insist – a bourbon! The main flavouring agent is peach, but there are also another 100 ingredients macerating in the spirit before it is given a long period of ageing. Peach and whiskey mix well. Maker's Mark's ex-director Jimmy Conn invented the Just Peachy (bourbon, orange juice, ginger ale, peach schnapps) as a long drink – although that seems rather a waste of Maker's to me.

What's intriguing about Southern Comfort is the way in which it has managed to cultivate such a wild and rebellious image. Maybe it's because it was Janis Joplin's favourite tipple, maybe because spirits from the Deep South are simply always reckoned to be rebel drinks. Whatever the case, Southern Comfort is the only liqueur that's managed this considerable feat.

The use of EMULSION

The drinking of the egg-yolk-based liqueur advocaat is a Dutch speciality. Its original incarnation was as a planter's drink in Holland's Brazilian enclaves, where the fruit of the abacate tree would be fermented and drunk. When the planters returned home they found that abacate trees were distinctly thin on the ground and, warping the original name to advocaat, decided to use eggs instead.

Production is dominated by Warninks, which goes though an estimated 60 million egg-yolks a year. The eggs are broken by machine, separated, and up to 70,000 yolks per hour can be mixed with the grape spirit, sugar, vanilla and an emulsifying agent. Thick, gloopy and sweet, it can be drunk on its own, diluted with lemonade or even eaten like alcoholic custard with a spoon.

Italy, inevitably, has a version of this liqueur as well. Called Vov, it's made with Marsala and is even thicker and sweeter than advocaat. One for sweet-toothed egg-lovers only.

The use of CREAMS

The same can't be said for Baileys Irish Cream, which claims to be the single most successful new spirit launch in the last 30 years and the world's top-selling liqueur. The creation of this sassy new kid on the block started when Gilbey's in Ireland didn't know what to do with a surplus of spirit. Someone had the bright idea of trying to make a bottled Irish coffee, and in 1975 Bailey's was launched to immediate success.

Bailey's is the polar opposite to Chartreuse or Benedictine. It doesn't come from an ancient heritage of herbal knowledge; it springs from twentieth-century technology, but that's not to do it down. Bailey's is not only a great technical achievement – an alcohol/dairy product blend that doesn't have any artificial agents, and yet doesn't curdle or go off in the bottle – but it tastes good as well.

It started an explosion of cream liqueur brands – some good, like Cadbury's or Amarula (*see* below), but with an excess of "me-too" brands. Even established liqueur brands have tried to get in on the act – you can now buy Crème de Grand Marnier, Cointreau and Tia Maria, none of which is a patch on its original incarnation.

One of the few that may last is the South African brand Amarula Cream. This is made from the distilled fruit of the marula tree, which is given three years' maturation in oak before being blended with fresh cream. Smooth and strangely fruity/toffeeish, it allegedly has aphrodisiac qualities. Certainly, Amarula has an advantage over many of its rivals in at least being made from natural ingredients and having a story to tell.

The attraction of cream liqueurs lies in the fact that they are easy to drink, they have little or no discernable alcoholic content and they are also softly sweet. In many ways they're the drinks world's equivalent of milkshakes. Some, like Baileys are rather good, but be careful of the cheaper brands.

The long history of liqueurs is littered with brands that jumped on a bandwagon and promptly fell off a few years later. The great brands simply carry on. They might not occupy a central part of anyone's drinking habits, but either on their own or in a cocktail they remain some of the most fascinating spirits around – whether you believe the stories or not.

BELOVED BY ELEPHANTS ...

... AND SOUTH AFRICANS

12 Cocktails

WHO INVENTED THE COCKTAIL? ANSWER: THE FIRST PERSON WHO DECIDED TO FIND OUT WHAT TWO OR THREE DIFFERENT INGREDIENTS WOULD TASTE LIKE WHEN THEY WERE MIXED TOGETHER. COCKTAILS ARE A PRODUCT OF EXPERIMENT, THE RESULT OF SATISFIED CURIOSITY. THEIR FORTUNES HAVE EBBED AND FLOWED AS PEOPLE'S TASTES HAVE CHANGED. SOME HAVE LASTED THE DISTANCE, BECOMING LEGENDARY CONCOCTIONS, OTHERS HAVE FALLEN BY THE WAYSIDE.

The history

Cocktails mirror the trends of their time; they are a barometer of society. They range from aristocratic concoctions to drinks of the people. They were the tipple for the "Bright Young Things" of the 1920s; the fuel that spurred Hemingway and Ian Fleming; that sharpened the wit of Dorothy Parker; that gave the disco era added froth and sparkle. Today they are cool, ironic and decidedly post-modern in attitude.

Their recipes have sealed friendships, but mostly cocktails are a matter of heated debate. No two people can agree about when they were first made, where the name came from, or even how to make them. Beware, you are entering a minefield.

The rum punches drunk in England by Boswell (*see* Rum, pages 92–111) were, in their own way, ur-cocktails, but the term first appeared in an American dictionary in 1806, meaning "a mixed drink of any spirit bitters and sugar".

That said, no one can agree where the name came from. Some argue it came from a horse-breeding term, refer-

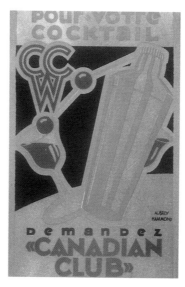

ring to a horse that was part thoroughbred and known as a "cocktail" because its tail was docked. Others have a fanciful tall tale that it was the name of an Aztec princess called Xochitl.

James Fenimore Cooper preferred the convoluted history of an inn-keeper called Betsy Flanagan, who stole her neighbour's chickens and served them to some of Lafayette's volunteers. She tied the tail feathers to mugs of drink and the French soldiers raised a toast of

"Vive le Cock-tail!" The most plausible, if rather prosaic, explanation remains the French term *coquetel*, meaning a mixed drink. The fact that other tales point to New Orleans using the term early in its life gives a hint that this might be the right one.

Many countries have contributed to the evolution of the cocktail, but America remains its spiritual home – the cocktail bar is the high temple, the barman a priest, the drinkers acolytes, genuflecting before the raised shaker.

The first high priest of the cult was Professor Jerry Thomas, a relentless showman and self-publicist, the Barnum of the bar, and his 1862 book *The Bar-Tender's Guide and Bon Vivant's Companion* contains the first recorded recipes of the craze that was beginning to grip America.

Thomas toured Europe, lugging £1,000 worth of silver bar equipment with him, showing off his dazzling creations such as the Blue Blazer, which would involve tossing a stream of flaming whiskey from mixing flask to mixing flask.

Decadent, depraved ....
and delicious

Cocktails have swung from sweet to dry throughout their life. In the early days, sweet was in. The main base spirit was gin, but the most common style at that time was the sweet Old Tom, rather than the dry gins that were being made by the end of the century. Bitters were also an integral part of all the early mixes – orange, Angostura and Peychaud all feature heavily in the recipes of the time, as do the sweet liqueurs that were widely drunk.

So when the good professor invented the Martinez, it wasn't the Martini we know today, but a sweet mix of Old Tom, sweet vermouth, maraschino liqueur and bitters.

The best gauge of how the cocktail continued its passage into the heart of American social life can be charted by the number of books that appeared on the subject. Thomas's greatest rival was Harry Johnson, who in 1882 published *New And Improved Illustrated Bartender's Manual, Or How to Mix Drinks of the Present Style*, with hundreds of recipes in it. Many – most of them, even – are forgotten. Barmen have taken the ones they wanted and modified them, while ingredients and tastes have changed. Shed a tear then for the Goat's Delight, Bishop's Poker and the Hoptoad.

By the time Johnson was penning his book, the swanky hotels of the day had caught on to the craze and become cocktail laboratories. New York's Waldorf-Astoria (home of The Bronx) was typical of its day in having a cocktail created for it. In fact, the Astoria was one of the drinks edging us closer to the Martini we know today, but it has languished in the shadows as other, newer drinks have taken centre stage.

American bars had begun to spring up in the fanciest European capitals, and new creations were soon spilling out of them, like The Sidecar which was invented in Paris in 1911. In London, the Ritz, the Savoy and the RAC Club all chipped in with their own contributions to the fast-growing lexicon.

The new dry gins were at the centre of the majority of the most successful, and by bringing gin to a wider audience, cocktails were the making of the spirit as an international favourite. Gin, recognized as one of the great mixers, had found its role, and without vodka to challenge it, had the field to itself.

Despite this, gin's homeland remained a tad aloof from the phenomenon. There were cocktail bars in Britain, but it was not appropriate behaviour to be seen in one. The country had to wait until the end of the First World War for cocktails to become truly popular.

Cuba and London

The end of the war brought an eruption of relief. The corsets of the Edwardian era were removed and young people, for the first time in Britain's history, began to rebel. This coincided with America starting its long experiment with banning alcohol, and so the focus of attention switched to Cuba, London, Paris, Venice and Berlin. Cocktails, however, remained quintessentially American. This was a time when the rest of the world was first bombarded with images of America. It was the birth of the movies, the first great explosion of jazz. Cocktails were bound up in this American spirit, and Europeans recovering from war drank them because they wanted to taste some of that sense of optimism and youth.

That said, in Britain cocktails remained slightly decadent. They were drunk by a small number of young middle-class artists and students. Cocktail parties weren't held in the working-class slums. Then the Second World War came and put paid to all of that frivolity.

In Cuba, meanwhile, a revolution was brewing. Cocktails had been made since the turn of the century when the Mojito, the Daiquiri and the Cuba Libre were all invented. During Prohibition, though, America decanted itself into Old Havana – literally, in the case of a Boston barman called Donovan, who transported his entire bar to the city Havana. And with the gangsters, movie stars and tourists came barmen, ready to learn from the recently formed Cuban Cantineros Club, an association and a school for cocktail makers.

Havana's hotels and bars were crammed with thirsty, partying Americans and the barmen responded. New recipes, like the Jai-Alai, the Ron

Fizz, the Santiago, the Presidente, the Mary Pickford and the Caruso flooded out of the Inglaterra, the Pasaje and, most famous of all, el Floridita, home to the greatest barman of his day, Constante Ribailagua – the inventor of the frozen Daiquiri. "When it comes to cocktails, Cuba is ahead of us all. American, French and English barmen could learn a lot here," wrote Albert Crocket in the *Old Waldorf Astoria Bar Book* in 1935.

Meanwhile, back in America…

That isn't to say that America had taken the pledge. In fact, drinking increased during Prohibition and, though underground, the cocktail continued. The reason that so many new recipes were created during this period is conceivably because the taste of the bathtub gin and vodka that was being produced desperately needed to be masked, so fruit juices, other spirits and bitters were added. Long drinks such as the Screwdriver were born around this time, for this very reason.

Those who could get their hands on good-quality English gin were beginning to develop a taste for drier drinks. It is around this time that the Martini first begins to move from the 2:1 ratio of gin to vermouth to the drier style we know today.

After Repeal, America picked up where it had (officially) left off before Prohibition. Cocktails grew even through the Depression, the rationale perhaps being that it made more sense to have one strong drink than a lot of little ones.

If gin had had it all its own way before the Second World War, then the arrival of white whiskey (as vodka was first called) was soon to change all that.

Over the years, vodka has outstripped its rival, muscling in on the Martini and dragging the title of hangover cure away from the Red Snapper made with gin and tomato juice to the Bloody Mary.

Some see vodka's rise as a triumph of no taste over flavour. It's certainly true that the vodkas that arrived in the United States and Britain after the war were miles away from the real stuff produced in Russia and Poland, but this flavourless base spirit allowed people to enjoy mixed drinks all the more. Vodka was new, it was light, it was cool. People have always looked for light flavours in cocktails. Even when the cream-laden drinks of the 1970s arrived, it was a virtually neutral base

BRIGHT YOUNG THINGS IN THEIR NATURAL SURROUNDINGS

that drinkers wanted. Brown spirits, most notably bourbon, may have been the base for many classics, but light remains most people's main criterion for a great cocktail. Vodka was the lightest of them all.

In the 1960s cocktails hit a wall. They had become an acceptable part of society, the businessman's drink, the politician's. In the 1960s, if you wanted to be rebellious you wouldn't sip a Martini – you'd let your freak flag fly and drop acid instead.

Cocktails remained quiet until disco arrived in the late 1970s and everything went silly again. It was all mirror balls, creamy drinks, spangly tops and Gloria Gaynor. The trendiest drinks were brightly coloured and had drag-queen names like Brandy Alexander and Pink Pussy.

In Britain in the late 1970s and early 1980s there was a mini-revival when post-punk people began listening to acid jazz and salsa and took to sipping classic cocktails, but it was always more of a pose than any great love of what they were actually drinking. At the same time, though, some drinks – the Piña Colada, the Black Russian, the Tequila Sunrise and the Margarita had escaped from the cocktail bar and made their way into pubs and clubs. The Wham! era of blonde highlights, tight shorts and fake suntans was defined by the irresistible rise of the Piña Colada.

In America, meanwhile, it all went badly wrong. It's Jimmy Carter who gets the blame for the downfall, with his speech complaining about the three-Martini lunch, although he was actually complaining about the tax-deductible lunch, not the Martinis!

There again, it's difficult to think of the Georgia peanut farmer being like FDR and mixing Dirty Martinis in the Oval Office every night.

This was the trigger for the Moral Majority to ride out and lynch anyone who dared to suggest drinking might not be all that anti-social. In time, cocktails became ensnared in the War Against Drugs and, as they did and people began to be scared of drinking them, so barmen tried to out-gross each other to get some attention. The names (and the drinks) got sillier – the Blow Job being a good example: a B-52 with whipped cream on the top that had to be drunk without touching the glass with your hands. Try it, and you'll see why it gets its name... If you weren't drinking dumb drinks, you were trying to pile as much alcohol in the glass as possible. Enter the Long Island Iced Tea.

Gary and Mardee Regan, in *New Classic Cocktails*, their essential guide to today's cutting-edge concoctions, define them as punk cocktails (that's the American cartoon version of punk, not the nihilistic UK one) but go on to say "without punk cocktails as an impetus we might never have seen some of these new classics... Punk cocktails smartly slapped the classicist bartenders across the face and screamed 'create, goddamn it, create'".

Then, in the mid-90s the classicists hit back. The Martini returned, with a new post-modern ironic twist along with the slice of lemon. They seem to be nostalgic for the past but, by being knowingly nostalgic, they are also detached and ironic. I remain unconvinced about much of the Martini revival, which has now reached ludicrous proportions. Gin and – at a stretch – vodka can make Martinis, but no other spirit can be used. If you want to make a tequila "Martini", go and find another name.

This isn't some purist, fundamentalist position. There are some that work brilliantly and, anyway, the whole nature of cocktails is that they change and shift with each generation.

Progress is to be encouraged, but what seems to be happening is that in the rush to create something new, many have forgotten the basic principle of any cocktail, especially a Martini, which is that the drink highlights its base spirit while being subtly enhanced by its flavourings. _There's_ the art of mixing a cocktail. It's about putting a new spin on perfection. A haiku in its mixing, satori when it is sipped.

The post-modern cocktail has come about as a result of there now being a greater range of high-quality spirits than ever before. The consumer and the barman are spoiled for choice. There's reposado and anejo tequila and fine mezcal, top-quality bourbon, premium gins and vodkas, and great flavoured vodka – and by that I mean the real Polish and Russian varieties, not the ersatz confected cheapies. All of this opens up a massive new range of possibilities.

It's wonderful to see this backlash against the morality of the late 1980s and early 1990s. It might not be two-fisted drinking, but people are sick of being told that everything is bad for them. Generation X wants to enjoy itself and, as we have seen in every chapter of this book, the desire for quality and flavour is what is driving the new push for the top end of the market. Cocktails are another manifestation of this – you can't make a great cocktail with poor-quality ingredients.

Why has it happened? Maybe it is simply because we just feel better about ourselves. After all, cocktails are drinks of celebration. Enjoy.

How they're made

When you read a cocktail recipe, it all looks so simple. Three ingredients, ice and a glass. How can it go wrong? Easily, is the answer. Here are some tips to ensure you won't mess things up.

How to make a cocktail

It's been said many times before, but it's worth repeating that a cocktail is a combination of three things:

● *The base spirit, which gives the cocktail its main flavour and identity.*
● *The modifier/mixer, which melds with the base spirit and transports it on to another plane, but doesn't dominate it.*
● *The flavouring. This is the smallest* element, but acts like the tiny detail that sets good clothes apart. It's the drop of bitters, the splash of coloured liqueur, the squeeze of a twist of lemon. Understand that, and you're on your way. Now the technical bit.

Shaking

First, an explanation of why you shake. It is to mix and also to chill the drink down, and give it a slight dilution, which helps to release flavours. The shaker, which should be made of stainless steel or glass, should never be more than half-filled with ice. Shaking actually doesn't take too long. A vigorous shake for 10 seconds will be ideal for the majority of cocktails. A simple indication is that the outside of the shaker should be freezing to the touch. If you shake for too long you'll end up diluting the drink. The contents are then strained

though the strainer so that none of the ice ends up in the drink. Only use fresh ice cubes in the glass.

Stirring

There's as much written about this as any part of cocktail-making. In general, stirring is used to marry flavours that go together easily, and to prevent the cocktail becoming cloudy. Whether you shake or stir your Martini is entirely up to you. As in shaking, this is another way to chill a drink down quickly. Half-fill the stirring glass with ice and agitate (15–25 seconds should do it). Normally, stirred drinks are strained into the cocktail glass, although a few are stirred in their final resting place.

Blending

Here, ice is whizzed up with the spirit and served unstrained, although the pile of mush that is usually served up as a frozen cocktail rather ruins the point of the drink in the first place, as all you do is freeze your insides and not taste anything. The blender is also handy for zapping fruit for Daiquiris.

Muddling

This means gently pressing and mixing some ingredients in the bottom of a glass, either with a pestle or the back of a spoon. It doesn't involve pulverizing them, just making a rough purée.

Layering

The heaviest part of a layered drink goes in first; the successive layers are gently poured in over the back of a spoon.

Ice

For some reason, this ingredient is rarely given a second thought. But water has a flavour too – and chlorinated water has a flavour that is enough to turn a potentially great cocktail into a hideous undrinkable mess. If the tap water tastes of chemicals, don't use it for ice. Use filtered water or, better still, bottled water. Ice cubes are normally used in shaking and stirring. Crushed ice is colder, but it melts and leads to quicker dilution. Freezing tonic water works, or you can make vermouth-flavoured ice cubes for the Martini.

Chilling glasses

Most cocktails call for chilled glasses. The simple solution is to keep them in the freezer, but if you don't have space they can be chilled down quickly by filling them with ice and water and leaving them to stand. When you are ready to use them, shake them so the freezing water chills the outer surface, then tip all the ice and water out. Try not to pick them up by the bowl, but by the stem.

Salting the rim

Don't bury the glass rim down in a pile of salt or sugar. The intention here is to coat the outside surface of the glass, not the inside. Moisten with lemon or lime juice, then carefully turn the glass side on in a saucer of the salt/sugar, or sprinkle the coating on to the glass while rotating it (make sure you have some paper to catch the mess).

Fruit

Always use fresh, washed fruit. One tip is to roll limes before cutting them or using them for Caipirinhas. This allows them to start releasing their juices.

How to cut and use a twist

Pare small strips from a lemon, ensuring that some white pith is still attached. Holding the peel between your thumb and forefinger, give it a quick twist so that some oil sprays from the skin on to the drink. Run the twist round the rim of the glass and drop in. Longer strips can be tied into a knot and dropped in.

Measurements

All the recipes are in the standard accepted US ounces. The Imperial British ounce is slightly smaller, but makes virtually no difference. If you are making cocktails at home, a US ounce is 2.8cl, an Imperial 2.5cl. For home mixing, an Imperial ounce is the equivalent of two-and-a-half tablespoons or six teaspoons.

It's worth getting a set of stainless-steel measuring spoons for teaspoons (tsp) and tablespoons (tbs). With practice, you'll end up knowing what an ounce looks like.

A dash is just what it says: the merest splash. When small additions are indicated (such as with maraschino), it's just a bit more than a dash.

Following a cocktail recipe is much the same as using a cookery book; you don't have to be restricted by the instructions. If you prefer more lemon juice, less (or more) alcohol, a different garnish, then go ahead and satisfy your own palate. Once you have mastered the basics, the world is your oyster (or bar).

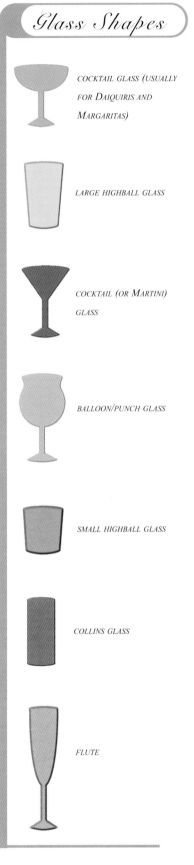

Glass Shapes

COCKTAIL GLASS (USUALLY FOR DAIQUIRIS AND MARGARITAS)

LARGE HIGHBALL GLASS

COCKTAIL (OR MARTINI) GLASS

BALLOON/PUNCH GLASS

SMALL HIGHBALL GLASS

COLLINS GLASS

FLUTE

Gin-based COCKTAILS

It's a sad indication of how disregarded gin is that this, the greatest mixing white spirit, is most commonly found lurking at the bottom of warm gin and tonic with a flaccid lemon sulking above. Gin deserves far better than that. It is an invigorating drink, bursting with a fresh mix of citrus fruits, heather and juniper that gets the taste buds working. Indeed, it remains the cocktail spirit base *par excellence.*

Gin was the fuel for the rise of cocktails, and remains the base of many classics. The Martini has already been discussed (*see* page 130–1), but it is also responsible for The Bronx, the Singapore Sling (which originated in the Raffles Hotel at the turn of the century) and the Gimlet, which is tricky to master despite its simple ingredients.

As ever with any naked cocktail, the Gimlet is about hitting the right balance, allowing the gin to shine but using just enough lime to take the edge off its neat flavour and transform it altogether. If it was good enough for Philip Marlowe, it ought to be good enough for you.

ALASKA

2 oz gin
splash Yellow Chartreuse
dash Angostura or orange bitters
lemon twist
Shake and strain into a cocktail glass. Garnish with the lemon twist.

ASTORIA

GIN AND LIME HARMONIZE
IN THE GIMLET

2 oz gin
½–1 oz dry vermouth

dash orange bitters
Shake and strain into a cocktail glass.

THE BUTTERFLY

2 oz gin
¼ oz Noilly Prat
¼ oz Blue curaçao
dash Poire William
Shake and strain into a cocktail glass.

BRONX

2 oz dry gin
½ oz dry vermouth
½ oz sweet vermouth
1 oz fresh orange juice
Shake and strain into a cocktail glass. Garnish with a cherry.

THE SILVER BRONX

2 oz dry gin
1 oz sweet vermouth
1 oz fresh orange juice
half an egg white
Shake well and strain into a cocktail glass.

CARUSO

1 oz gin
¾ oz dry vermouth
¼ oz green crème de menthe
Stir and strain into a cocktail glass.

CLOVER CLUB

2 oz dry gin
splash grenadine
1 oz lemon juice
egg white
Shake well for 30 seconds and strain into a cocktail glass.

GIMLET

2¼ oz dry gin
¾ oz Rose's Lime Cordial
Shake and strain into a cocktail glass.

GLOOM RAISER

2 oz gin
1 oz vermouth
2 dashes grenadine
2 dashes Pernod/absinthe
Shake and strain into cocktail glasses.

THE ORIGINAL MARTINEZ

2 oz Old Tom gin
½ oz sweet vermouth
2 dashes maraschino liqueur
dash orange bitters/lemon
Shake and strain into a cocktail glass.

CAJUN MARTINI

Paul Prudhomme
1 fresh chilli
1 bottle dry gin
1 oz dry vermouth

WHITE LADY

Slice chilli lengthwise, but keeping it in one piece, insert into the bottle of gin. Top bottle up with vermouth. Reseal and refrigerate for up to 16 hours. Strain into clean bottle. Refrigerate until well chilled. Serve in cocktail glasses.

MANDARINE MARTINI

Mayflower Park Hotel

1½ oz gin
½ oz vodka
splash Mandarine Napoleon
dash Cointreau
mandarin twist

Pour liqueurs into empty shaker. Coat and discard surplus. Add ice and other ingredients. Shake and strain into cocktail glass. Garnish with twist.

MARTINI THYME

Ted & Linda Fondulas

3 oz gin
¾ oz Green Chartreuse
1 sprig of thyme

Stir together the gin and Chartreuse. Strain into a cocktail glass and garnish with the thyme.

SMOKY MARTINI

2 oz gin
½ tsp Noilly Prat
dash to ¼ oz Scotch

Stir or shake and strain into a cocktail glass.

DIRTY MARTINI

2 oz gin
1 tsp Noilly Prat
splash of olive brine

Stir or shake and strain into a cocktail glass.

MONKEY GLAND

2 oz gin
2 oz orange juice
dash grenadine
dash absinthe/Pernod

Stir or shake and strain into a cocktail glass.

SCARBOROUGH FAIR

2 oz Plymouth gin
¼ oz Chambery
sprig of thyme
sprig of rosemary
sprig of flat leaf parsley
2 fresh sage leaves

Muddle sage, parsley and Chambery in shaker. Add gin. Shake and strain into a cocktail glass. Garnish with rosemary and thyme.

SINGAPORE GIN SLING

2 oz gin
½ oz Cointreau
1½ oz fresh lime juice
1 tsp each caster sugar, sugar syrup
¾ oz Cherry Heering
lime

Shake first four and strain into Collins glass. Top up with soda and float Cherry Heering. Garnish with lime.

STAR

1 oz dry gin
1 oz Calvados
dash Noilly Prat
dash dry vermouth
dash grapefruit

Stir and strain into a cocktail glass.

VESPER

3 oz Plymouth gin
1 oz Moskovskaya
½ oz Lillet Blanc
twist of lemon peel

Shake and strain into cocktail glasses and garnish with twist.

WHITE LADY

2 oz gin
¼ oz lemon juice
¾ oz Cointreau
1 tsp caster sugar
1 egg white

Shake and strain into a cocktail glass.

PINK GIN

4 oz Plymouth gin
2 dashes Angostura

Coat a chilled cocktail glass with Angostura. Discard excess. Top up with gin.

PINK GIN PERFECTED

Vodka-based COCKTAILS

Vodka can be used in any of the gin cocktails (there again, gin can be used in all of the vodka ones as well!). We have to thank vodka for giving cocktails a new lease of life in the post-war period – even if it did hasten the decline of gin. Now with high-quality premium vodkas from Russia, Poland, Holland and the United States, the spirit has a chance to show it does have a personality after all. This mix of classic and post-modern cocktails will gain something extra as a result. The new flavoured vodkas will also pep many of them up. Experiment!

COPENHAGEN

2 oz vodka

½ oz akvavit

slivered blanched almonds

Shake and strain into cocktail glasses and garnish with almonds.

COSMOPOLITAN

2 oz vodka

1 oz Cointreau

½ oz lime juice

splash cranberry juice

lime twist

Stir and strain into a chilled cocktail glass with sugared rim. Garnish with a lime twist.

CHAMBORD KAMIKAZE

Peter Meddick

3 oz vodka

½ oz Cointreau

½ oz lemon juice

½ oz simple syrup

½ oz Chambord

½ lime, sliced

lime to garnish

Place all ingredients (including lime) in large shaker with ice. Muddle violently. Strain and garnish.

JAMES BOND

1 oz vodka

dash Angostura

1 sugar cube

Champagne

In flute, soak sugar cube in Angostura. Add vodka and top up with Champagne.

FORTUNELLA

Oliver's, Mayflower Park Hotel

1 oz Ketel One

¾ oz Bombay Sapphire

¾ oz Caravella

splash Cointreau

splash Campari

1 tsp candied kumquat nectar

lemon twist and kumquat

Coat shaker with the Cointreau and Campari, discard excess. Shake and strain into cocktail glasses and garnish.

FRENCH MARTINI

2 oz vodka

dash Chambord

dash pineapple juice

Shake and strain into a cocktail glass.

HARVEY WALLBANGER

1½ oz vodka

3½ oz orange juice

¼ oz Galliano

Stir vodka and orange juice and strain into a Collins glass. Float the Galliano on top.

METROPOLITAN

2 oz Absolut Kurant

½ oz Rose's Lime Cordial

½ oz lime juice

1 oz cranberry

lime wedge to garnish

Shake and strain into a cocktail glass and garnish with the wedge of lime.

MOLOTOV COCKTAIL

3 oz Finlandia

½ oz Black Bush

½ oz Irish Mist

Shake and strain into cocktail glasses. (Finlandia, rather than Stoli, is ideal, as the distillery produced military alcohol used in Molotov cocktails during the Second World War.)

HARVEY WALLBANGER

SALTY DOG

ORANGE BLOSSOM

1¼ oz vodka

1¼ oz orange juice

dash orange flower water

Shake and strain into a cocktail glass. (Making this with eight parts juice to one part spirit is a screwdriver.)

POLISH MARTINI

1½ oz Wyborowa

½ oz Krupnik

dash apple juice

Shake and strain into a cocktail glass.

RUSSIAN BEAR

1 oz vodka

1½ oz cream

¼ oz crème de cacao

1 tsp sugar

Shake and strain into a cocktail glass.

SALTY DOG

2 oz vodka

2 oz grapefruit juice

Shake and strain into a salt-rimmed cocktail glass.

SEABREEZE

2 oz Absolut vodka

2 oz cranberry juice

1 oz grapefruit juice

Shake and strain into a highball glass.

VODKA MARTINI

2 oz vodka

dash Noilly Prat

lemon twist

Shake (or stir!) and strain into cocktail glass. Garnish with twist.

WHERE THE BUFFALO ROAM

2 oz Wyborowa

½ oz Zubrowka

dash Chambery

blade of bison grass

Coat shaker with Chambery and discard excess. Add ice and ingredients and shake. Garnish with blade of grass.

YELLOW FEVER

2 oz vodka

¼ oz lime juice

¼ oz Galliano

2 oz pineapple juice

Shake and strain into a highball glass.

The Collins Family

The three largest groupings also make three great thirst-quenchers. Any spirit can be used to make them. Sours are aptly named, as they have a delicious, mouth-puckering effect thanks to the higher percentage of lemon juice. Fizzes, allegedly first made as a hangover cure at the RAC Club in London, are long sours and perhaps easier to take for the uninitiated. Collinses are a variant on fizzes, which are stirred rather than shaken.

A Sour contains

¾ oz lemon juice

½ tsp caster sugar

2 oz spirit

Shake and strain into a sour glass.

A Fizz contains

¾ – 1 oz lemon juice

1 tsp caster sugar

2 oz spirit

dash Angostura (optional)

soda

Shake and strain into a tall glass, and top up with soda.

A Collins contains

¾ –1 oz lemon juice

1 tsp caster sugar

2 oz spirit

dash Angostura (optional)

soda

Place the first three ingredients in a tall glass half-filled with ice, and stir to mix. Top up with soda. Stir gently.

Tom Collins = gin
Colonel Collins = bourbon
Pierre Collins = Cognac
Joe Collins = vodka

Rum-based COCKTAILS

In recent times, rum cocktails have immediately conjured up images of badly made Piña Coladas or Daiquiris so cold that your innards were turned into a deep freeze. Naff, in other words. But rum remains a classic mixer – many of these recipes come from Havana's Golden Age, when that city was at the cutting edge of cocktail invention. The Mojito and Caipirinha are summer classics that refresh and stimulate. Both started life as people's cocktails, rather than creations of the swanky bars. Overproof white rum gives an undoubted kick that will keep you totally relaxed for the afternoon. Havana Club mixes well, while a gold rum will give extra weight and sweetness if that's what's desired. Once again, experimentation is the key. Recipes are guides, not rules.

BEE'S KISS

1½ oz white rum
1 tbs black coffee
1 tbs fresh cream
Shake well and strain into a cocktail glass.

CAIPIRINHA

2 oz cachaça (or white rum)
1 lime, quartered
1 tsp sugar syrup
Put lime and syrup in bottom of a large highball glass. Muddle well for a minute to extract juice and lime oil. Add ice. Stir. Add Cachaça. Stir again.

CASTRO

1½ oz gold rum
¾ oz Calvados
1½ oz orange juice
¾ oz lime juice
¾ oz Rose's Lime Cordial
1 tsp sugar syrup
wedge of lime
Shake and strain into an ice-filled Collins glass.

CENTENARIO

1½ oz gold rum
1 oz overproof white rum
¼ oz Kahlua
¼ oz Cointreau
juice of 1 lime

mint sprig
dash grenadine
Stir ingredients over ice in a Collins glass.

CUBAN ISLAND
(Schumann)

¾ oz white rum
¾ oz vodka
¼– ¾ oz Cointreau
¾ oz lemon juice
Shake and strain into a cocktail glass.

THE FLORIDITA

1½ oz white rum
½ oz sweet vermouth
dash white crème de cacao
dash grenadine
juice of half a lime

Shake over ice cubes and strain into a cocktail glass.

RONALDO

1 oz cachaca
1 oz gold rum
½ oz crème de banane
½ oz unsweetened pineapple juice
lime juice
lime wedge
Shake and strain into a highball glass half-filled with ice. Garnish with lime.

MAI TAI I

1 oz white rum
½ oz Cointreau
¼ oz Rose's Lime Cordial
1½ oz each of orange and

unsweetened pineapple juice

splash grenadine

½ oz gold rum

wedge of pineapple

Shake and strain into a Collins glass half-filled with ice. Add grenadine and gold rum. Garnish with pineapple.

MAI TAI 2

2 oz gold rum

1 oz Curaçao

1½ oz Rose's Lime Cordial

1 tbs Orgeat (almond syrup)

1 tsp sugar syrup

splash grenadine

½ oz overproof

wedge of pineapple and lime

Shake and strain into a Collins glass half-filled with ice. Add grenadine and overproof. Garnish with pineapple and lime.

MARY PICKFORD

1½ oz white rum

dash maraschino liqueur

1½ oz unsweetened pineapple juice

dash grenadine

lime twist

Shake and strain into a cocktail glass. Add twist.

MOJITO

2 oz white rum

1 tsp sugar syrup

half a lime

fresh mint leaves

soda water

sprig of mint

In a large highball glass, muddle the mint and sugar syrup. Squeeze lime into the glass and add lime half. Add rum and ice. Stir. Add soda water. Stir briefly and garnish with mint.

NAKED LADY

1½ oz white rum

1½ oz sweet vermouth

4 dashes apricot brandy

2 dashes grenadine

4 dashes lemon/lime juice

Shake and strain into a cocktail glass.

PRESIDENTE

2 oz white rum

¼ oz Cointreau

¾ oz dry vermouth

¼ oz sweet vermouth

dash grenadine

dash lime juice

Shake and strain into a cocktail glass.

PIÑA COLADA

1 oz Appleton Special/Overproof

½ oz Appleton 12-year-old

2 oz unsweetened pineapple juice

¾ oz coconut cream

crushed ice

Blend the crushed ice, white rum, pineapple juice and coconut cream together, then pour into a Collins glass. Top up with the 12-year-old rum.

RUM SHRUB

2 oz dark rum

1 oz shrub

1 oz soda

Fill wine goblet two-thirds with ice. Add rum, shrub and soda. Stir lightly. (Shrub is an old English speciality fruit and herb syrup – most often seen in the West Country.)

SEPTEMBER MORN

2 oz white rum

splash grenadine

1 oz lemon juice

egg white

Shake for about 30 seconds and strain into a cocktail glass.

YELLOW BIRD

1½ oz gold rum

½ oz overproof

¾ oz crème de banane

dash Galliano

¼ oz apricot brandy

3 oz unsweetened pineapple juice

¼ oz orange juice

Shake and strain into a highball glass half-filled with ice.

ZOMBIE

¾ oz gold rum

2 oz dark rum

¾ oz overproof

¾ oz Cherry Heering

1¼ oz lime juice

dash grenadine

¾ oz orange juice

Shake and strain into a large highball glass half-filled with ice.

LEFT: *Piña Colada*

Whisk(e)y-based COCKTAILS

Bourbon is a hugely versatile base spirit for cocktails, and it comes to life when given a dash of bitters. Try and find Peychaud bitters, it's worth the quest. The widespread use of bitters in many of these recipes points to the fact that this was one of the earliest spirits to be used in cocktails like the Old Fashioned and the Seelbach, which was only rediscovered recently when this elegant hotel was renovated. Many recipes call for rye whiskey. This refers to the true Kentucky rye, and not to Canadian whiskey. If you can't find a bottle, use bourbon instead.

RUSTY NAIL

AFFINITY

¾ oz Scotch whisky
¾ oz dry vermouth
¾ oz sweet vermouth
2 dashes Angostura
lemon twist
Shake and strain into a cocktail glass.

THE ALGONQUIN

2 oz rye
1 oz dry vermouth
1 oz pineapple juice
dash of Peychaud Bitters
Shake and strain into a cocktail glass.

BRIGHTON PUNCH

1 oz bourbon
3 oz brandy
¼ oz Benedictine
2 oz orange juice
¾ oz lemon juice
1 tsp sugar syrup
Shake and strain into an ice-filled Collins glass.

BROOKLYN

1 oz rye
¾ oz vermouth rosso
dash maraschino liqueur
Stir and strain into a cocktail glass.

HARPER CRANBERRY

2 oz I.W. Harper
3 oz cranberry juice
Stir into an ice-filled highball glass.

HORSE'S NECK

2 oz bourbon
2 dashes Angostura bitters
ginger ale
lemon twist
Coat a Collins glass with bitters. Add ice and bourbon. Stir. Add ginger ale and twist. Stir briefly.

OLD FASHIONED I

2½ oz bourbon
3 dashes bitters
½ tsp sugar syrup
splash water
half orange wheel
maraschino cherry
In a highball glass muddle the sugar, water, bitters, orange and cherry, lightly mushing up the fruit. Fill the glass with ice cubes and add bourbon. Stir.

SAZERAC

2 ½ oz bourbon
2 tsp absinthe/Pernod
½ tsp sugar syrup
3 dashes Peychaud bitters
1 lemon twist
Pour absinthe/Pernod into a highball glass, coat and discard the excess. Shake other ingredients and pour over ice into the glass.

THE SEELBACH COCKTAIL

Seelbach Hotel, Louisville, KY
1 oz Old Forester bourbon
½ oz Cointreau

7 dashes Angostura
7 dashes Peychaud bitters
5 oz Champagne
orange twist
Pour the bourbon, Cointreau and both bitters into a Champagne flute and stir. Add the Champagne and garnish with the orange twist.

SIDNEY

2 oz rye/bourbon
½ oz dry vermouth
splash Yellow Chartreuse
dash orange bitters
lemon twist
Stir and strain into a cocktail glass.

ROB ROY

1½ oz Scotch whisky
½ oz sweet vermouth
1 dash Angostura bitters
Stir and strain into a chilled cocktail glass.

RUSTY NAIL

1½ oz Scotch whisky
¾ oz Drambuie
Stir over ice in a highball glass.

TIPPERARY

1 oz Irish whiskey
¾ oz dry vermouth
¼ oz Green Chartreuse
Shake and strain into a cocktail glass.

Brandy-based COCKTAILS

If whisky is unknown, then brandy remains virtually unseen.

Still, brandy is quite capable of giving an elegant fruity kick to many great cocktails, ranging from the classic Sidecar, which was invented in Paris at around the time of the First World War, to the Brandy Alexander. Brandy also makes an appearance in some of the new post-modern creations.

Be careful when using Armagnac however as its rich and earthy qualities tend to overpower many of these cocktails. It is better to stick to a good VS – Martell, for example. On days when you are feeling particularly extravagant, you can always push the boat out and procure a bottle of VSOP.

AMERICAN BEAUTY

¾ oz brandy
¼ oz dry vermouth
¼ oz sweet vermouth
¾ oz orange juice
dash grenadine
port
Shake and strain into a cocktail glass and float port on top.

BRANDY ALEXANDER

1 oz brandy
1 oz brown crème de cacao
1 oz cream
2 tsp whipped cream
nutmeg
Shake first three ingredients and strain into cocktail glasses. Add whipped cream and sprinkle with nutmeg.

CORPSE REVIVER

¾ oz brandy
¾ oz Calvados
¾ oz sweet vermouth
Shake and strain into a cocktail glass.

DEAUVILLE

1 oz brandy
¾ oz Calvados
½ oz triple sec
¾ oz lemon juice
Shake and strain into a cocktail glass.

PRINCE OF WALES

¾ oz brandy
¼ oz Benedictine
Champagne
dash Angostura bitters
sugar cube
orange
cherry
Put sugar cube in a highball glass and soak with Angostura. Add ice, Cognac and garnish. Stir. Add Champagne and finally Benedictine.

SIDECAR

1½ oz brandy
¾ oz Cointreau
¾ oz lemon juice
twist of lemon
Shake and strain into a cocktail glass with sugared rim and garnish with twist.

STINGER

1½ oz brandy
¾ oz white crème de menthe
Shake and strain into a cocktail glass.

BRANDY ALEXANDER

Tequila-based COCKTAILS

The "new" reposado and anejo tequilas have opened up this branch of cocktails to a whole new world. The difference between these new tequilas and the old silver and gold brands that we had to put up with is considerable. Finally the delicate, pear and citrus flavours of blue agave are allowed to work their magic on these fine concoctions.

TEQUILA SUNRISE

CHAPALA

1½ oz tequila
dash triple sec
¾ oz lemon juice
1½–2 oz orange juice
dash grenadine
Stir over ice in a Collins glass.

EL DIABLO

1½ oz reposado tequila
¾ oz crème de cassis
½ oz lime juice
ginger ale or ginger beer
wedge of lime
Stir tequila and cassis over ice in a Collins glass. Top up with ginger ale or ginger beer and add lime wedge.

MALCOLM LOWRY

1 oz Chicicapa Mezcal
½ oz overproof white rum
¼ oz Cointreau
lime juice
lime twist
Shake and serve in a cocktail glass and garnish with the twist.

MATADOR

2 oz tequila
¼ oz Cointreau
juice of half lime
1 tsp sugar syrup
pineapple chunk
Shake over crushed ice and strain into a highball glass with sugared rim.

MEXICANA

1½ oz tequila
1½ oz unsweetened pineapple juice
¼ oz lime juice
dash grenadine
Shake and strain into a highball glass filled with ice.

ROSALITA

¼ oz dry vermouth
¼ oz sweet vermouth
¼ oz Campari
¾ oz tequila
Shake and strain into a cocktail glass.

SOUTH OF THE BORDER

1 oz tequila
¾ oz Kahlua
½ lime
Squeeze lime over ice in highball glass. Stir before adding spirits. Stir to mix.

TAPIKA

Tapika, New York, NY
3½ oz Chinaco Plata
½ oz Cointreau
½ oz prickly pear cactus syrup
1 oz lime juice
lime slice
Coat cocktail glass with Cointreau and discard, ensuring rim is moistened. Sprinkle rim with salt. Shake tequila, prickly pear syrup and lime juice, strain into glass and garnish with lime.

TEQUILA SUNRISE

2 oz tequila
3½ oz orange juice
dash grenadine
lime
Squeeze lime over ice into a large highball glass and drop into the glass. Add tequila and orange juice and slowly pour in grenadine.

TEQUINI

¾ oz tequila
¾ oz vodka
¾ oz Noilly Prat
dash Angostura
lemon twist
Shake and strain into a cocktail glass.

Champagne-based COCKTAILS

FIZZING AMERICANO

1 oz Campari
½ oz sweet vermouth
Prosecco/Champagne
orange wheel

Shake and pour over rocks in a highball glass. Top up with Prosecco or Champagne and garnish with orange.

BELLINI

Puréed fresh white peaches
dash lemon juice
dash peach brandy
sparkling wine

Stir peach juice and brandy in a Champagne flute. Top up with sparkling wine. Adding fresh mango purée makes a Bombay Bellini.

CHAMPAGNE COCKTAIL

Champagne
1 sugar cube
dash Angostura
twist lemon peel
orange

Place sugar cube into Champagne flute and dash with Angostura. Pour in Champagne. Add lemon twist and garnish with orange.

DUE CAMPARI
(Schumann)

¼ oz Campari
¾ oz Cordiale Campari
Champagne
¾ oz lemon juice

Shake lemon juice and Camparis and strain into Champagne flute. Fill with sparkling wine.

FRENCH 75

¾ oz gin
Champagne
¼ oz lemon juice
dash sugar syrup
dash grenadine

Shake first four, strain into flute and top with Champagne. (A French 76 is the same, but with vodka instead of gin.)

CHAMPAGNE COCKTAIL

Miscellaneous COCKTAILS

NEGRONI

LONG ISLAND ICED TEA

¼ oz triple sec
¾ oz white rum
¾ oz gin
¾ oz vodka
¾ oz tequila
½ lime
¾ oz orange juice
cola

Squeeze lime into a Collins glass, add ice cubes and spirits. Stir and top up with cola. (Replacing the cola with sparkling wine produces Anita's Attitude Adjuster, while replacing the cola with cranberry gives a New England Iced Tea.)

NEGRONI

1½ oz gin
1½ oz sweet vermouth
1½ oz Campari
soda
orange slice

Shake and serve on the rocks in a highball glass. Top up with soda and garnish with orange.

STRAWBERRY CREAM TEA

Equal measures of:
Kahlua
Baileys
Fraise
Vodka
Lassi

Blend and pour into an ice-filled Collins glass. Lassi is an Indian yoghurt drink. It gives this cocktail a lighter, cleaner flavour.

Appendix

The bartender's checklist

FRESH JUICE, FRUIT AND ICE ARE JUST AS ESSENTIAL INGREDIENTS IN A COCKTAIL AS QUALITY SPIRITS. KEEP EVERYTHING YOU NEED TO HAND. AND DON'T SKIMP ON THE DETAILS. IT'S THE LITTLE 'EXTRAS' THAT MAKE OR BREAK THE FINAL RESULT.

Equipment

Shaker
Mixing glass
Blender
Strainer
Measure
Waiter's friend
Corkscrew
Ice tongs/scoop
Stirring spoon
Measuring spoons
Cocktail sticks
Swizzle sticks
Straws
Ice bucket
Fruit press
Grater (for nutmeg, etc.)
Pestle (muddler)
Chopping board
Sharp knife
Paring knife

GLASSES

Cocktail glass (V-shaped
Martini glass)
Tumbler
Large highball
Collins
Wine glass
Champagne flute

Essential ingredients

ALCOHOLIC

Gin (keep in refrigerator)
Vodka (keep in refrigerator)
White and Gold rum
Tequila
Bourbon
Cognac
Blended Scotch
Dry and Sweet vermouth
Cointreau/Curaçao
Campari
Maraschino liqueur
Pernod/Absinthe
Drambuie
Green Chartreuse
Yellow Chartreuse
Kahlua
Champagne
Underberg (for hangovers)
Angostura bitters
Peychaud bitters
Orange bitters

The last two ingredients can be found in specialist retail outlets and are essential in any self-respecting bar.

OTHER

Tobasco/Worcestershire sauce
Fresh limes, oranges, lemons
Fresh fruit juice
Fresh mint
Maraschino cherries
Caster sugar
Coarse salt
Grenadine (made from pomegranates)
Rose's Lime Cordial
Mixers (soda water, tonic water, ginger ale, etc.)

Simple syrup

This is called for in a large number of cocktails. You can buy Sirop de Gomme, but simple syrup is easy to make as its name suggests. Take equal parts of sugar and water and bring to a gentle boil, stirring occasionally. When the sugar has dissolved and the syrup is clear remove from the heat and allow to cool. Then bottle and refrigerate.

Home-flavoured spirits

These are so easy to make that once you start you'll become hooked. Don't however fall into the trap of making all your home-made infusions from sweets and chocolate bars. You'll find savoury and fruit infusions much more versatile.

Vodka can be used for all infusions. Gin tends to work best with fruits, while tequila is good at picking up savoury flavours like jalapeno or citrus peel. Strongly flavoured herbs and pods only need a few days' steeping. Chillies need about one week, while citrus zest can take as long as a month. Check the flavour of the infusions regularly to see when they are ready to use. Vodkas can be sweetened with simple syrup.

High-strength Polish Pure Spirit is an excellent medium for maceration and extraction which can then be diluted with vodka to taste.

SOME OF THE ESSENTIAL

INGREDIENTS FOR THE

HOME BAR

217

Glossary of terms

ABV The alcoholic strength of a spirit measured as a percentage in relation to the liquid as a whole (i.e. 40% ABV is 40% alcohol, 60% water). See "Proof".

Aguard(i)ente Spanish/Portuguese term for spirit. In Spain and Portugal it refers to grape brandy, in Brazil and Mexico it is sometimes used to refer to a young sugar cane spirit.

Alambic/Alembic Old term for a pot still.

Alambic Armagnacais Traditional small continuous still used in Armagnac.

Alambic Charentais Traditional Cognac pot still.

Alquitara Spanish term for a pot still and a pot-still distillate.

Analyser The first column of a multi-column still.

Anejo Tequila/mezcal that has been aged in the barrel for more than one year.

Agave Family of Mexican desert lilies used to produce mezcal and tequila.

Age statement The age on a bottle of spirits referring to the youngest component in the blend/vatting.

Angel's share The term given to the spirit which evaporates from warehoused barrels. Known as "Duppies' Share" in Jamaica.

Aqua vitae The original term for spirits, meaning, "water of life". In Scottish Gaelic, it is *uisce beatha*; in Irish Gaelic, *usquebaugh*; and in Danish, *akvavit*.

Assemblage French term for blending.

Backset (aka setback or sour mash) In North America, the acidic residue from the first distillation which is added to the mash tub and/or the fermenter, totalling no less than 25% of the overall mash. It is used to stop bacterial infection and to lower the pH in the fermenter allowing, an even fermentation.

Bagasse The fibrous stalks of sugar cane, sometimes used as fuel for rum stills.

Batch distillation Another term for pot-still, or discontinuous distillation. The first distillation produces a low-strength spirit which is then redistilled and sepa-rated into three parts – heads, heart and tails – of which only the heart is retained.

Beading A simple method of assessing the strength of a spirit. When a bottle is shaken, bubbles (beads) form. The bigger they are and the longer they remain, the higher the strength.

Beer North American/Caribbean term for fermented "mash".

Beer still North American term for the first still in the distillation process.

Blending (1) Mixing different types of spirit; (2) Assembling different ages of the same spirit. In both cases the aim is to produce a consistent style.

Boise Extract of oak chips and spirit used to colour and flavour young brandies.

Botanicals The herbs, peel, etc. which flavour gin; the most important of them all being juniper.

Bouilleur French term for distiller.

Brandewijn Dutch term for grape spirit (burnt wine) which evolved into brandy.

Brouillis (aka Premier Chauffe) The spirit collected at the end of the first distillation in Cognac.

Cask strength A spirit which has not been reduced by the addition of water to the standard strength.

Chai Above-ground warehouse used for ageing Cognac and Armagnac.

Charcoal filtration Technique (used in Tennessee whiskeys and vodka produc-tion) which involves passing new spirit through vats or tanks containing granu-lated charcoal. This removes impurities and imparts a roundness to the spirit.

Charring The firing of the inside of a barrel. The flame opens up cracks in the surface of the oak, allowing easy pene-tration by the spirit, and also releases sugar compounds which aid flavouring and colouring of the spirit.

Chill filtration Filtering process done by lowering the temperature of a spirit to remove compounds which could cause clouding. It also has the effect of remov-ing some congeners.

Condenser The equipment which turns the alcoholic vapours into liquid form. Traditionally this was a spiral of copper immersed in cold water. Today, heat exchangers are used.

Congeners Chemical compounds found in a spirit formed during fermentation, distillation and maturation. They contain many flavour-carrying elements. The higher the alcoholic strength of a spirit, the fewer congeners present.

Cold compounding Method of adding concentrates of flavours to neutral spirit. A cheaper method than maceration and infusion, giving a cruder product.

Column still (aka continuous, Coffey or beer still) The type of still most com-monly used in continuous distillation. It works by forcing pressurised steam up the column where it meets the descending alcoholic wash, vaporizing the alcohol and carrying it up to be condensed.

Distillation The technique of extracting alcohol from a fermented liquid by heating it. Because alcohol boils at a lower temperature than water the vapour can be collected and condensed, thus concentrating the strength.

Doubler North American term for the pot still used for the second distillation.

Dram Scottish, Irish and Caribbean term for a glass of spirit.

Enzymes Organic catalysts which convert non-fermentable starches into fermentable soluble sugars. Grains such as malted barley and rye contain such enzymes and are added to other cereal crops for this process of conversion or saccharification.

Esters Flavour-giving chemical com-pounds, produced by the reaction of alcohol and acids during fermentation and maturation, that appear soon after the start of distillation.

Eau-de-vie (1) French term for young distillate (brandy); (2) French term for spirits made from fruit.

Faibles Low-strength solution of distilled water and Cognac used to dilute matur-ing brandies.

Fermenters Large vessels made of either steel or wood where the mash is turned into beer or wash.

Fusel oil A heavy congener.

Fut/Fut de chêne French term for a barrel of less than 650 litres.

Heads (aka high wines/foreshots/têtes) The volatile first runnings from the still during the second distillation. They are collected and redistilled.

Heart (aka coeur/middle cut) Term for the potable central fraction of the spirit in batch distillation which the distiller keeps.

Holandas Young Spanish brandy produced from a pot still (alquitara).

Infusion Process of extracting flavour from ingredients by gentle heating.

Maceration The process of steeping ingredients (fruits, herbs, etc.) in alcohol to extract colour and flavour.

Malt (1) A grain, usually barley, which has been stimulated artificially into germination and then halted by drying ("Malting"). The malt is high in sugars and enzymes; (2) Common term for a single malt whisky.

Maltings The building where malting takes place.

Marrying Process where recently blended spirits are placed in a large vat before bottling. The technique allows the different distillates to homogenize.

Mash The sweet liquid produced after hot water has been flushed through the base ingredient in the mash tub/tun to extract the fermentable sugars prior to fermentation.

Mash bill North American term for the percentage make-up of ingredients (corn, wheat, rye, barley) being used in mashing.

Molasses The thick black liquid that is left after sugar has been crystallized. It can then be used to make rum, rhum industriel, or neutral alcohol.

Mouthfeel Tasting term used for the shape and texture of the spirit in the mouth.

Neutral alcohol/spirit Spirit of above 95.5% ABV containing little or no congeners.

Nose The aroma of the spirit.

Oak The most common type of wood used for casks used in maturation. Oak is a strong, watertight wood which allows light oxidation. It also imparts a range of colour and flavour components to the maturing spirit. Different types of oak will give different effects.

Overproof Rum terminology for high-strength, unaged rum.

Paille French rhum that has been aged for less than three years.

Paradis Cellar containing the oldest and rarest brandies.

Peat A soft fuel made from compressed and carbonized vegetable matter – usually heather, wood, grass and occasionally seaweed. Its smoke, known as peat reek, is very pungent and when used in drying malted barley imparts its phenolic aroma to the malt.

Pina Term used to describe ripe agave.

Pomace *See* Vinaccia.

Pot stills Stills, usually made from copper, used in batch distillation.

Proof American measurement of alcoholic strength. A 100° proof spirit is 50% ABV.

Rancio The rich, pungent aroma with hints of mushrooms, cheese, dried fruit and nuts, which is created by the oxidation of fatty acids during the extended maturation of a brandy. It usually appears after 20 years or more.

Rectification Purification of a distillate by redistillation, giving a high-strength distillate with very few congeners.

Reflux The process in which the shape or control of a still forces alcohol vapours to fall back down the still to be redistilled. The end result usually produces a lighter spirit.

Reposado Tequila/mezcal that has been aged in the barrel for less than 11 months.

Retort A vessel used in batch distillation containing either the heads or tails of the previous distillation. The alcoholic vapour passes through the bottom of the retort heating the liquid and causing a second distillation.

Rhum Rum from French-governed departements (such as Martinique and Guadeloupe). Rhum agricole is produced from sugar cane juice; Rhum industriel is made from molasses.

Ricks The wooden frames that hold maturing American whiskey.

Solera Predominantly Spanish method of maturation and fractional blending, most commonly seen in Jerez and used for sherry and Brandy de Jerez.

Sour mash Another term for backset. A sour mash whiskey must contain 25% backset and the use of a lactic bacteria soured yeast mash which has been fermented for a minimum of 72 hours. All Kentucky and Tennessee whiskey is sour mash.

Stillage The non-alcoholic residue at the bottom of a still containing solids – which are processed for animal feed – and acidic liquid which in North America is used as backset.

Tails (aka low wines, feints) The unwanted end part of the second distillation. They are collected and redistilled.

Thumper A type of doubler containing water through which the alcoholic vapours pass.

Toasting The process of lightly heating the inside of a barrel, releasing sugars in the wood. A more gentle process than charring.

Vatting Scottish/Irish term for the mixing together of malt from one distillery. A "vatted malt" is a blend of malts from more than one distillery.

Vieux French term used for long-aged spirits like rhum or Calvados.

Vinaccia (aka pomace) The skins left after a wine has been fermented which when distilled produce grappa/marc.

Vintage Term referring to a spirit produced from a single year.

VS (aka ***) French term for the youngest grading of brandy, usually spirits which have been aged for a minimum of two and a half years.

VSOP French term for the second-quality grading of brandy, referring to a spirit which has usually been aged for a minimum of four and a half years.

Wash The fermented liquid which is ready to be distilled.

XO (aka extra, extra vieux, Napoleon, Reserve) French term for the top quality grade of a spirit which has usually been aged for a minimum of six to seven years but normally considerably longer.

Yeast A micro-organism of the fungi family which feeds on sugar converting it to alcohol and carabon dioxide. Yeast also imparts flavour compounds to the liquid.

Select Bibliography

This tome couldn't have been written without reference to a large number of books, articles, papers and websites. Space doesn't permit the inclusion of every single text, but a number of important reference works in the various subject areas are listed below.

BRANDY

Behrendt, Axel & Bibiana, *Cognac*, Abbeville Press, 1997

Brown, Gordon, *Handbook of Fine Brandies*, Garamond, 1990

de Bobadilla, Vicente Fernandez, *Brandy de Jerez*, SIMPEL, 1994

Gordon, Manuel Gonzalez, *Sherry: The Noble Wine*, Quiller Press, 1992

Long, James, *The Century Companion to Cognac and Other Brandies*

Nicholas Faith, *Cognac*, Mitchell Beazley, 1986

Read, Jan, *The Wines of Spain*, Faber, 1986

COCKTAILS, ETC.

Baggott, Matthew (Ed.), *The Hyperreal Drug Archives* (sourced from the Alchemy website http://www.levity.com/alchemy/find.html)

Berk, Sally Ann, *The New York Bartender's Guide*, Black Dog & Leventhal, 1997

Brown, Gordon, *Classic Spirits of the World*, Prion, 1995

Campbell, Joseph, *The Masks of God*, Arkana, 1991

Eliade, Mircea, *Shamanism*, Arkana, 1989

Embury, David, *The Fine Art of Mixing Drinks*, Faber, 1953

McKenna, Terence, *Food of the Gods*, Rider, 1992

Miller & Brown, *Shaken Not Stirred*, Harper (USA), 1997

Regan & Regan, *New Classic Cocktails*, Macmillan (USA), 1997

Robinson, Jancis (Ed.), *The Oxford Companion to Wine*, OUP, 1994

Schumann, Charles, *The American Bar*, Abbeville Press, 1995

Walton, Stuart, & Miller, Norma, *Spirits & Liqueurs Cookbook*, Lorenz Books, 1997

GIN

Doxat, John, *The Gin Book*, Quiller, 1989

Bayley, Stephen, *Gin*, Scope, 1994

RUM

Hamilton, Edward, *The Complete Guide to Rum*, Triumph, 1997

Lewisholm, Florence, *The Romantic History of St Croix*, St Croix Tourist Board, 1964

VODKA

Begg, Desmond, *Vodka*, Apple, 1998

Faith & Wisniewski, *Classic Vodka*, Prion, 1997

Hanik, Marian, *History of Vodka in Poland* (sourced from The Polish Vodka Website, http://wwweuro-indexcompl/polishvodka/indexasp)

WHISKY

Barnard, Alfred, *The Whisky Distilleries of the United Kingdom*, David & Charles, 1969

Booth, John, *A Toast to Ireland*, Blackstaff Press, 1995

Chisnall, Edward, *The Spirit of Glasgow*, Good Books, 1990

Craig, David, *On The Crofters' Trail*, Jonathan Cape, 1990

Daiches, David, *Scotch Whisky: Its Past and Present*, Andre Deutsch, 1969

Gunn, Neil M., *Whisky & Scotland*, Souvenir Press, 1988

Lockhart, Sir Robert Bruce, *Scotch*, Putnam, 1951

MacLean, Charles, *Malt Whisky*, Mitchell Beazley, 1997

Murray, Jim, *Complete Book of Whisky*, Carlton, 1997

Regan & Regan, *The Book of Bourbon*, Chapters, 1995

Steadman, Ralph, *Still Life with Bottle*, Ebury Press, 1996

Waymack & Harris, *Classic American Whiskeys*, Open Court, 1995

Index

Page numbers in *italic* indicate pictures.

Aalborg Akvavit 178
Aberlour 31, 32, 38, 39
absinthe 131, 160–3, 164, 165, 182
    cocktails 206, 207, 212
Absolut 132, *134*, 135, 141, 143, 144, 145–6, 149
    cocktails 208, 209
Absolut Kurant 148
Absolut Peppar 148
advocaat 197, *197*
Affinity 212
Africa 127, 179, 197
agave 152–4, 157
ageing *see* maturation
aguardiente 109, 154
Aguardiente Juanito el Camineno 109
akvavit 143, 178–9, 208
Alambic Armagnaçais 80
Alaska 206
alchemy 8, 10, 114, 180
alembic charnetais 75
The Algonquin 212
Allied Distillers 122, 124
Allied Domecq 51, 194
Altai 141, 144, 145, 146
Amaretto Disaronno *192*, 193
Amaro 175
Amarula Cream 197, *197*
American Beauty 213
American Colonies
    distillation history 13–14
    rum 94, 95
Ancient Age 59, 60, 64, 65, 143
Angostura Bitters 105, 177
    cocktails 129, 206, 207, 208, 212, 213
    gin 116
Anis del Mono 167
anise 160–7, 192–3
anisette 193
Anita's Attitude Adjuster 215
Antigua, rum 98
Aperol 176
apple brandy 173
applejack 173
Appleton 103, *103*, 105, *105*
Aqua Celestis 183
aqua vitae 12, 24, 27, 48
Arak 179, *179*
Ararat distillery 170
Archer's 179
Ardbeg 31, 32, 34, 35
Argentina 13
Armagnac 23, 79–82, 187
Armenia 170
Arnold de Villanova 11
Arran 36
Astoria 206
Auchentoshan 36
Aurum 189
Australia 109
Austria 174
Averna 176
Avicenne 10

Bacardi 97, 103, 105, 106, *106*, *109*
Bacardi, Don Facunado 97, *97*, 106
backset 59, 99
Baggott, Matthew 162
Bailey's Irish Cream 183, 197, 215
Baker's 64
Ballantine's 47
Bally 1986 109
Balvenie 31, 39
Barbados 94, 98, 104–5
Barbancourt distillery 108
barley
    bourbon 58
    Canadian whisky 66
    Irish whiskey 52
    malting *30*, 31–2
    whisky 27, 30–1
Baron de Sigognac VSOP 81
barrels *see* wood
Barton 59, 63
Basil Hayden 64
Bayley, Stephen 123
Beam, *see also* Jim Bean
Beam, Jacob 54–5
Beam, Jim 56, 59
Beefeater Gin 43, 118, 121, 122, *122*, 123, *123*
Bee's Kiss 210
Belgium 127
Bell, Arthur 46
Bellini 215
Bell's 47
Belvedere 143
Benedictine *185*, 186–7, 212, 213
Benriach 31
Berentzen 179
Berneroy 172–3
Bertagnolli 88, 89
Bisquit 75, 78
bitters 175–7, 200
Black Bottle 47
Black Bush 53, *53*, 208
Black Heart 97, 102
Black Isle 27, 40
Black Russian 202, *208*
Bladnoch 36
Blanton Single Barrel 64, 65
blending
    Brandy de Jerez 84
    Canadian whisky 66
    Cognac 76–7
    rum 102
    whisky 15, 28–9, 43–7
Bloody Mary 151
Bokma 125, 126
Bokvia 172
Bologne 107–8
Bols 126, 191, 194
Bols, Lucas 13, 112, 121, 125, 182, 192
Bombay Dry gin 124
Bombay Sapphire 117, 118, 119–20, 121, 123, 124, 208
Bonny Doon 89
Booker's 64, 65, 68

Booth, Sir Felix 116, 123
Booth, Philip 123
Booth's 123–4, *123*
Bosch, Vicente 167
botanicals
    genever 125–6
    gin 118–19, 120–1
    liqueurs 183, 185, 186–7, 192
    vodka 147–8
bourbon 23, 54–65, 196
    cocktails 68, 69, 212
Bowmore 31, 33, 35
Braastad-Delamain, Alain 74, *77*
Bradstreet, Dudley 115
brandy 14, 70–91, 154, 168–72
    cocktails 212, 213
    colonies 13
    liqueurs 189
    maturation 23
Brandy Alexander 213, *213*
Brandy de Jerez 83–6, 188–9
Braunsweig, Hieronymus 13
Brazil 109
Brighton Punch 212
Britain
    cocktails 200, 202
    rum 97, 102
    see also England; Ireland; Scotland
British Navy 95, 116
British Virgin Islands 108
Bronx 206
Brooklyn 212
Brooks, Alfred 46
Brown, Gordon 125
Bruichladdich 34, 35
Buchanan, James 46
"The Bucket of Blood" 151
Bullshot 151
Bundaberg 109
Bunnahabhain 34, 35
Bunuel, Luis 130
Burrough, James 116, 122
Bushmills 50, 51, *51*, 53
Butterfly 206
butts *see* wood

cachaça 109, 210
Cadenheads 97
Caesar 151
Caipirinha 109, 210, *210*
Cajun Martini 206–7
Calisay 177
Callwood 99
Calvados 172–3, 207, 210, 213
Calwood 108
Cameronbridge 43
Campari *169*, 176, 208, 214, 215
Campbeltown 36
Camus 78
Canada 66–7
Canadian Club 66, *66*, 67
Caol Ila *20*
Captain Morgan 97, 102, 109
Caravella 208
caraway 192
Cardenal Mendoza *83*, 85, 86, *86*
Caribbean 92–108, 96, 98, 103–8

Carillon Importers 124, 143
Carlos I 84, 85, 86
Carlos I Imperial 86
Caroni 105–6
Caruso 206
Casa Girelli Moscato 89
Cascade distillery 62, *62*
casks *see* wood
Castro 210
Catherine de Medici 12, 182
Catherine II, Emperess 139–40, *139*
Celts 10–11, 26
Centenario 210
Central Highlands 37
Ch. de Beaulon VSOP 78
Ch. Laubade 80, 81, 82
chalk, Cognac 74–5
Chambery 207, 209
Chambord 208
Chambord Kamikaze 208
Champagne, cocktails 212, 213, 215
Champagne Cocktail 215
Chapala 214
charcoal filtration 61, 62, 139, 146
Chartreuse *180*, 183, 185–6, *185*, *187*
    cocktails 164, 185, 186, 206, 207, 212
    crèmes 194
    Elixir 164, 185, 186
cherry liqueurs 190–1
Chichicapa 157
Chile 13, 171
China 8, 11
Chinaco 154, 156
Chinchon 177
chinguirito 154
chiringuito 92
Chivas Regal 47
Cinzano 131
Clarke's Court 108
Clear Creek 89
Clover Club 206
Clynelish 40, 41
Coal Ila 34
Cockspur 105
Coebergh 126
coffee liqueurs 194–5
Coffey, Aeneas 14, 21, 28, 42
Cognac 14, 23, 29, 70–8, 91
Cointreau 188, *188*
Cointreau cocktails
    brandy-based 91, 213
    gin-based 129, 207
    rum-based 210, 211
    tequila-based 158, 214
    vodka-based 208
    whisk(e)y-based 212
Col. Lee 63
Collins Family 209
Colonel Collins 209
Columbus, Christopher 92, *92*
column stills *see* continuous stills
Conde de Osborne 84, 85, 86
congeners 18, 20–1, 22, 145
Connemara 51, 52
Contini, Philip 89

continuous stills 14, 21–3
    Armagnac 79, 80–1
    bourbon 56
    gin 116
    rum 97, 101
    whisk(e)y 28, 42–3, 46, 49–50, 66
Cooley Distillers 50, *50*, 51, *51*, 52, 53
Cooper, Ron 154
Copenhagen 208
Cor, Friar John 12, 24, 26
corn
    bourbon 54, 58
    grain whisky 43
    Irish whiskey 52
    whiskey 43, 56, 58, 62, 65, 66–7
Corpse Reviver 213
Cosmopolitan 208
Courvoisier *71*, 72, *76*, 77, 78
Cragganmore 31, 39
Craig, Rev. Elijah 55
cream liqueurs 197
crème de cacao 209, 210, 213
crème de menthe 184, 194, 213
crème liqueurs 194–5
Crested 10 53
Cristal vodka 149
Crow, James 55
Cruzan 108
Cuarenta y Tres 187
Cuba 97, 98, 106, 110, 200–1
Cuban Island 210
Cuervo, Don José Antonio 154
curaçao 188, 206, 211
Cusenier 183, 191, 194
Cutty Sark 45
Cynar 176
Cytrynowka 148

Dailuaine 39
Daiquiri 110–11, 201
Dalmore *24*, 40, 41
Dalwhinnie 37
Damoiseau 108
Daniel, Jack 61, *61*
Danisco 143
Danska 143, 149
David, Elizabeth 96, 120
de Kuyper 126, 183, 188, 191, 194
Deanston 31, 37, *37*
Deauville 213
Del Maguey 157
Delamain 72, *72*, 76, 77, 78
Demerara Distillers 108
Denmark
    Akvavit 178
    bitters 177
    liqueurs 191
    vodka 141, 143, 149
Depression 29
Destilerias la Navarra 175
Dewar, John 46
Dewar, Tommy 46
Dickel, George 61–2
Digby, Sir Kenelm 120

Dillon 107
Dillon Tres Vieux 109
Dirty Martini 207
distillation 18–23
    Armagnac 80
    bourbon 59
    Brandy de Jerez 84
    Cognac 75–6, 77
    gin 118–20
    history 8–17
    Irish whiskey 52–3
    liqueurs 184
    rum 100
    tequila 157
    vodka 145–6
    whisky 32, 42–3
Distillers Company Limited
    (DCL) 47
Dom. de Boigneres 1984 82
Domecq 85, 170
Doxat, John 114, 115, 116, 129
Drambuie 182, 184, 195–6, *195*,
    212
Drostan, St 38
Dry Martini 130
Dubeid, Major Henri 162
Duboigalant 77, 78
Dubonnet 176
Due Campari 215
Dumbarton 43
Dunfermline 99

Early Landed Cognac 78
Eastern Highlands 39
Eaton, Alfred 61
eau de vie de genièvre 112
eaux-de-vie 173–4
Edradour 37, *37*
Edrington Group 43, 45
Edwards, Jerry 102, 104, 105
Egypt 8, 10, 160
El Diablo 214
El Dorado 108, 109
El Tesoro Anejo 156
El Tigre Aguardiente 109
Elijah Craig 63, 64
emulsion liqueurs 197
Endrizzi Chardonnay 89
England
    apple brandy 173
    colonies 13
    gin 114–24
    Pimm's 178
    rum 95–6
EPOM 167
Estonia 189
Etxeko 175
Evan Williams 90[degree] 63
Exshaw 78

Faith, Nicholas 75
Falimirz, Stefan 136
Famous Grouse 45, 46, *46*, 47
feints 32
Ferintosh distillery 27
fermentation
    bourbon 58–9
    rum 99–100
    whisky 31
Fettercairn 39
Filliers 127

Finland 142, 143
Finlandia 135, *142*, 143, 145, 149,
    208
Fizz 209
Fizzing Americano 215
Fleur de Bière 174
Flor de Cana 108, 109
The Floridita 210
Floryn 125
Forbes, Duncan 27
foreshots 32
Fortunella 208
Four Roses 58, 59, 63, *63*
fractional crystallization 18
France
    brandy 70–82
    Calvados 172–3
    colonies 13
    liqueurs 189
Frangelico 193
Frapin 76
French 75 215
French, John 183
French Martini 208
fris vodka 143, 149
fruit brandies 173–4
fruit liqueurs 188–91
Fundador 83, 84, 86
Fussigny, A. de 78

Galliano 187, *187*, 208, 209, 211
Gammeldansk Bitter Dram 177
genever 12, 112, 125–6
George T. Stagg 65
Germany
    bitters 176
    brandy 168
    kirsch 173–4
    Korn 179
Gernet Branca 176
Gilbey's 123, 124, *197*
gimlet 116, 206
gin 22–3, 112–31, 143, 200
    cocktails 129, 206–7, 215
    stills 22–3
Gin Sling 129
gin and tonic 128
Giovanni Poli Nosiola 89, *89*
Girvan Distillery *42*, 43
Glanadam 39
Glayva 196
Glen Garioch 31, 39
Glen Grant 39
Glendronach 39
Glenfarclas 31, 39, *39*
Glenfiddich 29, 39
Glengoyne 30, 31, 33, 37
Glenkinchie 36
Glenlivet *see* The Glenlivet
Glenmorangie 33, 40, *40*, 41
Gloag, Matthew 46
Gloom Raiser 206
Goldwasser 192
Gonzalez Byass (G-B) 84, 85
Gonzalez, General Manuel 154
Gordon, Alexander 115, 116, 122
Gordon's Gin *112*, *113*, 117, 118,
    120, 121, 122, 123
Gourmel 75, 76, 78
Gourmel, Leopold 78
grain

gin 117
    Irish whiskey 52
    whisky 42–5
Gran Duque d'Alba 86
Grand Marnier 183, 189, *189*
Grand Patis Lou Garagai 165
Grant's, *see also* William Grant &
    Sons
Grant's Black Barrel 43
grapes
    Armagnac 80
    brandy 170
    Brandy de Jerez 84
    Cognac 75
    grappa 88–9
    Pisco 171
grappa 87–9
Grassa, Yves 81, 82
Grassl, Martin 154–5
Gratte-Cul 174
Greece 8, 166
    ancient 10
    anise 160
    brandy 168–70
Grenada 108
grog 95
Guadeloupe 106, 107–8
Guatemala, rum 108
Gunn, Neil M. 26
gusano worm 157
Guyana, rum 108

Hacienda Sotol 157
Hadan Distillery *57*, 63
Haig, John 46
Haig, Robert 46
Haiti 108
Hanik, Marian 136, 137, 138
Harper Cranberry 212
Harris, Sean 120
Hart, Lemon 96
Harvey Wallbanger 187, 208, *208*
Havana Club 98, 105, 106
Hayden, Basil 55
heads 20, 32
hearts 20, 76
Heaven Hill 57, 58, 59, 60, 63, 64
Hebridean 196
Heering 129, 191, 207, 211
Henius, Isidore 143, 178
Henkes Aromatic Schnapps 179
Hennessy 77
Henry II, King of England 48
herbal liqueurs 185
Heron, Patrick 80
Heublein 134
Highland Clearances 27
Highland Distillers 33
Highland Park 31, 33, 41, *41*
Highlands 27–8, 37, 39
Hine 72, 77, 78
Hine, Bernard 75–6, *78*
Hooghoudt 125, 126, 143
Hoorbeke 127
Horse's Neck 212
House, Anthony M. 10
Houx 174
Hungary 176–7

Illicit Love 183
India 67, 179

Inishowen 53
Invergordon 43
Ireland 11, 23, 24–6, 48–53
Irish Distiller Group (ID) 50, 51,
    52–3
Irish Mist 208
Iron Jack 102, 106
Islay 32, 33, 34–5, *34*, *35*
Isle of Arran 36
Italy
    bitters 175
    brandy 168
    grappa 87–9
    liqueurs 189, 190–1, 192–3,
        197
Izarra 187, 194

J&B 45, 46, 47
J. Bally 107
J. M. 107
Jack Daniel's *22*, 61–2, *61*
Jacopo Poli Torcolato 89
Jacopo Poli Uva Viva 89
Jagermeister 176
Jamaica 96, 100, 105, 194–5
James Bond 208
James IV, King of Scotland 26
Jameson, John 49
Jameson's *50*, 51, 53
Janneau *70*, 80, 81, *81*, 82
Janot 165, 166
Japan, whisky 66, 67
Jarzebiak 148
jenever 127
Jerez, brandy 83–4
Jim Beam 59, 60, 64, 65
Joe Collins 209
Johnnie Walker 46, 47, *47*
Jose Cuervo 156
juniper 112, 118, 120, 121, 174
Jura 35, *35*
Just Peachy 196
Justerini, Giacomo 46

Kahlua 194, 210, 214, 215
Kentucky, bourbon 54–65
Kentucky Gentleman 63
Kentucky Tavern 63
Ketel One 143, 145, 149, 208
Kilbeggan 53
kill-devil 92, 94, 104
kirsch 173–4
Knob Creek 68
Knockando 39, *39*
Ko Hung 8
korn 143, 179
Krupnik 147–8, 209
Kubanskaya 141
Kümmel 182, 192

La Mauny 107
La Navarra 175
La Rojena distillery 154
Labat, Père 103
Labrot & Graham 59–60, *59*, 61,
    61, 64, 65
Lagavulin 31, 32, 34, 35
Lamb, Alfred 96
Lamb's Navy 97, 102, 109
Lang's Supreme 45
Laphroaig 31, 32, 34, 35

Laressingle 80, 81, 82
Larios London Dry Gin 127
Le Grande, Alexandre 186
lees 75, 77, 78, 99
Lemon Hart 97, 102
lemon liqueurs 190, *190*
Lepanto 85, 86
Ligon, Richard 94
Limoncello 190
Lincoln County Process 61
liqueurs 180–97
Lithuania, gin 127
Lochside 39
Locke's distillery 50, 53
Loiten Export Akvavit 178
London Dry Gin 124
Long Island Iced Tea 215
Longmorn 39
Lowitz, Theodore 139
Lowlands 28, 36, 42
Luis del Rio 157
Luksusowa 138, *138*, 143, 144,
    149
Lull, Raymond 10, 11–12
Lustau 86
Luxardo 191
Lysholm Linie Akvavit 178

M. de Caussade 81
Macallan 30, 32, 33, 39
McKenna, Terence 12, 94
Mackinnon family 195–6
Madrono 193
Magno 84, 85, 86
Mai Tai 210–11
maize see corn
Maker's Mark 57, 59–60, 63, 65,
    68
Malcolm Lowry 214
Malibu 193
malt whisky 27–8, 29, 30–41
malted barley, bourbon 58
malting 30–1
Mandarine Martini 207
Mandarine Napoleon 189, *189*,
    207
The Manhattan 68
maraschino liqueur 206, 211, 212
Margarita 154, 158
Marnier-Lapostolle, Louis-
    Alexandre 189
Martell 75, 76, 77, 78, *78*
Martell, Jean 72
Martin, John 150
Martinez 130, 200
Martini 201, 202
    gin 206–7
    vodka 135, 208–9
Martini & Rossi 130, 131
Martini Thyme 207
Martinique 94, 96, 98, 101, 103,
    106–7
Mary Pickford 211
Masataka Taketsuru 67
Mascaro 86
Maschio 88, 89
Matador 214
maturation 23
    Armagnac 81–2
    bourbon 60, *60*
    Brandy de Jerez 84–5

Calvados 172
Canadian whisky 66–7
Cognac 76, 77
grain whisky 45
liqueurs 184
malt whisky 33
rhum 103
rum 101
vodka 149
Mavromatis 166
Mayerne-Turquet, Theodore de 114
mead 11, 26
medicine 10, 11
anise 160, 164
juniper 113–14
liqueurs 180
Melnais Balzans 176–7
Mendeleyev, Dr 140
Mentzendorff 192
Metaxa 168–70, *170*
Metropolitan 208
Mexicana 214
Mexico
brandy 170
mezcal 13
rum 92, 109
tequila 152–8
mezcal 152, 154, 157
Midleton distillery 50, 51, 52, *52*
Miguel Torres Imperial 86
Millar's 53
Minero 157
Mint Julep 69
Mirabelle 174
Mith, Lars Olsson 141
Mojito 111, 210, 211
molasses
gin 117
rum 98–9
vodka 144
Molotov Cocktail 208
Mon Repos 108
monasteries 11–12, 48
liqueurs 180–2
Scotland 24–6, 27
see also Chartreuse
Monkey Gland 207
Monte Alban 157
Montenegro 176
Moors 10, 11, 83
Morgan, Jack 150
Mortlach 39
Moscow Mule 150
Moser, Antonio 88
Moskovskaya 135, *140*, 141, 143, 144, 149, 207
Mount Gay 92, 99, 102, *102*, 105, *105*

Naked Lady 211
National Rums of Jamaica 105
Negroni 177, 215, *215*
Nemunas gin 127
Netherlands
Brandy de Jerez 83
Cognac 72
colonies 13
gin 113, 125–6
liqueurs 192, 197
trade 14

vodka 143, 149
New England Iced Tea 215
Ngiam Tong Boon 129
Nicaragua, rum 108
Nicholl, Denis 10
Nikka All Malt 66
Nissebaum 149
Noe, Booker 57, 59, 60, 65, 69
Noilly Prat 131
cocktails 130, 206, 207, 209, 214
Nonino 87, 88
North British 43
Norway 142, 143, 178

Oban 37
obo mezcal 152
Ocumare 108
Okhotnichaya 148
Old Charter 58, 65
Old Fashioned I 212
Old Quaker 65
Old Tom gin 115, 130, 206
Orange Blossom 209
orange liqueurs 188–90
Ordinaire, Dr Pierre 160, 164
The Original Martinez 206
Orkney 33, 41
Osborne Dali 86
ouzo 160, 166, *166*, 167, *167*
OVD 97, 109

Pacharan 175
Paddy 53
Pampero 108
Parfait d'Amour 190
pastis 160, 163, 165–6
Patrick, St. 26
Patrick, St 48
Payne, Desmond 121
peat
Irish whiskey 52
malt whisky 31, 32, 33, 34
Pechuga 157
Pepper, Elijah 55
Pernod 160, *160*, 162, 163, 164–6
cocktails 206, 207, 212
Pernod, Henri-Louis 162
Peru 13, 171
Peter the Great 139, 192
Petiot, Fernand 151
Peychaud's Bitters 177, 212
Peyrat VSOP 78
Phoenicians 26
phylloxera vastatrix 15, 29, 72, *73*, 79
Pieprzowka 148
Pierre Collins 209
Pimm, James 178
Pimm's 178
Piña Colada 202, 211
pink gin 116, 177, 207, *207*
Pisco 90, 171–2
Pisco Sour 90
Pistorius column still 137
Plymouth distillery 115, 116, 118, 119, 120, 121, 123, 124, *124*
Poire William 174, 191, *191*
poitin 48–9
Pokhelbin, William 139
Poland

distilation history 13
fractional crystallization 18
vodka 136–8, 144, 146, 148–9
Poli, Jacopo 87–8
Polish Martini 209
Polmos 138
pomace brandy 89
Pomilio, Amadeo 189
Ponche 188–9
Popula 160
Port Dundas 43
Port Ellen 33
Portugal, colonies 13
pot stills 14, 20–1
Armagnac 80–1, 82
bourbon 59
Brandy de Jerez 83, 84
flavour 18–20
gin 118
grappa 88
Irish whiskey 53
rum 100
potatoes
akvavit 178
Great Famine 49
vodka 137–8, 144–5, *144*
Power's 53
Presidente 211
Prince of Wales 213
Prohibition 15, *56*
bourbon 56
Canadian whisky 66
cocktails 200, 201
gin 116–17, 122
Irish whiskey 50
whisky 29, 36, 47
pulque 152–4
Pulteney 40
Puncheon 105
Punt e Mes 176
Pussers 95

Quetsch 174

Ragnaud-Sabourin 78
Rain 143, 149
raki 160, 166–7
Ramsay, John 43
Real Hacienda 156
Red Eye 55, 63
Red Heart 100
Redbreast 53
reduction, Cognac 76
reflux 20
Regan, Gary 69, 202
Reid, Alan 43
Remy-Martin 77, 78
Revere, Paul 95, *95*
Rhazes 10, 11, *11*
rhum 94, 96, 98, 103–4, 106–8
Rhum J. M. 107
Ribailagua, Constante 110, 201
Ricard 147, 160, 163, 165, *165*, 166
Richardson, Rosamund 12
River Antoine 99, 102, 108
Rob Roy 212
Ronaldo 210
Rosalita 214

Rose without Thorns 183
Rosebank 36
Ross, Captain John 123
Roux, Michel 117, 124, 143
Royal Lochnagar 39
Royale Grenadian rum 102, 108
Royalty 143
rum 92–111
cocktails 110–11, 210–12, 214, 215
history 13
stills 22
rum punch 111, 198
Rum Shrub 211
rum verschnitt 100
Russell, Jimmy 59, 60–1
Russia
distilation history 13
vodka 134, 139–41, 144, 149
Russian Bear 209
Rusty nail 196, 212, *212*
rye
bourbon 58
Canadian whisky 66
Tennessee whiskey 62
vodka 144
whiskey 54
rye whiskey 56, 58, 65

Saint James 107
Salerno 10, 11
Salty Dog 209, *209*
sambuca 160, 184, 192–3, *193*
Samuels, Bill 57, 60, 63, 69, 132
Samuels, Robert 55
San Pedro de Oro Monolito 172
Sanchez-Romate 85
Sangrita 158
Sangster's Conquering Lion Overproof 105
Santhagan, René 170
Santo Domingo Albarradas 157
Sapin, liqueurs 193
Sauza *153*, 154, 156
Sazerac 212
Scandinavia, vodka 141–3
Scarborough Fair 207
schnapps 174, 178–9
Schrick of Augsburg 12
Schweppe, Jacob 116
Scotland
history 12, 13
liqueurs 195–6
whisky 24–47
Scott, Colin 43, 45
Seabreeze 209
Seagram 66, 67, 97
The Seelbach Cocktail 212
Senor Lustau 85
September Morn 211
Shapira, Max 57
sherry 84, *84*
Shijiro Torii 67
Sidecar 91, 213
Sidney 212
The Silver Bronx 206
Singami 172
Singapore Gin Sling 129, 207
Skrzypczak, Dr Boleslaw 144, 145, 146

Skye 41
Skyyy 143
slavery 92, 94–5
Slivovitz 174
sloe gin 191
Smirnoff 97, 132, *133*, 134–5, *135*, 141, 146
Smirnoff Black 141, 145, 149
Smirnoff Citrus Twist 148
Smirnoff Red 141
Smirnov, Piotr 140
Smirnov, Vladimir 134, 140
Smith, George 38
Smoky Martini 207
solera system 84–5, *85*
soma 92
Somerset Royal 173, *173*
Sour 209
"sour mash" 59
South Africa, brandy 170
South America
Pisco 171–2
rum 92, 108
South of the Border 214
Southern Comfort 196, *196*
Spain
bitters 177
Brandy de Jerez 83–6
colonies 13
gin 127
liqueurs 188–9
Mexico 152–4
Pacharan 175
whisky 67
Speyside 38–9
Springbank Distillery 31, 36, *36*, 97
Stag's Breath 196
Stalin, Josef 140–1
Star 207
star anise 160, *161*, 164
Starka 149
Stein, Robert 21, 28, 42, 46
Steinhager gin 127
stills 20–3
Coffey 14
Cognac 75–6
Scotland 27–8
see also continuous stills; pot stills
Stinger 213
Stolichnaya 135, *140*, 141, 144, 146, 149
Strathclyde 43
Strathisla 39
Strawberry Cream Tea 215
Strega 182, *183*, 187
Subin, Alan 124
sugar, rum 92–111
Suhoi 143, 146
Suntory 66, 67
Suze 176
Sweden, vodka 141, 143, 144
Switzerland, absinthe 160–2
Sylvius, Franciscus 112
Szczecin distillery 149

tafia 94, 103
Taggia, Martini di Arma di 130
tails 20, 32, 76
Taliesin 11, 26

Talisker 41, *41*
Tamdhu 31, *39*
Tanqueray 122–3, *122*
Tanqueray & Gordon *119*
Tanqueray, Charles 116, 122
Tapika 214
Tariquet 81, 82
Tatra 147–8
taxation
 USA 56
 vodka 139
 whisky 27–8
Taylor & Williams 65
Teacher, William 46
Teacher's *25*
Teaninich 40, 41
Temperance Movement
 Ireland 49
 USA 56, 62
Temperley, Julian 173
Ten High 63
Tennessee whiskey 23, 61–2
tequila 152–8
 cocktails 158, 202, 214, *214*, 215
Tequila Sunrise 202, 214, *214*
Tequini 214
The Glenlivet 38, 38–9, 39
The Singleton 39
Thomas, Professor Jerry 198, 200
Tia Maria 194–5, *194*
Tipperary 212
Tito's Texas Handmade 143, 149
Tobermory 37
Tom Collins 209
Tom Moore 63
Tonic Water 116
Tormore *38*
Torres 86
Touissant 195
Trepout, Marcel 82
Tres Magueyes Reposado 156

Trinidad & Tobago 105–6
Trinidad Distillers 102, 105
triple sec 188
 cocktails 91, 213, 214, 215
tsipouro 166–7
Tyrconnel 51, 53

UDV 58, 64–5, 65
uisge beatha 27
Ultraa 141
Underberg 176
Unicum 176–7
United Distillers 34
United Rum Merchants (URM) 96, 97, 100
United States
 applejack 173
 brandy 170
 cocktails 198–200, 201, 202
 gin 116–17
 grappa 89
 liqueurs 196
 vodka 134–5, 143, 149
 whiskey 54–65
 see also Prohibition
Up Your Nightshirt 183
US Virgin Islands, rum 108

Van der Hum 189
Vana Talinn 189
Venzuela, rum 108
Verdier, M. 79
vermouth 131
 Affinity 212
 The Algonquin 212
 American Beauty 213
 Astoria 206
 Bronx 206
 Brooklyn 212
 Cajun Martini 206
 Caruso 206
 Corpse Reviver 213

Dry Martini 130
Fizzing Americano 215
The Floridita 210
Gloom Raiser 206
Manhattan 68
Naked Lady 211
Negroni 215
The Original Martinez 206
Presidente 211
Rob Roy 212
Rosalita 214
Sidney 212
The Silver Bronx 206
Star 207
Tipperary 212
Very Old Barton 63
Veson Guildive/Guildire 94
Vesper 207
Vikingfjord 143
Vinvelli, Don Bernado 186
Vipre 174–5
vodka 132–51, 192
 Bloody Mary 151
 Cuban Island 210
 history 13, 15
 Long Island Iced Tea 215
 Mandarine 207
 Martini 201–2
 Moscow Mule 150
 stills 22–3
 Tequini 214
vodka-based cocktails 208–9
Voisin, Pierre 76, 78
Vov 197

Walker, Alexander 46
Walker, George 46
Walker, Hiram *66*
Walker, John 46
Wallace 196
Warninks 197
Wash Act (1784) 27–8

Wash Act (1823) 48
washbacks 31
Washington, George 54, 95
water
 bourbon 58, 59
 malt whisky 34
 vodka 145
 whisky 32
Waymack & Harris 55
West Indies Rum Refinery 105
Westerhall 108
Western Highlands 37
wheat
 bourbon 58
 Canadian whisky 66
 grain whisky 43
 vodka 144
Where The Buffalo Roam 209
whiskey
 cocktails 212
 Ireland 48–53
 liqueurs 195–6
 Tennessee 61–2
 USA 54–65
Whiskey Rebellion 54, *54*
whisk(e)y-base
 cocktails 212
 liqueurs 195–6
whisky 24–47
 barrels 33
 blends 15, 28–9, 33, 43–7
 Canada 66–7
 cocktails 212
 grain 42–5
 India 67
 Japan 67
 liqueurs 195–6
 malt 30–41
White, Gerard 57, 64, 65
White Lady 207, *207*
Wild Turkey 58, *58*, 59–60, 60–1, 64, 65, 68

William Grant & Sons 29, 39
William of Orange 114
Williams, Evan 54
Williams, Hugh 121
Winchester, Mike 32, 38
Wisniowka 148
W.L. Weller 58, 65
wood
 ageing 23
 Armagnac 81
 bourbon 55, 59–60
 Bowmore 35
 Brandy de Jerez 85
 charring 55
 Cognac 76
 Irish whiskey 53
 malt whisky 33
 whisky 33, 40, 45
Woodford Reserve 64, *64*, 65
wormwood 160–2, 163, 164
Worshipful Company of Distillers 114, 121
worts 31, 42
Wray & Nephew *93*, 99, 103, 105
Wyborowa 138, *138*, 149, 209
Wyborowa vodka, Where The Buffalo Roam 209

yeast
 bourbon 58–9
 rum 99–100
 whisky 31
Yellow Bird 211
Yellow Fever 209
Yukon Jack 173

Zar 143
Zeni 88, 89
Zoco 175, *175*
Zombie 211
Zubrowka 147, *147*, 148, 149, 209
Zytnia 138, 149

PICTURE CREDITS